Falling from Grace

Falling from Grace

Downward Mobility
in the
Age of Affluence

KATHERINE S. NEWMAN

UNIVERSITY OF CALIFORNIA PRESS
Berkeley · Los Angeles · London

University of California Press
Berkeley and Los Angeles, California

University of California Press, Ltd.
London, England

First California Paperback Printing 1999

Library of Congress Cataloging-in-Publication Data

Newman, Katherine S., 1953–
    Falling from grace : downward mobility in the age of affluence /
Katherine S. Newman. — 1st California pbk. print.
        p.   cm.
    Originally published: New York : Free Press, c1988. With new
Afterword and rev. ch. 2.
    Includes bibliographical references and index.
    ISBN 0-520-21842-6 (alk. paper)
    1. Social mobility—United States.   2. Middle class—United
States.   3. United States—Economic conditions—1981–   4. United
States—Social conditions—1980–   I. Title.
HN90.S65N48   1999
305.5'13'0973—dc21   98-38119
                                                              CIP

Printed in the United States of America

08   07   06   05   04   03   02   01   00

9   8   7   6   5   4   3   2

In memory of
Charles R. Newman
1927–1993

Contents

Preface

Hundreds of thousands of middle-class families plunge down America's social ladder every year. They lose their jobs, their income drops drastically, and they confront prolonged economic hardship, often for the first time. In the face of this downward mobility, people long accustomed to feeling secure and in control find themselves suddenly powerless and unable to direct their lives.

The experience of downward mobility may seem a strange subject of study for an anthropologist. The kind of data that researchers typically employ to chart patterns of mobility—statistics drawn from national surveys—are hardly the stuff of anthropology. Indeed, in the ten years since this book was first published there have been no other ethnographic studies of middle class Americans who have lost everything they have worked for. However, on closer scrutiny, downward mobility is a subject crying out for anthropological analysis. It is an experience as foreign to many in the United States as the lives of exotic peoples in New Guinea. Most Americans do not see how a catastrophic loss of place changes the way that husbands, wives, children, kin, and friends behave toward each other. They have never questioned whether the values embedded in American culture help those in trouble or make their lives more uncomfortable. And people who *have* lived through downward mobility are often secretive and cloistered or so bewildered by their fate that they find it hard to explain to themselves, let alone to others, what has befallen them.

In the midst of coping with an unexpected reversal in their material fortunes, the downwardly mobile must contend with the meaning of their fall, with the way it reflects on themselves and the larger society within which they live. This remains true whether the economy is in the doldrums, with unemployment high and the stock market crashing (as it was in the 1980s), or growing at great speed with record highs on the Dow Jones (as it is at the end of the 1990s). In good times and bad, people who are on the losing end of downsizing must contend with what their losses reveal about their moral character. Questions of meaning and interpretation occupy the heartland of anthropology. Hence, where other social scientists might be concerned mainly with the macroeconomic or statistical contours of downward mobility—its objective face—the anthropologist searches for the underlying cultural architecture that shapes the *experience* of "falling from grace." And when the topic is approached in this way, downward mobility emerges as much more than a collection of disturbing tales of outcasts from the middle class. It reveals a more general blueprint for American culture.

The downwardly mobile are a very special tribe. Some are heroes who find ways to rise above their circumstances; others are lost souls, wandering the social landscape without direction. But almost all are deeply sensitive to the lives they left behind. They spend hours reflecting upon what their old world meant and what the new one lacks. They therefore offer an unusual window on what it means to be middle class in America.[1] Yet, peering through that window, one discovers that middle-class culture is not uniform or monolithic. There are variations in the values and worldviews contained in the middle class, and they refract the experience of downward mobility in distinctive ways. Downward mobility brings these variations into sharp relief and focuses attention on the diversity of cultural forms that make up the American middle class.

My interest in downward mobility was inspired by several concerns—some worldly, some academic. The last decade has seen remarkable twists and turns in the ethos of American public life. The Carter years were suffused by the symbols of populism—the man of the people, dressed in a cardigan by the fireside, walking the streets of the capital during his inaugural parade. The 1980s brought stretch limousines and black tie back to Washington, symbols of a reawakened conservativism that emphasizes the individual over the community, laissez-faire over social compassion. With the refrain of Adam Smith's free-market economics in the background, America was said to be making great strides toward prosperity. This has been even more the case at the end of the century. With so many of our competitors in serious trouble (Japan, Indonesia, even France and Germany), the United States is roaring into the 21st century with high growth, unemployment at a historic low, and inflation virtually non-existent.

Yet the promise of success appears to be out of reach for many. And I do not speak here of the urban poor, who have always been on the dark side of the American dream. The farmers in the Midwest, the oil workers in Texas, and a host of unpublicized members of the middle class are also losing their grip on prosperity. Downward mobility is touching the lives of many people who never expected to find they had anything in common with the poor. The 1980s are calling into question that article of faith so deeply embedded in our national consciousness: that our material lives just keep getting better every year.

An examination of outcasts from the American middle class affords the opportunity to bring the insights and understandings of the anthropologist back to our own shores. Cultural analysis in America is a time-honored tradition: Margaret Mead, Franz Boas, David Schneider, and Louise Lamphere are but a few of the anthropologists who have written about American culture. But in recent years anthropology has gained greater public recognition for studies of exotic peoples in foreign lands. These are crucial contributions to the understanding of humankind in all its variety and are the foundation of what anthropologists like to call our comparative mission. Yet it was always said that the study of other cultures would better equip us to study our own. Along with many other anthropologists who are studying American society, I take that dictum seriously and attempt to apply it here.

Once intrigued by the issue of downward mobility, I began to see it everywhere, including in my own family. My grandfather worked for thirty years as a traveling salesman for a company that sold household appliances in northern California. He made the rounds of the retail stores that purchased the company's product line. His customers and the neighborhoods of the San Francisco Bay area he traveled were the core of his universe. The company was sold when my grandfather was sixty; he was soon fired, along with the other older salesmen. He lost his center of gravity, his feeling of worth. He died not long thereafter, a much sadder man than he had been during his working life.

His was not a tale of the Great Depression: It happened in 1959, an economic boom period in the United States. The more I looked, the more people like my grandfather I found hanging from the branches of middle-class family trees. It occurred to me that despite the tendency to think of these unfortunates as oddities, they might not be so exceptional. And I realized how very damaging the ideology of exceptionalism can be where downward mobility is concerned, for it can lead those who have suffered tremendous disappointment into debilitating self-blame, and it bequeaths to their children a host of anxieties about their own competence and security.

My analysis of the downward mobility experience is based upon more than 150 in-depth interviews of the sort anthropologists often call "focused life histories."[2] As is customary, I have concealed the identities of the people who shared their lives with me, changing their names, the cities in which they live, and other details necessary to protect their anonymity and privacy.

Acknowledgments

It took nearly four years to hammer these concerns into the shape of a book. Much of that time was spent in the company of my computer, but I was fortunate to have the help of many people as well, only a few of whom can be acknowledged here. First and foremost, I owe a great debt to the people who spent hours in front of my tape recorder, delving into aspects of their lives that were often stressful to discuss. They cannot be acknowledged by name, but I can thank them collectively, as well as the several organizations who helped me find them, including the Forty Plus Club of New York City, PATCO Lives, and the leadership of the International Electrical Workers Union local that represented the Singer Company workers in Elizabeth, New Jersey.

The Department of Anthropology at the University of California at Santa Cruz, provided a congenial atmosphere for my research in 1982–83. The American Association of University Women awarded me a postdoctoral research grant that enabled me to pursue this research full-time for one year. Columbia University's Department of Anthropology, Council for Research in the Social Sciences, and Junior Faculty Development Program facilitated this research in a variety of ways, not the least of which was their generous funding of summer grants and research leaves.

A number of my colleagues listened patiently while I thought aloud, the the truly hardy among them put in hours reading drafts of the manuscript. The late Robert Murphy, whose own research on the disabled is a model of anthropological scholarship on American culture, read every line despite his own busy schedule. Herbert Gans, whom many anthropologists would claim as one of their own although he is a well-known figure in American sociology, read and criticized my work in its early stages. Paula Rubel and Abraham Rosman took valuable time out from their sabbatical year to read the manuscript in full. Michael Kimmel dropped everything on short notice to give the book a thoughtful reading. I remain very much in debt to these colleagues, who contributed their own intellectual insights to my analysis. I have incorporated their ideas shamelessly here.

Many others read or discussed parts of this work and were unfailing in their help and support, including Elaine Combs-Schilling, David Schilling, David Halle, Louise Mirrer, Arlene and Jerome Skolnick, Philip Selznick, Doris Fine, Stephen O'Connor, Helen Benedict, Louise Lamphere, Carol Stack, Glen Elder, Jr., Judith Small, Bob Fitzgerald, Jill Suitor, Scott Feld, Eviatar and Yael Zerubavel, Alexander Alland, Jr., Elliot Skinner, and Myron Cohen. Professors Greg Duncan of Northwestern University, Suzanne Keller of the Department of Sociology at Princeton University, Ben Harrison of the New School for Social Research, and Michael Merrill of the Rutgers University Center for Labor Education generously contributed research materials. Bill Taylor, the director of PATCO Lives, proved to be a mine of information and assistance, as was Arthur Shostak of Drexel University.

I gratefully acknowledge three journals that published articles derived from this research: *American Ethnologist, Cultural Anthro-*

pology, and *Urban Anthropology.* The editors of these journals—Professors Shirley Lindenbaum, George Marcus, and Jack Rollwagen—and several anonymous reviewers made valuable conceptual and editorial suggestions and enabled me to put some of these ideas before my professional colleagues.

My original editor at The Free Press, Joyce Seltzer, pushed me mercilessly to express my ideas in an accessible form. If I have had any success in that endeavor, it is due largely to her efforts. She was, from the beginning, committed to the larger vision of the book, and her confidence in it kept me on track when the task seemed quite unmanageable. Charlene Woodcock of the University of California Press made many valuable suggestions which improved this second edition.

I was able to secure the help of several outstanding doctoral students in the anthropology department at Columbia University who worked with me as research assistants. Anastasia Karakasidou devoted several years of her own time to this book, remaining throughout the most dependable and intelligent colleague one could hope for. A number of others scoured the libraries for documentary materials, including Deborah Blincoe, Bill Bushell, Kate Dudley, Lawrence Hammar, and Andrea Pellegram. Shelley McDonough of Harvard's Department of Sociology mined the libraries and the Internet so that this edition would reflect the most recent findings available on downward mobility.

I have saved two crucial people to the end. It would be nearly impossible to thank my colleague and husband, Paul Attewell, in a fashion that genuinely reflects his contribution. He read every draft of every chapter many times over. He argued the ideas, pored over the writing, and pushed me to keep going. He lived this book just as I did, and it would not exist were it not for his intellectual commitment to the enterprise. My sons, Steven and David Attewell, have encouraged me from the sidelines from the beginning to the end of all my writing projects.

The second edition of this book is dedicated to the memory of my father. Charles Newman was no stranger to the ups and downs of the business world, but he bore these burdens with great courage. In more ways than one, he inspired *Falling From Grace.*

Cambridge, MA
September 1998

1

American Nightmares

DAVID PATTERSON was a practical man. All his life—from his youth in a run-down working-class district of Philadelphia to his adulthood in the affluent suburbs of New York—he had made rational decisions about the future. David had a talent for music, but he studied business. He had a flare for advertising, but he pursued a job in the computer industry. He wore his rationality proudly. Having steered clear of personal indulgence, he had a lot to show for his efforts: a beautiful home, two luxury cars, a country club membership, a rewarding executive job, and a comfortable, stable family. The Philadelphia slums seemed a million miles away and a million years ago.

When David's boss left frantic messages with the secretary, asking him to stay late one Friday afternoon, his stomach began to flutter. Only the previous week David had pored over the company's financial statements. Things weren't looking too good, but it never occurred to him that the crisis would reach his level. He was, after all, the director of an entire division, a position he had been promoted to only two years before. But when David saw the pained look on the boss's face, he knew his head had found its way to the chopping block. He was given four weeks of severance pay, the use of the company telephone credit card, and a desk in a remote part of the building for the month. Despite these assurances, the credit card was canceled a week later. The company made good on the severance pay agreement, but David was made to feel increasingly uncomfortable about the desk. So he cleared out and went home. Wasting no time, he set to work on the want ads every morning. He called all his friends in the business to let them know he was looking, and he sent his resume out to the "headhunters"—the executive search firms that match openings to people. David was sure, in the beginning, that it wouldn't be long before a new position opened up. He had some savings put aside to cushion the family in the meanwhile. He was not worried. By the third month of looking, he was a bit nervous. Six fruitless months down the line he was in a full-fledged panic. Nothing was coming through. The message machine he had bought the day after losing his job was perpetually blank.

After nine months, David and his wife Julia were at a crossroads. Their savings eroded, they could not keep up the mortgage payments on their four-bedroom neocolonial house. Julia had gone back to work after a two-year hiatus, but her earnings were a fraction of what David's had been. His unemployment compensation together with her paycheck never amounted to more than 25 percent of the income they had had in the old days. The house, their pride and joy and the repository of virtually all their savings, went up for sale. They reasoned that if the house sold, at least they could salvage some cash to support the family while David continued to look for a job. But their asking price was too high to attract many qualified buyers. Finally it was sold for a song.

Broke and distressed beyond imagining, the family found a small apartment in a modest section of a nearby town. David continued to look for an executive job, but the massive downturn of the mid-1980s in the computer industry virtually ensured that his search would bear no fruit. From Silicon Valley to Boston's Route 128, the shakeout in his field was stranding hundreds of equally well-qualified men. David could not get past the personnel offices of firms in other industries. He was not given the chance to show how flexible he could be, how transferable his managerial experience was to firms outside the computer field.

After a while David stopped calling his friends, and they ceased trying to contact him. Having always been sociable people, David and Julia found it hard to cope with the isolation. But with no good news to share, they didn't really feel like seeing old acquaintances. Friendship in their social circles revolved around outings to fancy restaurants, dances at the country club, and the occasional Broadway show or symphony in New York City. The Pattersons' budget simply could not sustain these luxuries anymore. For a time their friends were understanding, inviting them to dinner parties in their homes instead of excursions to places the Pattersons could not afford. But eventually the unspoken rules of reciprocity put an end to that. The Pattersons couldn't issue return invitations, and the potluck dinners of their youth were not a viable alternative.

David and Julia were almost relieved by the ensuing isolation. It had been a strain to put on a calm countenance when, in fact, they felt that life was falling apart. At the same time, however, they interpreted the sounds of silence as abandonment. When friends ceased to call, David was convinced this meant that they no longer cared what happened to him. At least they should try to help him, he thought.

Like many other executive families, they were newcomers to suburban New York. Only two years before, David's firm had transferred him from its California branch to its New York headquarters. The move east held the promise of a more important executive job for David and a taste of real affluence. The transition had not been easy, since the social barriers of suburban society were hard to penetrate. Making new friends was no small accomplishment, and after two years there were only a few they could count as close. But they weren't the kind of old friends one could lean on in a crisis, and this surely was a crisis.

Their two teenage children were equally disoriented. Like most kids, they had opposed moving away from the place where they had grown up. They made no secret of their fury at being disrupted in the middle of high school, exiled to a new state where they knew no one. The girl had become rather withdrawn. The boy had worked hard to make new friends, leaning on his father's prestige as a company executive as an avenue into the status-conscious cliques of the local high school. When the son first arrived, as David put it, "No one would even talk to him. He was looked upon as a transient. Everyone else in his school had been in the same area since grammar school." The son's efforts to break into the networks met with only mild success, and even then, it took nearly the entire two years before he felt on solid social ground. He had finally reached a comfortable plateau when David lost his job. The whole family was thrown into turmoil, and the prospect of moving surfaced once again.

This was too much. David's teenagers unleashed their fury: How could he do this to them? The whole move to New York had been his idea in the first place. Now he was going to drag them through another upheaval! How dare he interfere with their lives so drastically once again? How were they supposed to explain to their friends that their father-the-executive was unemployed? Conformity was the watchword in their friendship circles. Not only did they have to look right and act right, they had to come from acceptable backgrounds. An unemployed father hardly fit the bill. In fact, it threatened their standing altogether because it made it impossible for them to buy the clothes and cars that were commonplace in their social set.

David was accustomed to the normal tensions of life with teenagers. But in his shaken condition, he felt guilty. In retrospect, he agreed with his kids that the move to New York had been ill advised. But it wasn't as if he had had any warning of the debacle when they left the familiar comforts of California. He was simply doing what any intelligent man in his position would do: pursue every opportunity for upward mobility, even if the family is disrupted in the process.

Harder to contend with was the strain on his wife. Julia had long dabbled as a receptionist in art galleries, but her work had been more of a hobby and occasional supplement to the family budget than a mainstay. It had not been easy for her to pick up where she left off when the family moved to New York. Eventually, she found a part-time receptionist position, but her wages could not begin to cover the family's expenses. The move had bequeathed the Pattersons a staggering mortgage for a house twice as expensive as their old one. They could manage the bills as long as David was employed. But with his job gone, Julia's earnings could not stretch far enough. In one fell swoop, Julia found herself the major breadwinner in the family. Though she tried to find a job that would pay more, she had never thought of her work as a "career." She lacked the experience and stable employment history needed to land a better position.

It was the uncertainty of the situation that Julia found hardest to bear. She just could not tell when it would end or where they might land. It was difficult enough to batten down the hatches, cut purchases, and figure out a way to keep the credit cards from sliding too far into arrears. The family did not venture into the shopping malls any more, although this had once been a major form of weekend recreation. If she could figure out when things were going to bottom out, at least she would know what standard of living they had to adapt to. But, lacking any concrete sense of destination, Julia did not know how to begin the adjustment. Adjust to what?

Little help was forthcoming from the suburban matrons in the neighborhood, who—it appears—had never faced anything even remotely resembling this crisis. Where Julia expected to find sympathy and even offers of assistance, she found disbelief and not a little finger pointing. David could sense the damage this was doing:

> Since becoming unemployed there's really nothing, especially for my wife—no place where a woman can talk about things. There are no real relationships. She's hurt. People say to her, "With all the companies on Long Island, your husband can't find a job? Is he really trying? Maybe he likes not working." This really hurts her and it hurts me. People don't understand that you can send out 150 letters to headhunters and get 10 replies. Maybe one or two will turn into something, but there are a hundred qualified people going after each job. The computer industry is contracting all over the place and as it contracts, my wife contracts emotionally.

Secretly David worried whether Julia didn't share just a bit of her friends' attitudes. He could see the despair on her face when he would come home with no news to report. But on too many occasions, it seemed that her rage over the unfairness of his plight was mixed with doubt. She would bombard him with questions: Did you follow up on this lead? Did you call your cousin Harry about another? What did the headhunter tell you about that job downtown? David had few satisfying answers and after a while he began to resent the questions. Couldn't Julia see he was doing his best? It got to the point where he preferred taking a train into the city to look for work to riding with her in the car. Two hours together in the car with nothing but a bleak future to talk about was sometimes more than he could face.

The whole situation left David at a loss. No one was playing by the rules. He had credentials; he had experience; he was in a high-tech field that was touted as the wave of the future. Every time he turned on the news he would hear commentators lament the closing of the steel plants, the auto plants, and the coal mines. This was to be expected in an era when the United States no longer seemed able to compete in the world of heavy industry. But computers? They were supposed to be our salvation, and as a man who always kept one eye on the future, David had aggressively and successfully pursued a career in the field. How could he have gotten into such a quagmire?

The truth is, the computer industry was taking a bath in the mid-1980s. Thousands of employees had been turned out from Atari, Honeywell, Apple. Even IBM, the giant of the industry, had had to tighten its belt. David's entire division had been closed down: fifty people axed in one stroke. The industry shakeout was headline news in the *Wall Street Journal* and on the business pages of the major dailies. But it was only slowly seeping into general public consciousness, where computers still hold a special place as the glamour industry for the twenty-first century. The news had clearly failed to reach the Pattersons' friends. They were dumbfounded by David's disaster. High tech was the answer to the country's economic ills; computers were booming. How could David be having so much trouble finding a job? And what was the *real* reason he had lost his old one?

David could recite the litany of problems in the computer business so familiar to insiders. He could understand completely why his division, located at the market research end of the company, had been targeted as "nonessential" to its survival. In the beginning he told himself that his personal situation could be explained logically. Market forces had put pressure on the company, and it responded, as any rational actor in a competitive capitalist economy would, by cost cutting, aiming first at those activities that were most remote from the nuts and bolts of production and sales. Indeed, had David been at the helm, he argued, he would have made the same decision. For David Patterson is no rebel. He is a true believer in the American way of doing business. Up until now, it had satisfied his every ambition. Hence there was no reason to question its fundamental premise: In economics, as in life, the strong survive and the weak fall by the wayside.

But after months of insecurity, depression, and shaking fear, the economic causes of his personal problems began to fade from view. All David could think about was, What is wrong with me?

Why doesn't anyone call me? What have I done wrong? He would spend hours bent over his desk, rubbing his forehead, puffing on his pipe, examining his innermost character, wondering whether this or that personality flaw was holding him back. Could people tell that he was anxious? Were people avoiding him on the street because they couldn't stand to come face to face with desperation? Was he offending potential employers, coming on too strong? With failure closing in from all directions the answer came back "It must be me." The ups and downs of the computer industry and the national economy were forgotten. David's character took center stage as the villain in his own downfall.

*

David Patterson has joined the ranks of a little-known group in America, a lost tribe: the downwardly mobile. They are men and women who once had secure jobs, comfortable homes, and reason to believe that the future would be one of continued prosperity for themselves and their children. Longtime members of the American middle class, they suddenly find everything they have worked to achieve—careers, life-styles, and peace of mind—slipping through their fingers. And despite sustained efforts to reverse the slide, many discover there is little they can do to block their descent.

The lack of attention downward mobility receives—from policymakers, scholars, and the public—has little to do with its actual incidence. Its low visibility is hardly a product of size: About one in five American men skid down the occupational hierarchy in their working lives.[1] In recessions and depressions, their numbers grow at a particularly rapid rate. But downward mobility is not simply an episodic or unusual phenomenon in this country. It is a regular feature of the economic landscape that has been with us for many years.

Yet we hear very little about the downwardly mobile. Magazine covers and television programs focus attention on upward mobility, the emergence of the Yuppies, the exploits of the rich and famous, and in less dramatic terms, the expectation of ordinary Americans that from one year to the next, their lives will keep getting better. But many middle-class families are headed in the opposite direction—falling on hard times—and relatively little systematic attention is paid to their experience.

In the public mind, downward mobility is easily confused with poverty, and the downwardly mobile are mistaken for those who live below the poverty line. But the two groups are quite different. Nearly eight million American families are officially classified as poor, and they have been the subject of countless studies.[2] The poor *can* experience downward mobility—they can lose their hold on a meager, but stable existence and become homeless, for example—but many are at the bottom of the class hierarchy and some have been there for generations.[3]

The experience of the downwardly mobile middle class is quite different. They once "had it made" in American society, filling slots from affluent blue-collar jobs to professional and managerial occupations. They have job skills, education, and decades of steady work experience. Many are, or were, homeowners. Their marriages were (at least initially) intact. As a group they savored the American dream. They found a place higher up the ladder in this society and then, inexplicably, found their grip loosening and their status sliding.

Some downwardly mobile middle-class families end up in poverty, but many do not. Usually they come to rest at a standard of living above the poverty level but far below the affluence they enjoyed in the past. They must therefore contend not only with financial hardship but with the psychological, social, and practical consequences of "falling from grace," of losing their "proper place" in the world.

Besides confusing the downwardly mobile with the poor, Americans tend to overlook these refugees from the middle class because their experience flies in the face of everything American culture stands for. From our earliest beginnings, we have cultivated a national faith in progress and achievement. The emphasis on success has always made it difficult for Americans to acknowledge defeat: No one ever talks about the Pilgrims who gave up and headed back to England.[4] Our optimistic heritage stands in the way of recognizing how frequently economic failure occurs.

When academics study occupational mobility, most of the energy goes into trying to account for upward mobility. It is true that the majority of adults enjoy an upward trajectory in income and occupational status over the course of their working lives. Yet, despite the fact that a large number have the opposite experience, downward mobility is relegated to footnotes or to a few lines in statistical tables. Rarely is it treated as a topic in its own right.

When the media, in times of economic hardship, do touch on

the problem, they show sympathy for the victims but express bewilderment at their fate. The downwardly mobile are often portrayed as the exceptions that prove the rule. Occasional reminders of what can go wrong seem to strengthen the nation's assumptions about what constitutes the normal and positive course of events. Downward mobility appears, therefore, as an aberration.

What is worse, America's Puritan heritage, as embodied in the work ethic, sustains a steadfast belief in the ability of individuals to control the circumstances of their lives. When life does not proceed according to plan, Americans tend to assume that the fault lies within. We are far more likely to "blame the victim" than to assume that systemic economic conditions beyond the influence of any individual are responsible. This tendency is so pervasive that at times even the victims blame the victims, searching within to find the character flaw that has visited downward mobility upon them. Even they assume that occupational dislocation is somehow uniquely their problem. But the fact is, downward mobility has always been with us and exists in larger numbers than most of us realize.

American culture is rich in rituals and symbols that celebrate worldly success. The extravagant bar mitzvah, the debutante ball, the society wedding, and the lavish golden anniversary celebration all signal the value that Americans attach to economic achievement. Our symbolic vocabulary for failure is, by comparison, stunted. Downward mobility has virtually no ritual face. It is not captured in myths or ceremonies that might help individuals in its grip to make the transition from a higher to a lower social status—there is no equivalent to Horatio Alger stories for the downwardly mobile.

The fact that downward mobility happens so often, yet has not been institutionalized through social convention or public ritual, points to something very significant about the problem. Downward mobility is a hidden dimension of our society's experience because it simply does not fit into our cultural universe. The downwardly mobile therefore become an invisible minority—their presence among us unacknowledged.

This impoverishes public discourse about the problem. Even more important, it has a savage impact on the downwardly mobile themselves. Lacking social and cultural support, the downwardly mobile are stuck in a transitional state, a psychological no-man's-land. They straddle an "old" identity as members of the middle class and a "new" identity as working poor or unemployed.[5] They are in suspended animation. The chaotic feeling of displacement creates confusion that can only be resolved through reintegration in a new capacity. Yet the downwardly mobile are unable to find a "new place" that satisfies their expectations. Hence they are left hanging, with one foot in the world of the professions, the corporate empire, the realm of the economically secure, and another in the troubled world of the financially distressed, the dispossessed, and the realm of low-level occupations.

Hanging between two worlds is a distressing state of existence, for the downwardly mobile individual has to juggle two incompatible senses of personhood. On the one hand, he or she is a well-educated, skilled professional, accustomed to power, to deference, to middle-class norms of consumption. Yet behind the facade of the split-level executive home, the wallpaper is peeling, appliances are breaking down, clothes and shoes are wearing thin, and adults are venturing out to work at low-level white- or blue-collar jobs which afford no authority, no autonomy, no sense of self-importance.

Which self is the real and which the artificial for the downwardly mobile? Some cling to the old persona for years. When asked, they claim their previous occupations as engineers, vice presidents of marketing, or sales managers. But even after hundreds of interviews fail to rescue them from a bottom-level job, after the family home has been sold to pay off debts, after the sense of self-assurance fades to be replaced by self-recrimination, the torture of two selves endures. For the kids' sake, for the wife's sake, or simply for the sake of one's own sanity, it is hard to ditch yesterday's honored identity in order to make room for today's poor substitute. And one never knows, perhaps tomorrow's mail will bring news of a job interview, a passport back to the only occupational reality that makes sense.

Without any guidelines on how to shed the old self, without any instruction or training for the new, the downwardly mobile remain in a social and cultural vacuum. And society looks the other way because, frankly, it is embarrassing to see someone in such a state, and it's disturbing to treat the situation as anything other than an aberration. Any closer scrutiny makes us squirm, for it jeopardizes our own comfort.

This is not to say that there is no template for failure in American culture. Indeed, there have been periods when images of downward mobility were fresh in America's mind. The massive wave of farm foreclosures in the 1930s had a quality of collective public mourning: groups of worn and dejected faces surrounding the old homestead or the last tractor. John Steinbeck's *Grapes of Wrath* memorialized the plight of the dispossessed Dust Bowl refugees. We remember the fate of the Joad family, ejected from their land by the nameless, faceless, hated bankers.[6] The devastation of the Great Depression lingers in our historical consciousness. When the 1980s saw the United States facing the worst rate of farm foreclosures since the depression, the specter of the 1930s was a constant subtext. The beleaguered Midwest, America's breadbasket, recalled an old calamity suffered by others in other times. The words "not since the 1930s" were repeated again and again as if to assure today's farmers that they are not the first to see their livelihoods destroyed.

Despite the cold comfort of history's example, farm foreclosures are not rituals: They do not happen regularly enough to have acquired the character of a culturally recognized transition from one status to another. They are catastrophes, extraordinary events. They remind us of the calamities that can befall the nation, but they cannot structure the experience of individuals whose descent down the status ladder takes place in ordinary times.

The absence of socially validated pathways for dealing with economic decline has important consequences for the downwardly mobile. They often mourn in isolation and fail to reach any sense of closure in their quest for a new identity. Their disorientation suggests how critical culture is in "explaining" to individuals the meaning of their fate.

To a certain extent, the experience of downward mobility in middle-class America is the same for all of its victims. Catastrophic losses create a common feeling of failure, loss of control, and social disorientation. Most people who experience downward mobility long for the "golden days" to return; some genuinely believe they will. Those who have sunk far below their original social status simply don't know where they belong in the world. This is the core of what it means to "fall from grace": to lose your place in the social landscape, to feel that you have no coherent identity, and finally to feel, if not helpless, then at least stymied about how to rectify the situation.

But beyond this the commonalities cease. Some downwardly mobile people feel alone, others are part of a group; some blame themselves, while others point the finger elsewhere; some see their fate as capricious, while others find purpose in the midst of loss. These variations shape the "same" experience—that of economic dislocation—in different ways and suggest that while the downwardly mobile have all fallen from grace, the fall means different things to different people. Hence, to understand what the experience really means in American culture, we cannot simply focus on the David Pattersons. If the complexity of middle-class downward mobility is to be fully captured, the spectrum must be broadened beyond the archetypal white-collar manager.

The variation in subjective responses to dislocation is not random. The extent to which an individual feels isolated or blameworthy, rather than united in anger with others in similar straits, is not a function of individual personality. Americans experience downward mobility for a variety of reasons, and the reasons make a difference. The contexts or circumstances in which occupational displacement occurs influence how its victims understand their fate, how they explain it to their family and friends, and how they attempt to break out of it.

Collective Loss versus Individual Tragedy One critical contextual factor that shapes the interpretation of downward mobility separates those who have been cast down the occupational hierarchy as a result of a "mass loss" from those who find themselves in trouble individually. When the General Motors Corporation shuts down twenty-six plants across the country, (as was announced in the summer of 1998), the experience of the GM workers is quite different from that of an individual salesman who is fired for failing to sell his quota of widgets. The collective or mass experience of loss introduces a different dynamic of blame than the one that developed in David Patterson's mind. A single individual among the 29,000 can hardly hold himself responsible for plant shutdowns on such a scale.[7]

Collective loss focuses attention away from the individual largely because, in occupations where mass losses occur, work life has a collective rather than an individual character. Even in times of prosperity, the fate of most blue-collar workers is more a matter of their union's strength than it is one of individual behavior. Moreover, the organizations that bind workers into collectivities persist over time. People may groan over the ineffectiveness of unions, but the fact is that the United Auto Workers lives on even as General Motors closes plants around our ears. The persistence of collective organizations sustains a "group psychology," even in the face of individual misery.

Workplace versus Family   Although downward mobility often comes about in the context of the workplace, it visits other locales as well. Financial disaster often follows on the heels of changes in family composition.[8] Divorce is a primary cause of downward mobility for millions of American families. Women, many of whom have built careers as homemakers, find themselves suddenly displaced, pushed into the work force to support themselves and their children. The weak position of women—especially "displaced homemakers"—in the labor market translates divorce into downward mobility for many women: They cannot secure jobs that pay well enough to stave off financial hardship. But the locus of disaster in divorce cases is not the workplace per se. It is the family. When blame is assigned and fault is found, it is of a qualitatively different character than that which emerges from failures in the workplace. Occupational breakdown may be interpreted as a failure of the head; divorce is seen as a failure of the heart. As tragic as the latter may be, our culture teaches us that hearts can be fickle.

Hence divorce-induced downward mobility—which is primarily a woman's fate—is wrapped up in social conceptions of gender roles, the appropriate relations between parents and children, and the fate of the kids as innocent victims in a precipitous slide out of the middle class. Of course, these cultural dynamics can be affected even where downward mobility is not the product of a family breakup. But they take center stage when it is. Experiencing the loss of financial stability therefore becomes inseparable from a divorcée's perspective on marital relations and sex roles.

Arbitrary Fates, Intentional Actions   With hindsight, most people can construct a series of events that led up to their fall from grace. Even those who professed surprise when the disaster first struck often claim that, in retrospect, they should have seen it coming. This does not mean, however, that every victim of downward mobility believes that he or she could have intervened to reverse the situation. Nor does it mean that they accept the view that their own actions are responsible for, or related to, their demise. However, some groups *do* place themselves at the center of the drama, while others see themselves as sideline observers who were run down by a juggernaut not of their own making.

One might assume that the downwardly mobile who had a central role in their own fall from grace would be inclined toward self-blame, while those victimized by the arbitrary actions of others would be less so. This contrast holds true in some instances but not in others. When downward mobility results from the actions of a group committed to a cause, that group and its principles take the center stage, but the dynamic of blame shifts to "the enemy."

Strikes can potentially be interpreted in this way, since in addition to the pecuniary issues at stake, they may also be moral struggles. Individuals band together into picket lines, mass together in union halls, and engage in intensive, often heady debate over appropriate tactics. Brotherhoods of the embattled emerge out of these shared experiences. When strikes fail and strikers forfeit their jobs, they clearly cannot view themselves as innocent bystanders. But other meaning-systems are often invoked. Participants may walk a fine line between blaming themselves (or their leadership) for miscalculation and casting themselves as noble victims, sacrificing themselves for a cause.

Occupational Status The higher one climbs the ladder of occupational prestige, the greater the distance one can fall. At the same time, the more prestigious and highly paid an individual's job, the greater his resources to cushion the fall. These include everything from savings accounts and houses to skills, licenses, work histories, and support networks. Possession of and access to these resources affects the timing of downward mobility. For those who live close to the margin, the loss of a job can push the family into the abyss within a matter of weeks. For those whose lives are "padded," the transition can be staved off for years. Clearly, the cushions are not evenly distributed throughout the middle class. Those at the upper end are generally (but not always) blessed with backstops that can protect them, provide them with greater options, or allow them to be pickier about their occupational choices. Those at the lower end often find themselves on a one-way ticket out of the middle class within weeks. They do not have the luxury of waiting to find out whether they'll be able to find new jobs equivalent to their old ones.

Thus, in order to understand the variation in downward mobility within the middle class, we must consider a range of occupational "niches." For the middle class is a category so broad that it encompasses everyone from white-collar executives to elite unionized labor (sometimes called the labor aristocracy). Production workers in New Jersey's chemical plants may be working men on the job, but they are indistinguishable in many respects from their middle-class neighbors at home—neighbors who are teachers, policemen, or clerical workers.[9] Blue-collar workers who have "arrived" in the middle class by virtue of the life-style their incomes sustain have as much to lose when downward mobility strikes as do their white-collar neighbors.

A second, and growing, group in the middle class is the "new-collar" or "knowledge" workers. These people are not as affluent or as privileged as Yuppie lawyers or stockbrokers, but they are much more important in numerical terms.[10] Computer programmers, air traffic controllers, and lab technicians can be classified as knowledge workers. Their work is highly technical, they have skills and some credentials, but they often lack autonomy on the job. They are the kinds of workers Daniel Bell had in mind when he described the changing nature of the American labor force in his classic treatise, *The Coming of Post-Industrial Society.*

Professionals and managers are the occupational cream of the middle class. They are at the higher end of the middle-class continuum in terms of both income and prestige. Accustomed to being in control of others, the loss of authority is particularly hard to take. For them, moving down the occupational ladder often means becoming subject to the decision-making power of others.

The meaning of downward mobility for the American middle class can only be understood if the variations in attitudes and responses of each of these occupational groups are taken into account.

Tribes of the Downwardly Mobile

As members of the "middling classes," the people represented in this book have much in common: They share certain aspirations; they are one in their bitter disappointment and disillusionment at their fate; they must confront some painful realities in their own lives and those of their children.[11]

Survey data can document the incidence and economic impact of downward mobility.[12] But the *subjective interpretation* of the experience—what it means to those caught in its grip—is a matter of culture. The "worldview" of the American middle class is uniform in some respects, but it is cross-cut and internally differentiated in others. I have already suggested some sources of variation: mass versus individual loss, arbitrary action versus commitment-related dislocation, workplace versus familial breakdown, and the "wrinkles" introduced by occupational gradations within the middle class. The point is made more concrete in the chapters that follow, which examine four different groups of downwardly mobile, middle-class Americans: former managers and executives, air traffic controllers fired in the wake of a disastrous national strike, blue-collar workers caught in a plant shutdown, and divorced mothers.

White-collar managers are the highest-status group of the four discussed in this book. Although they were often sent packing as the result of corporate restructuring, they were more likely than the others to experience downward mobility as an "individual" plight.

The air traffic controllers are prototypical knowledge workers, whose technical training enabled them to secure high-paying, relatively prestigious jobs but whose lack of transferable credentials locked most of them into downward mobility. Unique among the four groups, the controllers took actions that led directly to their downward mobility.

The controllers confronted downward mobility as a collectivity, but not as one rooted in a residential community. By contrast, blue-collar workers caught in the shutdown of a 100-year-old Singer sewing machine factory in New Jersey exemplify the dilemmas of mass loss that are inseparable from a physical community. Finally, downwardly mobile divorced women provide a "familial" and a female perspective on economic dislocation.

Each of these groups affords an occasion to analyze aspects of American culture that go deeper than the experience of middle-class downward mobility. White-collar executives are creatures of meritocracy, who embrace the view that those who are worthy are rewarded and those who fail to reap rewards must also lack self-worth.

In undertaking a dramatic, illegal, and ultimately fatal national strike, the air traffic controllers demonstrate the importance of

Table 1.1. Dimensions of Group Comparison

	White-Collar Managers	Air Traffic Controllers	Singer Company Workers	Divorced Women
Status	upper-middle-class professionals.	"new-collar" or knowledge workers	blue-collar middle class	white-collar middle-class during marriage
Individual vs. collective loss	individual	collective	collective	individual
Arbitrary vs. intentional loss	arbitrary	intentional commitment led to firings	arbitrary	mainly arbitrary
Arena of loss	workplace and occupational identity	workplace and occupational identity	workplace and residential community	family

principles, causes, and commitment in American life. Despite public rejection, the controllers became true believers in a cause, a
cause that has sustained many of them through a skidding descent,
down the occupational hierarchy since 1981.

Blue-collar workers in Elizabeth, New Jersey, connect themselves to a tradition of craftsmanship and pride in product. For
them, downward mobility is embedded in the decline of craft
traditions that have been replaced by impersonal, instrumental
relations between workers and management.

Finally, divorced women place the family and changing nature
of gender roles on center stage in the experience of downward
mobility. Their subjective responses to dislocation also focus attention on the importance of "generational cultures" in our rapidly
changing, complex society. For although these women all suffered
downward mobility, their reactions can only be understood against
the backdrop of the generations they belong to. History marks
each cohort with particular memories and values, and the lives
of these divorcées testify to the folly of describing American culture
(or any culture, for that matter) as a timeless entity.

*

Meritocracy, commitment, tradition, and generational culture are
intellectual girders that connect the lives of these four groups of
downwardly mobile people to larger challenges and concerns in
American society. But these are particularly salient themes for
those who have slipped from the ranks of the middle class. In
the midst of the daily struggle to keep their heads above water,
to provide some sense of hope and continuity for their children,
and to fight off the depression that comes from relentless bad
news, the downwardly mobile try to salvage a sense of honor.
This is no easy task in a culture that measures its men by occupation
and its women by family roles (and increasingly by occupation
as well).

The salvage process does not occur in a vacuum. The tools
we use to make meaning out of an unexpected event are those
bequeathed to us by our culture. Human beings are meaning
makers who inhabit symbolic worlds that give form to experience.[13]
Much of the symbolic universe is taken for granted; it is second
nature. But when confronted with jarring realities, cultural assumptions—both shared and divergent—become somewhat
clearer. Downward mobility means a great deal to people who

live in a society that so closely connects occupation to self-worth. It might take on a different shape in cultures where kinship or descent from royal blood confers rank and a sense of self. The American dilemma is not necessarily shared around the globe. When we face it, we do so from the vantage point of our own culture, which provides an architecture of interpretation.

2

Downward Mobility in the
Age of Affluence

THE destruction of David Patterson's career is an example of what social scientists call intragenerational downward mobility.[1] It occurs when people who have attained a degree of occupational or financial success in their adult years see their achievements evaporate. They find themselves sliding down the socioeconomic ladder—they "fall from grace." Since David Patterson's experience flies in the face of American expectations for mobility, one wonders just how many people there are like him. If his is a unique or atypical case, a tiny undercurrent in a massive sea of upward movement, we need not be alarmed. It is quite another matter if we find that his fate is shared by many others. There are many ways of measuring downward mobility, but they all point to the fact that it is a widespread, chronic problem. In any year, millions of families are sliding downward.

In a national survey conducted every year by the National Opinion Research Center, between one-fifth and one-fourth of respondents report that their financial situation has been deteriorating. The numbers who say that their economic lives have "gotten worse" rises and falls a bit from year to year, but the NORC data show that financial deterioration affects millions of Americans in good years and bad.[2] Government statistics on income help explain why this is the case. As Figure 2.1 indicates, median income for men who work full time and year-round has declined substantially since the late 1980s. Women have come to the rescue in many families and because their earnings are considerably less than their male counterparts to begin with, they have not experienced this earnings slump. However, one look at Figure 2.2 show us that the vast increase in women's labor force participation has not been enough to smooth out the roller coaster ride that median family income has taken over the twenty years from 1976–96. The pronounced "dips" in this chart reflect recessions in the early 80s and 90s. Most families recover from the impact of these downturns, but some suffer the consequences of job displacement for a much longer period and never recoup the loss.

Overall, the average American has lost ground. However, the median income, like the "average American" is something of a

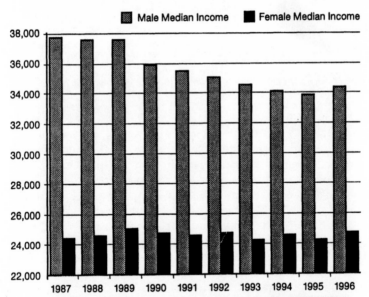

Source: 1991–1996. Historical Income Tables—Persons. Table P21: Educational Attainment—Persons 25 Years Old and Older Working Year-Round, Full Time, by Median Earnings and Sex: 1991–96. Income Statistics Branch, U.S. Bureau of the Census. Washington, DC. Calculated from the March Current Population Survey. Last reviewed 11/7/97.

Source: 1987–1990. Historical Income Tables—Persons. Table P22: Years of School Completed —Persons. Persons 25 Years Old and Older Working Year-Round, Full Time, by Median Earnings and Sex: 1987–90. Income Statistics Branch, U.S. Bureau of the Census. Washington, DC. Calculated from the March Current Population Survey. Last reviewed 11/7/97.

Figure 2.1 Median Income for Year Round, Full Time Workers 1987–96

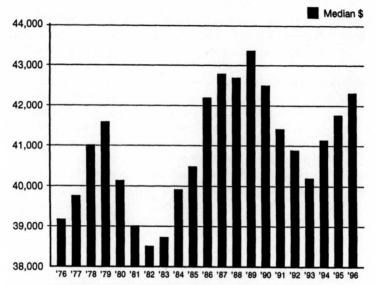

Source: Historical Income Tables—Families. Table F-7. Families (all Races) by Median and Mean Income: 1947–1996. Income Statistics Branch, U.S. Bureau of the Census. Washington, DC. Calculated from the March Current Population Survey.

Figure 2.2 Median Family Income 1976–96 (in constant 1996 dollars)

conceptual fiction. Behind these annual averages, some families are holding their own financially, some are streaking upward and others are taking a precipitous fall. Only by following a large number of actual families over time can the extent of downward mobility (defined by income) be accurately assessed. Researchers at the University of Michigan have done exactly that by following the fortunes of 5,000 representative families since 1968. Greg Duncan and his colleagues used this "Panel Study of Income Dynamics" to examine the experience of middle class families in order to understand how often they moved up or down the income ladder in recent decades. They concluded that more recent trends are running against families in the middle:

> During the 1970s, [middle class adults] faced roughly equal chances of moving up or down from the middle class. During the 1980s, however, their probability of falling from middle income to lower income increased . . . This subtle change in the balance of middle class movements means that middle class dreams of upward mobility . . . are becoming ever more distant.[3]

College educated adults and married couples were more likely to move up, families headed by young adults or minorities more likely to fall. Overall, downward mobility became more common.

Occupational Change Downward mobility can be conceived of as a matter of income loss alone, but it can also be defined as losing one's place in society. For most people in modern America, occupation is a crucial determination of social status, because in addition to money, a job confers prestige and sense of purpose. Hence we may speak of downward mobility in occupational terms when an individual has to take a job that is lower in prestige than the one he lost. Of course, occupational downward mobility often causes income loss; the two generally go hand in hand.[4]

If we compare the first job people take after completing their education with the jobs they have later in life, we get some idea of their mobility pathway. Most people expect that their first job will be but a stepping stone to later achievements and that they will experience an upward trajectory over time. This positive scenario holds for many, but others slip backward at some point in their careers. Technically, downward mobility could be defined as any slip in occupational status. Restricting our attention to serious cases, we might count as downwardly mobile only those people who fall so far down the occupational ladder that their present jobs are below their very first job.[5] A massive study of 33,000 civilian men in the 1970s shows that about one-quarter (23.2%) of the respondents between 21–53 years of age had suffered this fate.[6]

Unfortunately, this survey has not been repeated since the 1970s; hence there is no way to know for sure whether this pattern continued throughout the end of the 20th century. What we do know is that focussing on intergenerational mobility—the occupational distance between fathers and sons—upward mobility reached a plateau among Americans born in the 1920 to early 1940 period. Thereafter "there appears to have been no net upward mobility among white men born after 1950."[7]

Displaced Workers In periods of high inflation, it is entirely possible for individuals who are steadily employed to nevertheless experience an erosion in their standard of living. However, recessions bring about even harsher consequences since one of their by-products is an increase in unemployment. Two major recessions in the 1980s were followed by yet another in the early 1990s. Balance of trade problems, which find the U.S. importing

more goods than it exports, also exacerbated the outflow of jobs
to some degree. But the most significant push toward downward
mobility was a concerted push by American firms to lower the
costs of doing business. They out sourced work that had once
been performed in house, downsized the remaining workforce,
and tried to push more responsibility down to "empowered" line
workers or "high performance work groups."[8]

Between 1981 and 1986, nearly 5.1 million workers who had
been employed for more than three years with their firms, were
let go, becoming what the Bureau of Labor Statistics deems "displaced workers."[9,10] This is a particular kind of job loss, one owing to the disappearance of the job itself through plant closures,
insufficient work, or the abolition of a position or shift. There
are, of course, many other sources of job loss besides displacement: workers may quit or be temporarily laid off. A displaced
worker, as the BLS defines it, is one whose job no longer exists at
all. Since the early 1980s were characterized by double digit unemployment and daily headlines about the shutdown of manufacturing plants, it is hardly surprising that so many people suffered displacement of this kind. Ten years later, however, the
numbers did not look much more encouraging. Between 1991
and 1994, 5.2 million "long tenured" workers were displaced.[11]

Who are these people whose jobs have disappeared and how
have their ranks changed over the last twenty years? Steven Hipple, an economist in the Bureau of Labor Statistics who has analyzed data drawn from the 1980s and 1990s, tells us that there are
some pronounced differences between the decades.

> During the early 1980s . . . more than three-fifths of all displaced
> workers were in good-producing industries . . . By the mid-1990s, this
> proportion had declined to less than two-fifths . . . The share of job
> loss attributable to the growing services industry doubled from 9 per-
> cent in 1981 to 18 percent in 1993–94 (Hipple 1997:27).

Although manufacturing workers still experience displacement at
a higher rate than workers in other industries, that rate has been
falling over time. Employees in FIRE (finance, insurance, and
real estate) continue to fare better than manufacturing workers,
but they are seeing a steady increase in displacement rates.

This change in the distribution of displacement, has also had
an effect on the gender breakdown of the downwardly mobile.
Men are still more likely than women to be displaced, but women
now comprise an increasingly large share of job losers. That is

largely because manufacturing—the "old" source of displacement—was largely a male preserve, while service employment has a much higher representation of women. As women stream into this end of the labor market, they are showing up in the displacement data to a far greater degree than they once did.

Plant closures were the big news in the 1970s and 80s. They generated by far the largest proportion of job losses, consistent with the de-industrialization hypothesis discussed shortly. By the 1990s, white collar workers were joining the ranks of the dispossessed in much greater numbers than they had in the past. Manual workers still have it worse: their rates of displacement are consistently higher than their white collar brethren. But blue collar workers are experiencing a declining rate of job loss, while white collar workers are seeing an increase. Comparisons between the two decades bear witness to the shifting locus of downward mobility: "In the 1981–81 period . . . white collar workers accounted for less than two-fifths of the total job loss; by the 1993–94 period, their share had increased to three-fifths." (Hipple 1997: 29). Of particular interest for this volume are the trends for the category the Bureau of the Census lumps together under the heading "Executive, Administrative, and Managerial" employees. These are the David Pattersons of this world and they have been taking a beating. Table 2.1 shows us that their displacement rates have been trending steadily upward over the past fifteen years.

Millions of people lose their jobs every year, but only some of them become downwardly mobile. Most will find new jobs and the majority will do so at wage levels approximating the earnings they enjoyed before they were let go. When the economy is booming, the re-employment rate of displaced workers goes up and the time they spend searching for new jobs goes down. Clearly it is better to be displaced in good times rather than bad. Yet even in a relatively strong economy, some of the job losers will find themselves out of work for a long period of time and when they find new positions, they will be at substantially lower wages.

Americans who were displaced in the early 80s were unemployed, on average, for about four and a half months. By 1996, the median length of time without work was down to a little over two months for the two million workers who were displaced between 1993–94. This is a significant change for the better and reflects the fact that very low unemployment levels are the best medicine for displaced workers. Still, even in 1996, 7.3 percent of the nation's long term workers who lost their jobs were unem-

Table 2.1   **Displaced Workers by Occupation of Lost Job, 1981–86, 1993–94**

	Number/Percent Displaced 1981–86[1]	Number/Percent displaced 1993–94
Managerial and Professional Specialty	782,000 (15%)	667,485 (27%)
Technical, sales and Admin Support	1,125,000 (22%)	799,515 (33%)
Service occupations	254,000 (5%)	139,365 (6%)
Precision production, craft and Repair	1,018,000 (20%)	308,070 (13%)
Operators, fabricators and laborers	1,870,000 (36%)	493,890 (20%)
Farming, forestry, fisheries	80,000 (2%)	19,560 (.8%)

1. SOURCE: U.S. Bureau of Labor Statistics Press Release (October 14, 1986) "Re-employment Increases Among Displaced Workers" Table 6.

ployed three years later and over 14 percent left the labor force (ibid: 29). This suggests that even in good times, we find a large chunk of the nation's displaced workers experiencing a long period of unemployment.

Behind these average unemployment rates lie some important variations. While young workers are more likely to experience job loss in the first place, the older the displaced worker, the more difficult it is for him or her to find new employment at all. In the 1980s, only 41 percent of the displaced workers who were fifty-five to sixty-four years old found new jobs. For those over sixty-five, the picture was even less encouraging: only 21 percent found new employment. The same pattern holds today. 54 percent of the workers who were fifty-five to sixty-four in 1993–94 had found new jobs by the time they were surveyed again in 1996. 33 percent of the over sixty-five age group found new jobs. A movement from 41 to 54 percent (or 21 to 33) is a big jump in the right direction. But this still suggests that almost half of these older, but still working age, adults who lose their jobs—and even more of the seniors—experience long term unemployment or leave the labor force.

Race exerts an influence over the fate of the displaced. Blacks and Latinos are more likely to experience displacement in the first place. They sustain longer periods of unemployment once they've lost their job and their earnings losses are greater. Yet, the good news is that this gap is nowhere near as large as it was in the 1980s. Figure 2.3 charts the displacement rates from 1981–94 and clearly shows that the differences are narrowing as the rates of displacement decline overall.

While race has declined in significance, education has emerged as a major dividing line, though not in a completely straightforward fashion. As Farber has shown, more educated workers generally have lower displacement rates than the less educated, but their ranks have been growing among job losers.[12] Education still plays a protective role where downward mobility is concerned: once displaced, those who stayed in school longer recovery more quickly than those who dropped out. In the most recent studies, eight in ten of the displaced workers who had a college education were re-employed three years later in the most recent studies we have. Only seven in ten with less than a high school diploma found new jobs.

Unemployment causes downward mobility, particularly if it lasts a long time and pushes people out of the labor market altogether.[13] For most people, however, unemployment is a way-station. For them, the critical question is what their earnings and

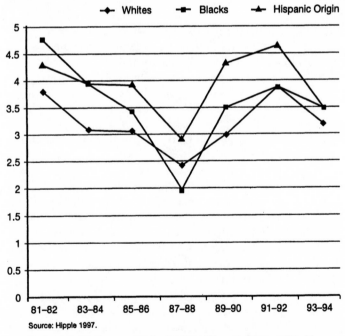

Source: Hipple 1997.

Figure 2.3 Displacement Rates by Race/Hispanic Origin, 1981–94

Table 2.2   Earnings in New Job Compared to Earnings in Lost Job For Workers Who Found Full-time Employment in 1986[1], 1996[2]

	Total Displaced (in thousands)		New Wage 20% or More below old wage (% of displaced)		New Wage Below, but within 20% (% of displaced)		New Wage = or above old but within 20% (% of displaced)		New Wage 20%+ above old wage (% of displaced)	
	1986	1996	1986	1996	1986	1996	1986	1996	1986	1996
All Workers	2,435	2,213	30%	33.9%	14%	19.6%	27%	24.6%	30%	22%
Construction	191	106	28	36.6	13	14.1	27	29.6	33%	19.7
Manufacturing	1,307	43	33	38.2	14	18.8	25	21.3	27	21.8
Transport/ Utilities	192	164	35	42.1	15	20.2	31	21.1	19	16.7
Wholesale/ Retail	296	408	21	30.4	14	21.4	26	16.5	39	31.7
FIRE	287	194	21	19.8	14	27.1	30	28.1	35	25
Government Workers	24	156	17	26.5	17	14.3	29	39.8	38	194

1. 1986 data: U.S. Bureau of Labor Statistics, news (October 14, 1986). "Re-employment Increases Among Displaced Workers."
2. 1996 data: Hipple, Steven (1997) "Worker Displacement in an Expanding Economy"Monthly Labor Review (December): 26–35, esp. p. 34.

occupational prospects look like after they land on their feet. In the 1980s, almost 30 percent of the country's reemployed displaced workers suffered earnings losses that exceeded 20 percent. That is, among those who actually found new jobs, almost one-third took a big loss in pay when they finally landed on their feet. As Table 2.2 indicates, the 1990s brought a slight jump in the proportion of displaced workers who sustained losses of this magnitude. In total, over half of the country's displaced workers lost salary even when they found full time jobs, with *more* than one-third losing more than 20 percent of their old income. Indeed, as one looks across Table 2.2 it is notable that in 1996, workers in almost all categories were *more* likely to suffer high wage losses (in excess of 20 percent) than they did in 1986. Even in a comparatively robust economy, downward mobility can increase.

Princeton economist, Henry Farber, has taken the most comprehensive look at the problem of job loss between 1981–1995. His conclusions are sobering:

Rates of job loss [in the 1990s] are up substantially relative to the standard of the last decade, particularly when we consider the state of the labor market. The increase has not been uniform. More educated workers . . . have seen their rates of job loss increase more than those of other groups. . . . The costs of job loss are substantial. Displaced workers have a large probably of not being employed . . . after displacement (about 35 percent on average). A substantial fraction of those re-employed are working part time . . . The decline in real weekly earnings . . . averages about 9 percent for workers [who find] full time jobs.[14]

How large then is the population of American workers who can be properly defined as downwardly mobile? We can hazard a rough estimate by combining: (1) those who suffered salary cuts which were 20 percent or more of their old wages, even though they found full time jobs; (2) those who remained unemployed three years after losing their old jobs; (3) those who could only find or elected part-time employment[15]; (4) and those who left the labor force altogether after they lost their jobs.[16] Adding these groups together, we find that about 46 percent of the "long tenured" displaced workers were downwardly mobile in the 1990s.[17] This compares favorably to the 55 percent who suffered losses of this magnitude in the mid-1980s. But it is not as substantial an improvement as we might have hoped for given that the mid-90s bequeathed the U.S. a much better economy than was in evidence ten years earlier. The overall point here is that even in fairly good times, a sizeable proportion of the experienced U.S. workforce that loses a job falls from grace.

Downward mobility can clearly be defined in different ways (income versus occupation)[18] and can be measured using different kinds of data (subjective reports of financial difficulty, longitudinal studies of family income, and studies of occupational change). Although these are very different yardsticks, each yields very large numbers.

Why are so many people suffering the dark side of the American dream? There are many reasons for large-scale downward mobility, ranging all the way from the faults and foibles of the individuals involved to systemic problems which plague our economy.[19] Each theory has its place, though pinning primary responsibility on character flaws is a weak explanation. When such a large segment of the population is affected, we need to go beyond the individual for the powerful forces that sweep the good and the bad, the hardworking and the self-indulgent into hard times.

The Nasty Side of the Business Cycle The most straightforward explanation attributes downward mobility to business cycles, alternating upswings and downturns in economic activity that have been the stuff of capitalist economies for several centuries. Business contractions are clearly major determinants of downward mobility because they generate unemployment. The recession of the early 1990s forced many prime age workers into downward mobility. Many economists see business cycles as necessary and natural: recessions cool inflation and bring prices and wages back into alignment. From this perspective, the human toll of unemployment is tragic but unavoidable.

The "naturalistic" viewpoint needs to be qualified, though. Business downturns may be as natural as storms at sea, but the Federal Reserve Board and the U.S. government bear some responsibility for their timing and severity, and so for the downward mobility they cause. In 1979 the business press was filled with calls for an engineered recession. The Fed obliged, causing a rise in interest rates—recession followed within months.[20] In the late 1990s, worries about the prospect of inflation led to frequent hints that the Federal Reserve Board would, or should, increase interest rates to cool economic expansion (through rising unemployment). Since the financial markets hang on Chairman of the Federal Reserve Board Alan Greenspan's every word, these occasional warnings sent the stock exchange into wild gyrations. The point is that the market alone does not dictate the forces that push people into downward mobility: public policy plays a significant role. This becomes clear when we compare the experience of different countries. The various OECD nations sustained quite different rates of unemployment throughout the 1980s and 90s in part because of the different priorities their governments placed on keeping unemployment low.

Even if downturns are sometimes needed, there is nothing inevitable about the harm that befalls those knocked down by them. Government politics that control advanced warning for workers prior to plant closures, that set levels and duration of unemployment insurance benefits, or that mandate retraining and job creation programs, make a significant difference in the degree of hardship experienced by displaced employees.[21]

The United States is conservative—some would say mean—in this regard. We provide 35 to 40 percent of an individual's prior wages for a period of twenty-six to thirty-nine weeks.[22] Most European countries (and Japan) offer support equivalent to 60 to 80 percent of previous earnings for nearly one year. The OECD has developed an index used to compare unemployment benefits across nations.[23] In 1995, the U.S. rated 11.8 on this scale. All of western Europe was more generous, ranging from the United Kingdom at 18.1 to Denmark at 70.7. Germany and France fell into the mid-twenties.[24] Many other OECD countries require companies to notify workers of plant closings several months in advance of the event—the U.S. generally does not. Private employers in other countries are more likely to cut back hours worked in order to save jobs or create new ones rather than lay workers off. Indeed, in 1997 French socialists pushed through legislation mandating a 35-hour work week in an effort to create new jobs and staunch rising rates of unemployment. Government treasuries elsewhere (for example, Sweden, England and Germany) foot the bill for training to a much larger extent than we do.[25]

Government supports provide some protection for individuals and families facing job losses.[26] They give people a more substantial cushion against downward mobility, allowing for longer periods of jobs search and retraining without major financial losses. In America, successive administrations have adopted a more hands-off or laissez-faire labor policy. The wisdom of this approach is a matter of political and economic debate, but its connection to downward mobility is clear. Americans who lose their jobs are at greater immediate risk of falling from grace than are their European and Japanese counterparts. (Though sluggish growth in European economies has pushed many of their workers into downward mobility as well.)

Post-industrial society The second half of the twentieth-century brought with it a transformation in the American economy perhaps as profound as the industrial revolution: the birth of post-industrial society. The hallmark of the new economy is a relative decline in manufacturing and an increase in service sector jobs. This shift has been quite dramatic:

> In 1945, at the conclusion of the war, the services industry accounted for 10 percent of nonfarm employment, compared with 38 percent for manufacturing . . . In 1982, services surpassed manufacturing as the largest employer . . . By 1996, the services industry accounted for 29 percent of nonfarm employment, and manufacturing, at 15 percent, was actually somewhat smaller than retail trade.
> (Meisenheimer 1998:22)

Figure 2.4 displays this dramatic change in the composition of our economy.

It is a simple matter to show this change has taken place; it is much harder to figure out what it means for American workers. Years ago Eli Ginzberg argued that the service revolution was responsible for the fact that our postindustrial economy had generated 21.2 million "poor" jobs compared to only 13.1 "good" jobs

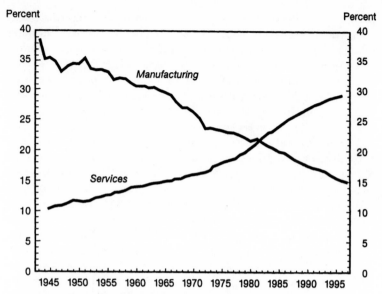

Figure 2.4 Share of nonfarm employment in manufacturing and services industries, annual averages, 1945–96

between 1950 and 1976.[27] But by 1996, service industries were paying on average 92 percent of the wages for manufacturing jobs. The narrowing of that gap could reflect a variety of trends: manufacturing wages have fallen (true) or good jobs in the services industries are growing faster than bad ones (debatable, but there is evidence to bolster this view). It is also possible that the economy is creating more high- than low-skilled jobs, but paying their occupants less—in essence that the connection between skill and income is eroding.[28]

Most likely these findings also mean that the whole category of "service" is just too broad to give us a very good handle on how the occupational structure is changing. At the very bottom of this sector, we find low-wage jobs like video tape rental; laundry, cleaning, repair; and, sadly, child care. When we cast a glance up the scale toward computer and data processing services, we see wages that are considerably higher than even the best paid manufacturing jobs. Anthony Carnavale and Steven Rose, economists at the Educational Testing Service in Princeton, have tried to bring some order to this chaos by dividing all jobs into three groups: elite jobs (managers and professionals), good jobs (supervisors, crafts, technician, police/fire, and clerical), and less skilled (operatives, sales clerks, service, farm).[29] Using this more nuanced model, they find a substantial rise in elite jobs and a decline in the share of less skilled ones. However, they also note that the pay of good jobs held by men—those in the middle category—is down significantly from the 1970s.[30] In contrast, managerial and professional positions have reached 30 percent of the prime-age (30–59) work force and their pay has risen.

If we add in benefits like health insurance or pensions it becomes even easier to see why the shift to services is problematic: services are far less likely than manufacturing jobs to provide these key benefits. Hence even if no damage had been done on the wage front by the movement from manufacturing to services, overall compensation would still be going down once these benefits are figured into the equation.

The good jobs/bad jobs debate is complicated by way we define the terms. If we focussed on wages alone (and forget about skill or occupational categories), we see a large increase over time in the share of employment that falls into the low wage category, an increase mainly experienced by men. In 1973, poverty level wages (less than $7.78 an hour in 1996 dollars) were received by 23.7 percent of all workers. By 1996, 30.6 percent of all workers earned wages that put them below the poverty line.[31]

Economists who argue that employment in the United States is becoming increasingly polarized do not envision a cataclysmic scenario of massive downward mobility. Instead they forecast a gradual process in which much of the burden of the postindustrial job structure would fall on newcomers to the labor force,[32] particularly the less educated of them, who will find fewer middle-income openings.[33] Recent evidence underscores the importance of this polarization thesis. Between 1989 and 1995, the U.S. lost 1.1 million jobs in the middle earnings category. We gained jobs at the high and low end of the earnings spectrum.[34] Hence those job losers who managed to remain in managerial and professional jobs did reasonably well, but those who did not (approximately 40 percent of the displaced workers who started out as managers) faced an occupational climate that was not particularly hospitable.

Wages are mimicking these growth patterns. The late 1990s economic boom was a blessing for almost everyone but it was especially beneficial to the highest income earners and, ironically, to those at the very bottom. Congress mandated increases in the federal minimum wage and that, plus a tightening labor market, improved the fortunes of those at the bottom of the occupational ladder. What happened to the people in the middle? As Figure 2.5 shows, they were the only ones who lost ground.

Deindustrialization Labeling a society as "postindustrial" does not, of course, explain why it is headed in that direction. For social critic Daniel Bell, postindustrialism developed in part in response to America's postwar affluence, which created great demands for services, and also because modern societies are becoming increasingly dependent on information and communication-intensive industries.[35]

Two labor economists, Barry Bluestone and Bennett Harrison, focus instead on forces leading to the decline of our "older" manufacturing economy. In *The Deindustrialization of America,* they call attention to the deliberate, systematic dismantling of American manufacturing industry by its own managers. The signs of the process are to be seen in the aging stock of plant equipment and the diversion of investment resources to foreign subsidiaries of American corporations. In essence, Bluestone and Harrison indict American industrialists for bleeding their own plants to death by failing to modernize. This practice occurred even in factories that were demonstrably efficient or profitable,

Figure 2.5 Losing Middle Ground

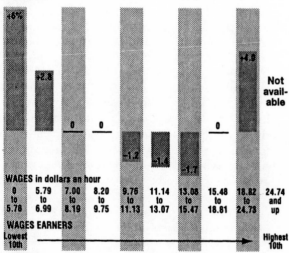

Americans earning in the middle of the wage scale saw their earnings decline since 1989, after adjustment for inflation, while the wages of those at either end have gained ground. The chart divides the workforce into equal segments and shows the percent change in the highest hourly wage for each segment from 1989 through the first half of 1998.

Source: Uchitelle, Louis. 1998 "The Middle Class: Winning in Politics, Losing in Life." New York Times Week in Review. Section 4, pp. 1 and 16.

but were nonetheless treated as "cash cows" and starved of needed capital investment.

Why would American manufacturing sound its own death knell? Manufacturers have been pinched by a profit squeeze whose origins lie both in increased foreign competition and in the postwar victories of organized labor. Unionized workers were able to bargain for higher wages, thus limiting the flexibility of management just as the competitive environment toughened. From management's perspective, the most effective way to respond was to cut and run. Labor and transportation costs are low enough to make it more profitable to produce cars in Korea and ship them to the United States than to manufacture them in America's heartland.

Even more ominous is the fact that the newly growing service industries are now also subject to capital flight. Satellite technology has made international data transmission relatively inexpensive, allowing for the same offshore movement of service jobs that has taken such a toll on domestic manufacturing. Data-entry, airline reservations, and other clerical jobs are being exported to the English speaking Caribbean, to Ireland, and even to the People's Republic of China, where wages are one-fourth to one-fifteenth of those earned by American counterparts.[36] Low-level white collar jobs are not the only endangered species: computer programmers in India are developing software for the U.S. market.

Organized labor is on the run. As plants move overseas and as imports increase their market share, wage concessions, two-tiered contracts (for everyone from steel workers to airline pilots) benefits reductions, and other "givebacks" have become widespread. The result is declining incomes for many who still hold onto their jobs and fewer well-paid openings for those who lose jobs to plant closures or relocations.[37]

Merger Mania Those near the top—the managerial labor force—also face increasingly volatile jobs markets and the prospect of downward mobility. The 1990s have seen a surge in the rates of corporate mergers, acquisitions, and hostile takeovers. As Figure 2.6 suggests, mergers have skyrocketed in recent years.[38]

The drama of corporate giants fighting one another for control of firms has serious consequences for middle managers who are rarely protected by the "golden parachutes" preferred to executives at the highest levels. When two corporate bureaucracies fold together, only one emerges in the end. Each middle man-

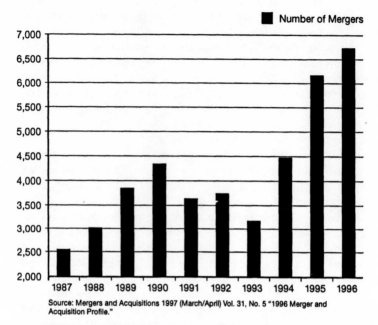

Source: Mergers and Acquisitions 1997 (March/April) Vol. 31, No. 5 "1996 Merger and Acquisition Profile."

Figure 2.6 Merger Completions 1987–1996

ager must wait, worry and pull available strings, hoping that he or she won't be replaced by the person who holds a mirror image position in the other firm.

Mergers are not the only threat to middle management. As foreign competition intensified in the 1980s and 90s, "lean and mean" became the watchword for many corporations looking to trim costs. *Business Week, Industry Week, Forbes* and *Fortune*—journals that keep their fingers on the pulse of the business community—were filled with characterizations of American management as "bloated", "inefficient," and "wasteful"—the work of managerial "empire builders" who bring on more staff than they need simply to expand their internal influence. They point with pride to the hundreds of firms that have attacked the problem by cutting the ranks of the white collar workforce. The American Management Association's survey of large firms shows that between 1988–1995, 18 percent of the job cuts they reported had fallen on the heads of middle managers, who made up only 5–8 percent of the work force. In 1997 alone, 32 percent of the job losses reported in the AMA's annual survey of large firms were sustained by managers or supervisors.[39] Many of the corporate leaders who led the way in downsizing management have argued that we have no choice

but to rid business organizations of these superfluous white collar workers if we are to succeed in the international arena.[40]

As managerial unemployment grows, it becomes harder for
displaced managers to find new jobs similar to those they left behind. Only 58 percent of the managers displaced in 1991–92 were
able to remain managerial or professional workers.[41] The rest
shifted, mainly downward, into new occupational groups.

The Demography of Downward Mobility Most of the theories
discussed above invoke economic factors—recessions, disinvest-
ment, mergers—as causes of downward mobility. But there are
other, noneconomic, ways to look at the issue. Demographers in
particular bring some interesting insights to these processes. The
economic fate of an entire generation depends upon its size relative to other generations. Put simply, individuals born into big
birth cohorts face tight labor markets because the sheer size of
their generation creates a glut of workers. In his book *Birth and
Fortune*, Richard Easterlin argued that this depresses wages for
that generation and intensifies the competition for good jobs.[42]
Generational size carries with it a cascade of potentially unfortunate consequences: delayed marriage, smaller numbers of children, and even higher suicide rates.

Demographic forces complicated the lives of the baby boom
generation, which presently accounts for about two-thirds of the
U.S. workforce. Born during a period of growing prosperity, this
generation developed high expectations for their adult standard
of living. However, because they are a huge generation, boomers
moving through the labor market have had a much harder time
compared to the smaller groups that came before or immediately
after. Downward mobility has been a problem for the boomers
because (1) many found career mobility blocked, even as their financial needs and family responsibilities increased; (2) competition for jobs retarded wage growth; and (3) because of the
weaker career prospects for this generation, families needed two
income-earners, pushing more people (mainly wives) out to
work. This placed even more pressure on the job market. To cap
the phenomenon, the size of the baby boom cohort created short-
ages in everything from child care (in their early adult years) to retirement homes (as they age).[43]

As MIT economist Frank Levy has shown in his most recent
book, *The New Dollars and Dreams*, we still face declining wage
growth for cohorts as they move through the life cycle: "A thirty
year old male high school graduate earned about one-third less

in 1995 (about $12,000) than his father had earned in the early 1980s." Why is this the case? Men's earnings were growing rapidly from the end of World War II to the mid-1970s. Thereafter they started going south. As Levy (in press) explains:

> In 1973 men who worked year round and full-time had median earnings of $35,000 (in 1995 dollars). In light of postwar experience, these median earnings shown have grown to about $43,–45,000 by 1995. But, in fact, prime age men who worked full time in 1995 had median earnings of $31,5000, with most of the downward pull concentrated among men who had not gone beyond high school.

As Figure 2.7 shows, each generation entering the labor market since the golden years of the post-war boom has found the going tougher. There are two measurements that matter. The first shows what happened to the median income of, for example, thirty-year-olds at different points in history. Starting from their peak in 1975, every decade thereafter was worse for thirty-year-old men. The same is true for their forty-year-old brothers.[44]

This figure also helps us examine the experience of cohorts—individuals moving through the life cycle. Here the story is one

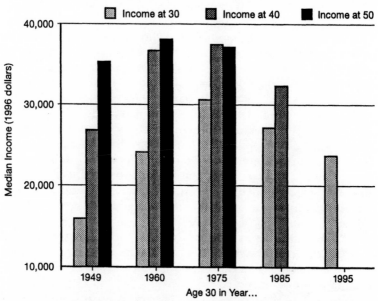

Source: Historical Income Tables P-7. Age Income Statistics Branch/HHES Division.U.S. Bureau of the Census.

Figure 2.7 Earnings for Five Cohorts of US Men

of slowing rates of income growth. Men who were thirty in 1960 saw a big jump in their income by the time they hit sixty in 1990. But when we look at the generation that moved from thirty to forty between 1985 and 1995 we see a much smaller increase in their earnings as they got older. Most people have at least a dim understanding of the standard of living their older siblings or parents enjoyed at the same point in their lives. The divergence in generational experience grates when today's thirty-year-olds find they cannot afford to buy a house, though their parents did with relative ease, or that putting their children through college will drain the bank balance, where other generations found their way to higher education without breaking a sweat. Slowdowns in economic growth have personal consequences that impact the mobility story and crystallize in generational frustration.[45]

Family Composition Changes in the composition of families and households also play a role in downward mobility. Getting married, having children, divorce or widowhood, and the employment status of wives, all affect the fortunes of American families. Perhaps the most important of these compositional changes for downward mobility is divorce. When divorced women are the sole or main source of family support, downward mobility usually follows simply because ex-wives cannot match the earning capacity of their ex-husbands.[46] Even now, women in the labor force earn only seventy-six cents for every dollar earned by men.

Only part of the problem can be attributed to differences between men and women in work experience and home related responsibilities.[47] Much of the differential is due to job segregation and discrimination. Pink-collar jobs, those predominantly filled by women, are disproportionately poorly paid, offer fewer prospects for advancement, and have weaker provisions for job security.[48] The disadvantages divorcees face upon entering the labor market are compounded by erratic or inadequate payment of alimony and child support.

One important aspect of the divorce process is the insensitivity of no-fault divorce to the nature of assets in the modern family. Tangible assets represent a declining proportion of family worth, while employment histories, educational credentials, and other aspects of "human capital" are increasing in value and importance. Yet when valuables are "equally" divided in no-fault divorce, this trend is not taken into account.[49] Even though bank accounts and homes may be divided equally, the diplomas, work experience, and skills are more likely to go with the husband. The employment experience of women figures prominently in the story of downward mobility quite apart from the messy problem of divorce. For decades, married women have been streaming into the labor force in growing numbers. Increasingly families *need* two working adults to sustain a middle class lifestyle. The cross sectional evidence in Table 2.3 shows that on average, families with non-working wives are sliding downhill, both in absolute terms and relative to dual–career families.[50] The demise of the traditional housewife is as much a matter of economic necessity as it is a response to changing social values.

Squeezes in the family life cycle—points at which the ratio of income to needs drops—are critical elements in the downward mobility story as well.[51] Two stages in adult lives tend to mark the onset of financial problems. The first is in early adulthood, typically under age twenty-five for blue-collar workers and a little later for professionals. This squeeze occurs because the cost of setting up an independent household coincides with a period of low income.[52] Expenditures on cars, appliances, furnishing, and buying or renting a home fall heavily at this point—thus many young couples find themselves struggling to make ends meet.

A second squeeze occurs when children reach the age that is most expensive to provide for: twelve to seventeen. This squeeze is more intense for blue-collar and lower-white-collar employees, whose earnings flatten around the point when their children become teens, than it is for professionals whose income curves continue to rise. Difficulties of this kind are temporary. Families recover as mortgages are paid off or children leave home. However, there are long term forces at work that have tightened the vise in recent years. The setting-up-a-household squeeze got tighter through the 1980s and 90s because the cost of home ownership escalated. Despite a decline in interest rates, housing

Table 2.3   **Median Income of Families 1976–96[1]**

	1976	1996	*Percent Change*
All married couple families	42,799	49,707	+14%
Wife in paid Labor force	49,476	58,381	+15%
Wife not in Labor force	36,397	33,748	−7%

1. SOURCE: Historical Income Tables—Families. Type of Families (All Races) By Median and mean Income. 1947–1996. Prepared from the March current Population Survey by the Income Statistics Branch / HHES Division, US Bureau of the Census.

prices continued to climb in the 1980s and 1990s. Hence while over 41 percent of American households headed by someone under the age of thirty-five owned a home in 1982, by 1996 that number was down to 39 percent.[53] The decline reflects both the drop in wages and the escalation in prices which, taken together, lower the fraction of young families that can afford to buy a home.

The second squeeze—the one involving the expense of teenage children—declined insofar as the average number of children per family dropped significantly after the baby boom cohort. In 1955, the average number of children under eighteen per family was 1.21. By 1997, that number was down to .91—a considerable slide.[54] Yet the cost of educating those children rose far faster than inflation. Especially for families intent on seeing their children through college, the gain from having fewer kids was offset by the higher price tag for educating them.

*

It would seem that David Patterson is not alone in his plight. Millions of Americans have met similar fates. Whether downward mobility is defined in terms of income loss or occupational dislocation or both, it is clear this is a problem that plagues a large proportion of our population in good times and bad. Divorce, coupled with relatively weaker prospects for women in the American labor market, pushes many single-parent families down the ladder. Some downwardly mobile families never find their way back into the labor force and remain unemployed for many years. Yet even those who manage to get new jobs typically find they must settle for less than what they were accustomed to.

For some this will be a permanent condition: they do not recover. Others spend months or years fighting their way back to square one. In time they may find the respectable positions they once had, but many lose years in the bargain and find it impossible to recapture the career advances that would have been theirs had they not been displaced. In both instances, the damage— financial and emotion—is lasting and painful.

If so many people are subjected to the downside of the American dream, if there are large-scale economic processes at work that ordinary folk cannot control, why do people like David Patterson come to see themselves as responsible for what has befallen them? And is his response the norm? We can only know that by looking beyond the statistical trends and into the lives of those who have fallen from grace.

3

Rejected Managers and the
Culture of Meritocracy

The cover photo of *Fortune* magazine carries a picture of a confident, elegant, powerful-looking man striding out the door of an unnamed corporate headquarters. His impeccable blue suit, conservative tie, and beautiful leather briefcase nicely complement his youthful, energetic face. This man is every inch the image of the modern executive, ready to take on the world. The accompanying headline reads: "Pushed Out at 45—Now What?" *Fortune*'s readers might be taken aback by this, but their nerves will be calmed by the cover's fine print: "Like many other managers, Silicon Valley's Joseph Rockom lost his $85,000 job but has bounced back." It seems that *Fortune* has discovered the phenomenon of managerial unemployment, but in keeping with the buoyant optimism for which it is well known, the magazine concludes that the casualties of corporate restructuring "have not lost [their] spirit," and that "most are winding up in new—and often better paying—jobs."[1]

Joseph Rockom's story is hardly cause for tears. Let go after seventeen years as a high-level executive at American Microsystems, he combined forces with a venture capitalist and founded a start-up company that manufactures computer workstations. He took a pay cut to $70,000, and where eighty people used to report to him, he ended up supervising himself alone. But *Fortune*'s readers will agree that Joe Rockom landed on his feet.

Although *Fortune* intended Joseph Rockom's story to typify the situation of the displaced executive, his successful comeback is by no means a universal experience. Many of the victims of corporate downsizing are far less fortunate. According to *Fortune*'s own research, 27 percent of the executive jobseekers remain unemployed for six months or more.[2] Government surveys show that nearly half of the displaced managers who do find new jobs go outside the managerial and professional occupations in order to obtain them. For every success like Joe Rockom, there are a substantial number of displaced managers who are either still drifting or are downwardly mobile.

Some are the victims of a business philosophy that regards the managerial work force as bloated and therefore ripe to be cut.[3] Foreign competition provides a powerful incentive for cost cutting even in an economy on the rebound. Other managers are refugees from the unprecedented wave of corporate mergers that has swept the U.S. economy in recent years. Computerization may also have lessened the need for middle managers.[4] But, perhaps most important, the business world is susceptible to fashions and fads, the latest of which appears to be "fewer levels of authority, with each manager controlling more people, and for participative management, with decisions pushed to lower levels of the company."[5] This shift from corporate organizations shaped like light bulbs ("with a lot of bloat at the top") to ones shaped like pyramids, can only mean one thing for middle managers: pink slips.

One might imagine that the downwardly mobile managers of the 1980s would be accorded some public sympathy for the dislocation they have endured in the middle years. But stories like those of Joe Rockom—which tell us that people who have what it takes in the first place will succeed even in the face of adversity—help explain why little public comprehension of managerial downward mobility is forthcoming. For *Fortune* magazine merely echoes the deep seated and widely shared belief in meritocracy that is the major motif of executive culture in America. It is a philosophy which promotes the notion that while many people will find themselves in occupational trouble, those who have the proper kind of determination and talent will succeed in the end. Edward Coffey, executive vice president of Bushell, Cruise and Associates, a New York outplacement consulting firm, counsels executives of all ages not to panic:

> Termination has become a fact of corporate life with little or no stigma. There is always another position, one that is often better paying and more satisfying. The key is to search for that new job methodically . . . and then to pursue it with confidence and determination.[6]

The credo of meritocracy is given full voice here: the displaced manager who fails to land on his feet must lack the necessary "confidence and determination."

*

This is not the first period in the nation's history when business executives have felt the sting of unemployment. In 1938, when the United States was still in the grip of the Great Depression, the American Writing Machine Company found itself the target of a successful takeover bid by another, larger corporation. Henry Simler, who had been president of AWMC, was one of the lucky ones. He survived the acquisition and was retained as a vice president in the parent company.[7] But many of his executive colleagues were less fortunate. They were forced out of AWMC and had to pound the pavement for a job in the midst of a steep recession. Seeing so many talented people in trouble motivated Simler to found the oldest executive self-help organization in the country, The Forty Plus Club of New York City, dedicated to the idea that resourceful managers can help each other find work. Today there are nine branches of this club in major cities across the United States.[8]

One might imagine that unemployed executives find comfort and safety in numbers. But this is not so. The Forty Plus Club in New York is awash in nervous anxiety.[9] The atmosphere is thick with tension as men and women pore over the daily want ads, wear their pencils down in the endless task of rewriting their resumes, and wait for the communal phone to ring with news of a job interview. When the phone does ring, people try to affect a casual, almost unconcerned air. But knuckles whiten until they know who the call is for, and disappointed members gaze up at the ceiling in hope of deliverance. The waiting is punctuated by the purposive activity of club members who drill the club's new recruits in job interview techniques, pass judgment on their résumés, and search by phone for job leads for each other.

The New York office is located in the heart of the financial district. The World Trade Center dominates the scene, its massive twin towers overlooking narrow streets bustling with international commerce. Professionals in pinstripes swarm around the city's major insurance firms and brokerage houses, while bicycle messengers weave their way around cars and pedestrians alike. Walking along the avenues around the Forty Plus Club, one rubs shoulders with the powerful and the pressured. Everyone seems to be in a hurry: Men and women with briefcases under their arms eat lunch on the run and are swallowed up in turn by the marble entranceways of New York's financial establishments.

Forty Plus members try to blend into this scene: They commute from home to the club and back during the same morning and evening rush hours that the denizens of Wall Street endure. They dress in suits and ties. But they are painfully aware that in the midst of all the frenzied activity on Wall Street, they have nowhere to rush to. After years of rushing to work, trying to meet deadlines or beat out the competition, they now find themselves with empty appointment calendars, and their greatest challenge is to kill time rather than find it.

The club aids in this effort to put structure back into structureless lives. It fills the days of the unemployed executives with constructive activities, tasks that give shape to the chaos its members experience. The club has a daily routine, an attempt to impose a sense of order and control through a ritualized imitation of work.[10] This helps, but in all their lives, most members of Forty Plus have never felt so lacking in control.

Mondays always commence with meetings. In the morning, everyone congregates in a large room cluttered with old furniture, ancient typewriters, tables overflowing with the *Wall Street Journal*, industry newsletters, and local want ads. Cigarette smoke hangs heavily in the air. The club president, who has himself been out of a job for two years, opens the meeting with a ritual query: "Have any of our members 'gone to jobs' in the last week?" On those occasions when the answer is yes, he takes his gavel and bangs loudly on a large brass bell. Much of the time, his question is met with downcast eyes and shuffling feet. Good news can be hard to come by in the Forty Plus Club, even though many members do eventually find employment.

To counteract the strained mood, the president moves on to introduce the new members. Every week some four or five new faces join the crowd in the downtown office. Members are accepted only after a careful review of their references and occupational histories. Forty Plus wants to convey to the business world a sense of elitism and exclusivity, to dispel any notion that they are a bunch of has-beens just killing time. Hence they only admit men and women who are over the age of forty, whose most recent employment was of a professional or managerial nature, and whose earnings exceeded $40,000 in the last year of formal employment.

The initiates are new to the club, but they are well seasoned in the ways of the unemployed. Most have already been out of work for six months or more; they have gone the route of the executive recruiting agencies;[11] they have filed hundreds of job applications; they have gotten nowhere. Most are surprised and demoralized by the fact that they have failed to find a job before coming to the club. The financial implications of prolonged unemployment have already manifested themselves, and their families are in various states of distress. Some are on the verge of losing their homes; others already have. Pounding the pavement by day, members must calm their families' fears by night.

Chancing upon the club's ad (which the *New York Times* runs without charge), they turn to Forty Plus as an avenue of last resort. Hence, when they stand to be introduced, they look at the seasoned members with a mixture of hope and despair. For the initiates are in the presence of the long-term unemployed and the downwardly mobile. The audience can sense their ambivalence. The tension is diffused by the president's ritual welcome: "We hope you won't be among us for long." New members stand to introduce themselves by giving a capsule summary of their occupational background. No mention is made of unemployment, but much is said about their aspirations for the future. While the old-timers may laugh and joke about each other, no sign of derision or lack of respect is shown to these initiates. Their shaky condition is tactfully honored.

The club's membership varies in terms of age, occupation, and family circumstances. Most are men in their late forties and early fifties. Nearly all are married suburban dwellers, with dependent teenage and college-age children. There are a handful of women, and though accorded respect in keeping with their executive status, they remain a minority. The club's atmosphere is quite masculine in tone. The range of industries from which the members derive includes insurance, high-technology fields (computers and electronics), high-volume retail sales, shipping, finance and banking, stock brokerage, oil and chemical industries, and high-level public sector fields (municipal and federal finance). Since heavy manufacturing is not well represented in the local area, managers from smokestack industries are rarely seen at this branch of Forty Plus.

Most of the seasoned members have been unemployed for one to two years. But there are some who have been "out" for much longer. Now dependent on borrowed funds, inheritances, the wages of spouses who previously had not worked for years, or the contributions of kin, they nevertheless continue to pursue job prospects commensurate with their previous experience as business executives.

The circumstances under which most of the club members found themselves thrust out in the cold mirror the statistical findings discussed in the previous chapter. Most had been terminated as a result of industry shakeouts in which companies affected by declining prices or sales (for example, in the oil and computer industries) or foreign competition had cut costs by shrinking their staffs. Others had been the victims of mergers and acquisitions, in which two management structures were collapsed into one and the extra individuals deemed expendable. Some merger refugees had been through the demoralizing experience of reinterviewing for their own jobs, of trying to convince higher management that they were best suited for the positions created by merger, only to find that someone else was chosen. This was particularly true for those who had worked in financial services (banking, brokerage, and insurance industries, among others).

A few had lost their jobs as a direct result of personal conflicts or charges of incompetence, but this was the exception rather than the rule. Even these people had been long-term employees who had worked five to twenty years for their companies prior to dismissal. They were not, therefore, drawn from the ranks of the inexperienced or from among those who had, in the past, had difficulty holding down a steady job.

Downward mobility and unemployment are not synonymous, but they are related.[12] Many managers spend time on the unemployment line at some point in their working careers. If they recover their footing quickly by finding new jobs that are equivalent in pay and prestige, they assume their old life-styles and identities with minimal interruption. They are not downwardly mobile. However, for those less fortunate, job loss has more perverse outcomes. Some people remain unemployed for such a long period of time that for all practical purposes their situation is permanent.[13] They are clearly downwardly mobile.

For yet others, unemployment is a way station to a lower-ranking occupation. These people do find new jobs, but not before spending substantial time in the purgatory of unemployment, unsure of the eventual outcome of their efforts to find new jobs. Unemployment translates into occupational downward mobility: people who face financial ruin because of prolonged joblessness are weak in "bargaining power." Many cannot afford to hold out for jobs befitting their real qualifications and background. So they take what they can get.

Approximately 25 percent of the Forty Plus Club members find new jobs that exceed the income they had before joining; another 25 percent break even; and the remainder take jobs below their old income, disappear altogether, or remain job searchers—often for years.[14] For the downwardly mobiles—both those who remain "permanently" unemployed and those who eventually find new, lesser ranking jobs—the time spent unemployed is filled with gnawing anxiety and crushing disappointments.

Middle-aged managers who have lost their jobs carry indelible memories of the day they were "let go." It is a central scene in the drama of downward mobility. With so much time on their hands, they replay these scenes over and over again in their minds, now berating themselves for having said the wrong thing, now recalling the acute embarrassment of being let go. Some suffered the humiliation of being fired on a Friday afternoon with a security guard standing over their shoulders, having been ordered to clean out the desks they had occupied for fifteen years or more. Many companies worry about the damage a disgruntled employee might do in the angry hours that remain to them in the workplace.

The way in which firings are stage-managed says a great deal about the kinds of social relationships that develop in business settings. Joe Malone worked for a recording company in New York City that he founded with a friend some twelve years ago. The firm was small but reasonably successful, and it allowed Joe to put his law degree (earned at night over the course of years) and his previous business experience to work. When the business hit a snag, Joe was maneuvered out by his former partner. He was cut loose without warning in a nasty screaming match that ended a twenty-five-year friendship. He can remember the conversation as if it were yesterday.

Joe is still fuming over the situation two years later, but at least he confronted his nemesis directly. In larger firms the bad news is often delivered in a more indirect fashion. Victor Katz worked as an economist for a major oil company. When the industry hit the skids in the early eighties, the personnel cutbacks were massive. Nearly 20,000 employees were let go in the course of six months. Even so, Victor was shocked when his division manager handed him the bad news. He never met the man who was actually responsible for the decision to let him go. To this day he still has no concrete idea who it was that lowered the boom. His immediate boss explained that there was nothing he could do to alter the orders that had come down from on high. The company was bent on reducing costs by "surplussing" expendable employees. The layers of bureaucracy in a large corporation protect those charged with holding down costs from seeing the damage they do to employees at close range. The fired executive thinks, How could they do this to me? But the question remains unresolved because it is never clear whether the decision makers knew anything about him or her as an individual or whether they simply fixed on the bottom line of the corporation's profit-and-loss statement.

Those who were able to face their executioners and those who were insulated from them by layers of hierarchy share something: They feel like crime victims. Their memories of being fired are suffused with a sense of frustration that they did not lash back, that they failed to defend themselves adequately, that they went out with a whimper and not a bang. Joe Malone does not feel this way; he said his piece. But virtually all the others at Forty Plus berate themselves for having failed to scream. They realize that the outcome of the situation would not have changed if they had played the scene differently. Yet they feel that an opportunity for some self-satisfaction has been lost once and for all. The episode remains forever lacking in closure.

It is customary in larger businesses to provide some kind of severance arrangements for managerial employees who are let go; generally they provide lump sums based on length of service.

A minority allow their former executives to continue using their offices, phones, and company credit cards, as a gesture of concern and support in the job searching phase they now confront. These arrangements are crucial both to the morale and to the financial health of managers, who can use the severance cushion to stave off the financial plunge that most other laid-off workers face. But they are not extended to everyone.

The public has an exaggerated sense of the benefits provided to displaced managers. William Agee's celebrated departure from the Bendix Corporation in the wake of a takeover by Allied was smoothed by the $4 million guaranteed income he received on the way out the door. But his experience was hardly typical. Golden parachutes, generous compensation packages awarded to executives in the event of corporate takeovers, are rare, the province of high-level management in big companies. *Industry Week* reports that only 15 percent of the nation's 665 largest companies had golden parachute clauses, and these only for top executive employment contracts.[15]

Smaller firms often escort managers out the door with little more than a handshake and a promise—reliable to varying degrees[16]—to provide references for future jobs. Among the men and women at Forty Plus, it was rare to find anyone who had been given more than four months' severance pay, and quite common to see long-term employees (ten years and more) dumped unceremoniously, with no thought given to their needs while hunting for a new job.

Severance pay is, of course, of considerable practical value. It buys time for people who have to make major readjustments in their lives and relieves the pressure of immediate financial catastrophe. At the same time, it is a potent symbol of esteem. Managers often fail to appreciate their own vulnerability to job loss, although they know that the world of business places the bottom line ahead of loyalty to employees. Still, they do believe in a code of honor in the corporate jungle. Severance pay recognizes the social responsibility of the corporation for an employee's well-being and expresses some gratitude for years of loyal service. For those who do not receive even this degree of recognition, the pain is deep: It suggests that people they trusted, organizations to which they had devoted many years, saw them as little more than instruments for making a profit.

Most displaced managers realized that their firms were experiencing financial difficulties. They had seen lower-ranking workers get fired. They were privy to boardroom discussions of the need to trim costs. Some had even been involved in the decision making over how best to downsize a "bloated" staff. But virtually none expected the ax to fall on them. Hence, with few exceptions, their response to their personal pink slips was one of shock.[17] For hours, days, even months, they really could not believe what had happened. And in the midst of their dismay, they faced one of the most difficult hurdles of the unemployment experience: breaking the news to their families.

This task was difficult enough for people who thought they would have no trouble finding new positions. It was far worse for those who had been bounced from troubled firms in troubled industries. The sinking feeling that they were in for a long bout of unemployment kept some from sharing the worst moments of their professional lives with family members. Jack Rigley, a refugee from the world of big oil, was so worried about the disappointment and upset the news would cause his family that he hid the fact that he had been terminated for nearly six months.[18] He continued to dress in a suit and tie every morning, leave the house, and stay out all day, returning home at the normal hour as if nothing had gone awry. Jack actually spent the days in coffee shops reading want ads or trying to make contact with old friends in the oil industry. Since Jack handled the family bank accounts, giving his wife an "allowance" to cover household expenses and doling out "mad money" to the kids on Saturdays, it was possible for him to conceal their declining bank balance, draw on his severance pay, raid the savings account, and keep the truth to himself for quite a while.

Rigley's experience is extreme, though he was not alone in his efforts to keep his fate a secret. Eventually, even he had to confess: As the months of unemployment persisted and the financial repercussions became more serious, he was faced with no choice but to tell the family, cut their expenses drastically, look for ways to borrow money, and liquidate whatever assets could be spared. But revealing the truth was, in his words a kind of "coming out of the closet." It was the first step in the symbolic stripping of his identity, for in confessing his predicament, he redefined himself in his family's eyes as someone unable to exert control over his own life and, by extension, the circumstances of theirs.

But most men and women did tell their immediate family members right away and calmed them with assurances that it would not be long before they would find new positions. Bolstered in most cases by the support of their families, reminded of their college credentials, their technical expertise, and their good reputations, they responded to the situation as a challenge.[19]

While the managers at Forty Plus were not pleased to be on the receiving end of pink slips, they were initially confident of their prospects. They had good references, contacts in their respective fields, and no reason to believe they would be in trouble for long. Indeed, Charles Knudson—formerly an executive with a transportation firm—decided to take his family on a month-long, expensive European vacation at that point.[20] For the first time in a long while, he had unencumbered time, a luxury sure to disappear upon starting a new job. His confidence in the future was infectious, hence neither his wife nor his children saw any cause for concern.

Confident that new jobs would be forthcoming, most Forty Plus members contacted friends and acquaintances in the industries from which they had come as a first step toward new employment. This proved easier for some than others, since different kinds of jobs produce different kinds of friendship networks.[21] Managers whose previous jobs brought them into contact with a large number of people outside their own firms had readymade networks to tap.[22] Joe Jorgensen had been booted from his position as a national sales manager. He had business acquaintances across the United States with whom he had dealt on a regular basis for fifteen years. It had been part and parcel of his responsibilities to get to know customers to whom he could direct his sales staff. When he found himself in need of a new job, there were plenty of people in fields allied to his own that he could call. By alerting them to his needs, he created a large cadre of remote sensors on the lookout for possibilities.

But George Mahoney, a computer scientist and engineer who lost his job managing data processing for a large New York bank, found that his contacts were basically internal. He was well known and respected by many important people in his own bank, but his job responsibilities had not involved frequent contact with counterparts in other banks. Kin were of little assistance because George came from a working-class family with little connection to the professional, white-collar world. Hence when it came time to search for another job, he was forced to rely almost exclusively on the want ads, hoping to capitalize on his skills and experience rather than on weak ties.

Corporate cultures sometimes curtail the extent and depth of friendship networks, even where structural conditions of work might, in another firm, promote them. Certain corporations are well known for their impersonal, bureaucratic atmosphere, where employees bolt for the door at five o'clock and where even managerial employees do not socialize together. They are often companies that require a high degree of geographical mobility of their managers, moving them every few years from one part of the country to another. While this may develop managers who have a greater command of organizational dynamics and a "national" rather than a "local" sense of corporate loyalty, it has the unintended consequence of decreasing the integration and attachment of the mobile manager into the local culture.[23] David Patterson, who moved across the country to take advantage of a promotion, found this out the hard way. Not wanting to disrupt his children in the middle of a school year, he moved to New York on his own until the family could join him. Two years later he found himself on the unemployment lines. When asked whether any of his workmates had helped him, he responded:

> No, they didn't do anything . . . I suppose they weren't really friends of mine. You know, I spent six months in a motel here before my family joined me. No one ever even invited me for dinner. I tried to make friends . . . but none of the company people ever made an effort. Can you imagine not even getting an invitation for dinner? That was such a lonely period. But it continued like that after my wife and kids arrived. That's just the kind of company it is.

Economic conditions are as important as corporate culture in determining how valuable a network is in finding a job. Managerial refugees from corporate downsizing usually found that contacts inside their old firm were of little help. Their friends had either joined the unemployment lines themselves, or were too anxious about holding onto their own jobs to stick their necks out to place friends.[24] Job losers in the high-stakes brokerage firms began to find this out the hard way in the fall of 1987, when Salomon Brothers chopped its highly paid work force by 12 percent, a harbinger of the dreaded "Black Monday" in October when the stock market crashed and billions of dollars were lost in the space of a day. As the lines formed around the xerox machines to pump out resumes, many turned to their networks in the business to find new jobs. But as one career counselor familiar with the brokerage scene pointed out: "Many people have been looking for help from other people, 'networking' to get into other firms. Now, though, their contacts are getting axed. With their contacts all in the same boat, their whole campaign shuts down very quickly."[25]

The employment picture was often surprisingly bleak even in healthy fields. The tendency for large firms to expand by acquiring other companies means that employment opportunities decrease for managers, even as the industries themselves are healthy. Departments are consolidated in those merged firms, and managers lose their jobs. Mergers also weaken the value of friendship networks in the job-searching process. Once again, those still on the inside are almost as vulnerable to the consequences of merger fever as those who are already unemployed.

Four phenomena—downsizing in individual corporations, declines in a whole industry, merger fever, and economy-wide recessions—together throw managerial employees into unemployment. The web of networks and contacts which are critical to career advancement in normal times, seems to falter when confronted with disruptions of this magnitude.[26]

Out of want, unemployed managers went beyond personal contacts in soliciting jobs. They scoured the want ads of the *Wall Street Journal* and found many opportunities to pursue: jobs for Vice Presidents and Comptrollers, for engineers and sales directors, for regional managers and research and development staff. Companies trumpet themselves in these ads as wonderful places to work, where there are prospects for rapid advancement. They all seem to be courting the fast-track, self-motivated executive who is looking for a new position. For executives recently dismissed, who think of themselves as successful people who have suffered slight setbacks, the *Wall Street Journal* is something of a candyshop.

Full of confidence, they send out batch upon batch of résumés and letters of inquiry. Commonly, Forty Plus members wrote 100 letters per month at the beginning of their job searches. They were staggered to discover how few bore fruit. Typically a hundred letters yielded a mere handful of interviews. The vast majority of letters went unacknowledged, even in instances where the job-hunters were certain that their credentials were a perfect match. But news of those few interviews was met with sheer delight.

Hopes soared. Husbands discussed with their wives the merits of one employer over another and the potential challenges of the job. Few could stop themselves from fantasizing about the future: where the family would move to, how best to manage the new commute, what kind of life-style the new salary would permit. The days up to the interview were a time of suppressed excitement for the whole family, with everyone trying to remain calm, and the job seeker concentrating on projecting himself as an executive prepared to weigh his options, rather than a desperate figure ready to jump at any offer.

The interviews themselves were dissected after the fact, sometimes with the whole family around the dinner table wanting to share in Dad's triumph. Every detail and nuance of the interview was analyzed for hidden meaning. And then everyone would hold their breath and wait for the phone to ring.

Abe Forman, a tall, broad-shouldered man, graying at the temples, put twenty years into the management of a large regional chain of grocery stores. He was pushed aside in the fallout from a merger, and he found himself pounding the pavement for the first time since his early twenties. In the eighteen months he searched without the aid of Forty Plus, several "live" possibilities presented themselves:

> I was interviewed for three jobs that I thought I had a good chance for. But the same thing happened every time. People would call and ask me to come and interview. I'd go and things would go fine. I had the experience they were looking for. The job was just right. They'd say, "We'll call you next week" and I'd go home and tell my wife that I thought our troubles were over. I'd feel just great. Such a relief to think that the whole nightmare was going to end.
>
> The next week would come, and I'd sit home waiting to hear from them. Nothing. No phone calls. Nothing. Friday would come and I'd start to say to myself, Maybe they just got tied up. But the week after would pass with no sign. Finally after a month, I'd call them back myself, even though I felt embarrassed. I just couldn't stand not knowing what was going on.
>
> They'd say, "Oh, the job disappeared," or "We decided to hold off on the job for another six months to see how our business is doing." They never even thought to let me know, and there I'd spent all that time going crazy at home and my wife and kids going crazy.

The etiquette of these episodes took on great symbolic significance for unemployed managers: Their treatment by potential employers was taken as a barometer of their worth. When employers courted them for interviews, the status they had once possessed was resurrected. When they were politely rejected, they were hurt. But when they were left in limbo, and only weeks later discovered that the job had evaporated or that another candidate had been given the nod, they felt far worse. Employers seemed to perceive them as so insignificant that they did not even warrant routine courtesy.

To compound the tragedy, most job seekers felt increasingly embarrassed in front of their own family members. Unable to contain themselves when live prospects developed, they had inadvertently raised the hopes and expectations of their wives and children. Entire families were riding an emotional roller coaster alongside the job hunter. When the jobs failed to come through, the discouraged manager had to face a roomful of disappointed faces. When these ups and downs happened repeatedly over the long months of unemployment, they had to nurse their own disappointment in the midst of the whole family's crushed expectations. As Abe Forman put it:

> How often can you put your family through this kind of thing? After a while you start to think about whether it would be better not to tell them anything at all. At least that way they wouldn't be so disappointed when things don't work out. But you want to share the good news or at least your hopes, otherwise it's just doom and gloom in the house. Either way it's a bad scene.

Disappointments were followed by crushing demoralization and shame. Battered in this way, the managers' optimism sank by several notches, only to soar again at the news of another prospect or additional interviews.

As months pass, as hundreds of applications go unanswered, and the number of new interviews shrinks from a trickle to none, the unemployed managers begin to realize with horror that the stigma of having lost their jobs, and the fact that they are applying for new ones as "unemployed persons," outweighs their many years of experience, formal credentials, and specialized expertise. Instead of being treated as experienced applicants ready for work, they are shunned as "spoiled goods."

Erving Goffman argues that social interaction is a kind of dramatic performance, in which people act out images of themselves.

In *Stigma: Notes on the Management of Spoiled Identity,* he examines the special problems encountered in the dramaturgical process by individuals who are, in some way, socially "damaged." Being unemployed is clearly a stigmatized condition in this society.[27] It broadcasts to employers that there is something not quite right about this person. It prevents the job seeker from constructing an appealing image of himself and throws the dramaturgy of the employment interview off-base. It is an untoward aspect of a manager's biography, which must either be hidden[28] or carefully explained lest it be taken as a sign of some deeper problem: This person seems intelligent and experienced, but is he an alcoholic, does he have an impossible personality, does he refuse to take direction from others? These questions would not arise were it not for the fact that unemployment as a social status is understood as a surface signal of a flaw hiding below. Hence unemployment forces its victims into a posture of "damage control" during interviews, when they are already under the greatest pressure to maintain a stage presence filled with confidence. They do not know whether to address the problem directly, and offer elaborate explanations for their unemployed state, or whether to remain silent on the issue.

Paul Armand, executive refugee from the international insurance business, had been out of work for nearly two years by the time he arrived at the Forty Plus Club. He found it hard to keep alive the network he had established over thirty years in the field:

> I keep in contact with people in the industry as much as I can, but that's not very much. You know what it is, it's the pride. It's hard to call up and say, "Hi, this is Paul Armand." You know what they think? Holy mackerel, it's Paul. Is he calling to ask me for a job? It's hard to make myself call under these circumstances. It's that stigma that's attached. Perhaps it's in my mind, but I feel it's there.

Paul, like most displaced managers, has developed extreme sensitivity to the nuances of eye contact and voice modulation in casual encounters with business associates. He reads negative sentiment into these exchanges where, perhaps, none is really present.

> You say "Hi, how are you doing?" and people look at you strangely and walk the other way. That happens a lot. . . . They probably feel that it's the same as when a beggar comes up on the street. They don't want anything to do with it. There's a general tendency

for people not to want to see the unpleasant side of life. . . . If they talk to you, they're afraid you're going to ask them for money or give them a sob story.

Paul is certain that he exudes his unemployment, that people he meets downtown can tell just by looking at him that in putting himself forward as executive material he is somehow living a lie. He subjects himself to the "third degree," examining his behavior carefully, trying to figure out what he is doing to project a stigmatized image, even though no one has ever told him point-blank that they think of him as a loser. Scott Budge and Ronald Janoff, counselors who run support groups for Forty Plus members, have described this syndrome:

> . . . A common expression of these feelings is the sense that a stigma of some sort is visible—that contacts, interviewers, or employers can "see" one's unemployment; that is, see *through* it to one's basic condition of worthlessness. Consequently each interview becomes a personal test on a deep level, a nagging worry about whether "he saw it" or whether one's overreaction to this anxiety itself led to an artificial presentation—which undermined the cherished rapport of an interview.[29]

The trauma of unemployment during the Depression provoked widespread feelings of personal inadequacy even though the official jobless rate skyrocketed to well over 25 percent. At these catastrophic levels, one might think that victims would identify with the masses of the unemployed and reject personal responsibility for their fate.[30] But in the mid-1980s, when managerial unemployment has yet to exceed 5 percent, it is little wonder that the unlucky few feel different and suspect that they can be easily identified.[31]

Loneliness dogs the heels of the unemployed executive. Those aspects of managerial life that were coveted before—autonomy, independence, and privacy—boomerang in the form of unwanted isolation. In upper-middle-class suburbs, the large homes of managers and executives are cloistered behind fences, widely separated by green lawns. There is little sense of neighborhood, even if the inhabitants know each other. Fourth of July barbecues are more likely to occur in the confines of country clubs than on the streets. Privacy is a luxury of the upper middle class, a sign of having arrived at a high station in life. It allows the privileged to control whom they interact with, refusing contact with those they do not wish to know. But the consequences of this privatized existence are profoundly negative once a family finds itself in trouble.

Managers typically socialize with their own class: They make friends with the lawyers who serve their companies, the managers of client companies, and fellow managers of similar rank from their own firms. Socializing revolves around an affluent life-style of expensive restaurants and nights on the town. Unemployment may not interfere with this social life in the beginning, but ultimately it begins to intrude. The club membership, the opera tickets, the summer vacations in Cape Cod, drop by the wayside, if not immediately, then eventually. With them goes the social context in which upper-middle-class friendship is sustained.

Friends are often understanding for a time and organize dinner parties at their homes so that the unfortunates can participate, but even this helping hand becomes uncomfortable for the unemployed after a while: Socializing requires reciprocity.[32] Before long, the unemployed manager begins to withdraw from his social circles, though he often feels it is he who has been abandoned. He finds himself feeling uncomfortable even among old friends.[33]

David Patterson is a congenial man who is easy to like. In the midst of relentless financial pressure, the threat of losing his house, and his inability to crack the job market, he could summon the energy to be friendly and outgoing. But he would slump in his chair when he talked about how isolated he felt in the wake of his job loss:

> All of a sudden everybody stops talking to you. It's like a disease. . . . Friends, associates, best friends . . . they start calling you less or stop calling you altogether. People don't know what to say. They think they're going to upset you, they don't know how to talk to you. This is when you need friends; people you can associate with.

David was the first to admit that he and his wife could not spare the money to go out to a movie, much less to the good restaurants they used to frequent. Yet he perceived his friends as having abandoned him in his hour of need and wondered whether he really *had* any friends: "The greatest thing someone can do is help you. The next best thing is try. . . . If they don't try, are they really friends?"

Social isolation has practical consequences for recovery: Weaker social networks mean fewer sources of job leads, references, or advice. In the managerial world, who you know is everything. Newspaper ads are of some importance in lower-level jobs, but for high-level positions, the "old boy" network—those subtle lines of influence that link like-minded and like-situated members of the executive world—generally dictates who will be given serious consideration and whose résumé will be tossed in the trash bin.[34] As the months go by in which the unemployed man is out of circulation, his ties become rusty. If years pass, as they have for many men and women at Forty Plus, the links to their old social milieu become, for all practical purposes, dead.[35]

On those increasingly rare occasions when long-term unemployed executives do rub shoulders with their old acquaintances from the workplace or the country club, the shame and embarrassment they experience transforms the encounter into an unpleasant reminder of failure, of status lost and a world they can no longer share. They feel their old friends pity them, an intolerable experience for men and women once accustomed to power, authority, and autonomy. Conversations are halting, the parties squirming with discomfort. The rejected manager backs away from his friends almost as quickly as they move away from him, yet he feels the sting of rejection.[36]

As the personal crisis deepens, the downwardly mobile manager finds himself increasingly alone with his troubles. He loses contact with his social friends; his former business associates steer clear of his calls; his day-to-day isolation makes it difficult to reach out and form new ties. Solitude closes in from all directions and shatters the social structure that undergirds the normal life of the managerial family.

Every aspect of the family's life becomes strangely different. Where once everyone was always too busy rushing off to social or business engagements to spend dinner together, upset adults and children now find themselves facing one another across the dining table, spending the evening hours together stuck at home. The ultimate victim of downward mobility is not just the breadwinner's occupational identity, nor even the checkbook and savings account, but the whole family's sense of normalcy. Nothing seems the same.

Although social isolation is widespread among displaced managers, it would be a mistake to conclude that unemployment and downward mobility have an identical effect on everyone. Income loss and unemployment can produce very different adaptations and problems for different kinds of people. An interesting contrast was particularly evident between the married men and the gay men at the Forty Plus Club. In many respects, gay managers were indistinguishable from their straight counterparts in age, in occupation, and in the extent of their downward mobility. Several gay managers had lost their jobs in the reshuffling that accompanied corporate mergers. They had been unemployed for approximately the same length of time, and as such were as committed as their straight colleagues to finding new jobs. But here the similarities stopped: The gay men were not as depressed, they seemed more optimistic, and they did not assume that their friends thought ill of them. Why were their responses so different, when their losses were so similar?

One answer is to be found in certain features of the gay community that buffer unemployed gays from some of the emotional hardships that their straight counterparts face. The most obvious of these is the lack of traditional nuclear family structures in the gay world. We are accustomed to thinking of the family as a "haven in a heartless world," and, indeed, many downwardly mobile family men found great comfort in the understanding embrace of their families. But security has its price. Once unemployed, difficulties in supporting dependents were an unremitting source of anxiety and guilt for married breadwinners. The gay managers were spared this: Even those who were involved in long-term relationships considered themselves financially independent. They did not have to come home at the end of a fruitless day of job hunting to face children and spouses whose worries were becoming increasingly difficult to quell.[37]

Gay executives also told a different story about the impact of unemployment on their social lives. People whose lives stand outside the family—whether gay or simply single—are often able to draw on "lateral" sources of support more easily than their married, straight counterparts. The gay men at Forty Plus had active social lives and very extensive friendship networks both before and after they lost their jobs. Even those embedded in marriagelike relations had a large number of friends whom they saw regularly. Gay managers were as concerned as anyone else about their standard of living, but their friendships were less dependent on being able to "keep up with the Joneses."

Lane Antonovich had been at Forty Plus for four months when we met, and had put in nearly six months of job hunting on his own before turning to the club. A young-looking forty-five, he had spent the past seven years in high-volume retail sales, climbing up the managerial ranks in a large firm before they parted company. Lane was now trying to make a career switch into the field of graphic design, a move that had not yet yielded any positive results. But he was invariably to be found bustling around the club, beautifully dressed, ready to lend a hand to others in need. His optimism made him stand out like a sore thumb in the midst of the depressing atmosphere at Forty Plus.

Unlike most other members, his financial problems had had only a modest impact on his life-style. Lane had a long-term lover and a large number of friends with whom he regularly patronized the opera, movies, nightclubs, and museums for which New York City is known. He could no longer afford to purchase these tickets himself, but rather than leave him behind, his friends (and his lover) took turns picking up his tab. To hear Lane tell it, this caused him no embarrassment. Of course, he looked forward to the day when he would not need to piggyback on their generosity, but this did not seem to weigh heavily on his mind.

As a gay man, Lane was part of an occupationally diverse community with strong ties of friendship. One of his best friends is a waiter, another a shop clerk, another a bureaucrat in an insurance firm. Their incomes vary considerably, as does their occupational prestige. Their homes range from exclusive co-ops to cramped studios in run-down parts of town. In virtually every respect, they are a more varied group than the comparable networks of the straight married men, most of whose friends were similar in occupations, income, and residence. What ties Lane's friends together, apart from personal histories, are their common sexual preferences and their cultural tastes. Lane's financial losses have had little effect on his ability to socialize with them. He is not embarrassed in their presence. On the contrary, they are sources of job leads, moral support, and a good laugh. One friend who is familiar with graphic design has helped Lane find small consulting jobs that may help him build a portfolio.

Lane is not a gay activist and he does not advertise his sexuality. He does not consider it a relevant aspect of his professional biography. He is, however, part of a network of friends, which provides an identity that stands apart from the workplace. It acts as a buffer against the trauma of unemployment and downward mobility both because the social structures that surround him remain stable and unaffected, despite his occupational turmoil, and because his community does not pass judgment on its members by reference to occupational success. It is hard to know whether this stability will persist should Lane continue his downward spiral indefinitely. But the contrast between his experience and the social isolation of his managerial counterparts in the land of suburban nuclear families is unmistakable.[38] It underscores several weaknesses in mainstream (straight) managerial culture under pressure: the narrow and fragile quality of friendship networks; the centrality of occupational success to self-worth; and the heavy responsibility that supporting a family places on breadwinners.[39]

As the months of unemployment slide by, the managers' nerves begin to fray. The days seem to grow very long, as tension alternates with boredom and loneliness. The silence of the house is punctuated by children leaving for school and returning home at the end of the day, by the wife coming in and out on her round of errands. Mail delivery is eagerly awaited, even when it brings little of interest. Many find themselves suffering from sleep disturbances, so they wake early in the morning and by 10:00 A.M. have already accomplished the job-hunting tasks for the day.[40] The kinds of activities they once looked forward to—reading the newspaper, nursing a cup of coffee, watching TV—now become daytime fillers, and a source of self-criticism. Men accustomed to the bustle of the office, the pressure of deadlines, the feeling of purpose and accomplishment, berate themselves for sitting at home "wasting time." The meaning of time shifts radically:[41]

> The unemployed individual is prevented from organizing time positively because "justifiable" nonworking periods are typically given their valuation through work: coffee-breaks, weekends, vacations, periods of business-related travel, illness, recuperation and retirement are all defined in relation to one's status as a working individual. Unemployment, unhappily renders free time "unjustified," an expansion of the underside of constant productive activity, of stolen moments of idleness that each working person engages in every day.[42]

Most debilitating is the fact that the idleness is, paradoxically, pressured. Every moment spent "doing nothing" is a moment in which a clock is ticking. Mortgage payments are due, banks are calling about credit cards in arrears, savings are slipping away. Anxiety alternates with lethargy, sleep disturbance with slow panic. Before long, they are completely preoccupied with their occupational dilemmas, unable to focus for long on anything else or anyone else. Mark Emmons, a former national sales manager in his mid-fifties, describes this period:

> At the beginning I had quite a few leads, interviews. And then there came a period of nothing. It was a time of utter mental turmoil for me. . . . I was at home all day typing up letters, sending out résumés. I felt like I was a rubber band that was wound up and stretched to the breaking point. Little things, things that would normally not bother me, really got to me. Nothing was coming through. I was bucking up against a stone wall. No matter which way I turned, nothing. I was very quickly falling into a bottomless pit. [Somehow I felt] I was on the outside looking in, that I had joined the group of those not wanted.[43] I had a feeling of complete uselessness, and I felt I was too young to be useless. The days were filled with uncertainty.
>
> It got to the point where I didn't want to get up in the morning. I would make myself get up and look for work to do around the house. . . . I started doing things to the house that didn't have to be done. I didn't want to drive anywhere, burn up gas, I would sit down and type letters. I'd make mistakes and do them over and get irritated. It was just one day after another, the same.

In the many hours they spend alone with their thoughts, displaced managers seek explanations for their job loss and their fruitless search for a new position. Simultaneously inquisitor and accused, they peel away the layers of their own personalities, delving deeper and deeper for the character defects or other failings that led to their demise.

Why does self-criticism often triumph? Why do good people sacrifice their most precious remaining asset—their pride in their person and its accomplishments, their self-worth—when they have already lost their social standing and economic security? An answer to this question requires an examination of both the psychological defenses that managers use to make sense of their condition and the cultural forces that undermine their attempts to maintain self-esteem. Executives *do* seek to defend themselves against self-blame, but their efforts are undermined by powerful messages embedded in managerial culture.

Categorical Fate

The downwardly mobile managers make frequent reference to the fact that they are caught up in larger currents of economic change. Many perceive themselves as victims of social forces beyond their control. Focusing on such forces provides a rational explanation for their personal plight, and simultaneously acts as a bulwark for self-esteem. Insofar as larger forces are at fault, the unemployed person is not to be blamed.

One particular version of this idea might be called "categorical fate."[44] It refers to situations in which an individual's misfortune is attributed to his or her membership in a group (or social category) that *is as a whole subject to victimization.*

One common expression of categorical fate involves age discrimination. Older managers could not help but notice how many other silver-haired people had found their way to Forty Plus. They realized that the younger members of the club were called for job interviews more often than they were. It did not require extraordinary deductive powers to realize that age translates into victimization.[45] Positive personal attributes of work experience, laudatory references, and intellectual capabilities seemed to be outweighed by their membership in a stigmatized social category: the older manager. As one executive woman who used to work on Wall Street put it: "Employers think that [if you are] over forty you can't think anymore. Over fifty and [they think] you're burned out." When asked why a particular job for which he had interviewed did not come through, another manager replied: "I had a long interview that I thought went well, but I didn't get the job. A year later I saw the man who interviewed me and I asked him why I didn't get it. He said, 'Well, we were looking for someone in their forties.' " In some industries, the cutoff appears to be even lower. As one refugee from Madison Avenue commented: "If you're in advertising, you're dead after thirty. Age is a killer."

This is a bitter conclusion to reach, but it does buffer the self-blame that might otherwise gnaw away at the managerial unemployed. A professional cannot help the fact that he or she is fifty-five years old. This is a fact of life that cannot be altered or seen as anyone's fault.

Another form of categorical fate derives from prejudice directed toward the unemployed as a group.[46] Many Forty Plus members had had occasional job offers or inquiries from headhunters, colleagues, and competitors in earlier years when they were employed as executives. Successful and established in their fields, they took these offers or expressions of interest as their due, as flattering confirmation of their vitality and accomplishments. But once unemployed, they experienced a terrifying contrast: a trickle of interviews immediately after being laid off, slowing to almost nothing as the months or years passed and their résumés clearly revealed the hiatus of unemployment.

It was inescapable in the minds of many that categorical fate was operating here, that their individual experiences were best explained by their membership in an ill-fated group. Employers were suspicious or averse toward unemployed professionals. As one fired manager explained: "More than any racial, religious, or gender bias, the prejudice against the unemployed is so strong that no matter what qualifications you had or how close your experience was to what they needed, the fact that you weren't working now was all that mattered."

Recruiters seemed to hold stereotypical views of the jobless as justly-fired incompetents or as shiftless. Hence, simply being unemployed cast a shadow of stigma over the job hunter:

> Once I was out of work three or four months, employment agencies and companies would get very suspicious. [They'd think] "You're in this hot field and you haven't been able to get a job for four months? There must *really* be something wrong with you," and they wouldn't touch you with a ten-foot pole.

Overqualification intensifies this form of categorical fate. Once an individual is perceived as "executive material," and has the work history to prove it, it is assumed that he or she could *not* do a good job in a lesser position. A computer specialist with extensive managerial experience found himself in this situation:

> Since I'd been in charge of an EDP [data processing] office, some employers felt that I would just be an officer and wouldn't be able to go back in and do programming. People with less experience had an advantage [in getting these lower ranking jobs]. Employers were afraid I couldn't take orders.

There is a cruel irony here. After much soul-searching and disappointment, some former managers realized that they would have to settle for positions below their managerial status, only to be rebuffed by recruiters who felt these hands-on jobs were below their rank. The symbolic blow of being rejected for positions they saw as below their dignity was severe. It deepened their sense of despair, for it appeared that even when they were finally willing to lower their expectations they were still subject to defeat.

Another form of categorical fate involved the realization that some managers were, unfortunately, in the wrong industry at the wrong time. Dave Netting, an engaging Ivy League graduate now in his late forties, worked for twenty-five years as an overseas manager of an American insurance concern. When, for personal reasons, he turned down yet another overseas assignment and found himself out on the street with only four months' severance pay, he knew his timing was bad. The insurance industry was suffering the consequences of risky business policies encouraged by the very high interest rates of the early 1980s. As the losses began to mount in the mid-eighties, companies found themselves in deep trouble. This set off a wave of mergers and layoffs, a terrible market in which to look for a well-paid job like the vice presidency Dave had left behind:

> The [companies] I contacted were all going through retrenchment. The biggest [was involved in a morass of internal] company politics. As a result people were being attritioned out of there. The number two [firm] was involved in a big scandal with [their] London [office] and didn't have any positions. Now they've merged with an international broker, and the dust from that merger is still settling. The number three broker is the one I used to work with, and I'm not going back to them. The number four broker has merged with another international broker, so there's fallout from there. There's just too much shake-up in the industry at this time.

Industry conditions were such that, as Dave saw it, even people with good reputations and strong contacts were unlikely to find positions. In fact, they were likely to find their friends in the business out on the street as well. This was a dismal scenario, but it has its comforts. Dave hoped for a turnaround in the field that would sweep people like him back into employment, but he did not hold himself personally responsible for the downturns of the industry. He saw himself as one among many perfectly respectable people who were victims of an unfortunate categorical fate: an industry downturn. They didn't cause the crash, even though they were paying the price for it.

The strength of categorical fate explanations depends in part on the extent to which relevant publics are aware of economic conditions. Fellow members of the industry know how much bloodletting has been going on in the insurance world. But Dave's next-door neighbor wasn't in the insurance field and was not particularly aware of the industry's condition. His mother-in-law only knew about it through Dave; she did not possess any independent means of confirming his perspective. They were therefore skeptical of his explanations for being unable to find a new job.

Explaining one's fate by reference to a categorical fate only "works" when the audience is aware of the group's victimization. This explains in part, why categorical fate as a "reading" of personal trouble is easier to sustain for blue-collar victims of a plant closure in the steel industry than it is, for example, for executives in the computer field. American steelmakers have been in trouble for such a long period of time, that most people are aware of their plight. They are part of America's fading dominance in heavy industry. As it happens, the computer field has also undergone a profound shakeout in the 1980s. But it is a retrenchment that is not widely understood in a society in which computers are supposed to be the wave of the future.

Seeing one's predicament in terms of categorical fate turns the blame away from the individual. It may limit some of the damage to one's self-esteem and perhaps stifle the onset of self-criticism. It is ironic, then, that some researchers view this kind of defense as cause for concern. They argue that the unemployed who focus on economic conditions or larger forces controlling their destinies are embracing "the sick role."[47] The concept of the sick role, originated by Talcott Parsons, argues that adults who become ill can "opt out" of normal responsibilities for their actions because they are the victims of circumstances beyond their control (for example, illness). By analogy:

> The unemployed role may contain certain benefits such as relaxation, sympathy . . . more freedom with one's time, etc. In sum, under certain conditions unemployment, like the sick role, may be a welcome haven from everyday obligations with the added bonus that, when unemployed, one does not even have to stay in bed.[48]

This implies that people who fail to blame themselves for being fired, settle back into a comfortable, apathetic unemployment. This is certainly not the case for most downwardly mobile executives.[49] Those who avoid self-blame and view their unemployment as the workings of categorical fate are hardly relaxed and certainly do not view joblessness as a "welcome haven." Most feel intense pressure to find a new job even though they do not hold themselves entirely responsible for losing the old one. Indeed, personal responsibility for getting back into the labor force is an unrelenting message at Forty Plus, and it is strong even in the minds of those who belong to groups that are subject to discrimination or ill-fortune.

Beyond providing a measure of self-assurance, categorical fate explanations render an otherwise chaotic and "senseless" situation somewhat more comprehensible. They point toward larger sociological labeling processes or toward large-scale economic changes to which we are all subject. Yet, even when categorical fates can be sustained among peers, managerial culture exerts a pull toward individualistic analyses of failure. Apparently watertight categorical fates can dissolve, especially under the influence of the business press, which reminds the unemployed manager that "You are out of a job, not because of impersonal forces, but because of your personal failings."

In 1987, the *New York Times* business section published an article written by a corporate headhunter that asked the tongue-in-cheek question: "How can the intelligent executive assure himself that the person he hires will be a genuine incompetent . . . ?" The writer, himself the president of an international executive search firm, answered his own question:

> Restrict yourself to hiring other people's rejects. . . . Make all your appointments from the unsolicited résumés that cross your desk. These, for the most part, are going to be directed to you by outplacement firms that specialize in finding employment for people whose present employers don't want them around any more. This is a rich pool, which, if carefully fished, can be relied upon to produce out-and-out incompetents over and over again.[50]

The unemployed manager who reads this passage cannot avoid the conclusion that it does not matter that mergers and downsizing are widespread, or that most layoffs are decided by seniority rather than ability.[51] The message is crystal clear: if you are unemployed, you are incompetent.

A similar message comes through in *Fortune* magazine's coverage of a workforce reduction at the Gradall Company of New Philadelphia, Ohio. Gradall chopped its payroll from 557 to 228 in 1982; among those let go were some thirty middle managers. The company's chief executive officer, C. William Gray, explained the nature of the layoffs: "There are flexible people and there are rigid people . . . and we used the depression to increase the

number of flexible people. Unfortunately, that had a bad effect
on some of the rigid people."
To which *Fortune* added: "Rigid people tend to be older."[52]
Gradall managers who were let go cannot be blamed for being
older, but can they help being "rigid"? Business culture intrudes
into a categorical fate explanation, subtly undermines it, and ex-
plodes the comfort it has to offer.

"Dead wood" is another buzzword by which managers with years
of seniority are magically transformed into incompetents. *Forbes*
bemoans the fact that too many firings are carried out on a seniority
basis: not enough "dead wood" is being cut out.[53] Merger situations
similarly provoke this imagery to describe long-term, loyal employees who are deemed redundant. In an article aptly titled "Planning
Executive Dismissals: How to Fire a Friend," the *California Management Review* suggests that these people are no longer "up to" the
demands of the new postmerger business world. It asks rhetor-
ically, "Can a medium-size firm afford to keep highly salaried
administrative 'deadwood' on the payroll?" Cast in this light, older
employees are seen as holding the company down, as parasitical.[54]
Executives who have the audacity to resist firing these long-term
employees are accused of allowing emotion to overwhelm better
business judgment: "Executives' emotional commitment to a project or a person can outweigh the actual implementation of required
business decisions from a strict cost/benefit perspective."[55]

*

As the mania for lean, mean management spread in the 1990s, it
became fashionable to condemn middle management en masse.
American business ills were chalked up to administrative bloat.
While this critique was most trenchant in the pages of the *Wall
Street Journal* and *Forbes*, liberals also joined the chorus. In his zeal
to defend the line worker against what he saw as the growing privileges of management, the late David Gordon repeatedly refers to
middle managers in the most derogatory terms: "fat," or "bureaucratic burden."[56] He decried this drag on the productivity of
American corporations and identified the managerial labor force
as the source of a wage squeeze pushing the bottom tiers into
working poverty. Gordon was a renowned figure on the academic
left whose sympathies clearly lay with the blue and pink collar
workers of the world; even he seemed comfortable lumping middle managers together with extravagantly paid CEOs as the con-
joint cause of corporate decline.

Few critics—on the right or left—have spent real time studying what middle managers actually do. Managers often play pivotal, but poorly understood, roles smoothing the rough spots in the decision-making process in large firms. Among those I have studied, middle managers routinely intervene to prevent the top brass from making mistakes based on a remote and often ill-informed appreciation of the problems facing their grass roots sales organizations, factories, or retail stores. Middle managers organize the voices that bubble up from hundreds of branch offices and push reforms through at the highest levels where this "white noise" cannot be synthesized or acted upon without the intermediate perspective that these "bureaucrats" bring to bear.

But none of these subtleties seem to have crossed the minds of those bent on blaming middle managers for all of the problems of American business. Instead, the treatment of managerial unemployment has become an exercise in self-justification. The business press avoids the conclusion that the well-being of some firms, or the free enterprise system in general, is often contingent on junking substantial numbers of loyal, hardworking employees—that success for some is contingent on hardship for others.

Labeling the unemployed as damaged goods undermines the force of fate, which points to age discrimination or industry downturns, leaving the downwardly mobile manager unable to link himself to millions in the same situation. Managers cannot hold on to a vision of their troubles as a "social problem"; instead, rejection is understood as a consequence of personal defects.

Manly Flaws The business press is not solely responsible for stigmatizing unemployed managers: Executives themselves play an important role in the process. Reflecting on their situation, many poke holes in their own defenses. Categorical fate convincingly explains why middle management is being cut nationwide, but it cannot easily account for why a particular manager was fired while others similar in age or background were retained.

George Peabody spent twenty-five years working his way up to the vice presidency of a manufacturing firm. Caught in the industry downturn of the early 1980s, Peabody found himself searching for a new job at the age of fifty-two, with a suburban New Jersey home and a comfortable life-style hanging in the balance. He recalls in detail the conditions that have bedeviled his field, leaving hundreds of competent executives out in the cold and few open doors to knock on. George has a number of personal friends in the same predicament, and he knows about many more. One might imagine that he would see himself as a victim of categorical fate, and this is partially true. But George knows that not everyone in the business was victimized: "Some people have been able to hang on. I just wasn't able to do that. Some of my friends had the same problems at work as I did and they kept their jobs. I did not."

Faced with "Why me, not him?" questions, managers are drawn toward more individualistic explanations, those that stress character or personal style as reasons for losing one's job in the first place and for failing to find a new one. It is a short distance from this to self-blame. But there are some characterological analyses that bolster self-esteem rather than attack it.

When Elliot Liebow studied black street corner men in his classic, *Tally's Corner*, he was struck by the way in which ghetto men sheltered their self-esteem behind a set of "shadow values."[58] Street corner men who moved from one failed marriage to another had an explanation: They described themselves as oversexed, incapable of limiting their physical desires to one woman. Failure in marriage became a virtue, the result of a "manly flaw," that of being too virile to be satisfied with just one woman.

Some downwardly mobile executives developed a managerial theory of manly flaws. They believe they were too aggressive, too rational, too smart, too experienced, or too committed to principle. These personal qualities threatened their superiors, gave momentum to their enemies, and led to their dismissals. Aggressiveness, rationality, and principled commitment (as opposed to political expediency) are praiseworthy attributes in American business. Executives are supposed to be tough and forthright; they are not supposed to bend with the wind. Hence to be fired for being too forthright is, according to the theory of manly flaws, a backhanded compliment. These unemployed managers frequently contrast themselves with those who managed to hold on to their jobs through political conniving and sycophantic behavior. They scorn the yes men and deride ex-colleagues who refused to make unpopular decisions.

The weak may retain their jobs, but at the cost of their integrity and self-respect, a price some displaced managers claim was too high for them to pay. Alex Kraemer has held several executive positions over the past ten years, both as the head administrator for a multimillion-dollar federal loan program and as an officer of a large Midwestern bank. These were positions of power and authority, and in Alex's view they came to him because he is a man who possesses the kind of personality that is required to "take charge." But the same traits led him into trouble:

> I stepped on toes [when I worked] in Boston and in my other job as vice president of the bank. You have to do that. There's no way you can be political. Playing that game is trying to keep everyone happy, and that doesn't always work. If you want to play it safe, and many people want to, you don't get a hell of a lot done. If you want to get something done you have to take a position.

If this is the genesis of Alex's job loss, it is also the explanation he finds most compelling in trying to understand why he cannot make it beyond the interview stage for executive positions.

> [A large investment house] was considering me for a job buying bonds. It turned out in the course of the conversation that I knew a hell of a lot more about bonds than the vice president. That killed the interview. . . . If you know more about the business . . . you don't get the job.

Alex sees himself as a person who easily intimidates others with his knowledge, his experience, and his forceful character. This is, in his mind, the main reason why he has been unable to find a job commensurate with his talents after nearly three years of unemployment, interspersed with short-term jobs as a machinist and an accountant for a small firm. His manly flaw is his take-charge personality and his unwillingness to "play political games."

It would be easy to dismiss Alex's invocation of manly flaws as boastfulness and puffery, a self-serving defense against the fact that he had been fired. But Jean Hartley's research on managerial unemployment in Britain cautions against wholesale dismissal of these explanations. Hartley compared the personality characteristics of unemployed executives to those of a control group of employed managers and discovered that the unemployed executives were *indeed* more assertive, more conscientious, imaginative, independent, and self-sufficient than their employed brethren.[59]

Discussions of management in the American business media are redolent with the image of the "individualistic, non-conformist, aggressive, anti-social" entrepreneur.[60] Despite America's romance with this entrepreneurial archetype, the age of bureaucracy may have rendered it maladaptive.[61] Modern bureaucratic organizations require conformity, predictability, and subordination of personal goals to institutional purposes in order to function smoothly. IBM is well known for demanding conformity from its employees: Its reputation in this domain is the subject of competitors' mocking television commercials that depict row upon row of men dressed in standard-issue pinstripe suits, mouthing identical phrases. IBM may be on the extreme end of this spectrum, but all bureaucratic organizations demand uniformity and team players to some degree.

This corporate demand for conformity places hurdles in the way of women and minorities who are aiming to reach the boardroom.[62] But managers who seek to emulate the Marlboro man also run afoul of corporate cultures bound by the trappings of bureaucracy and coalition politics. Noncomformists, whether defined by gender or by overly driving or individualistic personalities, are perceived as untrustworthy and are marginalized when promotion time comes. By extension, they are likely to lack the networks of supporters needed to protect their jobs when heads begin to roll.[63] They are square pegs in a world of round holes, and it is plausible that corporate shakeouts and downsizing are occasions on which some aggressive individualists are squeezed out by their tamer but more politically astute bureaucratic brethren.

The entrepreneur lives on in our folklore, our films, and our steady diet of television heroes. When advertisers want to attract us to their products, they feature the Marlboro man, not the bureaucratic conformist. Hence, when the unemployed executive seeks an explanation for his rejection and his subsequent problems in finding a new job, he turns to images that American culture posits as laudatory.

But the Marlboro man has competition for admiration. Alongside the rugged, independent hero lies the man of means, the man of position. Straight-arrow, get-tough personalities are laudable as long as they are also employed, clothed in Brooks Brothers suits, and housed in the appropriate two-story colonial. It becomes increasingly difficult for the unemployed executive to hold convincingly to the theory of manly flaws because those responsible for his rejection have all the goods, literally and figuratively. The boss who still has his job, his house, his Ozzie and Harriet family, and his prestige intact, has unmistakable advantages over the man who is unemployed, on the verge of losing his property, and trying desperately to answer the persistent questions of his anxious wife and children.

Managers can only make a convincing case for manly flaws when they can point to tangible evidence of success. In the upper middle class, the "goods" are often the measure of the man. Thus those who profess manly flaws explanations for their troubles also display a constant undercurrent of self-doubt. One moment they will say with conviction that they were just too strong for their superiors. In the next breath they wonder aloud at their inability to elicit any interest in their qualifications and reveal in halting phrases that they don't know whether they have the competence employers want or the perseverance to keep looking.

The ease with which potentially comforting explanations (categorical fate or manly flaws) for individual failure can be undermined helps to explain why displaced managers oscillate back and forth between seeing themselves as victims of forces larger than themselves and blaming themselves for expulsion from the world of the successful. They are not in rebellion against the business culture in which they have been nurtured. On the contrary, they are its true believers. They are trapped in a cultural maze that appears to contain exits, but in fact always returns to the same unpleasant conclusions. Escape is all but impossible, for it is a maze whose boundaries they fully accept. Because they have been steeped in the tenets of the managerial worldview, they cannot avoid its condemnation of their character or conduct. They prosecute themselves on its behalf, turning criticisms against themselves and against one another: victims blaming victims.

The Culture of Meritocracy

John Kowalski, a soft-spoken man dumped from his executive job after thirty years, was an active, organized, helpful member of the Forty Plus Club. He had been searching for an executive-level job for nearly two years without any real success. He had also watched men come and go from the club and had formed some thoughts of his own as to why so many were unable to climb out of the pit. While he might be expected to show understanding, even sympathy, for his "fellow travelers," he actually holds them in contempt in a classic formulation of "blame the victim":

I believe in the capitalist system. Private industry should make the products and the profits, and we'll all prosper. *If people at the club are not prospering, that's their problem.* They have to learn to live with it. If they're going to go out and work in a profit-making company, they're going to have to find out what their skills are and learn how to market them. . . . There's a place out there for all of us, it's just a matter of finding it.

John's is a personal statement, but it derives from a managerial theology whose foundation is a belief in *meritocratic individualism.* At the center of this doctrine is the notion that individuals are responsible for their own destinies. This idea, which owes its origin to Calvinist theology, carries into the world of work a heavy moralism.[64] One's occupation, or more precisely one's career or trajectory within an occupation, are viewed as a test of commitment, and the product of hard work and self-sacrifice. Cast this way, success is not a matter of luck, good contacts, credentials, or technical skill but is a measure of one's moral worth, one's willingness and ability to drive beyond the limitations of self-indulgence and sloth. It is this equation of occupational success and inner or moral qualities that rebounds on the unemployed manager's self-image, making him or her feel not just unsuccessful but worthless.

Driven by this imagery, occupational careers take on the flavor of a contest. Whether phrased in terms of Darwinian survival of the fittest or Adam Smith's confidence in the value of competition, this element of business culture regards a contest in which some fail, while others succeed, as a meritorious activity. For only through competition are superior ability and economic efficiency recognized, rewarded, and encouraged. Conversely, only through competition are the incompetent and the inefficient pushed to the bottom of the heap, as they deserve.

This glorification of competition also transforms the pursuit of wealth, and a narrow concern with economic profit over other social goals, into a socially responsible and hence morally admirable attitude. Under the discipline of the market, the pursuit of wealth leads to cost cutting, technological innovation, and careful allocation of investment. Society at large is well served because these processes result in cheaper goods and an increase in wealth. Respect for the bottom line represents neither selfish moneygrubbing nor an amoral neglect of social values. Rather it is a hard-nosed effort to reduce waste so that the commonwealth prospers.

This worldview is clearly comforting to those in management. It justifies the view that they rose to high positions because of sheer ability and hard work. It encourages the notion that social inequality is an expression of the natural order of things—not unlike the law of gravity. And it sanctifies a preoccupation with the bottom line, with profit over loyalty or other sentiment, as a constructive contribution to the common good, as economic realism rather than moral shallowness.

When the successful fall from grace, this ideology boomerangs. For if individuals are responsible for their own destinies, there is no one else to blame in case of failure. If the market rewards the competent and casts out the inefficient, unemployment is perforce a judgment of one's abilities. It is a testament to the strength of this business culture that unemployed managers assert and reassert these values, even though this brings criticism down upon themselves and others in the same predicament.

David Patterson's entire division was wiped out in early 1985. Fifty-five heads were on the chopping block, David's among them. Since then David has been faced with nothing but bleak prospects. One might expect that David would be furious with his company for having put him in this situation, that he would reject the bottom line logic that led his employer to sacrifice his career. Not so. David sees this as the natural state of existence in the corporate world:

> A policy is a policy and a procedure is a procedure. That's the way you operate. If you're part of the corporate world you understand. It doesn't make you feel better; it doesn't smooth anything, but that's the way you do it. You accept it . . . otherwise you can't work in that environment. . . . If I got back into the game, I'd play it the same way. And I would expect the same things to happen to me again.

George Marshall, another refugee from the insurance wars of the early eighties, echoes much the same sentiment in thinking about his job loss:

> Here I was in the business for so long and I had a good reputation. I never burned any bridges or anything. After all these years, the hard work goes down the drain. I've reached an impasse, a blind alley. It's very disappointing. I like to think I have some expertise to offer, and it's all gone down the drain. But the business world is pretty cut and dried. It doesn't matter what you've been doing for

twenty years, it's what you're doing now that counts. *The important thing is the bottom line. Rightfully so* [emphasis added].

John Kowalski spent the thirty years of his career with a trade association, moving steadily up the managerial ladder from assistant secretary to technical secretary to vice president. Finally in 1977 he crested to the top. The glory lasted for nearly four years and then it evaporated. John was demoted without warning:

I was told they were going to hire in someone else above me. So I was pushed out. They said you've done a great job and we want you to stay, but we recognize [that you might not want to under the circumstances], so you decide whether you want to stick with it or not.

John was given the choice of swallowing his pride and stepping down to a lesser position or leaving. Eventually he left, mainly because he couldn't work under his new superior, a man who was inclined to treat subordinates in a high-handed manner.

In the three years since leaving (during which Kowalski found only sporadic employment as a consultant), he has spent many hours trying to figure out how a job that had lasted for thirty years could come to such a sour end. He concluded that his bosses wanted a Marlboro man—a ruthless, take-charge guy. By contrast, John sees himself as an organization man, someone whose forte lies in getting people to cooperate with one another toward common goals, in smoothing ruffled feathers, and in making subordinates feel valued. Yet his belief in the competitive ethic and managerial machismo has led him to question his own character, to doubt the value of traits he once admired in himself, and to believe that, in the end, those who ousted him were right:

I'm beginning to wonder about my abilities to run an association, to manage and motivate people. It's clear from the setbacks I've had there that I have trouble projecting the image these people want. It makes me wonder whether I really do want another job as an executive. . . . I question whether I can manage four or five professional staffers.
Having been demoted . . . has to make you think. I have to accept my firing. I have to learn that that's the way it is. The people who were involved in it are people I respect for the most part . . . They are successful executives . . . So I can't blame them for doing what they think is right. I have to say where have I gone wrong.[65]

Though he has been on the receiving end of a bottom-line philosophy for nearly two years, John is entirely accepting of it and believes that middle managers like himself *should* be let go in droves if it will improve the posture of American business.[66] He argues that this is a sound approach, that those who are floundering in its wake simply have to tighten their belts, straighten up, and fly right. The fact that he himself has been totally unsuccessful at doing so does not hinder him from criticizing others in exactly the same situation. The twentieth-century Calvinism of the business world pushes John to accept his downward mobility as a moral judgment.

This is not a view confined to the ranks of those who have been unable to find new jobs. Victor Katz was trained as an economist and over the years developed an expertise in the plastics industry. Eventually he became a chief economist for the plastics division of a large oil company where he was responsible for forecasting the market. The oil slump that followed the collapse of the OPEC cartel put an end to his career: the company cut its payroll by 20 percent, aiming first at employees who were not central to its oil business. Victor found himself with six months' severance and an expensive surburban mortgage to contend with.

Despite a wealth of experience in economics and financial forecasting, he could not crack the labor market. Eight months later he had not landed a single interview, though he had responded to hundreds of job ads. The headhunters he had signed up with had produced nothing. It seemed that no one was interested in an older applicant. Victor was saved when, almost by chance, he landed a real, though modest, position with the federal government.

Although the job he finally found was the only "iron in the fire" after eight months of searching, he still maintains that he was the master of his own fate and that the men and women he left behind at Forty Plus were losers. His attitude toward those who remain unemployed is contemptuous.[67] He is anxious to be separated from them, to be considered a different kind of person. Victor argues that one must simply keep trying and that those who have yet to find rewarding jobs clearly have not been trying hard enough. His own fate, he believes, proves the point.

Like all cultural frameworks, meritocratic individualism provides a system of meaning through which individual experience is understood and evaluated. It shapes life by imposing explanations and moral tales; it creates a received wisdom. The main motifs of managerial culture involve the legitimacy of competition and hierarchy; the myths and heroes of the managerial world provide explanations for the prosperity and success of the few and the downfall of the many. Meritocratic individualism is more than an abstract philosophical doctrine. It is a culture which has the power to reach inside displaced managers and devastate their sense of self-worth. Its social Darwinist aspect provides a chilling answer to their incessant questions about why they have fallen from grace: They fell to their "natural" level. They got what they really deserved. Downward mobility is the crucible of self-doubt, an occasion for the culture of meritocracy to work its most profound magic on the vulnerable managerial self.

Climbing Out

The longer one is unemployed, the harder it becomes to climb out, and the lower the status of the new job is likely to be if one does become reemployed. This is the unavoidable but grim conclusion of governmental surveys. The raw numbers, however, give little sense of the drama of climbing out of unemployment, the obstacles and frustrations of finding a new job, especially when the end point represents downward mobility.

Unemployed executives suffer more than emotional trauma and financial loss. As joblessness stretches into months or years, many undergo physical deterioration as well. Prolonged anxiety leaves its mark. For some it translates into crows-feet or a permanent frown; for others, depression takes a toll in the form of nervous overeating and inevitable layers of fat around the middle. These problems are exacerbated by financial distress: Racketball games, which reduce the natural bulge brought on by age, go by the board. February cruises disappear to be replaced by winter pallor. Overweight bodies are forced into old suits, giving the long-unemployed manager a curiously overstuffed appearance.

Maintaining an appearance and demeanor that are consistent with an individual's claims to being a certain kind of person are crucial to success. In *The Presentation of Self in Everyday Life* Erving Goffman showed how social interaction is carefully stage-managed to prevent any information from emerging that conflicts with and thereby discredits an individual's public image. Central to a convincing performance are dramatic "props": the right kind of body, hairstyle, and dress. These props must confirm the social character a manager is trying to project to others: the broad shoulders, confident smile, and impeccable tailoring, enhance a vice president's claims to status and power. But where the match between performance and props is not quite right, discomfort and uneasiness result. Downwardly mobile managers often find they no longer look the part. Women executives who gain weight under stress do not suddenly become slim and svelte when a job prospect finally develops. Men who have avoided dental care for years in order to save money find that the damage to their teeth is irreparable. It is all very well to have a strong résumé; if your teeth are noticeably loose, this anomaly casts a pall of suspicion over claims to respectable status.[68]

Physical deterioration is not the only impediment to obtaining a new managerial job: One's biography must also be groomed and kept in shape. Downwardly mobile managers often take part-time jobs or night jobs that help pay the bills, while leaving them time to continue the search for "real" employment, for jobs that accord with their sense of true position. Members of Forty Plus have taken graveyard shift custodial work cleaning up the stock exchange and after-hours filing jobs in some of the downtown banks. They know instinctively that they must conceal the nature of these menial jobs and thus the facts of their fall, if they are to preserve their chances of rejoining the managerial-professional ranks.

The most common means of concealing inappropriate employment (or unemployment itself) is to present oneself as a freelance consultant. A number of Forty Plus members were working as delivery men or inventory clerks, but their resumes read "consultant."[69] This camouflage for unemployment or menial jobs is well-known among employers and probably functions more as a fig leaf for the ex-manager than a genuine deception. Self-styled consultants are dead giveaways as downwardly mobile, particularly when they must use post office boxes rather than legitimate business addresses.

Some ex-managers are very resourceful in protecting their biographies from the taint of unemployment. Herb Genet's résumé is a masterpiece of fakery. Rejected from the fast-track world of Madison Avenue advertising firms, he had been spiraling downward for nearly eight years. But you would never know this to look at his résumé. He has created a long string of business affiliations that "cover" all the missing years: he has been president of two firms, vice president of another. All three, he confessed, were absolutely bogus. But he had friends and family members who were willing to act as references, to confirm the track record represented in the résumé. Herb had worked out an entirely coherent—and totally fictitious—work history that showed a steady progression in degrees of responsibility, influence, and income. He knew exactly what the cultural rules were for producing the right profile. They include everything from a business address in the right part of town, to the appropriate position titles, to the right jargon to describe what a rising star would have done in such companies. There are few who have the nerve to use such a false résumé, and Herb himself felt a nervous flutter when he considered the consequences of being caught out in a reference check. But Herb also knows that the truth, which involved a variety of low-paid jobs and long stints of unemployment, would disqualify him from ever finding a "decent" job again.

Forty Plus, in keeping with the practices of most executive placement firms, urges its members *not* to lie and in fact places a great emphasis on honesty. Rather, the club admonishes job seekers to cast their work experience in the most positive light they can. They drill members in the fine art of boasting their own contributions to the successes of their previous firms. But the honesty approach works only so long as the rejected manager remains within a carefully circumscribed domain. A man cannot be out of work too long. He cannot take a job that is too far below his "real" rank, nor can he work in a job too far afield from his true profession.[70]

Prospective employers look for kindred spirits in the people they hire. They want to know that the newcomers will fit in. Above all, they want to know that what they see before them correctly indicates what is underneath or behind the appearances. When a well-dressed, comfortable, powerful man—a man like Joe Rockom from the cover of *Fortune* magazine—looks upon someone who is poorly dressed, whose teeth are bad, who has put on thirty pounds, or who looks tired and worn, he is not likely to feel confident about that applicant. When a boss interviews someone for a managerial job who has been working as a desk clerk to make ends meet, the social inconsistencies jar his senses. They cast doubt on the applicant's claims to being promising managerial material. The job seeker is typed as one of "them" and not one of "us."

In this way, the stigma of unemployment becomes a self-fulfilling prophecy: the more a person is in need, the less deserving he or she appears to be. Merely being among the unemployed already places an executive perilously close to a boundary line that must not be crossed if the person hopes to regain a foothold in the business world. When the executive's other props are in disorder, the task becomes insurmountable. Those unemployed who cannot stave off or disguise occupational and physical changes are pushed over the edge of acceptability, closing off the prospect of real recovery.

Paths to a New Job

Despite these hurdles to managerial reemployment, the majority of unemployed managers finally succeed in finding new jobs. But there are various pathways to reemployment, each of which leads to quite different destinations. Between January of 1984 and June of 1985, eighty-five members of the Forty Plus Club rang the brass bell, signifying that they had accepted an offer of employment. A quarter of these were making more money than they had in their previous job. Nearly half were making significantly less. The remainder found new employment at the same salary they had had one or two years before, at the time they had lost their jobs.[71]

The first, and most fortunate path, leads some back to their old specialties in the private sector. Managers who were younger, who had technically specialized skills, and who were unemployed for a matter of months, not years, were disproportionately represented on this route.[72]

A second pathway consisted of a move into the nonprofit sector or into government employment. Because it pays, on average, considerably less than the private sector does for managerial employees, the nonprofit sector welcomes managerial talent that has proved itself in large corporations. These organizations are less averse to downwardly mobile managers than are the Fortune 500. A similar situation obtains in government agencies. They are subject to the constraints of civil service examination scores and federal employment discrimination laws, tend to take credentials and years of experience at face value, and seem to give less weight to the right biographical trajectory or looks. Taken together, this means that both the state and nonprofit sectors become a haven for some surplussed managers, albeit at sharp cuts in pay.

Jenny White, a pleasant-looking fifty-year-old alumna of Forty Plus, who used to work for one of New York's largest stock brokers, is one example. After more than a year on the unemployment lines, she took a position as a middle manager in a nonprofit organization. Jenny was stunned that she was actually able to land this respectable if underpaid job:

> I was very depressed and gained a lot of weight [while I was unemployed.] It's amazing that I got this job, because not only is there prejudice against older people, there's prejudice against fat people. It turns out that nonprofits do hire fat people. We didn't have any fat people at [the brokerage firm]. Very few people who were old worked there either. Wall Street is very youth and looks oriented, and I'm sure I'd have no chance of getting a job there now."

A third route to reemployment—a skidding fall—is the most feared of all. Some Forty Plus members who were unable to find "appropriate" jobs took a series of progressively lower-status temporary jobs, only to find themselves trapped in a low pay cul de sac.[73] Jan Dreardon spent twenty-five years working for a regional planning agency. When government cutbacks in the early years of the Reagan administration led to the end of that job, he discovered that other public agencies in the field were in the same shape. Fifty-eight years old and without private sector experience to trade on, he struggled for two years to find a suitable position before accepting a part-time, temporary position as an accountant for a nonprofit organization. That position folded after four months, and he was out on the street again. Three months passed with nothing on the horizon. Finally, in desperation, he took a job as a sales clerk at Macy's.

> The money was really terrible, but at least it was a job. When I was unemployed I felt like I had no structure, I was just flailing around. When I worked at Macy's, it was such a pleasure to get up and go to work every morning. Just to have something to do and have some people to talk to was great. I even stopped thinking about my old job and my ambitions for a while.

He worked through the Christmas rush and was laid off. When we met, he was back at Forty Plus for the third time, looking forward to the next holiday season when he thought he could go back to Macy's. His story exemplifies a pattern that is familiar to many at Forty Plus: a skidding fall in which each job is qualitatively worse, farther afield from the person's field of professional expertise, lower in status, and less permanent.

While Jan's skid has entailed periodic bouts of unemployment, others land permanent low-status positions as delivery men or clerical workers. These jobs are, for all practical purposes, the end of the line, the final resting point of a skidding fall. Life returns to a semblance of stability for these individuals by the simple act of having a job to go to. But the men and women who fall into this abyss continue to apply for managerial jobs for many years, no matter how unrealistic the prospects of landing one. They still check the mailbox when they return home from a day of deadly-dull clerical work, hoping to find responses to new batches of inquiry letters. They steadfastly refuse to accept their actual occupations as their real social identities.

One might expect that the woes of downward mobility come to an end with reemployment. However this is not the case: Downward mobility changes the individual, leaving scars in the form of unfulfilled expectations and lurking fears. George Mahoney is a forty-year-old graduate of a prestigious college who specialized in computer science. Early on he decided he was interested in the business world, so with his high-tech training in hand, he put his computer skills to work in banking. He had several jobs with major banks in New York City, finally settling in an executive slot with a foreign bank whose major financial transactions were conducted in the Big Apple. He was earning $50,000 (in 1984) and had a staff of fifteen people. He reported directly to the board of directors and enjoyed daily access to the top brass at the bank. He was one of a handful of Americans in such a position, as others were occupied by foreign nationals who had come to New York from the bank's overseas headquarters. The axe fell without warning one day: George was let go in favor of an incoming foreigner.

He wasn't worried. He was young, he had credentials and work experience in a field experiencing high demand and short supply. Never in his wildest dreams did George expect to find himself at the door of the Forty Plus Club, but after nine months of blind alleys, he realized he needed help. What George lacked was a sufficient supply of executive-level contacts in other banks.

After a year of unemployment, he finally landed a new position, through the good graces of a former member of Forty Plus.

George's new job pays $10,000 a year less than before, but it is not an executive-level position and seems unlikely to lead in that direction. As a small fish in a big pond, he misses the "power" lunches and the feeling of significance. Most important, the new job does not allow him to exercise the highly specialized computer skills he developed in his previous job, and this is a constant source of disappointment. Smothered under layers of bureaucracy, his new position provides few opportunities to demonstrate to the powers that be just how good he is in his field.

George's experience is typical of many downwardly mobiles, and it tells us something important about the psyche of the modern professional. These are educated, skilled people whose self-esteem is generated not only by receiving hefty paychecks but by the day-to-day experience of tackling intellectual challenges, of solving complex problems. It is not financial deprivation that leaves George unsettled—he can manage on his present salary—but the lack of challenge in the work itself. He feels like a long-distance runner confined to a cell, or a musician without an instrument, his talents atrophying away.

The predicament of Gerry Smythe, a former comptroller who now works for the Internal Revenue Service, differs. Smythe audits corporations, drawing on decades of experience with tax law, accounting, financial forecasting, and market analysis. His job is skilled and his work challenging. What rankles him most is not that the IRS is getting these skills for a fraction of his former private-sector wage, but that his superiors don't realize that his work is so skilled and consequently give him little of the credit he feels is his due. When Smythe performs well and no one in the office notices, let alone applauds, he responds with mounting contempt toward his superiors. The only audience he finds for his triumphs is his wife. This situation leaves Smythe feeling unfulfilled, despite the intrinsic interest and challenge of his work. Smythe had the strength to overcome lengthy unemployment, but he is sorely tried by the benign indifference of his bosses.

Smythe's need for special recognition from his superiors is a common, though not universal, one among professionals and managers. Several decades ago, David Riesman pointed to a shift in the personality structure of the American middle class. Increasingly, he argued, this society was producing "other-directed" personalities, individuals whose sense of self, values, and goals were taken from friends and milieu, rather than from tradition or inner commitments.[74]

When a society takes other-directed personalities and then subjects them to an intensive socialization in business schools and in a business world that defines personal happiness and success in terms of being picked out of the crowd as a fast-tracker, having one's potential and achievements recognized in the form of rapid and frequent promotions—it is creating battalions of recognition-addicted managers.[75] They cannot thrive on the intrinsic satisfactions of a job well done, but only on a job left behind. Those who do get stuck in one position, even where their superiors like them, grow frustrated and bitter.[76]

For all the stress and disappointment people like Smythe have encountered at the hands of the corporate world, downwardly mobile managers are its product, heart and soul. The transition to nonprofit organizations or government service does not come easily to these men and women accustomed to the fast pace of the private sector. They experience a form of culture shock when they find they must shift gears into jobs that do not adhere to the credo of the bottom line. The downwardly mobile encounter profound differences in managerial style that they find hard to assimilate.

In Jenny White's mind, one of the main attractions of working for a big Manhattan stock brokerage firm was the lightning pace of the work. She learned how to hold two phone conversations at one time, place buy or sell orders on high-speed computers, and evaluate complex financial data in order to advise investors. Jenny is a career woman and she thrived on the razor-sharp minds and cutthroat mentality she faced at the New York Stock Exchange. She enjoyed the challenge, even though she was aware that the stock market was a volatile creature and that "bloodlettings were common in the brokerage houses." An economist by training, Jenny quickly acquired a taste for the demands placed upon her for rapid judgment and action, and the clear-cut way in which success is measured at the end of the day: in dollars and cents. She coined the phrase "performance culture" to summarize the ways of Wall Street, and while she freely admits that it was a source of pressure, she misses it.

When Jenny's career on the Street was cut short in one of its legendary bloodlettings in the early 1980s, she found herself unable to work her way back in. She took up a position in a well-respected nonprofit research organization. Her main complaints about her new job are not over salary or promotion prospects or lack of challenging work, although she has suffered in these areas. It is the strange organizational ambience of the nonprofit sector that perplexes and frustrates her most:

> [Nonprofits] don't think about costs as much as we had to in the stock market. There is always a big debate over every [policy], but whether it makes sense financially is only one of the tiniest little factors, rather than being the most important. Besides, things just don't get done as fast here, probably because [nonprofits] don't have to make money. That grates on me . . . They just don't have the performance culture. This is really irritating. You can do something, like suggest that a certain direction has to be taken in the organization, and nothing happens. You get no response or it takes a year to get one. You just know that nothing is going to happen.

Lack of attention to the bottom line, coupled with slow-moving change, is an anathema to individuals who are steeped in the Wall Street traditions of cost-benefit analysis and rapid decision making. They look on in wonder that such lumbering bureaucracies actually manage to remain "in business," since a similar posture in the profit-making sector would find an organization headed for extinction. Corporate refugees feel quite unsteady without the bottom-line philosophy. They must learn different rules and make major adjustments in their behavior in order to survive in the nonprofit world. Even after two years in her new position, Jenny cannot really let go of the corporate mentality that wants to be bold and decisive, when those around her are inclined to sit and discuss and come back in six months for more of the same. She must curb displays of impatience, no matter how deeply she feels it.

The lower salaries in the public sector and the nonprofit world mean that they cannot usually attract fast-track types. The reverse of this dictum is that the people who inhabit this slower-paced, more secure world are precisely those toward whom the corporate world casts a jaundiced eye. They are older, they are "allowed" to gain weight, and they do not have the driven, status-hungry demeanor familiar to those on Wall Street. Jenny fears that if she dallies long in the nonprofit sector, she will become a "nonprofit type" herself, which is not a positive image from her standpoint. She has carried inside the credo of the performance culture, and it pushes her to reject the world she now inhabits. Hence she continues to read the want ads and applies for jobs that would take her back inside its insecure fold.

Disappointment at their loss of salary, frustration over underutilized skills, aggravation over too little recognition or too few prospects for promotion—these are the more common refrains among reemployed downwardly mobiles. Underlying these specific complaints, however, are signs of a more complex residue of unemployment, a diffuse sense of anxiety and foreboding. The trauma of downward mobility shatters the manager's sense of safety and security about the world at the same time that it ravages his or her career and bank balance. This shows itself in many as a haunting fear of losing their jobs all over again and a sense of their present situation as temporary and fragile.

One response to this is to avoid becoming too comfortable in any new job, and to always keep one eye on the exit:

> I certainly have not stopped reading the newspaper ads. That's something I learned. Now I will not stay anywhere. [The sense of security] has been broken in my mind. I don't really trust it. It appears to be safe here, but it appeared to be safe at the [old firm]. So I'd move [if I saw a better job].

For others, these feelings cohere around the issue of loyalty. They portray the business world as a treacherous place, one that has ceased to value loyalty, and that has therefore forfeited its right to expect loyalty from its employees:

> When I first started working at [my previous firm], they never fired anyone. It was a cultural thing with them. Now it's a revolving door and it's gotten worse since I left. There's no loyalty . . . that's all gone now. It's just "get what I can get and get out." The social contract between employer and employee has frazzled.

Yet another reaction to the feeling of insecurity is to become very sensitive to office politics. George Mahoney's experience taught him some valuable lessons about the nature of infighting in the corporate world.[77] He is now inclined to play it safe and curry favor rather than speak his mind:

> I don't feel too solid anymore. . . . By keeping your mouth shut and trying to avoid controversy, that can improve your chances. . . . But you feel you shouldn't have to live in a slave-state mentality where you have to reflect the party line.
>
> I feel inhibited. You hope management would want to hear your ideas since you do have your professional expertise. . . . But you can see that the people who get promoted or get salary increases

are the ones who go along with what the boss wants rather than speaking out.

As long ago as the 1950s, C. Wright Mills pointed out that it is the lot of the white-collar man to be insecure about his prestige, to suffer what he called a "status panic": a lingering uncertainty about his social standing both inside and outside the world of the workplace.[78] George Mahoney discovered just how precarious the identity of the modern manager was when he lost his claim to it. Yet, having finally found his way back in to the managerial fold, he discovers what many who never experienced dislocation know: that dignity and authority on the job are not guaranteed simply by being gainfully employed. An imagined slight, a false step, the wrong word in the wrong ear can jeopardize a career and leave the fully capable out in the cold. It is a dilemma that never leaves the consciousness of the manager who has been through the experience of downward mobility.

Liminality

These are the words of the more successful displaced managers. They are not the skidders in menial jobs, nor the permanently unemployed. Yet even these people, who have landed decent new jobs, haven't really settled. Between the concrete frustrations of their new jobs (always subject to invidious comparisons with the old), and the nagging sense that they may lose everything again and be plunged without warning into the chaos of unemployment, they experience a sense of hanging in space, of waiting for something to happen, an inability to become rooted and accept their present condition as real, as permanent, as secure.

It is a testament to the centrality of occupational identity in business culture that downwardly mobile managers hold on tenaciously to a vision of who they "really" are based upon what they used to do for a living. Whether unemployed, or working in jobs that place them in the working or lower middle class, in their minds they remain displaced executives whose attitudes, desires, and expectations are closer to those of the typical manager than they are to those of the machinists, the delivery men, or the clerical workers alongside whom they now work.

No matter how much they cherish upper-middle-class dreams, their present lives and behaviors are, in most cases, a stark contrast to the days of yore: little socializing, spartan vacations, and few frills. But they do not feel at home with this stripped-down existence. It seems temporary and unreal to them, and for years they fail to reconcile the ways they think of themselves with the reality of their situation. Experientially, these downwardly mobile executives are condemned to drift in a limbo state: they do not seem to belong anywhere.

Anthropologists recognize this sense of hanging between worlds as an example of a "liminal" existence. Liminality is the experience of being stopped at the threshold between two states or identities. In simple societies, liminal states often develop in the context of "rites of passage," occasions when individuals move from one point in the life cycle (for example, boyhood) to another (for example, manhood). These rites are typically divided into parts. In the first phase of an initiation rite, boys and girls on the brink of maturity are taken away from their villages to isolated spots where they spend their days preparing for tribal rituals that will certify their standing as mature men and women.

During the first, liminal phase, the ordinary rules of social life are suspended. Because this is an extraordinary departure from normal life, it inspires in young people—just as it does in the unemployed managers—feelings of drift or chaos that come with the loss of a solid social role. The initiates are, for a time, living in a world utterly removed from their childhoods—but they are not yet adults. They are truly "betwixt and between."[79]

When they reemerge, they are welcomed into the society of adults through solemn ritual. Their liminal experience is therefore finite: It comes to an end when they emerge to take a new place in their communities. For the managers, by contrast, liminality lingers on. While managers hope to emerge and regain their old occupations and identities, neither they nor their families are sure whether or when this will occur. It remains an unrealized possibility, and because the liminal phase is so prolonged, it exacts a corrosive toll on self-confidence.

For both the managers and the tribal initiates, liminality is a time of seclusion. While it is possible to think of the social isolation of unemployed managers as an unintentional affair, the result of income loss or the estrangement of friends, this is not how the unemployed themselves experience it. They feel they have been actively shunned, placed at arm's length by their peers, just as surely as tribal initiates have been sequestered from the rest of the village.

Anthropology has given us an understanding of why tribal societies seclude initiates during the liminal phase, and why they avoid and fear contact with people who are in between. The very presence of liminal beings violates the sense of cultural boundaries so crucial to social order. They are regarded as dangerous or polluting because they defy classification, being neither boy nor man, girl nor woman.[80]

Taboos occur in situations where cultural categories that are normally distinct become blurred.[81] For example, anomalous creatures—animals that combine features that are usually separated—often become the subject of food taboos. Unemployed and underemployed executives are anomalous creatures too. Their existence is as threatening to the cognitive order of managerial culture as tabooed creatures are to some tribal peoples. The talented ex-manager is a living contradiction. How can there be a manager who is hardworking, experienced, intelligent—and able only to find a job as a file clerk?

The business press, which reflects the mores of the managerial world, often speaks as if there is no such anomalous creature, that these attributes cannot coincide in one person. The unemployed or underemployed manager must therefore be seen as inept, as dead wood, or as inflexible. Alternatively, his condition must be portrayed as purely transitional: He is rapidly on his way to better things. However, his former business associates cannot wish him away. They, who know his talents well, cannot look their downwardly mobile colleague in the eye because they cannot cope with the threat that his existence poses to their worldview. The very presence of Forty Plus members undermines the neat social categories of the bottom-line culture. Their fate inspires fear in others who may worry that they too will become living contradictions.

Some technologically simple peoples believe that close contact with an individual in a liminal state is contaminating. Technologically complex peoples often have the same response. Forty Plus members feel they are treated as carriers of a contagious disease. In a culture where people half believe that good luck can rub off, one also finds the lurking suspicion that to associate with the occupationally disabled is to court contamination.

Robert Murphy has argued that the physically handicapped in modern America are similarly shunted to the sidelines, shunned and avoided. People in wheelchairs are condemned to a liminal state:

The long-term physically impaired are neither sick nor well, neither dead nor fully alive, neither out of society nor wholly in it. They are human beings but their bodies are warped or malfunctioning, leaving their full humanity in doubt. They are not ill, for illness is transitional to either death or recovery. . . . The disabled spend a lifetime in a . . . suspended state. They are neither fish nor fowl; they exist in partial isolation from society as undefined, ambiguous people.[82]

When twenty-year management veterans are given until the end of the day to pack up and be gone, their employers are subjecting them to a similar form of quarantine. The boss fears that the newly fired will remind still-employed colleagues that they too could wake up one day to find themselves deemed expendable. Fired executives are living proof of managerial vulnerability. Hence they are rapidly pushed aside both by employers and by others who avoid the unfortunate, for fear that occupational calamity spreads like the common cold.[83]

Hence downwardly mobile managers are left hanging and socially isolated with no stable sense of who they are. Trained to see identity as a matter of occupation, yet unable to claim a place in the business culture they came from, they remain socially disabled and suspended in time. Some respond to this ambiguity by living in the past: they refer to themselves by job titles they haven't held in years. They take pride in professional credentials (Ph.D.'s, engineering diplomas), grown rusty from disuse. But after a time, this emphasis on the past comes to have a hollow ring.

Those who hold down jobs that are "below their station" are left without a new identity they can really accept. They are drifting even though their occupational and financial futures are, in fact, locked into the lower middle class. Even those who do earn decent money in "respectable" managerial jobs feel this sense of temporariness and unreality—their work is not what it once was, and they worry they may lose what they have in an instant. Thus, despite its varied outcomes, managerial downward mobility generates a floating, ambiguous, liminal condition that can be as permanent as that of the disabled.[84]

Managers in their forties and fifties cannot easily reconcile themselves to the notion that life will never return to "normal." Short of debilitating illness, they can expect to live another three decades or so. Time weighs heavily on their hands. They feel older than their years. Their deviant career path throws into high relief the contrast between younger, successful years and this middle-aged experience of failure and frustration. It is hard for them to avoid the conclusion that they were fast-trackers derailed too early in life. The rest of the world seems to define them as finished, old, washed up. After many years of fruitless attempts to recapture a rightful place in American society, they often come to see themselves in the same way.

What underlies the experience of managerial downward mobility is the damage it does to the victim's sense of identity and feelings of social embeddness. They lose a sense of who they are and thereby a sense of what they are doing in the world. And while the occasion for this upheaval in social identity is material—losing one's job—the factor that explains its dramatic repercussions is cultural.

Downwardly mobile managers are skewered by three beliefs that they hold dear: that occupation is the measure of a person's moral worth; that rewards flow to those who are really deserving; and that people are the masters of their own destinies. They are victims of their belief in meritocratic individualism as much as they are victims of economic adversity.

The distress that refugees from the managerial milieu feel is only partly a matter of income loss, or the destruction of a lifestyle. It is fundamentally the pain of being evaluated and found wanting. To be a downwardly mobile executive is first to discover that you are not as good a person as you thought you were and then to end up not sure who or what you really are. Uncertainty over self-identity eclipses the damage of self-blame. It is the rare person who can hold these features of managerial middle-class culture at bay, who can shield him- or herself from the disorientation of downward mobility. Only through culture can one gain a sense of identity, and only through culture can it be taken away.

4

The Downwardly
Mobile Family

Brutal though it can be, the damage downward mobility does to
a displaced manager is only the beginning of a longer story. Like
a storm gathering force, failure in the work world engenders
further havoc, first buffeting relations between breadwinner and
spouse, then spreading to the children. Economic foundations
are wrenched out from under the family, and emotional bonds
are stretched to the breaking point. In the end, even children's
values and plans for the future are drawn into the maelstrom as
they struggle to reconcile the teachings of meritocratic individualism with their parents' glaring inability to prove their worth in
the world.

As unwilling refugees from the middle class, children of downwardly mobile managers offer a unique window into the world
they have left behind.[1] Most had taken their old affluent life-
style for granted and did not understand the significance of what
they had had until after it was gone.

For Penny Ellerby, who was fifteen when the great crash came,
the most immediate and troubling impact was the change it
wrought upon the father she looked up to:

The pressure on my Dad was intense. From my point of view he just seemed to be getting irrational. He would walk around the house talking to himself and stay up all night, smoking cigarettes in the dark.

When things started to fall apart no one would tell my sister or me anything about what was happening. So all I perceived is that somebody who used to be a figure of strength was behaving strangely: starting to cry at odd times . . . hanging around the house unshaven in his underwear when I would bring dates home from high school. In the absence of any understanding of what was going on, my attitude was one of anger and disgust, like "Why don't you get your act together? What's the matter with you?"

Penny's father had been a successful show business promoter. He had invested most of the family's assets in a talent show that ran successfully for four years until its sponsors pulled the plug and sent his career into a tailspin. Penny remembers the spectacular crash that followed:

We went from one day in which we owned a business that was worth probably four or five million dollars in assets and woke up the next day to find that we were personally probably a half million in debt. Creditors called at the house and started to send threatening notes.

First he started a novel, but that didn't last more than two months. Then he went back into a public relations project, which also didn't work out. Then he tried to put together a series of college film festivals. Nothing worked.

Penny's adolescence came to an abrupt end at that point. Her father was unable to find a professional position of any kind. Tension between her parents rose to unbearable heights. Her dad finally left home, one step ahead of the bill collectors. She has not seen him for nearly ten years; for most of that time he has lived on the streets in San Francisco. Penny's mother managed to find a low-level clerical job but it could not begin to sustain the life-style she had known as the wife of a promoter. Today she lives in one of New York's tougher public housing projects and faces problems familiar to many a marginal wage earner: how to make ends meet and how to face the prospect of poverty-level retirement.

*

Downward mobility can occur as the result of a precipitous crash whose effects are felt immediately. Indeed, Penny's story demonstrates how rapidly, and how completely, downward mobility can undermine a family. But for most managerial families, the process is one of gradual erosion. Occupational dislocation may occur suddenly, but its consequences can take six or seven years to become fully evident, depending upon the resources the families can tap.[2]

When occupational disaster strikes, the first impulse is typically to contain the damage to the work world, and to continue as far as possible to maintain a sense of normalcy in the family realm. Hence families continue to pay the mortgage and send the kids off to school. But as months elapse without reemployment, and bank balances plummet, the attempt to maintain a normal lifestyle falters. What begins as a principled commitment to avoid defeatism and get on with life takes on a new character—the family starts to dissemble and hide its problems from the outside world, starting with small cover stories. Paul Armand instructed his son on how to describe his Dad's unemployment to his friends at boarding school: "In his school, everybody's father is the head of this and that. So I said, 'You just tell them your Dad was VP of a company and he just refused to go on an overseas assignment. . . .' I told him if anybody asks, tell them I started my own firm." This was, at best, a shading of the truth. Paul had created a "firm" on paper, but it was not engaged in any money-making enterprises.

The impetus to conceal, if not lie, sometimes comes from adolescent children. The world of the middle-class adolescent is consumerist, elitist, and exceptionally unforgiving of divergence from the norm. Teenagers want to look like, act like, and think like their friends.[3] The paradox of middle-class adolescents is that they must achieve individuality first and foremost by learning to look and sound just like "everyone else" their own age. Dress style and musical taste are only part of the cultural baggage American adolescents bring to the task of peer consolidation. Children of affluence—the sons and daughters of the managerial middle class—also rely upon their families' social position in seeking peer acceptance. Their fathers' occupation, and the life-style that it makes possible, is part and parcel of a cultural image they attempt to project.

When David Patterson moved his wife and two teenage children from California to Long Island, his children complained at first that they were looked upon, with some degree of suspicion, as "transients." To overcome the ill-will and cultivate new friends, Patterson's son boasted his father's status as an executive. The scheme worked, for local families were highly attuned to occupational prestige. Consequently, when Patterson received his pink slip, it threatened to undermine his teenagers' public identity and put their social acceptance by peers at risk. The children reacted with shame and with secrecy: They stopped bringing acquaintances home; they avoided discussing the family crisis with peers or school counselors. They became overwhelmed by the feeling that if their father's downward mobility became public knowledge, their own social standing would be destroyed.

The downwardly mobile managerial family jealously guards its public face, even if this means that everyone must eat a dreary diet so that the children can have some stylish clothes for school.[4] They cherish central symbols of belonging, like the family home, and families make considerable sacrifices in other domains to hold on to these valued possessions. Large houses are rarely traded in for something more modest until there is no other alternative.

Families avoid bankruptcy, both because they look upon it as the coward's way out of a disaster and as a too-public admission of failure and surrender. Dierdre Miller's father inherited a family firm that ran aground in the late 1960s. By the time Dierdre was a teenager, the firm was near collapse and the creditors began to hound Mr. Miller to pay up on his bills. It was clear to Dierdre's mother that they needed to declare bankruptcy to protect the family's remaining assets. But as Dierdre tells it, this was unthinkable:

> My dad wouldn't hear of the idea of declaring bankruptcy or of selling the family business. He felt he had a reputation to protect and that if he went bankrupt it would be destroyed. He used to tell me that you just have to meet your obligations, that you can't just walk out on people and companies you owe money to. I think he felt that if he declared bankruptcy he'd never be able to recover. It would be the end because no one would respect him.

Joan deLancy, a Wall Street lawyer, remembers that her father—whose career as an engineer bit the dust in the wake of defense department cutbacks in the early 1970s[5]—felt the same way:

> My father did earn money through various consulting jobs and short-term positions of one kind or another, but we didn't see much of it. It went toward paying off their debts. He could have walked away

from them by declaring bankruptcy, but he thought that would really seal his fate. Bankruptcy was too final, too much an admission of failure. Besides, it is not part of his character to walk away from responsibilities. As bad as things were financially, I think my parents were proud of the fact that they didn't take the easy way out.

As the financial slide worsens, the task of keeping up appearances becomes more difficult. Dierdre Miller's family lived in one of California's wealthiest suburbs before their troubles and continued to hold on after the crisis. She remembers that her mother would drive miles out of her way to spend the family allotment of food stamps in neighborhoods where her face was unknown. Though the Miller family was in serious financial trouble, with no money coming in to speak of, the mother's primary concern was maintaining face: "My mother wouldn't go down and apply for the food stamps. She made my father do all of that. She wouldn't have anything to do with [it]. She was real ashamed."[6] Mrs. Miller's strategy worked. For many years, outward appearances provided no clue that her family was poor enough to qualify for public assistance. The Miller children stopped bringing their friends home and virtually never talked about their family troubles to anyone.[7]

Eventually however, most downwardly mobile families find themselves in such financial straits that they can no longer camouflage their situation. Children begin to feel uncomfortable about the increasing visibility of the material differences between themselves and their peers, a problem that exacerbates the stigma of their fathers ending up in low status jobs.[8]

The Boeing company was Seattle's largest employer up until the late 1960s. In 1968, it shut down a large part of its operations, throwing thousands of engineers, draftsmen, and technicians onto a weak labor market. The Boeing slump spread like a wave through the supplier industries in the area, compounding the disaster. Alice Pendergast's father was a sales manager in a firm that made precision tools; their biggest client was Boeing. By the time Alice was thirteen, five years after the crash, the depth of the Pendergast family disaster had become clear, especially by comparison to her more fortunate friends:

My junior high school was situated right under this big hill where all the Seattle executives lived, and so I started going to school with their kids. It ended up that my best friend's father was the vice presi-

dent of the biggest bank in town. She lived in this house that seemed
like the most beautiful place I'd ever seen. I remember feeling really
awful because she had so much stuff.

I guess our standard of living was all right, given the bad money
situation. But I always felt we were quite poor because I couldn't go
out and buy new clothes like all my friends at school. Instead of
shopping at Nordstrom's, the high-class department store, we used
to go to K-Mart or Penney's. When I was a kid, trying to impress
my peers, it was awful. I remember going to school every day and
thinking, 'Well, I got this new shirt but I got it because it was on
sale at K-Mart."

Alice's dilemma is shared, in part, by all poor kids who rub
shoulders with the more affluent. But she suffered an additional
humiliation: She used to shop in exclusive stores, and therefore
fully understood the disdain the Benetton set have for K-Mart
kids.

It took a number of years before John Steinberg's family sank
under the weight of prolonged income loss. In the good old days,
John had enjoyed summers at the local country club, winter vacations in the Caribbean, and family outings to fancy restaurants.
The Steinbergs lived in a magnificent three-story house atop a
hill, a stately place fronted by a circular drive. Five years into
the disaster, and with no maintenance budget to speak of, it was
becoming visibly run down.

John remembers that by the time he was a college sophomore,
the paint was peeling badly on the outside. The massive garden,
long since bereft of a professional landscaper, was so overgrown
he could no longer walk to the back of it. The inside of the
house was a study in contrasts. Appliances that were standard
issue for the managerial middle class—dishwashers, washing machines, dryers, televisions—stood broken and unrepaired. The
wallpaper grew dingy, and the carpet on the stairs became thread-
worn. The antique chairs in the dining room were stained, the
silk seat cushions torn. Chandeliers looked vaguely out of place
in the midst of this declining splendor. The whole household
had the look of a Southern mansion in the aftermath of the Civil
War—its structure reflected a glorious past, but its condition told
of years of neglect.

The family car was a regulation station wagon, the kind designed
to haul a mob of kids. It aged well, but as John neared the end
of high school the car developed signs of terminal mechanical
failure. By this time, John's mother had taken a factory job in a

nearby town and was dependent on the old wagon to travel to work.[9] The starter motor went out at a particularly bad moment and, for nearly six months, the car could only function by being pushed out of the driveway and rolled down the hill until it picked up enough speed to jump-start in second gear. John remembers being grateful they lived on such a steep incline.

The Steinberg children had, in years past, accompanied their mother on her weekly shopping trips, for the fun of the outing and to make sure special treats found their way home. They would walk up and down the main street of their Connecticut town, stopping at the various specialty stores lining the prosperous commercial strip. Meat came from a butcher shop, bread from a fancy bakery, treats from the handmade candy shop, and staples from an independent, small grocery store. By the time John was in his late teens, the specialty stores were a thing of the past:

> I remember the first time I went with my mother to a big supermarket, a chain store we hadn't been to much before. She went to the meat counter and there were these precut packages of meat in plastic wrap. I had never seen meat set out that way before. We had always gone to the butcher and he cut the meat to order for us and wrapped it in small white packages.

There are many people in the United States and around the world who would be more than satisfied to eat at the table of the downwardly mobile managerial family. None of these people were hungry or malnourished. But food has greater significance than the vitamins it provides. That middle-class families can open the refrigerator and eat their fill is a demonstration of their freedom from want. The recent proliferation of "designer" foods and fancy delicatessens reveals the additional role of food as fashion and of gastronomy as tourism. And not least, food is a symbol of social status.[10]

For affluent adolescents wolfing down pizza, the connection between diet and fortune is obscure. They devote little energy to thinking about how the food they see on their own tables compares to the fare consumed by other, less fortunate families. Downwardly mobile children *do* learn about how high income underwrites a refrigerator stocked with goodies—when these items disappear. John Steinberg again:

> My family was the real meat and potatoes type. We used to have roast beef and steak all the time. After a few years we couldn't afford it and it was just hamburger and more hamburger. That didn't bother

me or my sisters. We were teenagers and we were perfectly happy with it. But I can remember one time my mother went out and splurged on what must have been a fairly cheap roast. It wouldn't hold up under my Dad's carving knife. It just fell apart. He was so disgusted he just walked out of the dining room, leaving my mother to face the kids. He was mad about having to eat that way.

Food, appliances, vacations, clothes, and cars—these basics of middle-class existence are transformed under the brunt of downward mobility. The loss of these items is not just a matter of inconvenience or discomfort. The lack of wheels whittles down each family member's freedom of movement and underlines a new dependency upon others. Dietary changes symbolize a shrinkage in the family's realm of choice. In a culture that lionizes independence, discretion, and autonomy, these material transformations become dramatic emblems of the family's powerlessness to affect its own fate.

But it is the loss of the home, the most tangible symbol of a family's social status, that is the watershed event in the life cycle of downward mobility.[11] In one act, years of attachment to a neighborhood and a way of life are abruptly terminated. The blow is a hard one to withstand, for at least since the era of the GI mortgage, owning a house has defined membership in the middle class. Home ownership is America's most visible measure of economic achievement. Adults who have lost their homes—to foreclosure or distress sales—have truly lost their membership card in the middle class.

It took nearly eight years from the time John Steinberg's father lost his job to the time they lost the house. But when it finally happened, the family was grief-stricken:

> Letting go of that house was one of the hardest things we ever had to do. We felt like we were pushed out of the place we had grown up in. None of the rental houses my family lived in after that ever felt like home. You know, we had a roof over our heads, but losing that house made us feel a little like gypsies.

Distress sales can free up capital and provide some cash reserves to draw on, but the financial relief is often short lived. The house is usually the last thing to go and debts have ordinarily piled high before that occurs. Hence the profits are already earmarked for debt relief. Moreover, the need to relocate finds the downwardly mobile family facing the same escalating housing costs that enabled them to pull a profit from their own home.[12] Rental accommodations anywhere near the family's original homestead are frequently costly. Indeed, rents can be much higher than the house payments on the old home, simply because it was purchased years ago, in the days of low mortgages and reasonable prices. These market factors ultimately lead the downwardly mobile in the direction of lower-income neighborhoods, where their dollars go farther but where the atmosphere is comparatively déclassé.[13]

The sliding standard of living the downwardly mobile endure constitutes a drift away from normal middle-class expectations and behavior. The family is growing more deviant over time—its resemblance to the "precrisis" era becomes increasingly faint. Some of the slide can be hidden through dissembling, lies, or cover-ups. The whole family goes "into the closet"—hiding the real situation from the outside world, trying to appear "straight" to their neighbors—while behind the scenes its life steadily draws farther and farther away from the middle-class norm. But there is a psychological cost to living in the closet: Relations between family members grow more intense, and new, sometimes arduous, demands are placed upon children.

Spinning the Cocoon

At the age when most teenagers were jockeying for the right to the family car and the chance to stay out all night, Janet Wilson was spending her evenings cooking the family meal and calming her younger sister's nerves. But her attempts at providing a normal family life were complicated by her unemployed father's mania for home improvement projects. In an attempt to keep himself busy, he tore out walls and ripped up floorboards in a half-baked remodeling effort. The project never seemed to end, and because the family had no money for materials to rebuild, Janet found herself serving food in a crazy cross between a home and a building site.

As the oldest child, Janet wanted to help, so she cooked and cleaned; she did the family laundry; and she found a series of part-time jobs. She found herself commuting four hours a day by train to a campus of the state university because she could not afford to move away to college.

While her classmates were tasting freedom in the dorms and living it up in the big city on the weekends, Janet was worrying about how to make ends meet and how she was going to pull her parents through this crisis. She found herself unable to connect with new friends, not only because she was a commuter, but because the unfolding tragedy back in Great Neck pulled her closer to her family. Her preoccupation with her father's depression, her younger sister's confusion, and her mother's increasing reliance on her as a confidante pushed aside any notion of a social life.

Children in downwardly mobile families find themselves drawing closer to their families because they feel they cannot "desert a sinking ship" and because their parents lean on them for emotional support. When they do pull away from the family—even temporarily—they feel guilty. Willing but unwilling, they become psychologically and emotionally bound inside a familial cocoon.

Drawing closer may be a natural response, but for adolescents in downwardly mobile families, it comes at precisely the time when their peers are moving out into the world, forging meaningful links with people outside the kinship orbit, developing identities apart from the family.

Joan deLancy, the Wall Street lawyer, marvels in retrospect at the way she worked her way through school and the amount of money she was able to send home to support her parents and younger siblings. It meant putting in three long days a week in class and working the other four in menial jobs. She never seemed to have the luxury of wasting time. Thinking it over ten years later, she believes she became too emotionally involved with her family's problems:

> You know, even though I managed to get out of the house and go to college, I can remember the nights I spent waiting by the phone for the call from my parents with news about my Dad's latest job prospects. I worried more about his chances than my own grades in economics, which probably had more impact on my own future. But I didn't feel I had a future independent of my folks. Every few months I would have to send money to keep them going. I felt that I had no chance to make my own life, that I would always be attached by this umbilical cord. But it was partly of my own making: I wanted to know what was going on. I felt guilty that I wasn't there to help out, even though I was out trying to survive for them and for me.

There is a curious parallel between this cocoon that envelops downwardly mobile children and a phenomenon seen among some financially secure middle-class families. In the latter case, one hears complaints that middle-class affluence removes responsibility from teenage children, "infantilizes" young men and women, fostering an unhealthy emotional dependency on their parents until they reach their middle or late twenties.[14] Parents groan about the "boomerang" generation, young adults who return to the nest and stay beyond the time when, in years past, they would have been expected to be independent. Parents send their kids out, but they keep coming back.[15]

In both the downwardly-mobile family cocoon and the affluent boomerang generation, young people in their late teens and twenties are tied to their natal families. In terms of emotional dependency, however, the two are opposites. For the boomerang generation, the grown children are dependent on their parents: They refuse to cut the apron strings. For downwardly mobile families, it is the parents who need their kids' emotional support. The parents have become dependent on their offspring in weathering the crisis. Their children want to be more independent, but a sense of responsibility and obligation pulls them back.

Downward mobility undermines middle-class expectations about the length of time a child can expect to draw upon the financial resources of the natal family. Financially stable middle-class families take pride in being able to launch their children's careers by putting them through college and sometimes through professional and graduate school as well. Though a heavy burden, supporting one's children well into their twenties is an expression of a distinctive American trait: the tendency to turn upward mobility into a multigenerational project.

When middle-class families hit the skids, this capacity to funnel resources to the younger generation is disrupted. Kids can no longer expect much financial help for their education. In essence, they are on their own. Financial independence begins in small ways, with children getting part-time jobs to pay for entertainment or leisure activities while living at home. These responsibilities escalate with age and the ever-sliding family fortunes. Teenagers may pay for their own clothes, gas, and car insurance. By their college years, some contribute money that help support the natal household's food and rent bills, while simultaneously covering their own personal expenses. This flow of resources from children to parents sometimes continues even after the kids have married and formed their own households.

John Steinberg regularly emptied his small savings account and sent it home to help clothe his younger sisters. He took a year out of college to work on construction sites and sent much of that money to his parents for their support as well. In his own mind, it was the only thing to do. But that did not make it an easy task:

> I was working at this lousy job trying to make enough money to support myself and send money home. Having a construction job in the summer is no big deal, but once fall rolled around and everyone else went back to the classroom, I really started to worry whether I would ever get back on track. I knew I didn't want to be a construction worker all my life, but it was beginning to look like the money would be needed for a long time. It was a very scary experience, because I felt my future was slipping through my fingers.

John's feelings that his own future was being sacrificed to support his family will easily be recognized by older readers, for it was not uncommon before World War II for children to contribute their earnings to the family.[16] But in today's middle class, such an arrangement is quite aberrant. Consequently, children feel they are unusually selfless and generous because they are going beyond the call of duty in contributing to the household. Parents feel miserable: Having to take money from a child reinforces feelings of failure they have already experienced in the job market. The cultural rules that govern relations between middle-class parents and their children dictate a top-down flow of resources in the family. Thus when parents do have to accept support from children, they do so with considerable discomfort and guilt. It leads the parties—parents and children—to feel that they are odd-balls and misfits.

The tight embrace of the family cocoon produces other reactions as well. In normal families, a membrane of privacy surrounds the parents, which effectively excludes children from many domains. Children are not ordinarily privy to the details of the household budget, for example. The aura of secrecy is tantalizing, and when children begin to make regular contributions to the household, the walls around the parental preserve can no longer be maintained. When children penetrate the adult preserve as advisers or adjunct decision-makers, they often feel a sense of power and respect ordinarily denied to children.

But incorporation into the family's power center can be uncomfortable for both parents and children. Parents wishing to retain control find they cannot do so. Their children, who are contributing their salaries to the household's pool of resources, expect to be consulted on decisions that used to be none of their business and bridle when decisions are taken without their consultation or are announced after the fact.[17]

Having now been admitted into the parental preserve, however, children often regret it. Intimate knowledge of the consequences of downward mobility can be frightening. As much as they want to exercise decision-making authority, they often wish they could retain a claim on unknowing childhood. Janet Wilson was proud to be a trusted "sub" parent, but she was also scared of what she learned as a result:

> Maybe it was because I was the oldest child or because role reversals had already occurred, but my mother always used to say you should know about our finances, how much the mortgage is, where we keep our information on the bank account. . . . This was kind of scary sometimes. You wonder what's so immediately dangerous.

Janet wanted to be trusted and treated like an adult. But deep down, she did not really want to know all the fine details. Information means responsibility, and she had reached the limit of her ability to cope:

> I was completely overwhelmed. Things got very bad at home financially. Finally, it was completely overwhelming and I was eventually hospitalized with a very bad clinical depression. It was awful . . . here I was in the hospital and we didn't have any money to pay bills.[18]

Janet's case is unusual only in that she finally collapsed under the weight of the strain. Otherwise, she is typical of downwardly mobile children who find themselves stretched between their desire to prove how adult they are to their parents by shouldering responsibilities beyond their years, and their desire to be like other middle-class kids: carefree and self-involved. Those who try to blend into the adolescent scenery feel guilty over the suffering they know is going on behind the closed doors of the family home. Those like Janet, who choose to accelerate their involvement in family survival, pay another kind of price. They find themselves in over their heads. Taking the role of adviser or confidante makes them privy to the debilitating worry and anxiety of adults whose lives seem to be falling apart. Yet the children lack the requisite experience to counsel their parents, who are twice their age and far more worldly wise.

Even more important, despite their willingness to contribute to the family's economic survival, they are unable to earn enough to reverse the situation. They can only mitigate its worst effects. Hence, "responsible" children of downward mobility are trapped in a no-win situation: The maximum effort they can contribute is not enough to halt the family's fall from grace.

Multiple Realities

Downward mobility interferes with the ability of parents and children to retain the kind of relationship that their middle-class culture deems natural, normal, and ordinary. It makes it hard for parents to be leaders because parental authority springs from financial control and the illusion of invulnerability. And it places new role demands on children that pull them emotionally closer to the family while forcing them to be financially more autonomous and responsible than their peers. These burdens fall unevenly, however, since downward mobility catches children at different ages and stages of development. Older siblings face different demands and have different experiences of the slide than their younger brothers and sisters.

Dierdre Miller is the second of five children, whose births spanned a fifteen-year period. Downward mobility bifurcated the Miller children into two groups. Dierdre was only seven when they moved into their five-bedroom house on an acre of land, but the comparison between the luxurious new environment and the previous one was clear enough. Her older sister was even more conscious of the difference. Throughout their middle teenage years, the two eldest girls knew little else but an insular community of wealthy people.

When the family firm began to fail, the sisters were at different points in the maturation process. The oldest one was almost on her own:

My oldest sister was affected by Dad's business losses because she knew how serious it was, especially in the family: how it drove a rift between my parents that never quite mended. In that sense she knew it was a horrible experience. But she was already out of the house, caught up in socializing. She was earning her own money as a lifeguard, so she wasn't affected financially in the same way.

Dierdre herself was on the cusp between independence and childhood, in the middle of high school, when the trouble reached crisis proportions. Hence she was old enough both to work for her father and to comprehend the full significance of his failing business. But it also meant that she remained home for only a few more years, during the early period in which the family's finances grew strained but were not totally transformed. She had left home by the time of the worst part of the slide. It was her younger siblings who remained behind during the hardest times:

> My younger sister really saw the brunt of it. She was in high school when they were on food stamps. . . . They still kept their house in [Atherton]. It was very ironic. They would go down and apply for food stamps, and here they were in this very expensive house and had three cars. . . .
>
> You could see the change most at Christmas. When I grew up there were these huge Christmas celebrations. There were so many presents it was just ridiculous. . . . Suddenly it was "What do you want for Christmas?" and [my mother] would buy us one present and it would cost around thirty-five dollars. She would try to focus on the younger boys a bit and try to get them more because she didn't want them to feel they were missing so much. But their whole experience of Christmas growing up was completely different from my memories of the same period in my life.

Dierdre's younger sister and her two little brothers were victims of the crash in the strongest sense of the term. They have never really known anything other than relative deprivation. In this respect, the three youngest children in the Miller family are products of a very different economic trajectory than the older siblings, who were once privy to good fortune only to see it disappear.

Financial difficulties create enormous strain in personal relations. In the Miller family, the parents came very close to a divorce after many years of escalating bitterness. The cracks in the family's stability developed over time, as the crisis deepened. As such, the younger Miller children were exposed to emotional disturbance for a longer period of time, and at an earlier point in their lives than their older siblings:

> My brothers grew up with my parents fighting like that. I don't think they ever knew the kind of household my older sister and I had as young children, which was very stable and happy. . . . We would do things together and go places together as a family. Once I left the house and my younger siblings were home, they never did anything together. They never participated together as a family.
>
> My father no longer ate with the rest of the family. When I was young we always ate together. Later on my mother would fix dinner for the kids and ate with them. She would fix a plate for him, and he would eat later. He never wanted to eat with [the rest of the family].
>
> I felt my younger brothers were missing something because my parents no longer got along and they fought all the time. They missed all the happiness. It was not a pleasant house to be in. I was better off out of it. They were too young to have a choice.

The experience of the Miller siblings might lead to the conclusion that the whole experience is easier on the older children than for the little ones, who must endure the daily costs of downward mobility for many more years. Realistically, there is no good vantage point from which to experience economic collapse; each position in a sibling set has its pros and cons. Older children do spend less time under the gun, and despite the tendency toward privatization that often follows from downward mobility, they are still usually more involved in peer groups than their younger siblings. However, precisely because the older children are poised for independence, it falls to them to shoulder adult responsibilities sooner than they expect to and to a more serious degree than their counterparts in "normal" families. They are more likely to act as confidantes to parents and, even though their earning power is weak, they face pressure to help support the family financially. And, most poignantly, they find *themselves* torn between trying to pull themselves out of the abyss of economic collapse and assisting their families.

Higher education is the ground upon which this latter dilemma plays itself out. Some downwardly mobile children delay college, others drop out in favor of full-time employment. One reported taking on numerous student loans which were immediately wired off to pay the family's bills. Others chose a less expensive college or commuted from home and had to forego the "college experience" for hours of part-time work. But all were caught in a dilemma of how much to sacrifice their own prospects for upward mobility in order to cushion the fall of the natal family. This dilemma can last for years: The older progeny of downwardly mobile families realize they may have to continue draining their bank accounts to help pay for the younger brothers' and sisters' food, clothing, or college tuition. (One has to go back to the immigrant generation in most families to find an analogous situation where young adults were torn between starting their own families and helping to pay for siblings and parents to come over from the Old Country.)

Despite these dilemmas and tribulations, older children also derive certain benefits from assuming the culturally aberrant position of "junior breadwinner," chief among them their parents' gratitude. A contributing child attains the status of near-hero, while the parents feel guilty both for needing the help and for "robbing" their progeny of their own independence or schooling. Partly in compensation for the guilt, parents lionize the older child who is shouldering the family's burden. This can, unfortunately, serve to exacerbate the feelings of inadequacy harbored by other children too young to make major contributions.

Janet Wilson was caught in this position. She supported herself through college and became chief cook and bottle washer and her mother's confidante. For this she won special praise from her parents, which only served to make her younger sister feel more inadequate: "My mother complained that my sister didn't do enough to help. She would say, 'Your older sister does all these things, why can't you?' That made my sister feel very guilty. Here I was her 'saintly sister,' and what was she doing wrong?" This is one element among several that breeds resentment in younger siblings in downwardly mobile families.

Youngsters often rely heavily on their older siblings for emotional support, especially when their parents are preoccupied with their own problems. When the older siblings leave the family home, they draw the wrath of younger brothers and sisters, who feel they are being deserted in the middle of a war. Since the young ones are often left uninformed about family finances, they may also be ignorant of the ways in which their older siblings have in fact continued to lend their support. Instead they feel they have been left alone with the burden of a disintegrating situation while others have skipped out on their responsibilities. Younger children also hear many family stories of the glorious past—years they missed out on—when there were foreign vacations, new toys and fun. Given this vantage point, their older siblings appear to be children of privilege and the younger ones unfairly deprived.

Parents and older siblings look upon the young ones with very different eyes. Feeling guilty because young ones have indeed been deprived of past affluence, they bend over backward to protect the little ones from the realities of the present. They tend to give younger children more toys or nicer clothes than they can really afford and are more tolerant of their material demands. Younger children sometimes emerge from this sheltered situation with a bizarre mixture of personality characteristics. On the one hand they are almost spoiled, on the other they feel deprived relative to their siblings. Dierdre Miller's youngest brother is a case in point:

> Whatever my youngest brother wanted when he was a kid, he got it, even though they didn't have the money. When he asked for something he just got it. If he lost something expensive, it was replaced. To me that was just amazing. As a result, he isn't happy with anything less than the most expensive items you can find. But since he was only seven, when they started on food stamps, he really thinks of himself as a poor kid. He's a mass of contradictions.

The perceptions of Dierdre Miller and her siblings illustrate the fact that downward mobility is not *one* experience, shared in common by the whole family. It is instead a mosaic of perceptions: adults preoccupied with certain problems, older children troubled by issues of special salience to them, and younger siblings confused by lack of knowledge yet acutely sensitive to changes in normal routine.

Beyond this *Rashomon* quality—in which each vantage point yields a different picture—one discovers that "the family" has not one history or one memory, but several. For the adults, the decades of financial stability and happiness which preceeded the catastrophe constitute the core of the family's history; these memories are kept burnished and form a sense of self and identity, even though they are at odds with the realities of downward mobility. For the youngest children, whose memories of the good days are hazy, fragmented or second-hand, the only meaningful reality is life since the fall, with overstressed parents and money in short supply. Older children with a foot (or a memory) in both worlds can contrast before and after, and therefore judge their parents differently than their other siblings.

For many years, social scientists considered the family to be a little world unto itself, a culturally homogeneous unit within which status and values were held in common, behavior regularized into roles, experiences and meanings shared. The downwardly mobile family—with its life chopped in two (before the fall, after the fall)—dramatizes the fact that this is not necessarily so. It encourages us to probe for the multiple realities interleaved within the home.[19]

Deviant Role Models

If the demands placed on children in downwardly mobile families are unusual by middle-class standards, the role models provided by mothers, fathers, and close kin are even more deviant. The downwardly mobile child grows up surrounded by adults under stress, people who have been pushed out of their accustomed way of life. It is inevitable that children observe these grown-ups and develop, through emulation or through opposition, values and aspirations about their own futures. Unlike most children, they are not faced with one set of relatively consistent role models, but two. They know the "normal" middle-class orientations toward things, and they know their own family's deviant fate. Out of this contrast, downwardly mobile youngsters perforce must pick and choose.

Married women constitute an ever-increasing proportion of the American labor force, and dual career couples are now common-place. But for the executives' wives—the generation of middle-class women who married and began their families in the 1950s—the admonition that a wife's place was at the hearth was taken by many as gospel. Few of these women had extensive work experience prior to the fall. Suddenly and without warning, the wives of downwardly mobile men found themselves on center stage in the family's battle for economic survival. The imperative for them to go out to work was clear, despite years in the home and in many cases with little in the way of professional or vocational credentials.[20]

But what kinds of jobs could older women, who were either new to the labor market or returning to it after a long hiatus, hope to find? John Steinberg's mother discovered the unfortunate truth while her husband stood on the unemployment lines. The first job she landed, after fifteen years as a full-time housewife, was as a bank teller. It didn't last long: Three months later the bank cut its white-collar staff and because she was "last hired" she was also "first fired." Next she found a position as a cashier in a high-volume chain store, but this too came to an end. Customer lines had to be kept moving at a fast pace, and lacking any experience with a cash register, she made too many mistakes. It was a traumatic experience:

> My mother lacked confidence in herself when it came to the work world. She had spent almost all her time with [her children] for nearly fifteen years and suddenly she had to get out there and hustle. She would get stomachaches from anxiety attacks and she had trouble sleeping.

After six months, she caught management's critical eye and was fired, a bitter blow particularly because Mrs. Steinberg was the only breadwinner in the family.

She next landed a job in a factory in a nearby industrial area. Each morning she drove from her house in the hills to work alongside working class women and illegal aliens, molding hot plastic amid conditions riddled with health and safety hazards—hardly the kind of experience women from the country club set were accustomed to.

After five years of poorly paid positions, Mrs. Steinberg finally landed a job in a large store where she could make a respectable living. At $20,000 per year, she still cannot restore the family to its former glory, but she can provide steady support. In the end, her success has been a small but significant compensation for the losses her husband endured. In her words: "I gained in independence. I have the added self-respect that comes from facing tough ordeals and managing to live through them, and not too badly, either. But I know that my husband lost more than I did, and I did not want to gain at his expense."

Not all wives of downwardly mobile managers were willing to

accept the transformation from domestic matron to wage worker. Some simply refused to step into the vacuum caused by their husband's employment. Dierdre Miller recalls that her mother tried working for a short time and then simply refused to go on:

> My mother never really looked for a job. She worked for a few months in my Dad's factory [to help him out] and then said that . . . she couldn't go back. That was completely crazy; she just didn't want to be down there. . . . Her attitude was that she was not meant to be working. The deal they made when they got married was that she would have a lot of kids and she would have a lot of money and he would handle work.

Janet Wilson's mother, who considered herself a serious artist, felt much the same way:

> My father really wanted my mother to find a part-time job at least. That brought up a lot of arguments. She finally did eventually look but she couldn't find employment. Partly she didn't want to work; she felt she already had a lot on her shoulders juggling [the family] books around. She also felt she was still taking care of the house.

For wives of outcast managers, downward mobility means much more than finding ways to cope with a smaller budget. It brings them under pressure to alter the patterns of their lives in rather profound ways and to take on new responsibilities. Some respond positively to this while others do not. When they do enter or reenter the working world, the role transformation is a source of both fear and pride. The fear comes from the knowledge that there is a family depending on them financially and that they cannot afford to fail. Pride takes longer to develop, but eventually the wives of downwardly mobile managers realize their efforts were responsible for keeping the family afloat.

The managerial father also experiences changes in his role vis a vis the family. The traditional division of labor in middle-class households finds fathers in charge of worldly activity and mothers primarily responsible for the domestic front. But the source of the father's authority in the traditional household is not simply his role as the provider of the paycheck.[21] It stems as well from his greater involvement in the external world, his presumed superior knowledge of the ways of mammon. What this division of labor communicated to children of traditional families was a vision of their fathers as almost omniscient, as the person in the household most likely to know the answer to questions about science, economics, political affairs. Dierdre Miller expressed it well:

> I think [my sisters and I] grew up thinking my father was a God, a perfect individual. We would go up and ask him anything and he would always know the answer. He was so incredibly bright. . . . And when he was prosperous, he thought of himself that way too.

This culturally-defined view of the father as the person "in charge" crashes head-on into the reality of downward mobility. If Dad is all-knowing, how is it that he has gotten the whole family into such a mess? Occupational dislocation rattles many middle class children into questioning their images of their fathers; they wonder whether they weren't sold a bill of goods. As one put it:

> I think the children in my family thought of my father as a God. And he promoted that image, so it wasn't something the kids made up on their own. One of the hardest problems for us was how to reconcile the image of the God with the reality of the falling-apart situation. It was also hard on my father to reconcile. I think some of my sisters still have an unrealistic view of my father.

This exaggerated sense of the father's knowledge, power, and competence sets the stage for a sharp contrast once he loses his job. For suddenly he becomes, not only human, but vulnerable, capable of doubt, of crying, of weakness.

The involvement of the "traditional" father in the world outside the home virtually guarantees diminished contact with his children. Careers are demanding and are predicated on the assumption that someone else (usually the mother) is taking care of the affective life of the family, not to mention its daily organization. As a consequence, many children of downwardly mobile families remember their fathers as distant, often austere, figures whose contact with them was limited to the hours after work and before bedtime. John Steinberg certainly saw his father this way:

> My father was very remote when I was young; the contrast with my mother couldn't have been sharper. My father was always off at work. When he'd come home, he'd sit down with the newspaper until dinner. It's not that we didn't talk at all; we did. But it was limited to dinner conversation for the most part. My mother was always home when

my sisters and I got home from school. We spent our time with her.

When unemployment strikes, and fathers no longer have offices to retreat to, they are brought into closer contact with their children simply because they are around the home for more hours. The consequences of this can be negative: children are exposed rather directly to their father's distress, which can be rather upsetting: Witness Penny Ellerby's story about finding her father unshaven in his underwear when she arrived home with boyfriends after school. But it can have positive effects as well: Fathers can become more closely acquainted with their children and close the gap that so often opens between a harried professional and his family.[22] John Steinberg, who is now in his early thirties and long gone from his natal household, remembers the transformation clearly:

> After his job disappeared, and the country club disappeared [my father] started spending time at home, and we got to know him. All of a sudden he was home when we'd get home from school. It seemed odd to us in a way; no one else's father was at home. But it was sort of nice to see him. I felt like I got a chance to get to know him. As the years have gone by, and things haven't improved much for him, that time we spent together laid some kind of foundation for sympathy that I don't think I would have if I'd never gotten to know him.

The change did not go unnoticed by fathers at the Forty Plus club. For some, unemployment was a blessing of sorts, for it allowed them to experience a degree of intimacy with their children that they had never had before. Alex Kraemer endured a skidding fall from the heights of success as a high-level bank officer to the depths of a manual-labor assembly-line job. In between he spent many hours hunting for a new position from home:

> I never would have been around my kids during these later formative years if I still held these high level posts. Maybe this is the best thing that could have happened to them. [Why?] Because I was there [at home]. I wasn't there before. When you're running a [bank] you can't be there. Don't kid yourself; I put in sixty hours a week at least. I wasn't there when my kids were very young and into their grammar school years. So maybe in some ways [my job troubles] are to their benefit.
>
> I know them better now. That brings personal satisfaction to me. When all is said and done, the kids make it worth it all. They can

hold their own. In the midst of a swinging community, they don't smoke dope or drink. There are things to be thankful for.

It is hard to quantify what is lost when a "normal" executive father loses touch with his children. Some kids conclude their fathers were not interested in them, and feel estranged from them for many years. By rearranging the whereabouts of fathers and creating a genuine need for a child's emotional support, downward mobility closes the gap and paradoxically points to one of the disturbing aspects of the stable, upwardly mobile executive family.

Children's reactions to these role shifts are filled with contradictions. Adolescent children often become self-appointed guardians of middle-class norms of behavior, particularly those that signify traditional sex role differences.[23] When fathers would try to help out with housework, to ease the burdens on now-working wives, they would sometimes run afoul of their children. Kids found it confusing and shameful when their fathers took on what they perceived as "feminine" tasks, particularly if this behavior was in full view of the local community. John Steinberg was embarrassed that his father took the family laundry out to the Laundromat™ when the washing machine at home broke down. Mr. Steinberg was happy to have the excuse to get out of the house. But John did not want his father to suffer the social stigma of doing "women's work" in public, nor did he want to be known as the boy whose father did the laundry while all the other fathers in the neighborhood were at work.

Watching their mothers and fathers struggle with new worlds of work and unemployment made the children develop strong opinions about appropriate male and female roles. Some, like John, reacted like traditionalists, uncomfortable with role change. Others, particularly young women, took a more "progressive" stance. Dierdre Miller's mother refused to work and began to nag her father: "They were fighting a lot and she was bitching a lot about money. You know, 'Where's the money? Where's the money?' That was a weekly event. He would come home and bring her a certain amount of money and it was never quite enough." This left an indelible impression and crystallized a set of values in Dierdre about the dependency of women and the nature of men's roles. Now in her thirties, she reflects back:

> My father's business failure shattered a lot of dreams at a young age, when I wasn't really ready for it. Now I'm real glad it happened.

In the 1950s I thought that a perfect life was in store. I thought
you lived in a perfect place with perfect weather and that you grew
up and got married and had a family and your husband took care
of you. You married a prince charming. That was all shattered for
me.
My mother really saw my father as perfect and when he fell apart,
she couldn't handle it. I decided that men were not perfect and that
they weren't going to take care of me. I was never going to let myself
get into a situation like mother, who was so dependent on my father
financially . . .

There is a critical subtext over the nature of gender roles running
through their accounts, one that differs from some feminist perspectives that focus attention on the burdens of women's roles
in America. Women who grew up in downwardly mobile families
see their fathers as victims and have sympathy with men as overbur-
dened breadwinners. Joan deLancy saw it this way:

When I think about the way this society forced men in my father's
generation to be completely responsible for their families, it makes
me furious. I've been in the professional world for a while now and
I know how much pressure is involved. It isn't something anyone
can easily handle by themselves. To hold your whole family's fate in
your hands just isn't fair. My father took that on himself because
that's what all fathers did then. As a result, my mother didn't really
know much about the working world. She had to find out the hard
way. It wasn't her fault, but the whole situation was terrible. It was
a bad way to organize a family's survival.

The trials of the Depression had the indirect effect of boosting
the position of women in the household, since women were often
the only ones able to find work.[24] The experience raised the expectations of the younger generation of the Depression era about
the future roles of women. This same pattern is reflected in many
of the daughters of downward mobility in the 1980s, particularly
those whose mothers went out to work. It was especially strong
in those instances where the mothers "came to the rescue" and
the fathers fell apart. Alice Pendergast's father sank into alcoholism
and an abusive state of existence when his job disappeared. Her
mother, the perennial housewife, rose to the occasion and became
the family's sole support. The effect on Alice is clear:

I always have had the feeling that women have to be strong and
that no matter what shit men give them, they're supposed to carry

on and take care of the family—that the woman is the important person in the family. If the man is there that's nice and if he's being helpful, that's nice. But a woman can do just as nice without a man as with one, and you can't count on a man.

This is more than an abstract philosophical conclusion. It is a conviction that structures their lives in adulthood. They are full-time workers, thoroughly invested in their careers, and have re-tained full control over their financial well-being, even though most are now married and mothers of their own children. Many have bank accounts in their own names, completely separate from those of their husbands, and typically contribute equally to the maintenance of their marital households, splitting the costs down the middle with their husbands.[25] The impetus for these arrange-ments comes partly from feminism but equally from their exposure to economic hardship and the debilitating pressures generated by the dependent female role. As Dierdre tells it:

> I think about whether I will be able to support my two children all the time. Not will my husband and I be able to, but will I be able to on my own? I don't want to burden him with that. Seeing what my father went through, the kind of burden he had to carry because he was the sole means of support, I would never put anybody through that. [My father's] drinking is a product of that, of the pressure of trying to bring home that paycheck and support so many children without any financial support from my mother. She didn't even think about contributing.

When an unemployed father finally lands a new position of lower status than before, his children come face to face with the relationship between their father's public identity and their own social status.[26] Discomfort over this new status does not necessarily imply that downwardly mobile children lose respect or admiration for their fathers. Alex Kraemer's children were not proud of his factory job, but they admire him for doing what had to be done:

> My kids can remember the good days, but they weren't upset with my holding positions that were beneath me. How many fathers were vice presidents of this and that who are now machining? They could see I was bringing in some small bucks. They were proud of the fact that I was willing to get down and do what I had to do. They understood the situation; they're not snobs.
> My kids respect me. I'm definitely the head of the whole family. During this whole period, no matter how badly the circumstances

have been, there's always been a need for someone to make decisions and to reason with the kids about things. That's been me. . . . The type of leadership I have in the family doesn't come from the checkbook. It's advice you give. It's holding the family together.[27]

Not every father is able to retain the respect and authority of their children. In some families, the children smolder with resentment over their lot and grow skeptical about their father's projections for the future. Alice Pendergast learned to have contempt for her father, concluding that he was a windbag and a loser:

Essentially my father was unemployed from about 1968 until 1976. That was when I was eight until I was sixteen. During this time there was a steady deterioration in the kinds of jobs he had and the kinds of social relations he had. At first, he had respectable jobs, jobs in his field, that he felt good about. But then he started getting involved in these real fly-by-night companies. These guys decided they were gonna be hotshot salesmen and they'd get their own little office and start up their own company. Things never worked out. But there was always *big talk* about how this was gonna be it, they were gonna earn so much money and this product was the best. . . .

When I was eight, I thought, great—father's going to do this and everything will be fine. . . . But as I got older and saw what my father had become I started thinking that he was fooling himself, that he was making mountains out of molehills, and that things weren't going to work the way he thought. I just kept thinking every time he got a new job, "Oh, God, here we go again."

The children of the managerial middle class are creatures of the culture of meritocracy. They have been taught that worthy people are successful, and that success is indicative of merit. Families in the hills have two cars and big houses and ski vacations because they are intrinsically smarter or more diligent than their counterparts in the flatlands. For children schooled in this philosophy, it comes as a rude shock that their fathers have failed in the most critical domain of life. Their culture pushes them to accept the condemnation downward mobility rains down on their parents. They may respect their fathers for continuing to try, for refusing to give up hope of returning to a "normal" occupation, but they cannot ignore the nagging suspicion that the family is in this fix because Dad is not, after all, the god he portrayed himself to be—indeed, that his own flaws pushed him down the social ladder.

What separates children who render harsh assessments of parental failures from those more inclined toward tolerance or sympathy? While individual personality clearly plays its part, there are other sources of variation, the most important being the extent to which children are incorporated into the worldly side of their parents' lives *before* downward mobility rears its head.

Dierdre Miller used to work for her father in the family business and from this vantage point she could draw her own conclusions about what had happened to his business:

> I first became aware of how hard things had become when my summer job changed. My Dad used to hire [my sisters and me] normally during the summers as a fun thing. We'd go in and kind of play around. But when I was sixteen he hired me to do what I would have called the production manager and the secretary's job. She used to do all the accounting and payroll, shipping and receiving.
>
> Every other phone call at the office was a bill collector and I was the one who had to put them off. I had to say, "Well, my father isn't here right now." I'd have to lie through my teeth. I got very good at it by the end of the summer.
>
> I realized fairly quickly what this meant. I had worked there when there were a lot of employees. At that time my father didn't really work in the back of the plant. He never lifted things; he never put on work clothes, he always wore a suit to work. But when things went bad, he worked in the back with the machinery. He would go and pick up parts rather than have them delivered. Anything to save a dime.

From this close vantage point, Dierdre could see that there had been a slump in demand for the firm's only product. She watched her father get his hands dirty in an effort to save the business. Her involvement in his workplace tempered the voice of meritocratic individualism, which pushes in the direction of blame:

> My exposure to the business led me to realize that a business could go wrong because of outside economic forces. It had nothing to do with my father's mismanagement. During the early sixties there was a slump in those industries he supplied and this had nothing to do with him.[28]

Few children have this kind of firsthand knowledge of their parents' business affairs, and it is no accident that Dierdre's example comes from a family firm. Elsewhere in the corporate world, children are held at arm's length from their parents occupational lives.

Yet there are other mechanisms for reducing the distance between home and work that can have similar effects. The more children are privy to discussions about the world outside home and school, and the ups and downs of their parents lives as working adults (rather than mothers and fathers), the broader the context they have for interpreting the crash.[29]

John Steinberg spent almost no time in his father's workplace, but he knew a great deal about the contracts Mr. Steinberg was negotiating, the problems he was having with engineers and suppliers, and his differences with the big boss. He gleaned this information sitting around the dinner table, where his father learned about the trials and triumphs of John's civic classes. When the crash came, John also had a larger context into which he could place the events, albeit one provided through his father's eyes. John's knowledge kept him from feeling that his father's situation had developed without warning and made him realize that the causes of the disaster were complex. His attitude contrasts sharply with that of Penny Ellerby, the daughter of the show business producer, who was confused by the information blackout that descended following the collapse of her father's business. She was not made privy to the details, and she did not understand what was going on. Hence, all she could see was that her father-hero was falling apart and acting oddly.

Conversation about the world of work, or the lack of it, is but one factor that tilts the balance of blame and sympathy. Another involves age (or birth position in a sibling set). Children who were in their teens at the onset of the crisis and then left the nest tend to have a different perspective than those who remained in the household for seven or eight years of increasing financial chaos and personality disintegration. Late adolescents more often view their fathers as victims of circumstances beyond their control. When the failures begin to accumulate, they cannot help but notice that their parents are drinking more, arguing more, and moping more. But they do have a prior history within which to place the stress-related behaviors. This does not make them forgiving of alcoholism, for example, but at least they have some idea of its origins.[30]

Younger children can lose sight altogether of the causes of

personality disintegration. They were not old enough to know the "real" underlying personalities of their parents, who may (ten years later) bear only a faint resemblance to the confident executives they once were. Younger children tend to draw conclusions from the behavior they see, rather than the history they are told about in nostalgic renditions of the family's past. They often conclude that the personality problems came first and the business disaster followed.

The Miller family exemplifies the way in which these internal age divisions shape different perceptions of blame:

> The girls, who were the oldest, were off in the world of the perfect father and perfect mother. My Dad was the important businessman and my Mom ran the house. And then both individuals fell apart. My mother became the bitch. When I was younger she wasn't like that, she wasn't screaming all the time. She has a temper, but this screaming all the time, at my father and the kids, was something new, something we could see came out of the way the business was falling apart.
>
> My brothers, who are nearly ten years younger, grew up with my father as a totally inept alcoholic. They have never seen him as a whole or good person. They see him as a disgusting individual who can't control his drinking, who screwed up their lives. Screwed up the business because of the drinking.
>
> I see it the other way around: the drinking was the result of the business screwing up. I see it as a chain effect: The business went under, my mother bitched at him, and then he drank. They don't see it that way. They see it as my father drinking, the business falling apart, and their relationship falling apart.

The vantage points of these children differ because of the differences in their ages, the length of time they have spent at home (in close proximity to their parents), the increasing remoteness of the precipitating cause of household tension (business disaster), and the increasing disintegration of household finances. These variables create separate realities, divergent visions of what came before and what came after the great crash.

Blood and Reciprocity: The Conundrum of Kinship

Downward mobility reaches out beyond the nuclear family, and distorts its relations with kinsfolk. Economic dislocation isolates the family from its old friendship networks, leaving the extended family one of the most important replacement for the atrophied ties to friends.[31] Cousins, in-laws, aunts and uncles can, to a certain extent, fill the gap left behind. Blood ties are often "thick" enough to endure, even in the face of the downwardly mobile family's embarrassment.[32]

But these relations do not always work smoothly, because kinship ties are not just a matter of family celebrations and socializing. Marriage brings two previously separate families together, and implies obligations and expectations that each side has of the other. When a married man has failed to take care of his wife and children, he is perceived as less than a real man. If his misfortune has also forced his wife out into an inhospitable labor market, where she occupies an entry-level job in a menial occupation, his wife's relatives are likely to be even more unhappy.

After conventional sources of loan funds have been exhausted, the prospect of turning to kinfolk as lenders of last resort also arises. Nothing queers family relationships faster. When a married man turns to his own natal family for help, or even worse, to his affines (in-laws), he is entering an emotional minefield: family can feel obligated to help, but resentful. Confusion and embarrassment can intensify over whether material help is a loan, a gift, a favor, or a right—self-abasement or a statement of love and sharing.

Anthropologists have long been interested in the effects of gifts, indebtedness, and exchange on human relationships. Indeed, perhaps the first classic ethnography, Malinowski's *Argonauts of the Western Pacific*, detailed the workings of an enormous system of exchange (the Kula ring) that linked a circle of island peoples in Melanesia through gifts of shells and bracelets from island to island. These exchanges bound trading partners together, acting to maintain social cohesion among groups that would otherwise be hostile.

Social bonds can be built on debt and on reciprocity, but they are not always comfortable ones.[33] Giving gifts places the receiver under an obligation, creating a bond between giver and receiver. It also creates an asymmetry between the receiver and the giver. An unreciprocated gift therefore makes the indebted person more and more uncomfortable as time passes. The balance may easily be regained, however, by completing an exchange. The obligation is cancelled out by a return gift, and the relationship returns to an egalitarian state as each side takes turns giving and taking.[34]

But exchange relations in the modern industrial family are

rather different from exchanges between semihostile clans, as the British anthropologist Edmund Leach has pointed out. In the modern family, exchange lacks the formal flavor of the Kula ring. Instead, it involves frequent but impermanent gifts (food, drink, hospitality), and there "is not close accounting of who owes what to whom, but there is a tacit understanding . . . that there is a moral obligation to balance things out over a long period."[35]

Within the family certain relationships presuppose no need for reciprocity in material exchange: Parents can give endlessly because they love and cherish. Because the relationship between parent and child is permanent, there is no cultural pressure for children to "pay back" material goods and thus cancel an obligation.[36] An ideology of altruism prevails that eschews balancing debts in favor of a generalized sharing, and notions of common property (or use) hold sway.[37] But even within the nuclear family, it can become problematic to determine which relations must respond to the demands of reciprocal exchange and which are covered by generalized sharing. Brothers and sisters are covered by generalized sharing while under the same roof, but once they separate into their own nuclear households, they may no longer feel bound by the same rules.

Sudden financial distress lays bare the ambiguities that surround these norms of obligation. For while the vertical ties between parents and children are, to some degree, clear enough, the lateral links—between siblings, for example—are hazy and imprecise. Is a man required to offer his help to his brother when the latter is in trouble? Or do his obligations end when the resources he might give to his brother come out of the funds he needs to pay his own child's college tuition? If he helps his brother, should he expect repayment, or would that constitute a violation of the generalized exchange in which they participated in their youth? What about cousins? The farther one strays beyond the vertical relations between parents and children or the circle of the nuclear family, the more difficult it becomes to determine the strength of the ties that bind. American culture provides little guidance in settling these matters, and under stable circumstances they do not arise.

Downward mobility pushes the issues to the fore, forcing a definition of the cultural rules that govern exchange with "insiders" and "outsiders." But even with those rules in place (reciprocity with outsiders, generalized exchange with insiders), the downwardly mobile who approach their kin for aid may find themselves caught in the middle of cultural contradictions. By borrowing, the displaced manager is in debt and by placing himself in debt, he subordinates himself to someone with whom he is supposed to have an egalitarian, generalized sharing, relationship—a close relative. By taking money, he also enters the realm of "permanent gifts," which are ordinarily governed by strict accounting, reciprocity, and repayment.[38] Not to repay is to subordinate oneself indefinitely and to welch on an obligation, to lose one's independence or status. But to attend to strict accounting and repayment in full is to label the lending kinsman an "outsider," someone from whom the borrower cannot receive in the intimate, familial way. The man who borrows from his relatives is therefore on the horns of a dilemma: If he fails to repay rapidly, he risks debasement. If he does repay, he risks unintentional insult to his kinsmen.

The insider's view of this dilemma was expressed by Joe Jorgensen, an unemployed manager at Forty Plus:

> I could never go to my family to borrow money. In fact, my in-laws don't know that I'm "out" [of work] because if they did they would offer to help me out financially. I don't want them to do that because if they did, they would never take the money back.
>
> I simply couldn't accept that. I would have to give it back. I have always been brought up that if anyone helps you in time of need, when you are able to, then you repay them in kind. You must show them your appreciation because nothing is coming to you in the world.

Joe was certain that the rules of family relations would cause his closest relatives, his sister and brother-in-law, to insist that he take help without letting him pay them back. He explained that you don't allow relatives to pay you back because that would transform a "gift" given out of love into a "loan." But accepting a gift without repayment has a hidden price: It tears away at a man's independence and pride.[39]

Joe knows this because he has been there before. Seven years before the onset of the current bout of unemployment, he was out of work for eight months and was suffering financially. To make matters worse, his car broke down, a serious setback for a suburban dweller whose line of work (in sales) entails extensive travel. His brother-in-law tried to come to the rescue:

> My car broke down and I had to have it repaired. My sister and brother-in-law drove up one Sunday in two cars and he put the keys and the ownership papers on the table and $100 under the keys. He said, "Here, use my car until yours is fixed." I said, "Josh, take

it back." He says, "Why? Your car is broken!" I said, "Josh, I'll go by train or bus. Because you will never take the money back." He says, "So what, you're more than a brother-in-law to me!" I said, "Josh, you know me. I just can't allow that."

One might assume that given his objections, Joe would prefer that the whole issue of help had never been raised. Curiously, this is not the case. He was delighted to know that Josh would offer to help. It signified just how much he cared:

> It showed me that he thought of me as more than a brother-in-law. It solidified my feeling that we were so close. I appreciated that so much, but I wanted him to realize that I'm a very independent person. His refusal to let me pay him back would tear down my independence, and I wouldn't allow that.

The symmetry of Joe's views is revealed in his comments about what he would do if Josh were ever in trouble. He allows that he would offer to help Josh the moment he needed it; the depth of his feelings for his brother-in-law are fully reciprocal. But would he allow Josh to pay him back? "Yes, for his peace of mind. If he would insist on repaying me, I would not insult him by not taking it back. But I would take the money and turn it over into something for his children as a gift."

Joe's ingenious solution to the problem of reciprocity and dependence would be to allow the hierarchical relationship of giver and receiver to be returned to equilibrium by repayment, but to retain the special quality of the gift by treating the repayment as a kind of sacred money, which can only be used for an altruistic purpose that would benefit Josh's family.

Many members of the Forty Plus Club share Joe's conviction that it is better to turn to impersonal institutions than to relatives in times of financial distress. For the downwardly mobile manager, impersonality is a buffer against embarrassment. Revealing financial problems to a bank officer is less troublesome than telling a friend or relative. Even more important, the prospect of having to default on a loan obligation, which is an ever-present possibility, is easier to contemplate if a bank takes the brunt than if a friend or family member stands to lose hard-earned funds.

Aspirations and Pathways

Children in downwardly mobile families watch their parents battling adversity and take on various responsibilities and worries of their own. They rarely sail through adolescence in an unreflective haze. Instead their senses are repeatedly jarred by conflict, disappointment, and incongruity, forcing them to develop beliefs and aspirations for the future in the light of their parents' fall from grace.

There is a great deal of variation in the conclusions that downwardly mobile children reach about the world they live in and their own place within it. But despite different attitudes and career aspirations, one finds a common core, a shared orientation among many of these offspring of downward mobility. Each expresses a psychological toughness, an earnestness, a sense of no-nonsense commitment, which marks them off from others.[40]

Though few would wish their experience on others, they credit their subsequent success in adult life to their determination to pull out of the vortex of failure that seemed to threaten their own futures. Alice Pendergast is now a student of social welfare administration. With little help from anyone, she managed to put herself through college and move on to professional training. She credits her experience with domestic disaster for her resilience in the face of adversity in her own adult life.

There is, however, a critical edge to her toughness. Alice has great confidence in her ability to surmount obstacles in her career, but she is awash in anger toward those who had it easy. As a high school student, Alice envied her "rich" friends, children of successful Seattle executives. These days she holds many of them in contempt: They lack drive and ambition and have, in her eyes, failed far lesser tests than those Alice had to endure.

> [My best friend in high school] flaked out; she took the easy way out. That makes me angry. It's really stupid; she has no excuse. I used to think she was so much better off than me, but now I think I'm just a bit tougher than she is. I've had to go through a lot more than she has.

The envy has not entirely disappeared, but it has been submerged under disdain for the ways in which a "normal" upbringing leaves people soft, with insufficient backbone. Alice's feelings of superiority are mixed with envy and fury toward people who had it easy:

> I hate going to school with all these upper-class people at [my university]. It seems like their fathers were [all] professors or doctors or whatever and I just feel like kicking them. How dare they be so lucky! It's stupid, but I'm just obsessed by how much money other people's parents have.

In part, this is simply *resentment* against the rich or privileged, but it also suggests something more profound—an insight into the ideological tenacity of meritocratic individualism in managerial culture. Alice and the other children of downwardly mobile managers have seen parents whom they love and admire bowed, and in some cases crushed, under the weight of economic adversity. They know that the good do not necessarily prosper in this world and that those who fail are not slothful, weak, or unambitious.

Yet these children of downward mobility struggled, took on part-time jobs, held parents' emotions together, and worked their way to whatever level of occupational success they attained. What took them enormous strength of purpose and sheer hard work, many of their peers—children of affluence—received as entitlements: good schools, cars, tuition money, time free from work to study. Children who had to "pull themselves up by their own bootstraps" feel emotionally tougher than their spoon-fed compatriots and believe that they have worked harder to get where they are. They are resentful of those who have not had to overcome the same hurdles: "The privileged ones do not deserve their comfort, they haven't struggled for it like us." And in giving emotional expression and moral dignity to their own climb out of downward mobility, they cannot help but recreate the *mythos* they know can be false: "Since we succeeded, we are better people; since others have not struggled, they are morally inferior." The Protestant ethic is renewed in the children of managerial downward mobility even though it has undermined their parents.

The offspring of downwardly mobile parents choose careers that express their own tastes, values, and abilities within a context of restricted choice, limitations imposed by lack of money, and family obligations. But for some of these people, an occupational trajectory is more than a ticket to a desired life-style. It can express a judgment—a rejection—of parental pathways that failed badly in years past. It can also constitute a means of erasing the stains of failure carried over from the parental generation. Careers, therefore, become symbolic statements, vehicles for correcting prior misfortunes or for setting the world aright as well as ways of earning a living.

One such reactive path finds the capitalist's child becoming a social activist, a reformer. Alice Pendergast believes her father's job was devoid of social purpose and that he mistakenly oriented his entire life toward the goal of getting rich. In her own life,

Alice has sought a respected position that will not only endow her with the status she lost as a child but will also express her sense of altruism and commitment to others:

> I feel that it is my duty to help other people. There are so many people in this world who don't understand what a problem is. I feel that I have to help the underdog. . . . I'm just one of those people who tries to take everyone under their wing. That's why I went into social welfare. It's my way of helping other people.

Dierdre Miller was raised in an environment that placed the highest priority on wealth and social position. Watching the anguish that the end of affluence caused, she concluded that there had to be other goals in life:

> Because I worked for my Dad and I saw what the bill collectors were doing to him and heard my mother yelling and saw what was happening to our home, how life was falling apart because of money, it became clear to me at fifteen that money was too important to them and that I would never let it become that important to me.
>
> When they didn't have enough money to buy my brothers' clothes and the kids couldn't go to the upper-middle-class school and look right, it would drive my mother up the wall. These values were warped.

Working her way through college, Dierdre decided to major in literature. She did not expect her education to lead directly to a career, but she felt it was enriching in other ways. It expressed her commitment to education in the purest, nonutilitarian sense. Ultimately she embarked on a career as a social worker, an occupation that provides a secure and steady living and is socially useful as well. She doesn't hope or care to be rich.

Both of these women rejected the business world for altruistic or aesthetic pursuits, having decided that their parents' goals did not justify the heavy costs they exacted on the natal family. But not every child of a failed businessman becomes a social worker. Reactive strategies can also lie at the opposite end of the spectrum: children sometimes dedicate themselves to becoming as rich as possible, as quickly as they can. This seems to be more characteristic of sons, especially those who remained in the family home long enough to witness the intense frustration of their fathers. The sons feel constrained by downward mobility and chafe at the lack of freedom to consume, to plan, to move. For them, downward mobility is a suffocating experience, and the only way out is to beat the world at its own game. As one young man joked, "Money may not be everything, but it surely buys a lot."

John Riordan was twelve years old when everything unraveled. Though his parents had started from fairly modest beginnings, by the time John was old enough to notice his surroundings, they had hit an affluent stride and were comfortably esconced in suburban White Plains. He had never known anything other than the life of the country club, family boat, and new cars every year. It took seven or eight years for the financial damage completely to transform John's life, but in rapid succession the country club and boat disappeared and new clothes became a thing of the past. One step ahead of the foreclosure notice, the family home disappeared. Thereafter the family moved from one rental to another. Abject poverty never struck, but insecurity and debt were everywhere. One thing John knew by the time he left home at the age of twenty-two was that he wanted to be wealthy.

Having observed how little protection educational credentials had afforded his father, John concluded that a college degree was not a ticket to wealth. In stark contrast to the rest of the kids in his high school who were virtually all college bound, John made a beeline for the get-rich-quick world of real estate. A single man in his thirties now, John earns more than anyone in his family ever has. He also spends it. Money burns holes in his pockets. His lifestyle is based on constant consumption: He owns a BMW, a townhouse back in White Plains, and a lavish wardrobe. John has dedicated his life to erasing the stigma that descended on his natal household. Indeed, he fantasizes about buying the family home back someday.

Dierdre Miller's younger brother, Paul, is equally concerned about getting rich quick. His childhood memories revolve around food stamps and the humiliation of living poor in a wealthy neighborhood. These days, Dierdre notes, her brother will settle for no less than the best of creature comforts:

> Paul is now twenty-four and still lives at home. He has very, very expensive tastes. I don't know if that's a product of the fact that he sensed he didn't get what he wanted as a child. But he has to have only the best. He has a thousand-dollar bicycle. He's into camping; he buys the best, a two-hundred-dollar sleeping bag. Money is no object.

Other children from downwardly mobile families are as intent on freeing themselves from the trappings of bureaucracy as they

are on making money. John Kowalski, dumped after thirty years
with the same manufacturer's association, has a son who has become a high-flying risk taker. John looks on in amazement as
his son turns out to be everything he is not: "My son is aggressive
and entrepreneurial. It's more important to him to make money
than my other kids. He's willing to gamble. He's done something
I could not have done and couldn't do even now." His son is
uncomfortable with lockstep organizations, allergic to the idea
of working under a boss's control. John was the essence of the
bureaucratic man; his son has moved in the opposite direction
by carving out an occupational niche that will assure his freedom
from the control of others.

Janet Wilson presents exactly the opposite picture. Her father's
years as a free-lance graphic designer were filled with unpredicta-
bility and insecurity for the family. Though Janet realizes he had
few alternatives, she is resolute in her conviction that she needs
a safer pathway. Her vision of safety is highly bureaucratic: the
church. She is pursuing ordination as a minister, a choice entirely
of her own making since her family has never had any contact
with this faith. Her motivations are somewhat reminiscent of Alice
Pendergast's: She wants to help other people. But she wants to
be swathed in a routinized structure:

> My parents think, If you want to help people why don't you become
> a doctor or a lawyer? That's great for some people, but for me the
> spiritual is important. . . . Besides, I think . . . my turbulent past
> made me want to find a path quicker, and it also made me afraid of
> taking risks. I've already been through the wringer.

The career pathways of children who have experienced economic dislocation in adolescence seem conditioned by their observations of what went wrong in their parents' lives. If their fathers
were embedded in bureaucratic organizations, they want to be
free from dependency on a boss. If the downfall came because
Dad was focused on making money, they are oriented toward
altruism. If Dad was an entrepreneur or practiced a trade known
for volatility, they seek the safety of a bureaucracy or another
kind of cloistered setting where there is safety in rules. These
strategies appeal precisely because they differ from the route followed by the family breadwinner.

However divergent their careers may be, children of downwardly
mobile families generally share one overriding concern: economic
security. No matter how critical they may be of their parents'

occupational trajectories, they share with them a desire for steady, dependable income. And they dread the prospect of fiscal trouble. Children of downward mobility are, in this respect, very similar to the "children of the Great Depression."[41] Most become nervous when they see their bank balances decline, and fidget over the prospect of debt.[42] Alice Pendergast clearly manifests these traits and she knows it, in part because her husband, who grew up in a stable middle-class family, is so very different:

> I probably spend about the same amount of money as my husband, but every time I spend it I feel so guilty that I can't enjoy what I've spent my money on. And I always worry that I spend too much. Every time we take money out of the bank, I look at the balance and think, "Oh, we've got fourteen more days until payday, what are we going to do?" and I get all upset about it. Mark just takes the money out and says "Okay, don't worry, we'll do fine."
>
> I don't actually need a lot of money for the rest of my life, but I don't want to worry about being poor. I don't want to have a time when I don't have any money. Because there were times like that when I was a kid and it was awful.

The fear of financial trouble intensifies as the children of downwardly mobile families grow up. They worry they may not be able to fulfill the responsibilities they have toward their own children any better than their parents did for them. Dierdre Miller:

> I tend to worry a lot about money. I have a simple attitude: I always think that I'll be poor and never have any money and that around the corner I'll get fired and the next paycheck won't be there. I worry about whether I'll be able to take care of my family, my kids, if that happens. How will we survive? Will we be able to live on welfare and still be able to maintain a household that will be good for the kids? Not fall apart emotionally because you're on welfare? . . . I'm not always sure that I'm strong enough to survive anything.

One might expect to find this attitude coming from a ghetto resident or a survivor of the Great Depression. The words come from a woman raised in one of the wealthiest towns in the United States.

The Pathologies of Downward Mobility

Downward mobility contributes its share to increasing rates of alcoholism, child abuse, and divorce. It is hard to know what proportion of these stress-related problems is attributable to economic dislocation, but we do know that when the economy goes sour, a whole host of family "disorders" increases. When we speak of pathological reactions to downward mobility, we must distinguish the common response patterns in these families from those that are exceptionally destructive. Many of these families display certain "garden variety" pathologies, including stress, high levels of alcohol consumption, marital tension, and depression. Others face more serious problems of physical brutality, incapacitating alcoholism, desertion, child abuse, the complete disintegration of the family, and in some instances, suicide.[43]

Despite parents' best efforts to hide the depth of their despair, many families eventually face the problem of chronic depression and drinking. Nothing seems to be working in Dad's efforts to find suitable work. Appliances and cars are breaking down, and there is no money to fix them. The kids want to buy clothes or toys that their friends have, but the budget won't stretch that far.

Seeking solace in the bottle is a common response to these circumstances. What may have started out as a socially acceptable level of consumption, perhaps including the three-martini executive lunch, becomes slurred speech, nodding out over the dinner table, hitting the bottle before noon, slowed reflexes, and a more belligerent, moody personality.

Alcohol abuse is hardly a problem unique to the downwardly mobile, but when the two problems coexist, the combination can be particularly demoralizing to the breadwinner and his dependent family. If it becomes severe enough, alcoholism can become a serious impediment to recovery from economic distress. It can lead to health problems the downwardly mobile family cannot afford either. A well-heeled executive may be able to check into a clinic to "dry out"; a downwardly mobile one cannot pay for the treatment.

Dierdre Miller's father began drinking heavily after his family firm ran into trouble. Where once her father would come home and talk with his family, after the business slid into the ground he would come home and hit the bottle. He became morose and would not communicate:

> By the time I left high school I would have open, horrendous fights with my Dad about his drinking. I would yell at him that he should

quit, that it was ruining his life and our lives. . . . After a while my brothers stopped bringing their friends around to the house. When they do, it's like my father doesn't exist. He's like a ghost in the house.

Dierdre's family fell apart under the combined brunt of financial failure and her father's drinking problems. She was understanding about the former, but her patience was severely strained by the latter. Like many other relatives of alcoholics, she assumed that her father could control his drinking if he chose to do so. Dierdre found herself arguing with her father about whether or not he really was an alcoholic:

> He always maintained that his drinking was under control because he knew he was doing it. He would say that he wasn't an alcoholic because he knew he was drinking as much as he was and chooses to do it. An alcoholic doesn't know this, he would tell me. Their lives fall apart, but his didn't. But to me, his whole life did fall apart because his family life was falling apart. . . . His children rejected him for his drinking.

Joan deLancy remembers that her father had always been a heavy drinker. In fact, it was a point of honor with him that he could "hold his liquor." Fifteen years and many low-level, dead-end jobs later, he has become an alcoholic. Joan and her siblings have endured many a social embarrassment as a result. Her father became a belligerent, intolerant alcoholic who was often insulting when told he had overstepped the bounds of polite conversation.[44] Before long, Joan stopped bringing friends home. Her older brother, George, developed a sullen, angry expression that would cross his face whenever he saw his father head for the liquor cabinet. Her mother was simply too distraught over the family's financial situation to pay much attention to the drinking problem. But, as Joan explains, the children felt quite helpless to affect their father's behavior:

> It always seemed to us that he was trying so hard to find a way out of the [financial] disaster that for years we didn't have the heart to confront him about his drinking. Besides, you couldn't very well say, "Stop drinking or you'll lose your job." He already had lost it. There wasn't very much for him to look forward to except lousy jobs and nothing important to do every day for years and years. He had been such an active man, always in charge. Now he's a broken man who still struggles along, but realistically I'm not sure there's anything

for him to look forward to. He was cut down in the prime of his forties and now he's in his sixties. I don't see what's going to change. The main reason I'd like him to quit drinking is that I'm worried about his health. But there are times when I think alcohol is just a sedative against the pain and disappointment. If he were clear-headed all the time, he might just feel worse.

Joan has felt torn on this count for many years. She believes her father's downward mobility might have killed a "lesser man." But she shares with Dierdre Miller the nagging suspicion that he could stop drinking if he really wanted to, and the irritation over her father's impossible behavior. Her brother is even more critical:

I get phone calls from my brother who gets hysterical, saying our father is not doing anything [about finding a better job than his present clerical one]. My feeling at this point is, I just want him not to crack up. As long as he can maintain his psychological equilibrium and continue trying to do whatever it is he thinks he ought to do, as far as I'm concerned we should try to back off and give him that space. My brother just can't do that.

Children of downward mobility who grow up under the persistent cloud of alcohol-induced problems sometimes develop puritanical attitudes about drinking. Some become complete teetotalers; others indulge on occasion, but with an underlying degree of anxiety that this may lead them to follow their parents' unenviable pathways in life. Alice Pendergast, whose father's drinking eventually destroyed the family, always felt awkward when her adolescent friends made drinking a weekend pasttime:

It wasn't that I wanted to be a goody-two-shoes. I was just so afraid of losing control. It was the kind of fear that made my stomach go into knots. I'm still like that. Even now, I just can't let myself get drunk. I feel like I'll fall into this abyss that I'll never get out of again.

Rationally I know that if I got drunk nothing would happen. I'd probably just have fun and act foolish and have a hell of a hangover the next day. But irrationally, deep down inside, I feel like I'd die if I do.

I know the reason I look down on people who are drunk is because of my father. Alcohol just destroyed him. He destroyed himself, but he used alcohol to do it.

Alcohol problems are but one aspect of the "normal pathologies" affecting downwardly mobile families. Adults and children must find a way to accommodate to flaring tempers, rage at the world, and the disorientation that comes from an apparent breakdown in the "rules" governing their fates and fortunes. Perhaps most difficult is the persistent depression that accompanies downward mobility. The home seems to be swathed in gloom. Because so much psychic energy is invested in occupational identity, accomplishments in other realms do little to eradicate the depression. Prospects of acceptable work are the only true antidote to the frustration, and these can be few and far between. As the dour atmosphere persists, communication patterns in the family change for the worse. Fathers find it hard to face the upturned faces asking how things are going. There comes a time when they simply do not want to be asked because they have little to report. Dierdre Miller's father simply withdrew into a private world and for years had little to say to his children. Unfortunately, the rupture this caused in relations within her family was so deep that even when his business life stabilized at a lower level, the emotional damage had been done:

> Now that things are going better with the business, my Dad comes home and tries to talk about it, but no one responds. My mother and brothers don't want to hear about it. All my mother wants to hear is how much money is coming in, not what he's doing, what he's producing. . . . He should be proud of his accomplishments, but no one is proud of him.

These "normal pathologies" illustrate common patterns of response to the persistent tension of downward mobility. Though they do not necessarily culminate in the dissolution of the family, families *do* sometimes disintegrate completely under the pressure. We have long known that low-income families that must struggle to get by suffer from high levels of marital instability. We are accustomed to the notion that this is a widespread problem in poor, black neighborhoods.[45] When middle-class whites face similar obstacles to a secure livelihood, they often crumble as well.

Alice Pendergast's family is one of the more extreme examples of the damage downward mobility can do to a family. The more menial her father's jobs became, the more he drank. The more he drank, the more violent he became.[46] He vented his rage and frustration on his wife and child, leaving "bruises the size of oranges on [his wife's] face," choke marks around Alice's neck, stains on the walls from the plates of food he threw in disgust, and the psychological damage that comes from living through a reign of terror. Alice's mother went to work to support the family as a clerical worker in a local insurance company. Though the family needed the money, Mr. Pendergast's dependence on his wife exacerbated his frustration:[47]

> The reason why my father drank and belittled and beat my mother was because he felt he had failed as a man. He wanted to reassert that even though he was being supported by this woman, he could still dominate her completely. And he did. Mentally and emotionally it just destroyed him that he couldn't be the man he expected himself to be.

Alice endured years of being thrown out of the house in the middle of the night, of going to school with sunglasses on to hide the evidence of beatings, and of begging her mother to extricate both of them from the hideous situation:

> She always felt she had nowhere to go. I remember all those times when I was little, I would say, "Why don't we just go?" She'd say, "I can't go, I can't live in an apartment. I can't give up this house. I can't support you. I'm not going to live in an apartment with no garden, a smelly little apartment." If anyone had dropped in status [from a well-to-do family to a browbeaten clerical worker], it was my mother. She just refused to drop anymore.

The trauma was all the more difficult to bear because the family became increasingly isolated from potential sources of support. Mr. Pendergast's belligerence drove friends away. Though Alice's parents had once had an active social life, by the time she was a teenager, nothing was left of it.

Her mother did finally ask for a divorce. But Alice will never get over the pain and suffering of the years she lived with her father. She counts herself lucky that she was able to pull herself together, work toward an education, find a husband, and leave Seattle behind. She is remorseful about her relationship with her father, whom she fervently believes loved her despite his brutality. He finally committed suicide, a final act of desperation that Alice connects to his profound disappointment over his inability to find a respectable place in society.[48]

Downward mobility strikes at the heart of the "masculine ideal" for the American middle class. When the man of the house has failed at the task that most clearly defines his role, he suffers a loss of identity as a man. When this is coupled with the admirable efforts of a wife to salvage the situation by going out to work, the man's response may be intensified feelings of impotence and rage culminating in abuse.[49]

Alice's experience is *not* typical of the downwardly mobile. With variable degrees of success, most families find ways to salvage a life in the midst of their frustrations. They weather the "normal pathologies" that stem from the destruction of their dreams, though not without cost. There is love and respect in many of these families, and spells of happiness puncture the anxiety and gloom. Many families fight off apathy, continually struggling to make ends meet, trying to build a good life in the teeth of adversity. But Alice's life is a reminder of how much damage can accrue when depression and a sense of helplessness brought on by downward mobility erupt into alcoholism and family violence.

Is Failure Genetic?

Even when they have found workable pathways in their adult lives, downwardly mobile children look at themselves as abnormal. They carry this self-image long after they have established their own families and live thousands of miles from their parents. Its persistence stems from a variety of sources, not the least of which may be the continued financial dependence of the parents on their children. As parents age, the consequences of their loss of retirement benefits loom large in the lives of their adult children, who feel the pressure to provide for a decent old age. Hence there are real, practical reasons why downwardly mobile children cannot put the experience behind them as a thing of the past.

But there is also a psychological dimension: Adolescents who experience a precipitous drop in economic status feel singled out. They think of themselves as victims, though it is not always clear to them who or what has victimized them. They believe that they are unlike their peers, and they continue to see themselves as products of a uniquely unfortunate experience. After all, they are *not* products of the Great Depression, when the whole country was in the throes of economic disaster.

Faced with the same worries as their "normal" counterparts in their adult lives—the hurdles of promotions, bar exams, academic tenure, or partnerships—the progeny of downwardly mobile families ruminate over whether they can make the grade. Driven to succeed, running hard to escape the fate of their fathers, they obsess over whether failure can be genetically transmitted.[50] This is not to be taken literally: They do not believe in a gene for financial disaster. But they become anxious whenever they notice personality resemblances between themselves and their parents and wonder whether these similarities will push their own careers in the direction of downward mobility. In Alice Pendergast's words:

> What scares me is the thought that I could actually become him. That I'll be a loser, that I won't have any friends. That I won't be able to find a good job. That I won't get along with my family or be brutal and abusive. That I'll be an alcoholic. The whole bit. I just think I'll be just like him, only a woman. . . .
>
> I think about my father every day of my life. Everything I do is consciously in reaction to him. I try very hard. That's why I'm in graduate school . . . because I wanted a good education. I don't want to make the same mistakes as him. But I have to tell you that when I get near an unemployment agency, the first thing I think is, I'm going to be here when I'm forty-five. I am really scared that everything I've worked for is just going to fall apart at a bad time, just like it did for him.

At some level the products of downward mobility believe that failure can be transmitted through the generations. Hence even if all outward signs point to successful careers, they continuously scan their lives for evidence of the crash to come. This nagging conviction keeps them off balance and insecure.

*

Most people who have aspirations for success doubt themselves at one time or another. But when the adult children of the downwardly mobile confront these fears, they are of a qualitatively different character.[51] For they have seen the consequences of failure close at hand; they know all too well what is destroyed when people lose their toehold in the class structure. The experience undermines their sense of security, or more properly, their ability to judge how stable or vulnerable their occupational positions really are. For when, in the midst of a comfortable, easy going life, everything falls apart, children never quite recapture that feeling of safety again. Even if, in their own adult lives, all outward indications are that things are going well and success is just around the corner, they worry that it is all a mirage. After all, everything appeared to be fine years ago, and yet everything collapsed before their eyes.

Suzanne Keller, a distinguished sociologist at Princeton University, once described how she felt when as a child she watched the social order in Austria disintegrate under the Nazi invasion.[52] Her privileged grammar school was mainly populated by Roman Catholics, but there were a few Jewish children as well. All were united in their dislike for one boy known as an obnoxious bully. As the German invasion gripped Austria and the "new order" of Nazism swept through Keller's school, the bully appeared with a swaztika emblazoned on his arm. He began to order Jewish children around and taunt his schoolteachers. Keller watched in stunned amazement as authority figures cowered in his presence.' All around her, Keller saw adults, who were supposed to be the bedrock of life, the people in charge of the world, waver indecisively or fall apart.[53]

These memories have colored Keller's life ever since. Like other victims of trauma, she cannot forget what upheaval meant, and deep down she does not feel safe even though she has been a senior professor in a prestigious university for twenty years. She always keeps a possible refuge in another country to which she could flee. Permanence and stability remain doubtful concepts in her mind, the legacy of having observed the social order collapse before her eyes.

Downwardly mobile children are internal refugees. Like Keller, they never feel totally safe. They cannot trust the appearance of success, since they suspect that they harbor a slow virus for downward mobility.[54] Like Sisyphus, the higher they climb, the more urgently they sense they are about to fall.

5

Brotherhoods of the Downwardly Mobile

When the downwardly mobile managers looked for the causes of their distress, the answer that echoed back from the surrounding business culture was, if anything, condemning. Meritocratic individualism seemed to say to them: "You would not be in this mess unless there was something seriously wrong with you." Suspended between incomprehension and this accusatory message, managers were left bewildered, defensive, and self-critical—victims of their own culture.

But this is not the fate of every downwardly mobile refugee from the middle class. There are situations in which people who lose their jobs bring to bear other versions of American culture—perspectives that bring richer meaning to the experience of downward mobility, that bolster pride rather than destroy it. Economic losses, the pain of losing one's place in society, and the guilt at plunging the family into hardship remain. But under certain circumstances suffering is understood to be noble, and downwardly mobility—while no less unpleasant—loses its arbitrary, purposeless, or condemnatory face.

In August 1981, President Reagan fired nearly 12,000 striking air traffic controllers and shut them out of their chosen profession. Because the controllers were well-paid professionals who lacked credentials for equivalent employment outside air traffic control, the president's order locked them into a long struggle with downward mobility. It is a battle many have lost. They have seen their savings disappear; their homes go to foreclosure; their wives go out to work; and their dreams of a middle-class life-style dashed. But the controllers understood these losses in a very different way from their counterparts among the managers and executives. They see themselves as men and women who were prepared to sacrifice what they had in the name of higher principles. Downward mobility is the price they paid for standing up for what they believed.

The strike crystallized polarities in American culture between self-interest and self-sacrifice, between money and honor, between loyalty and betrayal, between private good and public virtue. To understand how the controllers took from this cataclysmic event a sense of purpose and meaning that has sustained them in the years thereafter, it is necessary to look backward to the strike itself and the character of the controller world. For the features that bound them together into a close-knit brotherhood were born in the workplace, forged in the heat of the strike, and kept alive as they struggled for public vindication and a new place in the occupational hierarchy.[1]

Civilian air traffic controllers are almost entirely employed by one branch of the federal government, the Federal Aviation Administration (FAA). The air traffic control system has had a long history of labor-management problems, and was plagued throughout the 1970s by sick outs, slow downs, and other demonstrations of dissatisfaction with working conditions, compensation, and managerial inadequacy.[2] Complaints continue at the end of the '90s as antiquated equipment, insufficient public investment, and governmental ignorance threaten the safety of travelers. In the 1970s negotiations between the controllers' union, the Professional Air Traffic Controllers Organization (PATCO), and the FAA produced so few results that a strike was planned to take place after contract negotiations in 1981.[3] This was a bold act, for it violates federal law for civil service employees to engage in a strike. When the 1981 contract talks broke down, PATCO President Robert Poli, with over 80 percent support in a strike vote, called for a walkout. President Reagan gave the 11,500 controllers who answered the strike call (out of a total of 17,000) forty-eight hours to return to work. He warned that those who failed to heed this order would be fired. While some responded to the threat, the vast majority stayed out and walked the picket lines, believing that the nation's air traffic system could not function without them. The president fired them all and barred these long-time veterans of the civil service from federal employment of any kind. Nevertheless, most remained confident that this was a temporary setback and were sure they would be rehired as the system faltered and airports shut down.

This did not happen. The FAA ordered immediate restrictions on airport traffic, grounded general aviation planes, spread the density of the remaining airplanes out over longer hours to reduce peak traffic density, pressed military controllers into civilian service, and called upon the managerial ranks to man the towers. Despite delays, airplanes continued to fly (albeit in reduced numbers). As months passed, it became clear that the strike had failed. Public support for the controllers' efforts was nil, labor support was weak at best, and the president remained adamant that strikers would not be allowed back to work.

The losses sustained by the controllers as a result of this debacle can best be understood against the backdrop of their prestrike world. Most controllers had grown up in working-class households and gained their introduction to the profession during military service. The generation that participated heavily in the strike was drawn largely from men who had enlisted (rather than been drafted) during the Vietnam War.[4] Some did so out of conviction that the American presence in Southeast Asia was justified; others simply felt they had to stand by their country in its time of need. Many enlisted because military service provided a means of learning a trade, a route out of small-town America, and an option for working-class teenagers who were not college bound.

Whatever their motivations, military enlistment put them on the opposite side of the political fence from their college-age contemporaries who took to the streets to protest the war. They joined conservative politicians, veterans organizations, hard hats, and many others who looked with horror at the upheaval on the nation's college campuses.

Once under arms, they entered air traffic school and eventually found their way to the military airport towers and radar control centers of Southeast Asia, the United States, and Europe. Here they stepped into an occupational culture somewhat at odds with other parts of military life. Controllers were "cowboys" in the midst of regimentation. Taking their cues from the devil-may-care fighter pilots, military controllers viewed themselves as daring, skilled professionals dedicated to disaster prevention in the air. Privately they had little use for their superior officers or for the trappings of military routine: Their cool nerves were what mattered.[5]

Military duty provided an avenue to upward mobility. It was common knowledge that military air traffic control experience could be parlayed into a working-class dream: a high-paying civilian air traffic control job that required no educational credentials beyond a high school diploma. There was a catch, however. Only one civilian employer could make the dream come true: the federal government. When their tours of duty were completed, these military controllers returned home, took the civil service test for air traffic control, and with the aid of veterans' preference points, joined the civilian ranks of the Federation Aviation Administration.

Their introduction to the FAA began with a grueling standardized training program. From all over the country, would-be controllers converged on a single training school in Oklahoma City for eighteen weeks of high-pressure memorization, testing, and simulated experience with radar screens. It was a thoroughly exhausting ordeal; many trainees failed and were dropped from the program then and there. Oklahoma City was the crucible of a national controller community, for it took people from different parts of the country and pushed them through a "boot camp," giving them uniform training and a common outlook as survivors of a tough competition.

The completion of training saw them off to FAA facilities around the country, ranging from radar approach control centers (which monitor and guide traffic between airports) to airport towers (which control landing and takeoff patterns), where on-the-job training continued for another four years. Flunk-out rates were high: Over 50 percent of those who began never finished. Dismissal could occur at any point along the path. Those who finally achieved the rank of journeyman controller felt tremendous self-confidence in their technical expertise, skill, and intellectual powers. They were an elite who had survived extraordinary pressure and excelled in a job few others could do, as three strikers in northern California attested:

I know I did a job that only one out of a hundred people could do. It was fantastic and I accomplished it. I memorized a map of every single street in California and the altitude of every single mountain. . . . I was able to give you thousands of frequencies from memory, give you distances between every single city . . . I had all that memorized and applied to a three-dimensional pattern and had instant recall of all those facts. . . . Our facility controlled more airplanes in a year than the entire countries of Austria and Switzerland. . . . That's something you take with you. That's the pride the controllers have. . . .

The responsibility was important. . . the knowledge that was required. It wasn't a job that everyone could do. Our failure rate was well over 50 percent. You were unique, being able to make it through the programs.

Working the airplanes was a charge for me because I happened to be real good at it. I got a personal satisfaction when I could push back from a busy sector and know that I did something that a lot of people couldn't do. . . .

This emphasis on intellectual capacity was particularly gratifying for controllers, most of whom came from blue-collar families where work was more a matter of physical stamina than brainpower. As the first and often the only members of their families to hold well-paid white-collar jobs, they gained the admiration of their kinsmen and the personal satisfaction of knowing they had lifted their own families out of the blue-collar world. These working-class boys were now earning an average of $35,000 per year in an intellectually challenging and respectable profession.[6] John Nelson's father works on a Ford Motor assembly line and makes a good living. But when John became an air traffic controller, he was the object of everyone's admiration:

People were very proud [of me]. Our family and relatives were proud. My dad used to get a kick out of telling his friends that his son was a controller. People would say, "Ahh. . . ." I enjoyed telling people [I was a controller] too! It made me have more respect for myself.

These experiences of upward mobility produced self-styled conservatives who were believers in the "pull-yourself-up-by-the-boot-straps" version of the American dream and patriots of the "America: Love It or Leave It" variety. Dissent, in either political or social terms, was not a part of their culture. On the contrary, material success and satisfying work bred sentiments of gratitude, loyalty, and pride in their country. Some described themselves as conservative Democrats (owing largely to their blue-collar family backgrounds), but many were registered Republicans. Indeed, PATCO was one of the few organized labor groups to support Ronald Reagan's election bid in 1980. This, then, was the raw material that formed the air traffic control work force across the country.

The organization of the occupation itself reinforced their uniformity of outlook and strengthened the bonds between individual controllers. The task of controlling air traffic involves more teamwork and interdependency than do most professional occupations. As planes pass from one sector of airspace to another, they have to be "handed" from controller to controller. Staff have to coordinate their actions, and trouble in one person's sector quickly creates problems for his or her neighbor. During periods of peak density ("rush hours"), this interdependency is tested to the limit. Split-second decisions must be made, and the margin for error is very small. Any mistake can result in a catastrophe, a prospect that never leaves a controller's mind. In tight situations, the quick intervention of one's teammates is critical: No controller can operate successfully without the help and support of his colleagues.

Crew members frequently become fast friends. Teams stay together for years. They are assigned to rolling shifts[7]—eight hours on, eight hours off, eight hours on again—which find them working and relaxing at odd hours. This shift structure makes it hard for controllers to spend time with people who are not part of their work world and encourages socializing with workmates instead.[8] As one New York–based controller put it, "You're almost like brothers . . . and sisters. You become so close and you rely so much on each other that there's just a natural gravitation outside the job as well as inside."

Controller culture was sustained in these islands of tightly knit teams, but the work also generated a sense of brotherhood within much larger groups that transcended particular towers and control centers. Controllers who sat at screens in Fremont, California, were in constant contact with their counterparts in the airport towers of San Francisco, San Jose, Los Angeles, Oregon, and Hawaii. Controllers working on Long Island communicated with others in New Jersey, Philadelphia, and Washington, D.C. They rarely met face to face, but they knew each others' voices and, as the clamor for a strike grew in the late 1970s, local controllers came to see themselves as part of a nationwide brotherhood.

Controllers are responsible for guiding planes across the skies, but this does not begin to capture the feel of the experience. Theirs is a world not of mundane routine but of intense emotions— of adrenaline rushes and gnawing tension interspersed with boredom (as the traffic subsides). The pace of work lurches from soporific to frantic and back. Sitting in darkened rooms, watching bright blips move across the radar screens, they cannot forget that each blip represents four hundred people whose safety depends on their words and actions.[9] They have to be capable of visualizing this complex spatial information, for distressingly often radar screens "go down" without warning, leaving controllers "blind." They continue directing planes through their sectors, keeping them spaced apart, with only radio contact, slips of paper, and memory as their guides.

With this kind of pressure a constant companion, one might imagine that controllers disliked the job, but in fact most had a love-hate relationship with it.[10] The relentless test of their mental capacities was welcomed. They drew immense satisfaction from knowing that they could handle the cognitive complexity and extraordinary responsibility: "The more tension that builds up, the more cool and rational we got about each move we made. Most people would blow their cools, but the controllers were the opposite."

But the pressure had its downside. Fear of causing a major accident is always present, and this pressure increases steadily as more and more planes jam the sectors. Rolaids and aspirin circulate like candy. At the end of a work day, many have difficulty calming down:

> There was a tremendous problem with letdown. You'd climb that mountain, and your body was just too tired to bring you down from it. A few hours later you'd be climbing that mountain again, and it would go up and up and up and it never came back down.

Controller folk culture celebrated this unusual work world. Its central theme focused on a Hemingwayesque image of the controller as "tough guy," the man or woman unruffled by stress. But like Hemingway's characters, controllers were subject to many pitfalls born of constant stress: alcoholism, ulcers, drug abuse, burnout, a slowing of reflexes, an inability to concentrate. Most of these problems were seen as avoidable if the individual was careful. Others, stemming from advancing age, were regarded as the inevitable misfortunes of the controller "life cycle." While most people see their jobs as stretching on until retirement, controllers knew that their time "in the saddle" was limited. After the age of forty, slowing reflexes made it difficult to perform at peak levels:

> You knew at some time in your career that you were going to peak and then slide down the other side. There was a tendency to help these [older] guys, to carry them along, the weaker ones. You'd keep them off the busy positions during the rush hours. Because you knew one day your time would come. . . . One of the biggest fears of the job was worrying about when that day would come. It's a young man's career, a young man's job.
>
> Those [older] guys had given their all at the worst times. They had worked the positions when you sat there and ate your lunch and they didn't move for ten hours. . . . You knew that even though these guys weren't as good as they once were, you knew that at one time they were much better. There was a lot of inner respect for them. Knowing all along that you would go along the same garden path, and hoping you wouldn't.

The Failure of the Strike

Air traffic control is an extraordinary occupation. It skims the elite from among thousands of applicants, puts them through grueling years of training, leads them into a work life of exceptional satisfaction and great stress, and leaves "old" men burned out at forty-five.

One would not expect people who had passed through this kind of socialization to be disinterested in their work conditions or timorous toward management, and they weren't. Air traffic controllers held strong opinions about how the system should be reformed and were assertive (their opponents would argue, even arrogant) in expressing them. The 11,500 well-paid, securely employed strikers did not risk their jobs in 1981 without serious grievances and very high levels of frustration.[11] They complained about antiquated computers that would black out during rush hours; rolling shifts that left them bleary-eyed with exhaustion; rules that ensured that only a fraction of the work force would ever see retirement benefits; and lower wages than controllers in other parts of the world.[12]

The strikers anticipated widespread public support for their cause and were shocked when newspaper and television coverage of the strike put the spotlight on their wage demands and underplayed their concerns over safety. Coming at a time of rising unemployment in the early 1980s, the salary increases they were after appeared excessive. Hence the strikers were met with public indifference or resentment, a cold shoulder from organized labor, and barely disguised hostility from the White House.[13] Controllers huddled together for months in meetings of union locals as they watched and waited for the call to return to work. It never came. In the meantime, the months without income bit deeply into family treasuries.

In the end, the strike was a disaster for PATCO, for the individuals who lost their jobs, and for the families who no longer had FAA salaries to depend on. Its long-term consequences were devastating: Five years after the strike, 70 percent of the fired controllers were still suffering income losses, with more than one-third reporting that their income was "much lower" than it had been during their years with the FAA.[14] Over 30 percent had incomes low enough to qualify for food stamps and federal school lunch programs. Over half of the strikers' spouses "had to go to work." Thirteen percent lost their homes. Two-thirds of the fired controllers found they had been blacklisted, particularly by defense contractors who might have been able to put their skills to use but whose contracts were largely with the federal government. Strikers were told in no uncertain terms that their "kind" need not apply.

Perhaps even more than income, the strikers lost a valued occupational identity and the opportunity to work at a job they treasured for its excitement and intellectual challenge:

> It's hard to explain [why the job means so much] to someone who doesn't do it. . . . The best way I can put it into words is that it's instantaneous mental gratification. There are not a lot of jobs you can get that from.
> There's not a lot of things in life you can get that from. . . . It's hard to get air traffic controlling out of your blood. . . . It's something I was trained to do, I enjoyed doing, I was compensated well for it. Deep in my heart I enjoyed it. I probably miss the job itself more than I miss the money and the friendships.

While 93 percent of the striking controllers had found some type of employment by 1986, most were unable to maintain the same

level of occupational status they had enjoyed as air traffic controllers. One-fifth ended up at the lower end of the occupational
spectrum: in clerical or sales, service sector jobs, and unskilled
manual work. It came as a rude shock to these skilled professionals
that so many could do no better than minimum-wage jobs.[15] Stan
Norton, who put in fifteen years in a New York area control
tower, was staggered to discover how far he had sunk:

> I got a job for a while doing inventory in a local factory . . . counting
> parts. I couldn't believe I was doing this. It was something high school
> kids do after school. It really hits you that you're not qualified for
> anything else. After all the years in the service and everything else,
> air traffic control is the only thing you're really qualified to do.

Most of the controllers lacked college degrees, having entered
the military directly from high school. As mature family men
and women, they were not in a position to forego income in
favor of returning to school to upgrade their educational qualifications. Face to face with credentialism, Stan and his fellow strikers
discovered that their prospects were limited:

> I'm stuck on a rack. Either I become an air traffic controller again
> or I'll be doing menial labor for the rest of my life. I don't think
> there's anything in between. . . . I could stand on top of the roof
> and yell, "Hey, I'm intelligent! Hey, I can separate airplanes! I'm
> sure I can learn to do whatever you want me to do." You know, it
> doesn't matter . . . they're not interested.

The strikers' occupational prospects were hampered by the high
levels of unemployment prevailing in the United States in the
months following the strike. By early 1982, when most of the
strikers made forays into the job market, they had to compete
with more than 10 million other job seekers, as the national unemployment rate climbed to 9.7 percent.[16] Job seekers faced a "buyer's
market," and the controllers were perceived as troublemakers who
were narrowly trained in skills that were not transferable to other
occupations.

Alongside financial problems, unemployment, and downward
mobility, the strikers were faced with public condemnation. In a
New York Times editorial published six months after the strike
began, PATCO President Robert Poli pointed to some of the
more potent "insults" hurled at the strikers:

> I suppose no public employee who strikes should expect public sup-
> port, but in this case there were a number of factors amplifying that

natural bias. First, the strike was not only illegal, it was perceived to be an open challenge to a president who had just survived [John Hinckley's 1981] assassination attempt and was at the peak of his popularity. Second, the strikers were shown as bearded militants with fists raised. Third, the union itself was hoist on the petard of its own contract demands. Few people looked past the demand for a $10,000 raise. No one seemed to listen when we talked about the real issues.

It was all wrapped in such a pretty media package. There was a good guy who stood for principle and order [the president] and a bad guy who represented greed and lawlessness [Mr. Poli]. One of the saddest parts of this tragedy is that a group of people whom I know to be decent and generous will forever be branded as irreverent malcontents. [Poli, 1982]

This was the rather dismal view from the top of the union leadership. The rank and file were equally stunned by the vehemence of the public condemnation. As two California-based controllers put it:

The hurt that I've seen, the ruthlessness, the vindictiveness, the cruelty . . . that will never leave me. . . . To see people called . . . lawbreakers, criminals, thrown into federal prison, brought away in chains and all that.[17] Nobody ever [thought to themselves] why would 70 percent of a well trained, highly paid work force, knowing they were violating the law, do that? Well [they thought] we were criminals [or] brain damaged.

We were seen as a bunch of young, snot-nosed controllers. [The public] saw us making big bucks and said "What the hell have [the controllers] got to complain about? Here I am breaking my back." The government painted us as a bunch of greedy kids looking for a $10,000 pay raise.

Strikers were variously described as amateurish and inept in their conduct of the strike (by the leadership of organized labor), as self-seeking and greedy (by other rank-and-file unionists unwilling to back their salary demands), and as undeserving (by higher-paid pilots). Perhaps most difficult for these veterans of the Vietnam War, they were viewed as unpatriotic lawbreakers who flouted a solemn oath not to strike:

I don't know how many times I was told, "Mister Poli, I understand all these [problems the controllers are having] that forced you to strike, but you broke your oath!"

In the battle for the hearts and minds of Middle America, the

Administration won uncontested when they raised the oath issue. No matter how often we explained why we had to strike, the people of this country place a high value on oaths.[18]

The stigma had been created by the public relations campaign waged by the White House in the heat of the strike. But it refused to fade. In the wake of the union's court-ordered decertification, the resignation of its leadership, and the strikers' slow but inevitable drift toward other jobs, these images petrified. They became a "permanent" stain on the controllers' honor, a stigma foisted upon them by unsympathetic neighbors, potential employers, and the man in the street.

In descriptive terms, the words *financial distress* and *occupational dislocation* barely scrape the surface of strike's impact on the controllers and their families. Some have divorced, others have lost homes. At least nine suicides have been attributed to the hardships and disappointments engendered by the strike.[19] Many controllers now believe that they will never regain their prestrike standard of living. Even those who do not see the abyss of downward mobility as a lifelong problem believe it will be many years before they regain the ground lost since 1981.

Yet fired controllers experienced the loss of their jobs and social status in ways that differ sharply from managers and executives who, on the face of it, underwent the same descent into downward mobility. The controllers were not suffocating in self-blame or in doubt of their skills, aptitudes, or self-worth as many managers were. Nor did controllers wander in an existential wilderness asking, "Why me? Why did this happen?" They did not perceive themselves as incompetents or dead wood. Instead, the striking controllers developed a distinctive perspective—a symbolic framework—that gave meaning to their downward mobility. And this meaning enhanced, rather than undermined, their self-esteem. Controllers fought downward mobility both by finding jobs and, even more critically, by finding dignity in their experience. And this made a world of difference.

The strikers enjoyed several important advantages over the displaced managers. First and foremost, they had someone to blame. Their job loss was directly traceable to President Reagan and his FAA director, J. Lynn Helms. They made the decision to fire the strikers, prosecute some, take away their pensions, and lock them into downward mobility by ensuring that they would never work as controllers again. The controllers could turn their anger and hatred toward real external enemies rather than turn their fury inward.[20]

Even more important, the fired controllers had one another to lean on. Where displaced managers and their families retreated "into the closet," air traffic controllers sought one another's company or attended the meetings of PATCO locals that continued for many months after the strike. In the face of noncomprehending neighbors and kin, they could turn to people who had shared their experiences and commitments. And they still do. Seven years after the end of the strike, newsletters distributed by successors to PATCO—for example, the United States Air Traffic Controllers Organization and PATCO Lives![21] —kept strikers abreast of legislative and political developments that bore on their prospects for reinstatement. Although the strike has now become the stuff of history, reunions still take place every August even now and the popular press continues to benchmark every major strike against the experience of the controllers.

Through these mechanisms, the strikers have formed an enduring national community even though they have moved into other occupations. It is a community born of collective struggle and defeat, but one whose solidarity continues to cloak each individual with the knowledge that he or she is not alone.

Most important, the strikers were able to draw on certain themes and ideas in American culture that lent dignity to their actions and made sense of their suffering. The "America: Love It or Leave It" loyalists reformulated prior visions of conformist patriotism into a new kind of patriotism suffused with struggle against the injustices perpetrated by a vengeful government. Unlike the themes of meritocratic individualism, which undermine managers in their struggle with downward mobility, another set of ideas— equally drawn from American tradition and culture—sustained the controllers through an experience that was, on its face, equally devastating. As brothers in a moral protest, rather than individual victims of impersonal rejection, controllers found self-respect in their loss, a redemption that was not available to downwardly mobile managers.

At the most general level, controllers came to see their personal financial and occupational losses as sacrifices they made for a just cause. Moving away from flag-waving visions of the patriot, they situated their actions in a vision of America as a land of honorable rebellions. Their search for meaning has placed the strike on historical ground, vindicating the controllers by linking them to great struggles of the past.

While the controllers' strike was but one example of hundreds of labor-management disputes in America's industrial history, in its aftermath it took on a highly moral character. The strike ceased to be an effort to gain personal benefits and metamorphosed into a quest for human rights; a test of loyalty; and a struggle for professional altruism. And the strike's unfortunate outcome—permanent downward mobility—was interpreted as a tragedy whose roots lay in a division between the government and the people.

The Struggle for Human Rights

It might seem surprising that overwhelmingly white, politically conservative Vietnam veterans would understand their plight by analogy to the black civil rights movement and the notion of equality embedded in human rights, but in fact these became important strands of their symbolic reconstruction of the strike.

The civil rights movement of the 1960s was, in its own time, the subject of controversy and passion. Since the death of Dr. Martin Luther King, Jr., it has been enshrined in the minds of many mainstream Americans as the quintessential expression of the obligations ordinary citizens have to challenge injustice, even when this involves breaking the law. The Selma march, the Montgomery bus boycott, and the memories of clergymen and schoolchildren being hauled off in Mississippi police vans, have come to symbolize a decidedly American practice of holding the country to a higher moral standard than that embodied in the simple "rule of law."

The controllers placed themselves in this grand tradition and argued that the laws that prevented them from engaging in labor strikes were analogous to the Jim Crow traditions of the South before the victories of the civil rights movement. The analogy gathered force from the fact that controllers had to break federal laws forbidding strikes in order to obtain their "natural rights." George Jacobs, a white controller from the San Francisco Bay area who now works as a delivery man, explained:

> A hundred years ago if I was black and I was an American citizen, I didn't have rights because [those in power] said I didn't. The same thing is true for government employees. You don't have these rights

[to strike] because somebody says you don't. I never agreed with that. I never will . . . I still believe that what we were doing was right.

Another white controller, who was a political conservative, a self-styled "American hawk," put it this way: "I equate our strike with the civil rights movement. Just because there's a law doesn't mean it's right. Sometimes the law has to be changed."

Injustice was written into federal labor law just as it was embodied in anti-civil-rights doctrines (for example, separate but equal). Forbidden to strike, controllers were denied the most elementary tool in collective bargaining and were therefore unable to pursue their goals in the same way that millions of unionized private-sector employees can. The main issue of the strike was therefore seen by many as a question of "equal treatment" and a reversal of their status as "second-class citizens."

I was in a union for six years and every time we bargained with the employer, the employer had the hammer and said, "Hey, I'm the boss. You ain't got any rights, you're a government employee. You don't have the right to strike. . . ." They took away my rights as a citizen of the United States. . . .

When I enlisted into the FAA, I signed a lot of papers because it was the only way to get the job. [There was] paper saying I was an indentured servant or a second-class citizen or that I gave up my constitutional rights because I was a government employee.

I believe that the constitution gives equal rights to all citizens without exception, and that Congress shall pass no law that will take away from any group of citizens, rights and privileges enjoyed by the rest. The "no strike" law is a violation of the constitution.

There can be little doubt that pecuniary issues were significant grievances. But as the strike went down to defeat, the issue of rights took center stage, and the tainted question of money receded.[22] The symbolic interpretation of the struggle shifted along a cultural axis that unites avarice and public virtue: namely, that "demanding higher wages is one of the things one must virtuously struggle to win the right to do."[23]:

I figured $40,000 a year was a good salary and I was happy . . . I saw us lose money to inflation and I didn't like it, but I knew what I had. I have enough relatives around that made seven dollars an hour to know that eighteen dollars an hour was pretty good even if inflation was eating away at it. So the issue was never money to me. I had rights as a human being and as an American citizen; *that* was the issue.

How does one go about securing human rights in a society where the law does not guarantee them? American history provides the answer: civil disobedience. Nonviolent, peaceful abrogation of the law in the name of a higher principle was the hallmark of the civil rights movement. The controllers' strike was, retrospectively, understood as a tactic of nonviolent resistence to oppression rather than one side's attempt to win a labor dispute. By calling on the legacy of Martin Luther King, the controllers placed themselves squarely within a tradition enshrined in modern civics texts as a positive force for the good in American history. From the Boston Tea Party to the Underground Railroad (which brought slaves out of the South in the Civil War era) to the struggles of the suffragettes, the United States can be viewed as a country built upon the civil disobedience of oppressed groups in their fight against the power of unjust government. The controllers tapped into some of the most powerful moral themes in American culture: those that demand that individuals stand up for their rights, fight injustice and oppression, and sacrifice their comfort and social standing for a higher cause.

During the year of the strike, this theme was driven home through America's support for Solidarity's struggle to gain recognition as a legitimate trade union from the Polish regime. The United States—with President Reagan at the forefront—extended warm support to Solidarity activists, admiring their courage in the face of repression. The nightly news covered the Gdansk shipyard strikes, the courageous behavior of the Solidarity leadership, the arrests and harassment meted out by a hardline government, and the hopeful faces of Solidarity sympathizers with their fingers outstretched in the victory sign. In lauding the Polish struggle, Americans underlined their support for illegal but highly moral (nonviolent) actions of Poles in support of human rights, and in particular, the rights of workers to organize and strike.

The irony was not lost on the controllers that the same kinds of actions on their part resulted in public condemnation, felony charges, and prison terms for some PATCO leaders. While U.S. politicians were busily hailing labor activists behind the Iron Curtain they were excoriating the controllers:

Being stripped of our profession and livelihood for our crime of civil protest, was a perfect example of Reagan's vindictiveness. . . . At the same time, he was asking Americans to light a candle in their windows and pray for the workers of Poland, who were doing the same thing!

The difference between the Polish government and the U.S. government is that Lech Walensa got his job back. . . .[24]

Loyalty

Though the struggle for rights was the most common interpretation of the strike, many controllers saw the main issue as one of loyalty to their fellow workers. Even those who had serious reservations about the strike itself, felt that they had to stand alongside their colleagues:

I didn't think [the strike] was a good idea at all. I thought it was a loser. I knew from the get-go what the outcome would be. I had a gut-level feeling for it [but] it came down to a question of personal integrity. Personal loyalty. You saw where the battle lines were drawn and who the people were that you just had to stick with. Whether you believed in the cause or the outcome of that battle, the battle existed. You saw the two groups of people: who was going out and who was staying.

Those that went out were the best controllers, the people I associated with because of their professional standing. The people that stayed were those I felt should have been replaced anyway. I couldn't have stayed at work regardless of the outcome. I couldn't have worked with those people and looked myself in the eye.

This was not an invention of the moment. The controllers had been loyal on many occasions in the past. During the war in Vietnam they were the patriots who "stood by their country when few others would do so." They expressed the same value when they went out on strike:

I do not regret my decision. I did not make it lightly or in haste. I would like very much to return to work as a controller, but only if everyone who went out on strike is allowed that opportunity. I would rather be outside the gates with those who had the courage to stand up than inside the control room with those who crawled.

Because they were loyal to their ideals and principles, the controllers were therefore thunderstruck to discover that they were being described in the media as disloyal or anti-American. One official of a New Jersey PATCO local expressed his outrage:

> I knew one guy on strike who had the Purple Heart. I knew one guy who had the highest civilian honor awarded, the Medal of Honor. [sic] He gave it back he was so upset at what happened. We're not unpatriotic malcontents, we're really not. Eighty-five percent of the controllers that went on strike were Vietnam veterans. I know personally a guy that went on strike with two Purple Hearts, a Silver Star, all kinds of medals from flying in Vietnam. He didn't like the war, but he fought it because that's what his country told him to do.
>
> I have always supported the United States and will always [do so] in the future. I have very deep patriotic feelings. But I feel that the country has turned around on me and said, "You rotten so and so" [They think] I'm as bad as Nixon, and I'm not!

Many of these veterans believe that the legal and social harassment they faced was harsher than that meted out to men who fled to Canada rather than face the military draft during the war in Southeast Asia: "Deserters and draft dodgers can be forgiven, but we can't? A guy who goes on strike for his beliefs gets thrown away like a used-up whore [and] can't be forgiven after four years?"

The strikers see themselves as loyal to the country, loyal to their fellow controllers, and ironically as one of the few groups who were "loyal" to President Reagan during his first election bid. Quite apart from whatever political sympathy they may have had for the Republican party, the controllers supported him because he had publicly backed their cause prior to his election in 1980. While on the campaign trail, Reagan wrote to PATCO president Poli:

> I have been thoroughly briefed by members of my staff as to the deplorable state of our nation's air traffic control system. They have told me that too few people working unreasonable hours with obsolete equipment has placed the nation's air travelers in unwarranted danger. . . . You can rest assured that if I am elected President, I will take whatever steps are necessary to . . . adjust staff levels and work days so that they are commensurate with achieving a maximum degree of public safety.[25]

Reagan's public acknowledgment of the controllers' prestrike grievances won him their electoral support in 1980. In return, they expected him to make good on his promises. Once elected, he betrayed them: "I'm upset with President Reagan. I know people say, 'Well, he made a campaign promise and politicians aren't meant to keep them.' Well, how come I'm supposed to keep my oath [not to strike]? How come it only works one way?" The controllers turned the loyalty issue back on the president and argued that he was the one who was disloyal; he was the one who had violated a public pledge.

The controllers' view of the strike as a proving ground for loyalty draws strength from broader themes in American culture: An individual may be called upon to stand by his friends, and if he is a worthy person, he will do so despite reservations about the wisdom of their commitments or actions.[26] The notion that an honorable person could not have followed any other course of action derives from the belief that integrity resides in commitments to friends, particularly friends who could be depended on in the stressful everyday life of the radar station.

Strikers claimed the high moral ground. Measuring their own actions against those of the president, where the virtue of loyalty to one's fellows or fidelity to public promises was concerned, the controllers came up shining and the president appeared to be the turncoat. The president left his commitments behind in the wake of political expediency—no match for loyalty or principled commitment in the hierarchy of morally acceptable motivations. And if downward mobility was the price to be paid for responding to loyalty's call, then so be it.[27]

Professional Altruism

Professionalism was another aspect of the crusade that controllers remembered throughout their struggle with economic dislocation. It was their desire to claim the mantle of a professional identity that justified the strike and transformed occupational dislocation into a sacrifice for a worthy cause.

Professionals are defined by the specialized knowledge they possess, the autonomy they enjoy, and the altruism or public service that is intrinsic to their work.[28] Controllers were clearly knowledgeable: At least five years' worth of training had been invested in them, not to mention the accumulated wisdom based on years of job experience.

Autonomy was far more problematic. Controllers were hamstrung by procedures they were unable to change and confined by the hierarchical structure of the civil service. They lacked meaningful access to the decision-making process in the FAA and saw that their views (on safety standards, flight routes, and so on) were routinely ignored. One dismissed controller, working as a groundskeeper four years later, described the frustrations involved when technical professionals like himself were controlled by bureaucrats:

> We had no say in what we were doing. They built a new radar (the New York Tracom) in 1977. Now we went over there to test the equipment out. Even though we gave our opinions . . . they totally disregarded everything we had to say. People were writing regulations for controlling airplanes who never controlled airplanes in their lives. That's ludicrous. How could I tell a doctor how to operate if I'd never operated before? That's what they were doing.

Controllers were denied the professional autonomy and control over their work lives that their skills and responsibilities "entitled" them to. Thus the strike, for some, was viewed as an effort to realign authority in the workplace; if not to create autonomy, at the very least to allow controllers input into the decision-making process.

In the aftermath of the strike, controllers amplified the third element of professionalism (altruism and public service) by emphasizing the public safety issues underpinning the strike. They began to speak of themselves in terms familiar to those in the "helping professions":

> I thought of [my job] as a moral obligation. You sit there and you separate airplanes and you have a moral obligation to keep those people safe. If you don't for whatever reason, you're wrong. I took that to heart, and I felt that was the most important thing in the world, just separating those airplanes. The FAA's rules and bureaucrats were interfering in my ability to do that.

Controllers cast themselves as guardians of public well-being in the air—indeed, as the only parties to the nation's air traffic system who were concerned, first and foremost, with safety. They had only the most cynical views about the FAA and the commercial airlines on this score, since they could recall violations of FAA rules that had been swept under the rug and episodes in which they had been *ordered* to overlook safety regulations. Controllers regarded themselves as the only professionals who had "the big picture" on how the skies were managed, who had neither a fiscal nor a political stake in the way in which the system was structured. Thus professional altruism became an important image in the controllers' reconstructions of the strike: The only way they could gain greater autonomy and control over the workplace was to strike for it.

Their analysis drew upon a cultural "script" for scandal in public affairs: that of the "whistle-blower." In the annals of whistle-blowing there are many examples of technical professionals pitted against political authorities. The engineers who protested the launching of the space shuttle Challenger, only to be overruled by NASA officials sensitive to political pressure, constitute but one recent example of an archetypical drama: the confrontation between the honorable technician and the vested interests.[29] The script for scandal equates the technician with purity and the politician with self-interest.

All labor strikes are struggles of sorts. But since they usually revolve around wage demands, job security, or other self-interested goals, they lack the moral force of a crusade. What made the controllers' strike different was their view that public safety hung in the balance. If controllers had to continue working impossibly long hours with faulty equipment and insufficient rest in between, the public would face the resulting intolerable risk. The controllers saw the strike, then, as an example of a familiar story in which the selfless expert attempts to protect the public good. This is the stuff of a moral crusade, and as such it serves as a continuing reminder to the controllers that downward mobility is a selfless sacrifice for a worthy purpose.

The Government vs. the People

Populism is a political philosophy that surfaces time and again in American history. In the late nineteenth and early twentieth century, populism gave birth to political parties that issued scathing critiques of American politics. They argued that political and economic power were vested in an unrepresentative elite, and that democracy properly implemented should serve the common man.[30] Though the Farmer's Alliance and the People's Party failed to survive, their populist philosophy has bequeathed to us an enduring language of antigovernment sentiment.

It is one of history's ironies that presidents can be elected on the grounds of antigovernment sentiment. Ronald Reagan's 1980 bid for the White House stressed his position as an outsider to "politics as usual" in Washington. He equated "outside" with "the people" and "inside" with an unholy alliance of "vested interests" and "big government." This populist formulation was, of course, not uniquely Reagan's. Jimmy Carter before him had traded on his status as an outsider from Georgia. Reagan was so successful in portraying the federal government as the antithesis of the people's will that even after his reelection in 1984, he continued to cast himself as the outsider, a warrior against big government and entrenched interests in the capital city.

Given Reagan's central role in squashing the strike and firing the controllers, it is hardly surprising that they regard him as their chief enemy. But the terms by which he was redefined— from the strong, conservative leader to whom the controllers threw their support in 1980 to the main villain in their demise—derived directly from the populist rhetoric that was Reagan's stock in trade: Controllers argue that the president was an "insider" who does not represent "the people."[31] The distinction is important, for it provides a symbolic framework within which the controllers seek redemption from "the people" even in the face of governmental disdain. As one striker who used to work in the Fremont, California, FAA facility put it:

> I've given up on the government in the sense of "they the government" not "we the people." I've given up on the government as those elected officials who've gone to Washington and become cocoons and live in their little worlds. Anything that attacks them [as the controllers did], they kill. But the people of the United States are not that way. The people are still the great United States that everybody thinks of. And I'd like them to know that I'm not what [the government] tells them I am. That's very important to me.

The populist opposition between the government and the people resolves the tension between the controllers' self-image as individuals who stood by their country and their public image after the strike as lawbreakers who deliberately violated an oath against strikes. The controllers claim they have remained loyal to the people, not the government. It is the government, they argue, that is not to be trusted and the government that is deserving of condemnation, not the controllers. The administration's conduct during the strike would have been sufficient to sustain this view. Scandals that have enveloped the White House since the early eighties served to bolster their perspective:

> One of the biggest bastards in the whole thing was the head of the FAA, J. Lynn Helms. Where is he now? He's had his own legal problems . . . defrauding the government, securities and exchange. He called us one of the biggest [bunch of] criminals ever, and look at him.
>
> I'm fired from my job and sitting here trying to do the best I can and where's J. Lynn Helms for all the crimes he did? Tell me where the justice is in this world?

A significant number of Reagan appointees had to resign because of alleged corruption or improprieties (including Burford and Lavelle from the Environmental Protection Agency [EPA], Donovan from the Department of Labor, Thayer from the Department of Defense, and Bess, the former head of NASA) and still more came under investigation (including Attorney General Meese and former advisers Michael Deever and Lyn Nofziger).[32] As the controllers surveyed President Reagan's tenure, they argued that he epitomized their view that America is a society whose masses are good and true, but whose power elites are ruthless and corrupt. The powerful do not play by the same rules as the common man (read the controllers) and they mask their power by manipulating the news media, preventing ordinary people from discovering their fabric of lies. Reflecting on the strike three years after the fact, Harry Cherlin, a twenty-year veteran of the Philadelphia control tower, explains how it reshaped his perception of power and politics in America:

> We were killed by the media. Why? Who licenses the press! If you've got a multimillion-dollar TV station and you're dependent upon the government to give you a license . . . are you going to do anything to hurt the government? If the truth doesn't get in the way of the [owner's] license, then he'll be glad to give you the truth, but if it gets in the way, you can bet . . . he's going with the money, not the truth.
>
> [The strike] changed my perception of how absolute the control is that is exercised over this country and the people's way of thinking. [The government] controls all the information so [it] can control how the people respond. . . . It was very educational for me. There were things that were totally untrue that were being put out [through

the media] for a specific reason, to draw a specific response. How well it worked!

Organized labor comes in for a similar critique. It is viewed *not* as the champion of the working man, but an institution which is part of the power structure:

> These big union guys like Lane Kirkland . . . they're management. They didn't support us with money or on the picket lines. . . . The leadership sits around making seventy, eighty thousand a year and telling people what to do. Let's face it, unions aren't what they used to be.

Politicians, the rich, and the leadership of organized labor all are part of a power structure controllers now see as corrupt or self-serving. However, by distinguishing the people from the "power elite," the controllers have retained their faith in America, exonerating the people from responsibility for the striker's plight. Instead, the public becomes the chief victim of manipulation:

> Ninety percent of the people in my neighborhood sit back and watch that TV and believe what they read and hear. They are being totally manipulated. Prior to the strike I had never been in a situation where I knew what was [actually] going on. I only knew what I was being told. When the strike came, for the first time I was in a position to know . . . and [compare it] to what was being told [in the media]. The difference was incredible. Most people didn't get to see the truth about the strike.

If the people did not know the truth, their condemnation of the controllers was based on ignorance. Ignorance can be corrected if the "truth will out"; the people will then redeem the strikers.

The view that the press manipulated information on behalf of a hidden power structure is not an explanation of the controllers' own invention. It is part of a generally available repertoire of political discourse and discontent. The controllers appropriated the populist vision from American's cultural mainstream and claimed vindication for their acts in its name.

The Plight of the Misunderstood Crusader

These four themes—civil rights, loyalty, professional altruism, and the populist struggle—melded together into a set of ideas that framed the strike as a crusade for certain ideals. The costs of the crusade (economic disaster, status loss, occupational disenfranchisement) for the strikers were thereby rendered acts of personal sacrifice. Sacrifice is an honorable act; indeed, it calls forward laudatory qualities of integrity and commitment to ideals. These are the rallying cry of the nation in times of war, when men and women are asked to lay down their lives in defense of the country. American culture places sacrifice for a cause on the highest pedestal, as an act deserving of respect and honor. Controllers claimed this imagery as their own.

However, sacrifice requires recognition of the cause: It must be understood as an altruistic action by the community in whose name it has been committed. This recognition is delivered unambiguously during conflicts in which there is a consensus over the threat to America's interests (for example, World War II). It is less clearly defined where national convictions waver or change, or where significant groups demur (for example, the war in Vietnam). And, when the public denies legitimacy to a cause, the acts of its leaders cannot be popularly defined as altruistic sacrifice. Instead, the protagonists suffer the reverse fate: They are labeled scoundrels.

Yet there are mythic figures and episodes embedded in American culture in which individuals criticized by society are belatedly recognized as having been on the side of the truth. The Western (film) exemplifies the peculiarly American idea of the misunderstood crusader—a man who sacrifices for the sake of the common good, is shunned by the public at the time, and is only later acknowledged as society's true hero. The plots of films like *High Noon* or *Seven Just Men,* convey this essential message.[33]

Air traffic controllers appropriated the role of the misunderstood crusader. They see themselves as people who suffer now but who will one day be recognized as having worked for the common good. Elliot Nielson, a thirty-five-year-old striker who put twelve years into air traffic control and now works as a delivery man, put it well:

> It will take a long time to change things. Look at the blacks and the way they suffered in this country. . . . It took a long time to change things for them; it took one hundred years for the civil rights movement to really take place. I hope it won't take one hundred years for the air traffic controllers to benefit from what we did, but I think eventually it will benefit them. It will benefit the public too even though they don't know it now.

The misunderstood crusader is a symbol for causes that do not receive public support. Drawing on this archetype, controllers feel confident that they were "right," even though society did not understand them at the time, and hope that they will be recognized and redeemed for their courage in the future. It links the controllers to many other social movements involving unsung heroes or belatedly credited leaders. It enables them to interpret their bitterly resented personal losses as the price they have had to pay, as others have paid before them, for standing up for a set of beliefs:

> I had always been brought up to do what you have to do, what you think is best and right. My father [who opposed the strike] always said, "You are the first person you have to look at in the morning. If you can't look yourself in the eye you're in a lot of trouble. You must follow your own conscience." That's what I did during the strike. Someday I hope people will understand that.

Controllers sought public support for their actions. But the crusade had private dimensions and a domestic audience as well. For more was sacrificed than the controllers' well-being and occupational identity. Many families saw their standard of living slide at least as dramatically as that of the displaced managers. For example:

> My family and my wife [have] suffered a great deal from the strike. We don't have the things that we would have had if I'd stayed working. I almost lost the house twice. . . . The only way I save the house now is I rent the downstairs apartment out [it's illegal]. We need new furniture, but no one will let us use any charge accounts.
>
> My wife probably would never have had to work if I was still a controller. She had to go to work because there were times when I didn't work for months at a time. I couldn't get hired.
>
> [My kids] saw that they couldn't get the things they wanted. They used to say, "Daddy, can I have a quarter or a dollar?" and they always got it and now they can't. The TV broke down and we didn't get a new one; we watch TV on a ten-inch black-and-white we picked up at a garage sale for ten dollars. They're not starving, but we don't have steak like we used to. The thing I worry about more than anything is that if my kids want to go to college. . . . I don't think I'll be able to send them.

From the very earliest point of the strike, however, there was a participatory role for families of controllers to play. The same controller continued: "My daughter was eight, my son nine, and the baby was two when the strike happened. They came out to picket with us and wore T-shirts that said, 'My daddy is an air traffic controller.' "

There were others who stood on the sidelines and could not understand why their fathers and husbands "threw away" steady, secure, high-paying jobs and subjected them to such devastating losses. The misunderstood crusader seeks redemption from them and from society at large. He seeks validation in the eyes of those who may now, in their ignorance, see him as the villain or the fool.

I just hope when [my children] grow up they'll realize what I did and respect me for my values. If you're not a person of your word and if you have no values, you don't have self-respect. And if I have nothing else, I have self-respect. In my heart I know I was right, no matter what the outcome. My kids will always admire me for that and respect me for the stand I took.

Participation in a crusade means forever being part of a brotherhood of hardship. On important ceremonial occasions (weddings and funerals), strikers see each other; when air crashes occur, they call each other. The hot line maintained by a striker-supported organization called PATCO Lives in Washington, D.C., rings without ceasing when reports critical of the present air traffic control system hit the press. Several thousand veterans of the strike subscribed for years to *The Lifeline*, which kept them informed of events in Washington, D.C., of court cases involving controllers, and of the new pathways strikers found for their professional lives. Many still socialize with friends they knew from their days with the FAA. A powerful bond ties strikers together, even those who have never met before. As one put it, "When I meet a controller for the first time, I feel like I know him. Even if he worked two thousand miles away from me, I know what he's been through because of the strike, and I feel like he's an old friend."

This sense of camaraderie and shared tragedy unites the controllers and allows for some comfort in the midst of their economic troubles. But cleaving together does more than provide a salve for old wounds. It fuels an ongoing social movement. For in many ways—some only interior, others quite public—many controllers see themselves as participants in an enduring struggle. The strikers are "believers" who have a cause they must carry on until they achieve the public vindication the script calls for. This can only be the case if the strikers' views on the defects of the air traffic control system (and their complaints about the working conditions of controllers) are proved to be correct in the final analysis[34]:

> It matters to vindicate my people. I think this will happen. I think history will prove that . . . the people who went out [on strike] were not just malcontents, but that there were real problems with the system that could have been resolved.[35]

In early March 1986, PATCO Lives! took to the radio and television airwaves to publicize the first government report that raised an alarming specter of an overworked system staffed by inexperienced controllers. The report was the first official recognition of the controllers' complaints.[36] Veterans of the 1981 strike brought this news to public attention because the ethos of crusade that continues to grip them years after the ill-fated strike demands that they scan the present for evidence that their actions in the past were legitimate. In the official reports, and newspaper accounts of "Trouble in the Air,"[37] they find ample evidence to warrant saying: "I was right all along." Indeed, the fact that the FAA's working controllers formed a new union in 1986 to press for redress of the same grievances that led to the strike boosts the outcasts' claims that the system itself is in fundamental need of an overhaul.[38]

Not only do strikers try to prove the air traffic system unsafe, they also seek to show that a host of characters (organized labor, the government, the public) were wrong about the strike and wrong about the strikers' "character defects" (disloyalty, ineptitude, and so on). Reading backward, they see the strike as a watershed event that forever altered the landscape of American labor relations. The controllers are hardly alone in this view: Labor defeats as remote as the failed 1987 strike of the National Football League players were traced to the PATCO debacle. The controllers' strike is an instance of "original sin" from which the decline of unions, the "givebacks" in contract negotiations in many industries, and the hard luck of the once-inviolate commercial airline pilots directly followed[39]:

> You can do anything you want to the labor force now because we didn't stand together. It's that simple. . . . If the airline pilots [who

did not lend their support to PATCO and have subsequently been harshly treated in their own labor negotiations] had refused to cross the picket lines, the strike would have [been a success]. They made a mistake and they're paying for it now. Labor made a mistake. . . . I believe in unionism. But for unions to survive in this country there will have to be a rebirth of unionism . . . they'll have to get back to the standards we once had.

   The days for organized labor are over. The very thing that happened to PATCO is happening all across the country. . . . Middle-class America is on its way out.

Although many controllers families continue to suffer serious income decline and stress, controllers point to the success stories among their colleagues as further evidence that they were all "made of good stuff." As one former PATCO official put it:

   I'm proud of [my people]. . . . In spite of all the prejudice and blacklisting they were faced with, they're doing real well. Once we broke into places like Rockwell, Lockheed, and companies like that our people performed so well they were promoted right away. Many of them own their own businesses and some went back to college. A lot of them are not making as much money as they used to, but they will some day. . . . They are talented people.

Controllers share with their managerial colleagues a belief in the notion that worldly success is an indication of self-worth. If the controllers survive and prosper despite overwhelming obstacles, it confirms their basic strength and moral worth—qualities that they argue were there all along. As one Texas controller put it:

   I was indicted [for participating in the strike]. The FBI took me away, the news media lied and printed . . . wrong information. I was convicted of contempt of court and my picture was splattered on the TV. I was blacklisted and could not secure employment. . . .
   I started a wholesale business in March of Eighty-two and swore to myself that I would not rest until I created a million-dollar business. We went over a quarter million in Eighty-three. Several supervisors [who did not go on strike] from [my old control tower] live on my block and they expected to see a "For Sale" sign go up on my property. Instead they began to see a Lincoln Continental parked in the driveway.[40]

The retrospective interpretation of the strike has transformed the meaning of downward mobility from the self-blaming experience it is for the displaced managers and their families into an experience rich with integrity and the drama of sacrifice. The change was achieved not simply by unifying the controllers around ideas meaningful to themselves. Rather, they identified and elaborated existing readings of the wider culture within which they live. Public opinion may regard the strikers as a group whose foolish actions or greedy motivations were responsible for their firings, financial disasters, and downward mobility. But the controllers saw their fate as the price they paid for standing up for their principles and do not fault themselves for having lost to a more powerful and less worthy opponent. "Putting oneself on the line" for a cause is, in one reading of American history, the highest of callings, the noblest of actions.

Participation in a crusade cushions the blows of downward mobility because it gives meaning to hardship. It transforms simple loss into sacrifice. It provides for the confirmation of traditional values: standing for principles, for loyalty, for self-respect as a professional. American culture dictates that these are things worth struggling for and allows controllers to see themselves both as victims and as heroes. Vindication may take a lifetime, but the symbolic legitimation provided by the figure of the misunderstood crusader is a reservoir of strength available to those mistakenly identified as outlaws.

*

American political culture draws upon a history that contains complex and often contradictory symbols about consent and dissent— on the one hand emphasizing conformity, loyalty and consensus, on the other hand legitimating the primacy of individual conscience, individuals who stand against the crowd, and distrust of government. Both perspectives can be understood as forms of patriotism even though they are somewhat at odds with each other. And both are deemed legitimate by the American mainstream.

On the basis of their prestrike political orientations, it would have been difficult to predict the pathway of interpretation chosen by the controllers in the aftermath of the strike. They shifted from a fairly conservative, conformist orientation to a more populist or reformist vision, finding legitimation for their crusade and salve for the wounds of downward mobility in the latter. But the crusading reformer is not a quirky invention that makes sense to the controllers alone. On the contrary, it is recognized by Americans as one legitimate reading of our political heritage and a proper statement about the values that motivate upstanding citizens in our own time. Because the misunderstood reformer is a familiar and laudable character in mainstream American culture, his example confers dignity on the downwardly mobile controller who sacrificed everything in his name.

As Bill Taylor, the director of PATCO Lives put it:

> The why's of the PATCO strike are finally being reported and the issues now have a chance to be heard. People are paying attention—and [they're] remembering who it was that tried to tell them all of this a long time ago. Today, millions of Americans are being educated on the issues for which 11,400 principled people sacrificed their careers.
>
> And it's all happening because we wouldn't let it die. Of all the things we've done in these past four years this has been the most important. We didn't let it die. And because we didn't, some of us may still be reinstated, but more importantly, all of us will be vindicated.[41]

In 1995, hundreds of the original 11,000 strikers were called back to the Federal Aviation Authority. The fourteen-year gap was too much for many of them. Air traffic control is such a stressful occupation that even on a good day, it takes a young person's stamina to manage the skies. Besides, given the tenacity and determination of the strikers, it comes as little surprise that by 1995 many had made successes of themselves in new professions they preferred. While the recall owed itself less to vindication than to the Clinton Administration's desire to cement relations with organized labor, it is testimony to the powerful resonance of the 1981 strike that this is the means the White House chose to make a symbolic statement. It continues to be a watershed moment for organized labor and the one historical "turn" invoked when major labor disputes erupt. From the 1997 United Parcel Strike (a victory for labor) to the General Motors walkout of 1998 (a stalemate at best), the memory of the controllers remains alive in the minds of those who walk the picket line. And the language of sacrifice—for workers threatened by runaway shops, outsourcing to Mexico, or the wholesale shutdown of plants—remains a potent narrative for redefining labor disputes into causes worth fighting for.

6

Blue-Collar Workers
and the Abandonment
of Tradition

The company was God, the company was the mother, the father, everything.
—Fourth generation Singer employee

Many victims of downward mobility suffer the indignities of financial loss in isolation, their families hidden among more prosperous neighbors in suburban communities. But sometimes downward mobility takes on a communal character. When steel mills close their gates, oil fields fall silent, and farm areas experience epidemics of foreclosures, downward mobility engulfs entire communities. The blight spreads from the shuttered factory to the town beyond its gates, undermining the firms that supplied the factory; the restaurants, supermarkets, and clothing stores where workers used to spend their money; and the public sector, which must struggle to support schools, police, and fire departments on a reduced tax base.

The plant closures and downsizing that plagued the country over the past several decades appear to signal a fundamental change in the structure of the American economy.[1] Workers displaced from manufacturing industries often find that the industries themselves no longer exist on these shores. Hence equivalent jobs are nowhere to be found. The economic consequences of deindustrialization have been amply documented.[2] What remains to be explored is the subjective experience of mass, community-based downward mobility—the ways in which plant closures affect the *identity* of workers and the communities they live in.[3]

For the connection between a community and its industries runs deeper than paychecks and tax revenues. A manufacturing plant can become a moral bedrock, an institution that anchors a town's special character, weaving the fortunes of many generations together. When something so fundamental to a community's sense of self disappears, the consequences are more than economic—they call into question deeper commitments of loyalty, stability, and tradition. The haunting shells of once-bustling factories and silenced coal mines provoke the unemployed survivors and their neighbors to wonder whether the world they live in hasn't changed in fundamental ways—for the worse.

Thus, in the midst of coping with the practical, personal consequences of economic dislocation (the familiar litany of occupational degradation, income reduction, economic insecurity), blue-collar workers also face the question of where (or whether) they belong in postindustrial America. Do they have a place in a society that was once built around steel mills, auto factories, and appliance manufacturers but that now appears destined to become a service and high-tech economy? Is their middle-class lifestyle—a level of comfort only recently available to "the working man"—destined to become a thing of the past?[4] Their dilemma is fundamentally different from that facing managerial workers or air traffic controllers. The latter groups know that, whatever their personal troubles in finding employment, modern America needs people like them. But blue-collar men and women cannot respond with equal certainty: They face replacement by robots or by low-paid workers in runaway shops around the globe and absorption into a service economy that promises them less money and less job security.

The experience of a plant closure becomes a focal point for evaluating the "kind of world" the workers inhabit, and the shutdown is viewed as a harbinger or symptom of industrial transformations that victimize the working man and woman. Workers reflect warmly on the "good old days" when permanent shutdowns were rare. Dwelling on the past, however, is more than an excursion in nostalgia. In reconstructing their own history, remembrance becomes an act of criticism and a source of explanation for why modern America is not what it should be. From memories a moral analysis unfolds that locates blame for the shutdowns, and for the sorry state of industrial America, in a failure of traditional values. For while tradition is often seen as a conservative force,[5] it can also be a powerful resource for criticism.[6] It provides a language within which downward mobility can be seen as the consequence of our society's abandonment of what is best in our industrial heritage.

Elizabeth, New Jersey, is, in many ways, typical of industrial America. It has seen periods of tremendous prosperity, presided over by the nineteenth-century captains of industry, and periods of sharp decline, occasioned by the abandonment of the area by manufacturers bent on lowering their labor costs by relocating to areas where unionism is weak and wages are low. Older people in Elizabeth (now in their seventies and eighties) remember the town as a place of grandeur, where ladies and gentlemen in fine dress promenaded down the main avenue on Sunday. Younger people are likely to think of the city as fossilized, a run-down place centered on a main street whose marquees and billboards have the dated look of the 1950s.

In 1873, the Singer Sewing Machine Company found Elizabeth an attractive place to establish its flagship factory, moving there from cramped quarters in lower Manhattan.[7] For the next 100 years, the Singer company, a major multinational corporation since the mid-nineteenth century, dominated the city of Elizabeth. The plant produced consumer and industrial sewing machines that were sold all over the world, pausing only during the years of World War I, World War II, and the Korean War to produce munitions. Singer became the spine of the local economy, providing jobs and a secure life for generations of townspeople.

Singer's extraordinary success rested on its near monopoly of the sewing machine market. When first introduced in the Victorian era, the sewing machine was an expensive item—costing the equivalent of today's car.[8] But Singer's products lasted a lifetime, and with innovative marketing, "buying on time," and a reputation for excellent service, the company turned the sewing machine into a mass-production commodity, an item no newlywed bride would do without.[9]

Flushed with success, Singer's manufacturing empire spread worldwide, with plants in Scotland, Canada, France, Italy, Brazil, Australia, Germany, Mexico, and a factory in Russia that was expropriated during the Revolution. Yet Elizabeth remained the heart of the Singer Company, since it was the largest of its American factories.

The Elizabeth factory was one of the largest industrial facilities in the United States up until World War II, but the postwar period was one of steady decline. Before the war, Singer controlled 70 percent of the world sewing machine market. By the early 1950s, the company could claim only 33 percent of the American market and only 20 percent of the international business. The company's problems were exacerbated by the accelerated entry of women into the full-time labor force. Singer's most important customers disappeared into the workplace and had less time for domestic sewing. This, coupled with the increased availability of inexpensive, ready-to-wear clothing, diminished the market for the machine.

These losses spurred Singer to diversify,[10] and to search for ways of lowering production costs. Like many other firms, it began to move its American manufacturing operation overseas— to Italy, Taiwan, and Brazil. Eventually, the company initiated a slow but relentless dismantling of its sewing machine business. Today Singer no longer has any manufacturing or retail outlets in the United States.[11] The name that for generations was synonymous with the sewing machine no longer produces it at all.

The shift in corporate strategy did not bode well for the Elizabeth plant. Investment in the plant's equipment stagnated, and employment shrank. In 1980 the Elizabeth factory stopped manufacturing consumer sewing machines, and 850 workers were laid off immediately. Despite various rescue plans, layoffs continued until in 1982 the last of the plant's work force—about 700 people—were sent home. After nearly one hundred years of continuous operation, it was all over.

Singer's Place in Elizabeth's History

A series of articles written in 1939 for the *Elizabeth Daily Journal,* the leading newspaper of the then-booming industrial center, chronicled the dominance of the Singer Company in Elizabeth:

> The steady pay of Singer's built Elizabeth. During nearly every year from 1873 to 1920 the factory took on from 100 to 200 additional employees. Paying wages that were high those days and keeping its

men busy the year 'round, the company made it possible for its employees to build and own their homes. The acquisition of wealth and property by the factory's employees followed a regular pattern. When they first came here they rented flats and laid aside as much of their earnings as they could. With their savings and a building loan account they bought lots, erected two-family houses, moved in downstairs and rented the second floor. When they paid off the building loan mortgage they moved upstairs as a mark of their prosperity.[12]

By 1939 nearly 5,000 workers staffed the Elizabeth plant, one quarter of all those who were engaged in industry in Elizabeth. These numbers grew as World War II boosted demand for the plant's manufacturing capacity.[13]

The company made special efforts to attend to its civic image and to cultivate ties with the town. During the 1930s, Singer built a mammoth recreation complex that became the center of Elizabeth's social life. With a paternalism we now associate only with modern Japanese industry, Singer made special efforts to recognize the births of employee children. Company representatives attended every employee funeral, paid toward the burial expenses, and sent flowers. Scholarships were offered to children of employees. The company sponsored a "veterans club," which was open to those who had worked a minimum of forty years in the Elizabeth plant.[14]

Some of the flavor of this period is captured by interviews printed in the *New York Times* on the occasion of the plant's demise:

"Working at the Singer plant was a way of life," said Mr. Finkel, who was there for 44 years. "It was the natural thing for a young man coming out of high school to do. Everyone in town seems to have worked there at some point."

A machine operator and first-baseman, Mr. Finkel recalls that the company recruited top athletes during the 1930s, 40s and 50s from nearby high schools and other companies to work for it and play ball.

"Everyone in town went to those games," said Sophie Kobylinsky. Mrs. Kobylinsky also has fond recollections of company dances on Friday and Saturday nights during that period, to which women were not admitted without bringing cookies and cakes, with the company supplying drinks and beer.

"Singer's recreation hall was the center of social activity for the whole town," she said. Harry James, Jimmy Dorsey and other top bands played at gala company affairs.

Mayor Thomas Dunn recalls that thousands of people used to gather at the plant each year for a springtime demonstrations by the company's fire department in which a house specially built for the occasion was burned to the ground.[15]

The Singer plant underwrote the development of a middle-class blue-collar community, where production workers became homeowners, sent their kids to private parochial schools, and enjoyed a taste of the American dream long denied past generations of factory workers.[16]

The Economic Effect of the Shutdown

The Singer plant put Elizabeth on America's industrial map: It had a reputation for being a leader in innovative production technology.[17] The shutdown dealt a serious blow to the city's identity, since for nearly a century "Singer was Elizabeth and Elizabeth was Singer." Its fate seemed to symbolize the sorry state of industry in the Northeast, since it came amid almost daily reports of factory shutdowns in areas long known as the nation's workshop.

Against this depressing background, the Singer workers faced the fact that their "employer for life" was gone. Though the shock still reverberates in Elizabeth today, it was not unexpected. Plant closings are often sudden events—one day a factory is humming with activity, the next day it is an empty cavern—but for the Elizabeth plant, the end came in the form of a slow bleed and staggered waves of layoffs. As a result, the people who stayed to the end were largely longtime employees hoping to work enough months to hold on to their retirement benefits. Younger and less senior workers had long since left or been let go.

The range of financial and employment problems confronting the Singer workers was considerable.[18] Some families were only minimally affected, while others were in such dire straits they had to send their children away to live with relatives who could afford to take care of them. A host of factors—workers' ages, seniority, skills, and numbers of dependents—determined the degree of financial distress facing Singer families.

Workers who were close to retirement qualified for partial pension benefits.[19] For example, men and women who were fifty-five when the shutdown occurred held on to 60 percent of their retirement income and forfeited the rest. Given losses of this magnitude, many needed to find new jobs but found themselves on the receiving end of age discrimination and gave up after months of trying.[20] They became resigned to a lower standard of living, waiting for the day they could file for Social Security benefits (at age sixty-two). Their standard of living was reduced to the basics; comforts like vacations were put aside indefinitely; and the problems that attend the loss of health insurance in an older population remained a constant worry.

Employees under fifty-five lost all retirement benefits. Since Singer people often began work in the Elizabeth plant in their teens, this meant that individuals who had worked in the plant for over thirty years were unable to collect a dime in retirement. Unemployment compensation, which lasted for about eighteen months, helped, but by the middle of 1984 these benefits were, in most cases, completely exhausted.[21] Many of these were middle-aged workers whose children had left home, hence their financial burdens were less onerous than their fellow workers who were younger. When the plant closed, many of these families had only the income from spouses who were still employed to rely on. The shift from dual-earner to single-earner households was a hardship, since it generally took two workers to sustain the middle-class lifestyle so important to the Singer employees. While most found ways to meet their basic expenses, they faced prolonged insecurity, the loss of their seniority, and the prospect that the only new jobs they could hope for were in the service sector.[22]

Those men and women who were too young to qualify for any retirement benefits *and* who still had dependent children at home were in the toughest situation. They faced an inhospitable job market, since the local area has seen many of its major industries flee, a point not lost on the Singer workers:

> You don't do any job finding when there aren't any jobs available. The area has been going downward in manufacturing for a long time. Jersey has lost hundreds of thousands of jobs in manufacturing over the years. This county alone had tremendous, big manufacturing plants. All these things are practically gone.

Minorities and immigrants, many of them Cuban and Haitian women, confronted discrimination or prejudice based on language barriers. Those who found new jobs often experienced steep losses of income and status, for inside the Singer plant they had risen to positions of responsibility. The experience of Elena Morales, who worked her way up in the Singer plant from an assembly-line worker to a quality-control inspector, was fairly typical:

> I collected unemployment for a year. After [that] a Polish friend of mine who has a dry cleaning business asked me if I wanted to work for her part-time . . . She wasn't paying me too much money . . . but I stayed with her for two years. . . . And then I worked in a restaurant . . . until 1983. Finally I found [my present] part-time job in the airport cleaning the airplanes. I started as a cleaning lady.
>
> Losing my [Singer] job had a tremendous impact on me. I didn't have nothing. We still have bills and things. My husband had a job, and he had all the things on his shoulders. . . . Factories are the worst in my mind now. . . . Nothing is secure anymore . . . I think all the companies are going to close.

Because she lost the seniority she earned during her sixteen years at Singer, Elena found herself at the bottom of the job pyramid where perks are few: She works the graveyard shift, she must take her vacations at inopportune times, and she knows that if layoffs come, she will be vulnerable once again.

The financial effects of the shutdown on Singer families were hard to weather and many families suffered long-term losses that were difficult to rectify. This situation provided fertile ground for reflection over why the shutdown had occurred.[23] For up until the announcement of the closing, the workers had simply observed the ups and downs of factory life. Once plans for the closure were confirmed and workers began to assess what this would mean for themselves and their families, they spent a great deal of time discussing among themselves how such a fixture in the community could simply disappear, and what this signi-fied about broader trends in industrial America. These two is-sues—the shutdown of the local plant and the changing nature of the national economy—became intertwined in a discourse of blame.

In Singer's glory days, the firm celebrated its image in self-promoting in-house publications, in its civic good works, and in its expansive buildings.[24] But by far the most important aspect of the company as far as the Elizabeth workers were concerned was its paternalism. Singer was more than just a place to work, it was a traditional way of life. Men and women who are now in their seventies and eighties remember their own parents' and grandparents' lives as revolving around the factory. From the late 1800s through the post–World War II period, family "chains" three or four generations deep spent their working lives in the factory. Men and women found their future spouses in the plant. When their children were old enough to work, parents manipulated whatever networks of influence they had to bring them into the factory. They did the same for their grandchildren, nieces, nephews, and cousins. Thus, while jobs were not inherited, recruiting from longtime "Singer families" was quite common. Joe Schultz remembers it well:

> I started working at Singer's in 1935. That was my first and only job I ever had. I worked there forty-seven years and one month. I was one of many people in my family. My niece worked there. My two brothers, my father. You see, Singer's in the old days, it was a company that went from one generation to the other. If there was a good worker in the family, they kept hiring them. It was like a family, like a lot of factories years ago. I know many families who went through there, probably through four generations.

Most of the old-timers owed their Singer jobs to family reputation and ethnic solidarity. Nepotism benefited the workers in that it offered them a degree of influence over the economic fate of their family members. It benefited the company by creating incentive for reliable work: Failing to perform on the job jeopardized not only the individual, but his or her relatives.

Before World War I, it was not uncommon for children to begin working at the factory at the age of ten or eleven, hiding from school board inspectors when they came looking for truants, standing on wooden boxes to reach the machinery. Even later, workers routinely spent forty years or more in the plant before retiring.[25] For them, a Singer job was synonymous with lifetime security. During the Great Depression, while many in Elizabeth lined up for the soup kitchens, Singer wages protected employees from the worst of the hardships. In some respects the old-timers were grateful to the company for seeing them through the Depression. In other respects they came to expect this kind of treatment from Singer, seeing it as a company that undertook lifelong commitments to workers. Ethel, who retired from the plant in the late 1970s after nearly forty years of employment, captured its "cradle to grave" character well:

> We called [Singer] the old soldiers' home. You went in there. You
> died in there. People didn't quit unless they were really looking for
> something higher, if they had a better education or something. Most
> of the people there were born in Elizabeth, they worked in Elizabeth,
> they died in the Singer Company.

Security was of central importance to the Depression generation,
as it was to their children who entered the plant after them, but
industrial leadership and pride in the product were also significant
aspects of Singer's identity. The workers thought of themselves
as part of a manufacturing giant. There was no part of the world
too remote for a Singer sewing machine and no company that
could compete against Singer.[26] Hence the solid blue-collar families of Elizabeth prospered just as the company prospered, partners
in an industrial dominance that owed its origins to traditions of
excellence and craftsmanship.

> We took pride in our work. We did it not because we were told to
> but because we wanted to do it right. You did it yourself. It was
> your job, and you made sure you did it . . . right. . . . It was a
> pleasure to go to work. As a matter of fact I couldn't wait to go to
> work in the morning.

Older workers remember a strict labor discipline and an unforgiving attitude toward those considered unreliable or whose work
was below the quality standards set by the company.

This was the factory culture into which older Singer workers
were inducted and the tradition they passed on to new generations.
However, as the workers caught in the shutdown began to reflect
on how such an institution could pass from the scene, they began
to construct another history. It was the tale of how these traditions
were forsaken, a morality play in which Singer's abandonment
of tradition caused the company to lose market power. And the
same misguided moves repeated over and over again in factories
across the country, spell the end of American dominance in industrial manufacturing.

The Devaluation of Craftsmanship

The old-timers did not feel that Singer was special for its time;
they believed that the general orientation of American business
in the past was one of loyalty toward the work force and pride

in one's product. But Singer turned its back on these values, adopting the tools of "scientific management" as a method of pushing its work force after the war. Craftsmanship was sacrificed in the pursuit of increased productivity and diversification.

In 1949 the plant union—the United Electrical Workers—took the Singer labor force out on strike. The workers walked the picket lines for six months, one of the longest strikes in the history of the industrial United States at the time.[27] When the dust settled, the company installed a new system for measuring productivity on the shop floor that drastically altered the calculations that set a worker's pay. The new "standards system" was the death knell for the craft ethic. Workers had to compete for jobs with favorable base and incentive rates and were forced to speed up in order to exceed the "standard" (or quota) and earn a decent wage:

> At the beginning . . . we had the old piecework system. It was good. They treated you good, you know what I mean? But then after 1949, after the strike, that's when it all started with the standards system. Then things started to really change down there. You had to fight, you had to fight for your dollar. There was no two ways about it. We made more money on some jobs. Some jobs you just couldn't make it. And it created problems for the workers and problems for the company. I believe that the standards system was the ruination of the Elizabeth plant.

Social relations in the plant underwent a fundamental change for the worse as a result of the new "incentive" system. Production workers could not afford to be helpful to each other:

> The whole atmosphere was different. [Before] there was times where they would let you go, maybe get something in a different department, help out. But when the standards system come in, whatever job you were on, you were stuck on that job. You lost contact with a lot of people in the plant. I worked there thirty-eight years. [After the standards] there's a hell of a lot of people I didn't even know worked there even though I was there at the same time! You just lost contact with people in the place. . . . You didn't have time to talk to them.

The emphasis on productivity went hand in hand with the erosion of quality:

> When I started there, everything was quality. And it had to be done right and if it wasn't done right, you got it back to do. When the [standards] system come in, they tell you to check one out of every . . . ten pieces or one out of every . . . thirty pieces, so you didn't

care about the other twenty-nine pieces. And if those twenty-nine pieces turned out to be scrap, [the company] wound up with scrap.

The closure of the plant in 1982 was, in the minds of the old-timers, the inevitable long-term consequence of the measures taken in 1949 to boost productivity. They see the standards system not as a spur to productivity, but as an act of betrayal, a sign of distrust, and a wedge that drove management and workers apart.[28] Management "forgot" that it was the craftsmanship of the Elizabeth employees that gave Singer its preeminent position in the sewing machine market. Since the machine had always been an expensive investment for a family, the company's reputation for dependability, high-quality manufacture, and superior service was critical to its success. By speeding the work pace up to the point where it became impossible to maintain quality production, management turned its back on the special relationship it had with its blue-collar workers, set the stage for a downward spiral in the machine's quality, and effectively forfeited its competitive edge in the world market. As one engineer put it:

> The standards method of manufacturing was not something that promoted quality in a machine. It was set up so that if you do things very fast, you get paid for it. If you made ten units you got paid for ten units even though the ten units didn't work. It was the same all the way through the company. So Singer's quality image dropped. And their service image dropped, so instead of saving money on service they were saving money on inventory, parts, and all this kind of stuff. It really was quite an unpleasant situation. When I went out in various places and someone would find out I worked for Singer, I'd begin to get all the horror stories [about broken machines].

The workers' emphasis on craftsmanship seems at odds with a popular conception of modern plants as monotonous assembly-line operations where "deskilled" drones bide their time until the final whistle blows.[29] The image of the contemporary factory as deadening does not capture the complexity of the Singer plant, which retained under one roof a mix of skilled and unskilled workers, of complex and routinized systems of production, of highly particularized work (machine setups and repair) and routinized assembly work.[30] Nor does it capture the essence of workplace culture where even routinized work can be imbued with a spirit of craftsmanship born of pride in the finished product rather than of control over the labor process.[31] Singer workers, from the lowliest needle grinder to the engineers in research and development, were proud of what they made and proud to be part of a factory with such a rich history of industrial leadership. John Kolombotovic, who spent forty years in the Singer foundry casting iron, describes some of the machines manufactured in Elizabeth:

> I don't know how many industrial machines we made, but the main one . . . (we called it the Two eighty-one) was the old workhorse. That machine, it was proven. They were using that machine in most of the garment industries, maybe for the last fifty years now. It was always a reliable machine. All of a sudden Singer comes out with this new electronic machine with all the push buttons and you watch it work. It was so fast you couldn't even see the needle going up and down. I forgot what the revolution per minute was [but it] was a . . . beautiful-looking machine. Oh my God, a beautiful machine.

For these workers, whose formative experiences included World War II and the Korean War, pride in product, pride in their company's eminence, and love of country became fused together. Their labor, and that of their families, pushed Singer to its one-time domination of the international sewing machine trade and contributed to America's metamorphosis into the most productive and powerful nation in the world—triumphant in war and triumphant in the marketplace.

That might was built on a traditional ethic of hard work, craftsmanship, and commitment. And, generalizing from their own experiences at Singer, they believe that American industry, and American society in general, has forsaken these values. In a historical irony not lost on this generation, they point to Japan as a place where commitment to quality and a bond between labor and management still holds: "The Japanese companies, they stick by their workers. They have jobs for life and they don't just shut down plants and let their people go. And look how well they're doing! They're wiping us out!"

This a particularly difficult comparison for the generation of World War II to swallow, though they freely offer it as a lesson for American industry. They are doubly frustrated by the decline in their own fortunes and the growing dominance of the country they fought against. George Antonio, who saw the war from a battlefield vantage point noted ironically: "The Japanese tried and failed to get me during the war. They couldn't do it. Now they've done it through their production."

Singer workers argue that quality manufacture was ceded to the Japanese because American workers were pressed into production methods that gave priority to numbers and speed over the craft mentality. The mighty giant of American industry has fallen because fundamental values have been swept aside in favor of high productivity or cheap labor. John Kolombotovic expressed this view:

> The American economy is going downhill, and this is a very bad thing. Not only the sewing machine industry, but also other companies are moving to the foreign countries to save money. This is wrong because now there are a lot of jobs today that only a few people still know how to do. If we have to start these industries all over again it will be too late. This is bad for the country.

The Disloyalty of Management

Why would Singer's management set the stage for the "end of quality" through the standards system? Workers argue that after World War II, the pattern of recruitment to high-level management jobs moved away from the selection of experienced, seasoned "sewing machine men" toward managers with no commitment to the machine or to the people who produced it.

In the long distant past, top management in the Singer corporation was drawn from the ranks of people intimately familiar with the Elizabeth factory. Workers harbored no Horatio Alger illusions that industrious production workers would be elevated to the presidency; they recognized that engineers and supervisors were the ones who climbed the managerial ladder. But the managers who worked their way up through the ranks knew the Elizabeth plant from the inside. They had a healthy respect for production workers and recognized their contribution to Singer. Perhaps even more important, they were themselves "sewing machine men." They knew the machine; they knew the customers; they were familiar with the design process and its testing. They were not Wall Street wizards bent on managing the sewing machine trade in the same way they would a toothpaste company.

The old-timers considered good management to be a kind of craft where people "paid their dues" and put down roots in their knowledge of a product. But by the early 1950s, Singer began recruiting executives whose business experience was completely unrelated to sewing machines, financial men who could spearhead diversification into other industries. For many of the old-timers, this was a telling sign that the Elizabeth plant was headed for the industrial graveyard. An engineer in the plant—who took early retirement after almost thirty years with the company—saw Singer's move toward financial management as a terrible mistake:

> [I think] that anyone coming in [at the top] should start at the engineering level or lower and gradually work up, and by the time you get to that [executive] level you really know what is going on in the company. And then you know how to manage it. But Singer began to bring in outside management into the sewing machine business . . . from anywhere. The theory was that if you can manage anything well, you can manage anything.
>
> They brought in people from various types of industry entirely, who didn't know anything about [sewing machines]. They'd give them about two years to set the world on fire, and when they hadn't set the world on fire, then they're gone and the next guy comes in. So it was just a vicious cycle for twenty years or so. Revolving door policy. All the top management came in from outside, stayed two or three years, and they'd get dumped and the next one would come, and you could watch the company going down the hill all this time. . . . Most of the top management hadn't been there long enough to have a feel for what this all meant. During the last few years there was nobody between me and the president of the company who knew what a sewing machine was.

In 1975, the Singer Company hired yet another new president, Joseph Flavin, who came to the company from years of high-level management experience with IBM and the Xerox Corporation. Flavin's 1987 obituary notes that he was regarded by Wall Street as an "astute planner" who "oversaw [Singer's] evolution from the world's best-known manufacturer of sewing machines to a military contractor."[32] He was praised for his farsighted recognition that the company needed to "overhaul its identity" and pull away from the "sewing machine culture" that had shaped it throughout its history. Flavin was a man whom workers (particularly union leaders) regarded as the epitome of everything traditional management was not. He "knew nothing about sewing machines." He was a "white-collar man" who had no loyalty to the Elizabeth workers. As one union official and longtime Singer worker commented:

> To this day I don't believe that the people in the corporate management at Singer know how to run this business. They know absolutely

nothing about sewing machines. . . . I don't think that [the president] knows what a sewing machine is. I really don't.

The new president had no stake in preserving the Elizabeth plant and therefore either made no efforts or, according to some, actually blocked efforts to find alternative production work for the plant when sewing machine sales faltered and the red ink began to flow. Some even felt that he closed the plant down because, like others of his white-collar ilk, he did not want to associate with blue-collar people:

> I don't believe he was ever enthused about this factory here. I believe that he is a country-club type of a person, and I think that probably it is below his dignity to work in an area such as this. He probably would prefer having a factory or a facility directly across the street from a golf course. . . . I don't think that he fits in with the kind of people that live here.

Indeed, when in 1978 Singer moved its headquarters from nearby Manhattan to Stamford, Connecticut—the chrome-and-glass enclave of insurance companies—many Elizabeth workers looked askance, perceiving the move as another indication that senior management wanted nothing to do with the dirt and heat of manufacturing. The highest levels of management seemed to be working overtime to create distance between themselves and the "people who made Singer what it is." Management's geographical separation from Elizabeth made it increasingly difficult for plant loyalists to find sympathetic ears for their ideas on revitalization.[33] Distance made it all the easier to neglect the factory's need for modernization, which the workers realized was crucial if they were to remain competitive:

> Their responsibility [toward this plant] was like [the responsibility you have] when you buy a home. If you bought a home and you lived in it and you never fixed it, someday it is going to fall down. And all that is going to be left is for somebody to come and pick it up and dump it into a truck. That is exactly what happened [to this plant].

The workers' craft ethic was not opposed to technological progress. On the contrary, they berated management for putting profit before investment, failing to modernize the plant's antiquated technology:[34]

> I'm a tool and die maker, and I know how things were going in the outside world as far as technology, and . . . I know that they were

making no change whatsoever in the technology in the plant as far as tools were concerned. Nothing was being bought, they were just maintaining what they had or not even maintaining what they had.

This belief was widely shared:

> If our industries in the rest of the nation are the way that they were at Singer's then we're in a lot of trouble. And it seems like that's exactly what's happening. Our steel industry, there probably isn't a steel company now in the United States that has the potential that Japan has. We don't even have electrical furnaces yet. There were machines at Singer's, hand-operated machines, or perhaps belt-operated machines, that were probably there when they first built Singer's. And that was sad. There was no attempt, there was no vision, to look ahead and say, "Hey, we must retool." They didn't do it. And because they didn't do it that was one of the reasons that they had problems in later years.

Instead, where new technology was implemented, it expressed a penny-wise and pound-foolish attitude toward speed and quality:

> We produced the finest sewing machine in the world, but that was before they went onto full-scale assembly-line production. That's why you get a lot of lemons. If they had kept the old system, in other words, if you produce that sewing machine, and you put your ticket on that sewing machine, and that sewing machine came back, they went after you. Now the fellows working on this conveyer system, if the hole wasn't drilled deep enough or whatever, if he couldn't get that screw in, he took his hammer and slammed it in. When the conveyer system first started you didn't get too many machines back, but after awhile, God, they were getting thousands back.

The worker's criticism of management parallels their view on craftsmanship on the production line. As they saw it, the Singer Company needed "sewing machine men" for management because this was crucial for maintaining pride in one's product. The loss of the managerial craft ethic inevitably diminished the company's commitment to sewing machines, its drive for technological superiority, and its loyalty to the Elizabeth plant (hence its closure).

In the end, the workers were angry, but not surprised, to learn that Singer was getting out of the business it was best known for. It seemed symptomatic of everything that is wrong with modern American business. For in the "old days" a company's name, its identification with a product, meant everything.[35] But in the postindustrial society of rapid mergers, acquisitions, diversification, and the erosion of "craft" management, these traditions are being abandoned. It is becoming increasingly difficult to identify a product with a company; no one knows who produces anything anymore. Cars sold as Chryslers are made by Mitsubishi; U.S. Steel becomes USX; luggage companies own wineries; and conglomerates like United Technologies must broadcast elaborate commercials simply to explain to the public who their constituent companies are.

With this kind of anonymity in the marketplace, Singer people argue, comes a lack of identity and a lack of responsibility. We cannot hold anyone accountable for poorly made products when it is no longer evident who makes them. Hence the Singer Company is seen as a symbol or an example of a much broader trend away from traditions that gave American companies valued reputations for quality work and dependable service.

The blame also falls on new kinds of managers—the MBA types, familiar with takeovers and tax law but ignorant of the products their companies manufacture. While Singer workers are not familiar with the details of life in other factories, they sense that the shift toward "modern" management has occurred everywhere in America.[36] They read their own experience as indicative of a fundamental transformation in the corporate world away from values of lifetime commitment to a firm, and knowledge or experience as the basis of advancement, to a world based on more ephemeral qualities; an emphasis on personal career at the expense of the firm, and the elevation of "textbook" education over experience. Harold Brown, a manager who had worked his way up from the shop floor, described one of a series of fast-track financial types brought in to cut costs and turn the factory around:

> I think probably one of the biggest mistakes was to bring in the management they had. . . . They brought another fellow in from another company to manage the plant. In order to produce so-called results, a lot of the figures in the monthly budget were distorted. He stole money from one place to another, moved it over so he could balance budgets in other areas. . . . About a year later [he] was let go.

Julia Alvez, a former quality control inspector, put it more bluntly:

> I think that this is one of the reasons Singer's closed down: There were too many people that had college degrees there. Today you need too much on paper to tell you "I am a doctor, I am an engineer." But those people [on the shop floor] know something without having a school degree. They used to make those old machines work.

The abandonment of tradition has transformed industrial America into a place these workers hardly recognize. The transformation is a failure of morality and not simply a shift in business strategy.

Race, Ethnicity, and the Dynamics of Blame

Elizabeth has been a community of immigrants since the seventeenth century. Its founding predated the Revolutionary War and the main thoroughfare, Broad Street, is bounded by markers of eighteenth-century churches burned down by the British during the War of Independence. Though Broad Street's monuments are emblematic of a collective American heritage, the small print on the street sign says "Latvian Way"—a nod to the importance of ethnicity in Elizabeth.

The Singer labor force mirrored the ebb and flow of immigrants to Elizabeth. After World War I, Germans settled in Elizabeth in large numbers and with their reputation for skilled hands domi-nated the factory work force. Eastern Europeans followed in their wake, forming the lower tiers of the factory stratification system. With the coming of World War II, the tide of immigrants shifted. Italians, Spaniards, and Portuguese joined their brethren from Poland, Czechoslovakia, the Ukraine, and Ireland, settling in New Jersey communities already brimming with immigrant workers.

Recruitment into the plant was strictly an ethnic affair. And since these jobs were coveted for their steady pay, power accrued to ethnic brokers who could guarantee access to the plant. Walter Barry, a professional union organizer who was in charge of the organizing drive that brought the Singer plant into the United Electrical Workers in 1943, remembers how strong the control of the ethnic leadership was:

> [The union organizers] had to learn the ethnic background [of the Singer workers], where the Slavs, Poles, Germans, Italians and other ethnic minorities lived. We cultivated the societies [social clubs], the gin mills, and the other locations where the workers hung out and attempted to learn who the key [ethnic] leaders were . . . inside the various [shop floor] departments at Singer.
> . . . There was a padrone system. The leaders of the various ethnic groups would bring in friends from that group and would have control over them.[37]

Ethnic groups were "marked" by a collective reputation: as hard workers, skilled workers, or lazy workers. At times these stereotypes were tinged by nativism or racism. Yet they could stress the positive as well:

> Of all the people that came in with the [Hispanic] group, I was surprised, you know who were the best workers? Portuguese people. They are polite. They have done their job right. If they have done something wrong, they were willing to do it over, whereas some of the other people didn't want to do that.

Alongside the European immigrants were the internal migrants, whites from industrial areas of the United States hit hard by the Depression and blacks brought from the agrarian south by company recruiters to handle the worst jobs in the plant.[38] The foundry in the Elizabeth plant employed over 1,000 men who made cast-iron parts for the sewing machine; they were virtually all black. It was hot, dirty, physically taxing work, and for a long time it was the only part of the Elizabeth plant where blacks could get jobs. Segregated from the rest of the work force, they remained confined to the foundry until after World War II. In the late 1950s and 1960s, blacks moved out onto the factory floor, to better-paid and less arduous jobs.

Beginning in the 1960s, the sources of immigration to Elizabeth shifted again, this time to include Central America and the Caribbean. These men and women were among the youngest members of the Singer work force at the time the closure was announced. For, by the 1960s, the sons and daughters of the white ethnics no longer automatically entered the factory gates, preferring instead to join the civil service or find white-collar clerical work. Cubans, Haitians, and native-born blacks filled the resulting gap.

The immigrant groups who came to Elizabeth before World War II remember Singer as a place in which people with different cultural traditions mixed easily.[39] However, postwar newcomers to Elizabeth, particularly blacks and Caribbean immigrants, were seen in an entirely different light. When analyzing the demise of the Singer plant, ethnic antagonism became fertile ground for scenarios of blame that laid responsibility for the closure at the feet of "undesirable" nonwhite workers. Many, though by no means all, of the older workers blamed the work habits or attitudes of newer generations for the decline of the plant:

> Things really changed inside the plant in the early sixties. The workers would fight; there were stabbings. It never used to be like that. It was different people coming in. There were different kinds of ethnic

people at Singer there all the time and we never had a problem. [But by the sixties] it was just a lower class of people, that's the only way I can explain it. You can't go walking down [by the plant] now. We used to go walking at noontime to Elizabethport; we thought nothing of it, it was perfectly safe. People kept their houses up, their lawns nicely mowed, flowers growing. Then it changed. . . . Everything changed. The people moved out and these other people moved in, and that's the kind of people who were hired.

Many white ethnics saw a chasm of values between themselves and the newer workers. Where they had taken pride in their work, they felt that the recent entrants didn't. From this they concluded that the quality of the plant's product was suffering. As one Singer veteran put it when asked whether she thought the plant had to close:

I don't know. . . . I know some of the best work had been done and . . . I guess over a time the workers they had weren't doing the work too well. The old-timers were leaving, retiring. The new element in there . . . they weren't doing the work properly. Puerto Rican people and coloreds too, they have a different conception of working. They don't have the same idea of conscientiousness, somehow. All they're interested in is the money part. They don't care about what's going to happen to the company or that you should do a good job. This doesn't enter their minds. I think this is one of the factors [in the closing].

Irony abounds in these remarks: the European immigrants who flooded into the factory in the 1920s and 1930s were poorly regarded by the skilled German workers who dominated the plant at that time. Mediterranean and Slavic immigrants, in particular, were singled out as dubious material for a work force. Nevertheless, some descendants of the once-stigmatized groups looked upon the immigrants of the 1960s and 1970s and the native blacks as bad workers and blamed them for the shutdown.[40]

The entrance of these newcomers into the plant work force coincided with a number of other events that exacerbated the tendency to "point fingers" at ethnic and racial minorities. The slowdown in the sewing machine trade; the advent of federal equal employment opportunity laws mandating affirmative action hiring; and the worsening of race relations in the area surrounding Newark, New Jersey,[41] in the wake of the disastrous riots of the mid 'sixties all took place during the time these nonwhite immigrants joined the shop floor. The conjunction of these events, mixed with a climate that had always prompted ethnic stereotyping, led to a "politics of blame" that was racially and ethnically loaded.

By far the most incendiary aspect of ethnic relations was the publicity given to federal guidelines for equal employment. The refrain of reverse discrimination was frequently raised by white workers who followed the public debates of the early 1980s over appropriate remedies for employment discrimination:

> We more or less had to hire a certain amount of [blacks] and for a time, Singer would cater to them more and they would get away with more. If they did bad work, instead of letting them know about it, they would cover it up. But if you [a white] had done bad work, they'd lower the boom on you. And this made for a lot of hard feelings. They tried to give them better jobs and everything else. Because the government was telling them you gotta hire [someone of a particular race]. Sometimes you'd . . . feel angry toward them. Why should they come in and take over the best jobs just because the government says you gotta hire them? We figured you hired a person for their qualifications, not for their color. I don't think that's right.

Hiring quotas seemed an affront to Singer's tradition as a nepotistic employer. The company had always hired people on the grounds that they came from "Singer families," if not by blood, then by fictive kinship connections of church membership, common language, and cultural ties. Equal employment opportunity regulations were perceived not only as offering preferential job prospects for particular ethnic groups but as a bureaucratic attempt to interfere with patrimonial traditions:

> My grandfather, my father, myself, my niece and nephew after, and my mother's brother worked at Singer. You see, it was a regular family there because the company used to hire families. When these [blacks and Hispanics] came in, the companies were told they had to hire them if they wanted government contracts. I heard that a couple of times. Singer's and a lot of other companies had nothing against these people. I had a lot of good workers in them too, you know. But Singer's, like many other factories around here, when they got a good working family, they kept them.

Many resented this tampering with tradition. From this angry posture they envisioned a causal chain: The government insisted on preferential hiring and the end of nepotism,[42] which brought minorities onto the factory floor, ruined the quality of workmanship, and pushed Singer out of a leadership position in the sewing machine market.

The tendency to attribute Singer's decline to the changing character of the work force was exacerbated by the declining economic position of Elizabeth as a whole, particularly the area around the port where the plant had been located. One former Singer worker described the transformation of Elizabethport (the local name for the Singer neighborhood):

> The area that is our ghetto used to have a lot of hard working people in it, a lot of whom worked at Singer's. That's the Elizabethport area. Now there's no jobs, and when there's no jobs the whole area deteriorates, restaurants move out, taverns move out, candy stores move out, and that's the end of the neighborhood.

Like many other northeastern industrial cities, Elizabeth had been a boom town during the world wars and the Korean conflict. Thereafter, however, a familiar pattern of industrial decline began to take its toll both in terms of factory flight and increasing poverty in urban areas.[43] The neighborhood around the Singer plant, which had once thrived with single-family homes and facilities that catered to the workers (e.g. diners), hit a steep decline. It became a ghetto of poor minorities with a run-down housing stock, cracked sidewalks, and boarded-up buildings. Today, Elizabethport has a reputation as an eyesore and an enclave of danger.[44]

It goes almost without saying that minorities and immigrants did not perceive themselves as the root of all evil in the plant. If anything, the immigrants saw themselves as the Protestant ethic incarnate, as hardworking, nose-to-the-grindstone workers bent on getting ahead. They tended to put the blame on certain older white workers. Maria Ramirez, a native of Cuba who began working at Singer in the mid-1960s, commented on the work attitudes of immigrants compared to their well-established counterparts: "The new-timers were not like the old ones. Because most people that came from another country, they work automatically. They tell us to do this and we do it and never ask the reason why we are doing it. . . ."

Julia Rodriguez, a Portuguese worker, agreed:

> I spent 13 years of my life [at Singer]. I worked very hard. I always tried to do my best. You know a lot of factories go out of business because they made bad parts, scrap. That was a big problem at Singer's;

there was a lot of scrap. I never had rejects in my job. I used to repair many parts from the [older people] making them bad.

First-generation immigrants in the plant often remarked that as a group they had "carried a heavier load" than the older white ethnics who had "slacked off." They did not see their presence in the Elizabeth plant as a bow to government mandates. They were the salt of the earth, the core of the factory's productivity. If anyone or anything was to blame for the shutdown, in their view it was the tendency of the Singer Company to take advantage of cheaper labor and weaker unions elsewhere in the United States and abroad.

Downward Mobility and Blue Collar Culture

Downward mobility wears many faces in American society. For the managers, its appearance is individualistic and the experience is fundamentally a lonely sojourn. For air traffic controllers, downward mobility was a sacrifice for a cause, endured by a brotherhood tied together by a common fate but not by common residence The Singer experience reveals yet another side to downward mobility: Its meaning is bound up with a community of residence. The loss of a family's livelihood is therefore intertwined with a town's loss of identity, for Singer was Elizabeth and Elizabeth was Singer for the better part of one hundred years. And Singer itself was both a plant that produced sewing machines, and a way of life suffused with distinctive traditions.

For the Singer workers, the plant closure was a moral drama with a message. If we forsake our traditions, particularly those that have to do with craftsmanship, with pride in what we produce, we will reap a sorry harvest of confusion and economic disarray. They say that the country must remember on whose backs the industrial preeminence of America was built, and honor their contributions by continuing to implement the values that "made us great." The older workers, in particular, interpret the loss of the Singer plant in terms of the spectacle of America's declining hold on industry worldwide.

Though conservative in orientation, the Singer workers were not in favor of turning the clocks back or fossilizing industry. They were not opposed to change per se. What they criticized was industry's abandonment of core values. As Joseph, a forty-three-year veteran of the Singer plant, put it:

This factory had been here for 125 years. The whole Singer empire started here. Along comes [the new president] and he forgets all these things. He forgets that without an Elizabeth there would have been no Singer at all. We could have failed years ago. If the people here had not been conscientious, if they didn't pride themselves, if they didn't do what was required of them, Singer would have failed many, many years ago. . . . We did not fail because of our own inadequacies. We failed because [the management] failed us.

The old-time members of the Singer rank and file have spent many hours considering the question of who was to blame for the shutdown. Some, like Joseph, place responsibility at the feet of management for failing to invest in the plant or for pushing workers so hard with the standards system that the quality of the product declined. Others, point to the vulnerability of American-made products to foreign competition. Many articulate these explanations while simultaneously laying blame at the feet of racial groups they consider undesirable. None see themselves as personally responsible for the shutdown. Indeed, one would search in vain for self-critical statements so common among white-collar workers, "If only I had done something different. If only I had taken a different job, gotten a better education, or moved to some other community."

In this regard, Singer workers present an interesting modification of the American work ethic. They do believe in that aspect of the tradition that dictates that hard work is the key to success or at least security, though they do not measure this in terms of occupational prestige but in terms of steady, well-paid work. Yet they reject that aspect of the work ethic that proved so corrosive to the displaced managers. Singer workers do not hold themselves personally responsible for their own fate. Singer old-timers do fault individuals (and sometimes ethnic groups) they regard as shirkers: Those people are to blame for their unemployment or downward mobility. But as long as people are working hard (as they believe they were themselves), they cannot be held blameworthy if the factory closes and they lose their jobs. They see themselves as fundamentally at the mercy of remote decision makers (sometimes too amorphous to name). These inaccessible authorities control their fortunes.

The workers' perspective is grounded in blue-collar culture.[45] The Singer workers have rarely experienced the twists and turns of their work lives as matters of individualized action. In the old days Singer would hire hundreds at a time; during slow periods it would furlough just as many. These were group issues. When contracts were negotiated, the union spoke with one voice on behalf of everyone in the plant. Although individuals could be called to account for poor workmanship (and thereby be singled out in some sense), the union protected them in the name of the social whole. Shop floor solidarity, no matter how cross-cut by ethnic and racial divisions, promoted group orientation when faced with management intransigence.[46] Bolstering these sources of collective identity was the depth of Singer's connection with the city of Elizabeth and its residents. With kinship chains of workers four generations deep, the connection between the plant and any given worker (particularly the older ones) seemed less a matter of individual endeavor than of "blood ties" and tradition.

The group orientation was helpful in some respects when the plant closed because it meant that individual workers rarely faced the kind of self-recriminations felt by other victims of unemployment.[47] But the shared fate of the group had a negative aspect too. When economic loss occurs on a mass scale, affecting a whole town, it can be much harder for individuals to recover than when unemployment occurs on an individualized basis.[48] Singer workers who had to find new employment often found relatives and other members of their support networks in identical trouble. The local area was a poor place to try to rebuild since whatever resurgence was occurring was in comparatively low-paying service sector industries. These circumstances undoubtedly exacerbated racial antagonisms, since competition was keen for what remains in the way of jobs.

After decades of boomtown prosperity, Elizabeth faced the reality of deindustrialization as factory after factory closed its gates. Over time this altered the psychology of the Singer workers as they considered the city's reputation. Once known for its hardworking blue-collar people and industrial innovation, it was now known as a crumbling, decaying place of the past. The Singer closing exacerbated this sense of decline and created an aura of gloom.

The city's decline and the shutdown of the plant took on broader significance for the blue-collar workers, who have begun to wonder what this portends for their "kind." They have begun to wonder whether they are needed any longer in the postindustrial, service-dominated society. Thus the problem of finding a new job is embedded in a larger symbolic question: Do we have a place in postindustrial society or are we now wholly superfluous? Many Singer workers who are reemployed, in many cases in jobs related to the booming Newark Airport, have already found an answer.[49] Their destiny has been to join the growing ranks of service employees, and their new jobs are lower in salary, less secure, and less likely to come under union protection than their Singer jobs were. They have had to start all over again accruing seniority, and they face an unpredictable future.

Even those who have found new jobs with comparable wages and benefits and who do not therefore worry about near-term "extinction" are concerned about commitment. They wonder how much of themselves they should invest in their new jobs in case those should disappear someday too. One skilled carpenter who had found a new job in the construction industry wondered how confident he could be about its longevity:

> I'm not really scared about my situation now since I found a good job. But what if I put in ten years to this job and then they close down? I'd get nothing for retirement. I'd really be in trouble. It's just not like it used to be, when you stayed with a job until you retired.

While they once thought of themselves as settled for life, they now realize that nothing may be settled at all. They are people who felt an identification with Singer. Now they question how much identification any worker should have with his or her employer.

> The company made their money in this area and they became a worldwide financial power through the work of the people in Union County, New Jersey. And then they let them down like a bunch of garbage. . . . They used the community. . . . There's such a thing as takers and there's such things as givers. [Singer's] were the takers, and most large corporations are takers, except public relations covers it.

In coming to grips with the pragmatic consequences of the plant closure, the Singer workers have had to evaluate what the loss means to them and how it reflects upon fundamental changes in the American economy. They have done so by turning to the past—to tradition—not as a source of nostalgia but as a source of critique. Singer's history is one of profit and glory, they argue, because it cleaved to certain values basic to industrial dominance:

loyalty, craftsmanship, nepotism. Having forsaken these traditions, it was only a matter of time before the factory would close. As they read about the hundreds of shutdowns that have occurred in the last decade, the wholesale erosion of mining and steel towns, and America's balance-of-trade problems, they argue that these tragic outcomes are the ultimate "payment" for the collapse of these blue-collar traditions and values.

7

Middle-Class Women
in Trouble

Women are in double jeopardy in terms of downward mobility. Some, like their male counterparts, lose well-paid jobs and plunge from the middle class for that reason.[1] But for most middle-class women, one must look closer to home to find the main cause for downward mobility. It is in the aftermath of divorce that once-secure women find themselves sliding right out of the middle class. When men, who enjoy far greater earning power and job mobility than their wives, no longer contribute to household support, the "female-headed" families left behind are pushed into downward mobility.[2]

As Richard Peterson's research (1996) has shown, men experience a slight improvement in their standard of living following divorce, while women sustain a 27 percent standard of living decline.[3] Losses are particularly steep for middle-class women because they have more to lose than their poorer sisters.[4] Hence divorce, while a hardship for most people, often spells a dramatic slide in the standard of living to which most white-collar, suburban families are accustomed. They often face the prospect of moving to cheaper surroundings or the end of a secure hold on a college education for their children, all of which can have serious long term consequences.

A series of obstacles stand in the way of divorced mothers as they struggle to maintain a decent standard of living for their children. High on the list of hurdles they face is the difficulty of securing child support payments from fathers of their children. According to a Census Bureau study in the early 90s, 11.5 million single parents have custody of their children, though only 6.4 million have agreements in place for child support. Half of those single parents (3.2 million) received either partial support or none at all.[5]

Labor market segregation adds to the woes of the divorced woman trying to support her family, particularly if she has interrupted her career to raise small children.[6] For, as she returns to the job market, she often finds her prospects limited to jobs that are sex segregated and poorly paid. If her children are young, she must find child care for them while she is working, which increases the cost of supporting a family. Clerical workers, waitresses, sales clerks—these are the jobs open to women who lack professional credentials—and they do not, by themselves, pay enough to sustain a middle-class standard of living. And despite recent improvement in America's attitude toward working women, their wages are still comparatively low: In 1998 women still earned only seventy-six cents for every dollar earned by men.[7]

Legal reforms implemented in the 1970s—the end of alimony and the rise of no-fault divorce—once hailed as the equitable solution to property settlements, have only exacerbated the situation.[8] Among the most valuable property built up during marriage is the occupational training, the track record on the job, and the professional licenses that accrue to men while their wives are at home raising the family.[9] With these credentials, men can hold on to a middle-class lifestyle after divorce, while their wives are left behind with half the financial assets but without the occupational wherewithal to a comparable standard of living.[10]

These economic facts have contributed to "the feminization of poverty."[11] Welfare rolls are increasingly filled by women and their wages are still comparatively low: in 1998 women still earned only seventy-six cents for every dollar earned by men.[7]

children who have been abandoned economically by husbands and fathers. Many of these families were low income to start with, but a growing number of single-headed households are outcasts from the middle class who have suffered a wrenching dislocation. They have seen the end of affluence not in the guise of a pink slip—which is hard enough to bear—but in the form of marital dissolution. They must find their bearings as members of the new poor, while simultaneously coming to grips with the painful emotional loss of husbands and fathers. For these women and their children, downward mobility is cloaked in the disappointment of failed marriages, the financial irresponsibility of ex-husbands, and the difficulty of reconstructing the family in a new form which is still perceived as damaged.[12]

Jacqueline Johansen found all this out the hard way. She was married for twenty-five years to John Johansen, a dentist in northern California. She worked for a time to put him through school, but her main career was raising three children, something to which she devoted her full attention during the years John was compiling a professional track record in dentistry. His income continued to increase over the years, and it supported an affluent, country-club lifestyle. When he left Jacqueline for a younger woman, John was earning a big salary; Jacqueline was "earning" nothing, though she maintains she was working pretty hard. The divorce was a bitter affair, with lawyers battling on both sides. Once the dust settled, Jacqueline had the huge house (and a huge mortgage to go with it) and monthly support payments that will terminate when her children, who are in their mid- to late teens, turn twenty-one. Since Jacqueline lacks a college degree, she has only been able to find a part-time clerical job that pays a small salary that cannot begin to cover the expenses of three children and a big house. She is having trouble making ends meet and the child support payments are becoming increasingly erratic. She is adamant that her children go to college, but she has no idea how she will manage to pay for it. The pressures are enough to keep her awake at night, but her skills are not enough to do very much to change her long-term prospects for recovery. Slowly, but surely, Jacqueline is seeing the end of her tenure in the middle class. And, since she is forty-seven, it seems unlikely that things are going to improve with time.

Jacqueline's story has been repeated over and over again across the country. It has been the subject of countless academic studies and government reports. Politicians and advocates from women's groups have termed the situation a "public disgrace" and have warned that the nation's children are at risk.[13]

When downward mobility is generated by occupational disaster, the finger of blame must be pointed at forces that are in some sense abstract. But where divorce is the culprit, the causal connections are quite direct and personal. In these families, downward mobility is cast not in terms of the job market, the crisis atmosphere of a strike, or the changing nature of the American economy. Instead, dislocation is seen through the intimate lens of family life. Husbands who vowed to love, protect, and support their wives, now maneuver to protect their incomes from the demands of alimony or child support. Wives accustomed to the comforts of middle-class life—nice homes, good schools, freedom from worry and want—now see these mainstays pulled out from under them by the very men who were their most intimate and trusted partners.

Precisely because downward mobility is bound up with forces internal to the family, cultural concepts of what the family should be—of how men and women should treat each other, of what parents owe their children, and what adults can expect from their own parents in times of crisis—come to the fore. However, these expectations are not static and unchanging. Where family and gender roles are concerned, American culture has shifted, diverged, and turned back upon itself even in the space of this century.[14] Each generation of middle-class divorcées understands its fall from grace differently, through cultural expectations that are shaped by historical experience. Each cohort carries distinctive ideas about what women should expect in their own lives and the lives of their children.[15] The generations of American women who live side by side today, bring to every experience—be it downward mobility or good fortune—the aspirations and hopes that are born of the formative experiences they have had.

Middle-class divorcées of the 1980s belonged to two distinct periods of the nation's history. The members of the two generations whom I interviewed had much in common—they had all been homeowning wives of white collar husbands and were now divorced single mothers.[16] But they were daughters of different eras and therefore members of different cohorts. Hence they confronted the transition to downward mobility from different cultural vantage points.[17]

Depression Women

Women born in the late 1920s through the 1930s belong to a generation that, perhaps more than any other in recent memory, has experienced extremes of income and life-style: They could be called "children of the Great Depression" or "adults of affluence."[18] Their childhood was spent in grip of the most spectacular economic downturn in recent history. Their adult lives saw the country through its most impressive economic rebound: the post–World War II boom. This extraordinary biographical trajectory, from hardship to comfort, gave them a distinctive perspective—a generational worldview—which shaped their perceptions of divorce and downward mobility in their adult lives. But their story begins with the dark days of the 1930s.

The Depression cut across America's class boundaries: Financial disaster and traumatic downward mobility reached right into the stable middle class and took a devastating toll on much of the working class.[19] Economic insecurity and occupational dislocation spread like a virus throughout American society, with the burden falling most heavily on lower-income groups.[20]

Children of the 1930s were victims of economic deprivation in large numbers. Yet even those who escaped grinding poverty remember their fathers reduced to the dreaded dole. Their mothers were worried women who scrimped on the basics and took in laundry to earn extra money, trying to keep up hope when despair was epidemic and reason for optimism very scarce. From these childhood experiences, the Depression generation developed a keen appreciation for the difficulties of raising a family on too little money, insufficient and monotonous food, inadequate clothing, and the anxieties that these frustrations cause. Life had a precarious quality, and the insecurity of the period left its mark.[21]

Jennie Ames is in her fifties and the mother of two children. A slight, almost frail woman, she has lived most of her adult life in coastal California. But she was born and raised in the Midwest during the hard times when Dust Bowl refugees were dispossessed from the land, and poverty spread through the nation's breadbasket:

I grew up in the thirties on a farm in Minnesota, but my family lost the land during the Depression. After several years on the dole, Dad became a mechanic for the WPA. But we had to move around a lot. We never had any fresh fruit or vegetables during that whole time. At school there were soup lines and food handouts.

Jennie's mother raised chickens and took in washing to supplement the family's meager income. Ultimately her parents split up, and Jennie's mother went to work in a steel yard in the Northwest. Jennie came into adolescence in government housing. With the farm long since lost, her family never had a home of its own again.

Girls like Jennie, who grew up in hard times, were of necessity drawn into the family economy to help make ends meet.[22] As Depression households struggled to make what they could not buy—to can food, to sew clothes—girls were often pressed into household service, to take on chores that were, in times past, considered adult responsibilities.[23] Their contributions to family survival meant that the impact of economic loss was vividly clear to them even though they were just young girls in the thirties.

The 1950s, the period when most of the Depression women married and started their families, offered a stark contrast and a welcome relief to the economic uncertainty of the households they grew up in. Where their fathers struggled to earn a living as farmers, tailors, and laborers, their husbands—many of them beneficiaries of the GI Bill—donned the white collar of the engineer, the lawyer, the dentist, or the corporate manager. Money was a bit tight during their early married years, but they think of the time with nostalgia—the dinners of hot dogs and beans now remembered for the ways in which mutual sacrifice solidifies a marriage. Financial difficulties soon passed. Riding the wave of the postwar housing boom, inexpensive mortgage money, exploding birthrates, and the rising expectations of a whole generation of upwardly mobiles, Depression women ultimately laid claim to something their parents could only dream about: a suburban home.

To be a married woman in the middle class of the 1950s was to be sheltered from the world outside the home, preoccupied with endless mountains of diapers, neighborhood kaffeeklatsches, and the daily dilemmas of child rearing. Despite the fury later expressed by feminists over the segregation of women from the "public" sphere, and sarcastic portrayals of suburban matrons as mindless devotees of Tupperware parties, many women found the traditional nurturing role satisfying and rewarding. They were only too glad to leave responsibility for the family's economic survival to their husbands.

When, years later, these women found themselves on the receiving end of a divorce, the home-centered orientation of their generational culture left them quite unprepared to take on the role of breadwinner.[24] They had very limited experience with the paid labor market during the years of their marriages, and few had marketable employment skills at the time of divorce.[25] Most of these divorcées had dependent adolescents to take care of and were at the age where their career prospects were hardly glowing. They had not expected to need careers, since their generation defined occupational success as a man's concern. Now that it was their problem to support the family, they were ill equipped to do so.

Women of the Sixties

By the time the next generation of women was born, the hardships of the Depression were history. The middle class was in full bloom, with high expectations for continued prosperity. In contrast to the Depression generation, the women I interviewed who were born after World War II and into the early 1950s spent their childhood years in homes free of economic hardship.[26] Their fathers were white-collar managers or professionals, and their mothers were typically full-time homemakers.

These postwar women married in their twenties, and by the time they divorced, most had one or two young children. Their labor-force experience was more extensive than the Depression generation: Most had worked until the birth of their first child and intermittently thereafter, supporting husbands who were busy completing college degrees. While they had somewhat more education than their Depression-era counterparts, few had finished college.

Products of the affluent fifties and sixties, this younger group did not experience the steep ascent in income and standard of living common to their older counterparts. They left the middle-class homes of their childhood for comparable lifestyles as married women. Thus, while both generations of women ended up in roughly the same economic position during their married years—middle-class wives with white-collar husbands—the trajectories that brought them to this point were quite different.

Marilyn Harris grew up in the Los Angeles area in the 1950s and 1960s, where her father was a successful accountant and her mother worked on occasion as his assistant. The five-bedroom, three-story house Marilyn lived in testified to the family's secure position. Looking back, Marilyn sees herself as having been cosseted and pampered, but no more so than the other girls in her neighborhood, who routinely had cars of their own and wardrobes bursting with the latest fashions.

When Marilyn got married at the age of nineteen, she quit school and took a job as a receptionist to support her husband while he finished a business degree. His career as a CPA and a real estate investor made it possible for them to move from their newlywed apartment into successively larger San Fernando Valley ranch houses. The couple steadily accumulated the resources and property that Marilyn was entirely familiar with from her own upbringing. When her marriage collapsed in the late 1970s, Marilyn found herself face to face with economic hardship for the first time in her life: "I grew up in the middle or upper middle class. If my parents had financial problems, I didn't know about it. I had everything I wanted. All of a sudden, here I am with three kids and no money. It's a total shock."

The Depression generation was seasoned in the ways of economic dislocation, while for Marilyn, and most other postwar daughters of the middle class, divorce was their first taste of hardship. Little in their background had prepared them for it; downward mobility was not part of the plan.

No description of the younger generation would be complete without emphasizing the political culture that swirled around them in the late 1960s and early 1970s. The era of political idealism and youthful rebellion that followed on the heels of the civil rights movement and the War on Poverty catalyzed a generation of students unwilling to follow the counsel of their elders. The "war at home," the campaign to wrest American troops out of Vietnam, polarized the nation but provided many young people with a feeling of involvement and political commitment. The feminist movement burst on the scene, challenging traditional dictates that kept women cloistered in the kitchen and away from the boardroom. It was a period of intense turmoil that irritated many but provided a distinctive shape to another generational culture. For while the war in Vietnam slowly takes its place in history, the legacy of the period is found in a spirit of social change that the "Sixties generation" has carried into its adult years.[27]

While upward mobility was a key element in the lives and experiences of those women born into the depression, liberal politics and social concerns provided a language for the sixties women. As Todd Gitlin, a sociologist who was once the leader of the Students for a Democratic Society (SDS), has expressed it:

> [The sixties] generation sought to remake the world and themselves. Many were the routes, many the extravagances. No authority was exempt from scrutiny, affront, devaluation. It became normal, though not universal, to experiment with drugs, sex and politics. Closets, minds and roads to transcendence, glory, utopia and sheer fun were opened.[28]

One did not have to be a political activist to glean from the experience of the 1960s a feeling that life could and should depart from tradition. Even those women who initially followed paths familiar to their mothers—marriage and a family—were influenced by social movements that promised change, particularly feminism. It bequeathed to them a language for casting their lives in the aftermath of divorce as dedicated to "autonomy," "independence," "self-determination," and "equity." For some the discourse of the 1960s became meaningful only after the fact. But their generational culture bequeathed to them attitudes, values, and symbols they drew upon in their time of need.

The Meaning of Economic Loss

Dramatic income loss followed on the heels of divorce for both generations of women. Their household incomes fell to levels approximately one-third to one-half what they had been during their married years, which approximated what was then the national average for divorced women from middle-income groups.[29] The dynamics of downward mobility were similar for the two generations, but their perceptions of the experience were strikingly different. For those raised in the Depression era, the steep losses and plummeting standard of living provoked fear and anxiety. They worried and fretted over how to make ends meet. Yet they were hardly strangers to bad times. Having come through the Depression, these women knew how to budget, bargain hunt, and bake; they were able to cook inexpensive meats or to stretch meals. They had an eye for sturdy goods and were able to make new clothes and mend old ones. They had sewing machines—virtually all of them Singers—an item considered essential for a married woman's household in the late forties and the fifties, and they knew how to use them. Even during the affluent years of their married lives, they had managed household finances with the caution borne of an early brush with relative deprivation.

The pragmatic advantages of early exposure to hardship were more than balanced by the harsh memories the Depression women had of their early encounter with economic disaster. Divorce thrust them backward, against their will, into the kind of life they had deliberately set out to leave behind years before. For those whose husbands initiated the move toward divorce, financial calamity added insult to emotional injury. Yet even those women who were the prime movers in divorce were shaken by the backward slide from stable middle class to uncertain poor, in part because it was such an unwelcome reminder of the past.

Jennie Ames, the Depression child whose family farm went under, was married for thirty years to a man who made a living as a civil service engineer. They lived a comfortable but not opulent life in a sleepy coastal town, until the children grew up and the marriage dissolved. Jennie had held intermittent part-time jobs as the children reached their teen years, but she was never a serious career woman. The end of her marriage found her with very little to live on and very little to work with in the way of job skills. She found a part-time receptionist job for a local doctor, which helped. Nevertheless her standard of living plummeted to the point where the end of the month barely saw her to the end of the food budget. And all this had a disquietingly familiar ring: "You know, I've been there. I've seen some hard times and it wasn't pleasant. Sometimes when I get low on money now, I get very nervous remembering [the Depression] and all those years we went without."

For many women in the Depression generation, the meaning of downward mobility crystallized in their feelings about the family home, their almost desperate concern to hold on to it at all cost. For Jacqueline Johansen, the dentist's ex-wife, the prospect of having to give up her house was depressing in the extreme because it was a tangible representation of personal accomplishment:

"Sometimes I think I should sell my house so I'd have some more money for the kids. But I just can't do it. It took years to afford this place. We had to work hard and save to get it. I just can't see giving all that up."

Jacqueline took pride in her home as a visible legacy of her family's entry into the burgeoning middle class of the 1950s. Becoming a homeowner meant more to her than just having a roof over the family's head or a sound investment. It was for her, and for others who grew up on farms gone to foreclosure or in crowded city tenements, a statement of arrival. The prospect of seeing this anchor of middle-class life stolen away in the wake of divorce was frightening. For those who were, in the end, forced to sell, it was a bitter pill to swallow.

Donna Sanders spent all her married life in the Pacific Northwest, where her husband worked in his family's lumber business. They were married for over thirty years when everything fell apart. Donna held on to the home they had lived in, but three years after the divorce became final, her ex-husband stopped making the mortgage payments. Though Donna took him to court, the judge refused to press him because business was bad. Donna had no choice but to sell: "I lived in that house for twenty years. I raised all my kids in it. I really loved the place and it broke my heart to have to sell it, especially since I can't afford to live anywhere as nice as that. I probably never will."

For Donna, the family home meant security, a rock upon which to build a life in the mainstream middle class. It was a refuge from the vicissitudes of the outside world. Beyond this, the house symbolized her family's long-term integrity through time and across generations. Holiday gatherings in "the family home" were ritual occasions that reaffirmed the continuity of the family. Without it, the family had no center: no familiar place for children to come home to once they have left the nest, no repository of memories of growing up or growing old. As another divorcée resistant to selling out commented: "I want my grandchildren to be able to come here, to know this is the family home." This is a sentiment close to the hearts of most intact families; it achieves even greater salience when marital disruption threatens to destroy a family's sense of integrity and stability.

The Depression generation made great sacrifices in other areas of domestic spending in order to hold on to their homes after divorce, even when they might have been better off (financially) had they sold out. However, those who kept their homes while their bank accounts dwindled could not afford to maintain them properly. Over time, the appearance of the houses deteriorated, a transformation house-proud women were loath to see. Jacqueline Johansen held on to her house, but she had to sit by and watch it grow shabbier with every passing month: "I have no money to fix up the house. Everything in it is destroyed now. The roof leaks and I can't afford to fix it. It was my dream house; now the image is being destroyed and I can't do anything to stop it." Shingles fall off, paint peels, carpets wear thin, and fancy towels go threadbare. These barometers of decline force a daily confrontation between a woman's expectations for a life of comfort and the truth of downward mobility. The more run-down the home, the more mothers feel their grip on the middle class slipping. Powerless to stop the decline, they find themselves unwilling witnesses to the gradual destruction of their own dreams and aspirations as they are expressed in their homes.

Downward mobility evoked a rather different response from the sixties generation. While they certainly felt the brunt of income loss, they had neither the past history of the Depression years to remind them of financial hardship, nor a background of hard-fought ascendance into the middle class. They did not speak of sliding backward. On the contrary, their perspective of downward mobility was shaped by the sixties with its emphasis on nonmaterialistic lifestyles.

Although they were upset and angry about the day-to-day trials of making ends meet, there was an undercurrent in the sixties women that found some positive value in the need to scale back on consumption. Divorce and downward mobility forced them to live a more meaningful existence, one that stresses the value of friends, education, or personal autonomy over the value of things. Many spoke in disparaging terms of the "consumerism" of their married years and lamented the focus on material "things" (fancy homes, cars, clothes) that had dominated their marriages. Too little time had been devoted to the "real" or important things in life. As Marilyn Harris put it: "Money destroyed my marriage. All my husband wanted was to accumulate more real estate. We had no emotional relationship. Everything was bent toward things. Money to me now is this ugly thing." In the aftermath of divorce, she wanted to rid herself and her children of these "warped" values, replacing them with more "authentic" preoccupations:

Sometimes I feel that I don't want my kids to see all that material junk on TV. I don't want them to want all those things. The world is sick from all that stuff. . . . People are the most important thing, not all the possessions. I hope the experience of living without will help my children to learn that.

Downward mobility caused them to reconsider the superficiality of their married ways and to develop alternative lifestyles. The cultural framework that emerged out of the tumult of the 1960s downplayed symbols of middle-class status and highlighted minimalist concepts of material well-being.[30] It played up the value of self-enhancement, of natural living, and of human relations. In a sense, divorce pushed them back toward the values that lay at the heart of their generational culture.

Sixties women faced less rewarding consequences of downward mobility, but they were qualitatively different from those that preoccupied the Depression generation. The mothers in the sixties cohort were less worried about losing their own grip on the middle class. Their anxieties were reserved for their children, for the ways in which their kids were unfairly deprived by an abrupt descent into downward mobility.

Gina Palmino, an administrative assistant in her mid-thirties, is raising her sons in coastal northern California. In the aftermath of her divorce, she has been able to hold on to her Victorian house, but the quality of life she can provide for her children causes her concern:

It really hurts me to have to say to my kids, "I'm sorry but that's enough orange juice for now." I hate to have to limit them—they're growing and they need things. But orange juice is expensive and I have to ration it . . . I know that I had a lot of things that I'd like my kids to have now.

Where the Depression generation focussed on the meaning of downward mobility for their own class identity, Gina's generation worried about how relative deprivation was affecting their youngsters. The difference can be explained in part by the divergent positions in the domestic cycle the families occupied when they divorced.[31] Sixties mothers, with young children to care for, were burdened by a sense of responsibility to provide the comforts considered important in the life of a young middle class child—books, toys, clothes, healthy food, and the like. Having experienced the benefits of middle-class life in their own childhoods, they felt they owed it to their kids to reciprocate across the generations. Downward mobility made it almost impossible to follow through.

Because the sixties women were raised in secure surroundings, they lacked survival skills that came naturally to the Depression generation. Some were angry or frustrated that they had had so little experience in "coping with the real world" and blamed their own parents for sheltering them. Karen Stein grew up in northern California, the daughter of a prosperous lawyer. By the time she was sixteen, she had her own car, her own phone, and little exposure to want:

> I grew up in very comfortable surroundings. . . . My background really affects me now. I was never prepared for how to deal with the situation I find myself in now: a low income and raising three kids. My parents just didn't prepare me for reality. I got cheated out of that training.

Karen's confrontation with downward mobility, and the realization that she was poorly equipped to contend with it, led her to impress on her own children a greater dose of realism than she had been raised with. She was especially adamant about the need to sharpen her daughter's survival skills, lest she become too easily dependent on men in later years: "I don't want my kids to ever have to be dependent on anyone, especially my daughter. . . . I don't want her to go through what I went through. [This] is a very important experience. My kids will all be better off for what they've had to go through."

The idiom within which the sixties generation reacted to downward mobility was clearly at odds with that of the Depression women. The difference in their ages, points in the child-rearing cycle, and prospects for reemployment and remarriage played an important role in the divergence between the two generations of women. But these differences were articulated in terms of the values and expectations born of the historical periods in which each group came of age.

Men, Money, and the Meaning of Parental Responsibility

Of necessity, downwardly mobile divorcées went to work, and were justifiably proud of keeping their families afloat financially. Yet most had no choice but to retain economic ties to their ex-husbands in the form of alimony or child support. These payments were generally slow or delinquent in coming, court orders notwithstanding.[32] Mothers tried to remedy the situation through costly visits to lawyers in an attempt to pressure their former husbands into compliance. Most despaired of changing the situation, either because the expense of prosecuting a delinquent spouse was prohibitive or because they worried the judge would alter the original decree to their detriment.

Mothers in both generations looked upon fathers' failures to meet their financial obligations as a shocking disregard for the material and emotional welfare of their children.[33] Since fathers were no longer present in the day-to-day lives of their children, money became a symbolic barometer of their continuing affection and nurturance.[34] Signs of resistance—delayed payments, bounced checks, legal maneuvering—were taken as indications that fathers no longer cared what became of their children:

> When my ex-husband doesn't send money for the kids it makes me feel like . . . how can you have children, how can you produce a family and then turn your back and not even worry about where their food is coming from? That's not the way a real father should act! A real father doesn't stop caring about his kids just because he isn't there anymore. . . .

Some researchers have argued that as a group, divorced women are frustrated by their continued dependence on former spouses.[35] But generalizations of this sort ignore the differences between generations in what they expect of relations between men and women, even in the aftermath of divorce. The depression women were *not* resentful of their financial "dependence" on ex-husbands. As Donna Sanders saw it, alimony was an entitlement for the years she devoted to child rearing and homemaking:[36]

> We were married for thirty-two years when we got divorced. I raised four children, and during that whole time I worked hard for the family and didn't do much that was just for myself. All I asked for after thirty-two years was four years of support so I could try to go back to school and make something of myself. . . . I think he owes me for all those years. I did my "job," now he should do his and take care of me at least until I can take care of myself.

The financial distress and plummeting standard of living simply compounded the Depression generation's emotional isolation and despair at having to face a harsh world all alone. Being forced to take on responsibility for their family's financial well-being was at odds with a lifetime of expectations built around being taken care of.[37] Their marriages had shattered, but their traditional view that a woman's life is to be lived in the company of a man did not die. Their desire to be sheltered from the world and "saved" from the permanent fate of downward mobility grew stronger as the depth of their economic slump dragged them farther and farther away from the middle class. They resented their former husbands for putting them through downward mobility, and hoped to find white knights who would pull them out of the quagmire. As Jacqueline Johansen put it: "Not having money means 'I'm it.' Everything has to come from me. But I don't want to work . . . what I really want is to be rescued by a man. It wasn't my choice to be independent and I don't like it." Remarriage appeared to be one of the few avenues out of downward mobility and none of the Depression women were worried that it would make them unnaturally dependent.

Sixties women had a different perspective.[38] They were adamant about the importance of holding their ex-husbands to their child support obligations, but they *did* resent having to rely on them. The dependency seemed to drag out the unequal power relations that often characterized their married lives. Marilyn Harris grew increasingly bitter about the way she had to beg and cajole her ex-husband to give her the funds she was legally entitled to:

> [My ex-husband] controlled everything having to do with money when we were together. For me it was always, "Can I have this? Can I have that?" I had to ask for money to buy underwear. I was negated. That was one of the biggest problems in our marriage: his control over money. I hated it then, and I hate it even more when it happens now. He never willingly gives me what he owes [in child support]. He makes me ask for it and plead.

The sixties women searched for a plan of "liberation," a way of gaining the credentials necessary for careers that would generate enough income to free them from dependency. They confronted downward mobility as a form of bondage and a form of freedom: they had to manage with fewer resources but they could control what they had more completely than they had in their married lives.[39] Getting their hands on the money they were due was a source of continued irritation, but once it was theirs, they were delighted to discover that, for the first time, they were entirely able to control the expenditures in their own households.[40]

Statistics show that younger divorcées are far more likely to remarry than older ones.[41] Yet, the sixties generation was deeply ambivalent about the prospect. The women's movement of the 1970s had made its mark on them in the form of an urge to be autonomous and self-sufficient.[42] Remarriage, or a "long-term relationship," was fraught with danger. It could reverse the control they had come to enjoy over the domestic environment in the wake of divorce and render them once again creatures of dependency. As one young woman put it: "It's hard for me [now] to take money from anyone. . . . I want to be self-sufficient and not owe anybody anything. . . . I want to be in a place where I don't need someone to take over my financial problems. If I ever get married again, I want to be pretty . . . stable." Forging a new emotional life was an important priority for the sixties generation, but they were wary that reestablishing intimate ties with men would compromise their developing sense of independence. Romantic partnership, if it was to happen at all, would have to develop on an egalitarian footing.

How Thick Is Blood?

Downward mobility also transformed the relations between divorced mothers and their parents. Before divorce, financial relationships between married daughters and their parents were confined to occasional gifts that did not have to be reciprocated.[43] After divorce, some parents began to make regular contributions to the maintenance of their divorced daughters and dependent grandchildren.[44] This proved to be a vital safety net, but it was only available to the younger divorcées, who could be redefined as daughters again. They received money, clothing, free child care, and food from their mothers and fathers on a fairly routine basis.[45] These resources enabled them to indulge (occasionally) in "essential luxuries": items that would be routinely available in comfortable middle-class homes, but that would have been out of reach for downwardly mobile divorced households on their own steam.

To avoid compromising their daughters' autonomy, grandparents would define the assistance as presents to their grandchildren. These "presents" often made the difference between meeting the family's needs and going without. Yet the sixties women discovered that only one set of grandparents was likely to come through: their own parents. Their ex-husband's parents quickly dropped out of the picture. American kinship is, in anthropological parlance, bilateral.[46] That is, we trace our descent equally through the mother's and the father's bloodlines, and a child is equally related to both sets of grandparents. Yet the skew in the help offered in the wake of divorce shows how weak the link can be between grandchildren and their paternal kin. The bonds between children and their father's kin are fragile in the face of the strain divorce imposes between divorced women and their former in-laws.[47]

There were clearly practical benefits to the rekindling of financial ties between the sixties women and their parents. The extra money made it possible to pretend, on occasion, that divorce had not irrevocably shut them out of the middle class. But emotional and symbolic considerations were equally important. Divorced women are an anomaly in the kinship system of the middle class, since they are neither fully daughters nor fully wives. The disruption of social identity causes divorced women—of all generations—to feel somewhat at sea. The Victorian stigma that once surrounded divorce has faded in the face of the large proportion of American marriages that founder. Divorced women no longer suffer the "taint" of immorality that surrounded them in earlier times, but they walk through a cultural badlands nonetheless.[48] For although the single-parent family is now a widespread form, it is not fully integrated into the cultural landscape. The divorced mother and her children are perceived as "not whole" since "the couple" stands at the center of middle-class notions of the nuclear family.[49] This provides the impetus for divorced women to reclaim the only position in the family structure to which they remain legitimately entitled, that of the daughter.

Yet culture intervenes to determine who among divorcées can successfully recapture this place in the kinship system. The sixties generation could lay claim to daughterhood since they were still young enough to fit the image of the subordinate that is the lot of all "real" daughters. The Depression women were rarely so fortunate. Women in their forties and fifties with older children do not fit the bill of the dependent, subordinate daughter. Even if they want to be reincorporated into their families of origin, they are beyond the threshold of our cultural conceptions of daughterhood.[50]

Parents of Depression generation divorcées were not in a position to help them in matters material or social. Now elderly, they had survived the 1930s as adults (not as children) and were lower in economic status for most of their lives than their adult daughters, who reaped the benefits of the postwar boom. By the time their daughters were divorced and in their forties and fifties, these parents were retired, and living on social security—a very modest income that left little extra to turn over to a struggling divorcée. In fact, many of these mature daughters were under pressure to assist their elderly parents.[51]

There is a tragic irony here. The older her children, the greater the expenses a divorced mother faces in raising them. Yet the older the divorced mother, the more problematic her job prospects.[52] Typically therefore, the Depression women were faced with higher expenditures for households and weaker career possibilities than the sixties women. Yet the Depression generation was hamstrung by symbolic and material barriers that made it all but impossible to get help from their kinsmen of the sort routinely available to younger divorcées with small children. What's more, they could not expect to fit back into their parental households and weather downward mobility in the understanding embrace of Mom and Dad. They were, compared to their younger counterparts, on their own.

Since downwardly mobile divorcées face financial adversity, one might expect they would turn to the kinds of adaptive strategies sustained by the poor, who live in a constant state of economic insecurity. Urban anthropologists have described the ways in which the poor develop complex networks of exchange partners—friends and family—to make it through the month.[53] Clothing, food, money, furniture, and child care circulate among sisters, mothers, cousins, and unrelated women-friends in poverty areas. Partners in exchange, who respond to a constant stream of requests for help, know that they have a network of beneficiaries they will be able to rely on when they are themselves in need. These networks act as real "safety nets" through the spreading of resources from those momentarily blessed with a small surplus to those who are caught up short. The obligation to reciprocate guarantees that today's "giver" can expect to be tomorrow's "receiver," should she need to call on an exchange partner for help. These are adaptive responses to the fluctuating resources that the urban poor have to contend with on a daily basis.[54]

The social organization of middle-class families works against the kinds of reciprocal exchanges that are the lifeblood of the urban poor.[55] "Lateral" sharing networks—exchange links to siblings, cousins, and "family friends"—do not surface in the middle class. Poor families do not restrict their networks to blood relations or marital ties, strictly defined. They expand the universe of exchange to include friends and neighbors who, in time, become close enough to achieve the status of "fictive kin," described in phrases like "going for cousins" or "going for sisters." By contrast, the flow of resources to a middle-class divorcée is narrow, where it exists at all. It comes from only one source—her parents—on anything approaching a regular basis. And it is not really an exchange, for the divorced woman is not obliged to reciprocate. Indeed, it is a cultural condition of receiving this aid that she be defined as a dependent, (even if she no longer lives in her parents' home), and dependents are not bound by the conventions of reciprocity.

The truncated structure of the middle-class mothers' support network differs from the expansive system of families in poverty for several reasons. Poor women (indeed, poor families) are forced to keep constant watch over their economic environment, maximizing their range of options within a widespread network, because although they never know precisely when they'll need help, they do know that day always comes. They give, knowing that they will someday need to receive, because their world is defined by scarcity and unpredictable crises. By contrast, middle-class women encounter financial stress as a sudden shock, not as an expectation. Intact middle-class families are virtually never involved in reciprocal exchange because the majority of them do not face unpredictable bouts of scarcity.[56] Hence when divorce strikes, middle-class women find themselves lacking the built-in support systems which poor women have had to maintain throughout their domestic lives. People adapt to foreseeable crisis situations; when crises are not part of the repertoire of daily experience, they are caught unaware and unprepared. And despite the widespread occurrence of divorce in the middle class, it remains an event for which few middle-class people prepare in advance.

Support networks also depend upon the control which participants exercise over economic resources. Poor black women are the linchpins of sharing networks in part because historically they have enjoyed better job prospects than black men and because

they are the principal recipients of government benefits. These
are meager resources, but they are more dependable than those
that flow to ghetto men, whose jobs tend to be seasonal, poorly
paid, and prone to frequent layoffs.[57] Men are important in another sense: Through the father of her children, a woman gains
access to a whole new range of swapping partners—his female
relatives. But because they do not control dependable resources,
men are not central figures in resource networks. These factors
combine to place poor, black women at the center of the exchange
systems that sustain their households.

Middle-class women rarely occupy the same pivotal economic
role in their marital households. They spend many more years
in nuclear families where husbands are the principal wage,
earners.[58] They do not control the principal resources of the household in the same way that women who are recipients of public assistance income do. In this respect, middle-class women occupy a
less central location in the economic structure of their communities and their families prior to divorce. Hence, even if they have
social ties that could serve as the raw material for a sharing network, they lack control over the resources that might potentially
flow into the system.

Middle-class women also tend to lack the independent social
ties that are the foundation of a sharing network. Their predivorce
friendship patterns revolve around couples. This leaves divorcées
little raw material to shape into an exchange system when downward mobility looms ahead. Those "women friends" they do have,
who might potentially fit into support networks, are often helpful
in a pinch, but they are off limits where money is concerned.
Middle-class culture sharply separates the realms of friendship
and money. This cultural barrier leaves middle-class women unable to link themselves effectively to others who might cushion
the blows of downward mobility.[59]

Children of Divorce

Downward mobility is an unavoidable fact of life for the "divorced
child," and there is evidence to suggest that the greatest relative
deprivation of all descends on middle class children who are bystanders to broken marriages.[60] But children's responses to downward mobility vary according to the particular strategies their

mothers elect in accommodating to financial troubles, and according to the children's ages at the time of divorce.[61] Because they were young and not yet members of peer groups that might dilute the intensity of the mother-child bond, the children of the sixties divorcées were very close to their mothers. The absence of their fathers generated in many of these young kids a fierce attachment to the one parent still at home: Mommy.[62] Mothers and their young children were brought together in a particularly intimate, dependent, and emotionally charged environment. This afforded the kids a close vantage point from which to observe just how hard it was for their mothers to cope with financial stress.

Young children could see that their mothers were worried and preoccupied over how to make ends meet.[63] "We can't afford it," was a refrain most frequently heard when they went shopping for food, clothes, or toys. The message was not lost even on very young children, who tried to reassure their mothers that they could "do their part" for family survival. Jane Morgan, a secretary struggling to get by on a part-time salary and sporadic child support had a six-year-old son and a four-year-old daughter. She found herself unable to provide for them in the ways she felt most appropriate and could not hide her frustration:

> My son heard me crying one night and asked what was wrong. I told him I was upset that I couldn't give him the things he wants, like a bicycle. I felt he deserved to have these things and it wasn't fair to have to deny him. He put his arms around my neck and told me not to worry. He said "It's worse for you, Mommy."

Young children were not forever tolerant of hardship, but they were capable of offering sympathy beyond their years.

Like the progeny of downwardly mobile managers, the children in divorced families were influenced by an early brush with financial hardship as they developed their own values. Ironically, they were often at loggerheads with their mothers. The sixties mothers, who were "products" of middle-class affluence (and the counterculture of their own youth), downplayed materialism. They wanted to see their children develop "alternative" values, to learn to appreciate the more important things in life. Their children, who had experienced a fall down the class ladder of American society, were adamant about finding a way out of disaster. Where children in other families seemed to be focused on superheroes and Barbie dolls, the children of downwardly mobile divorced families seemed to be unduly fixated on the desire to get rich. As Marilyn Harris explained: "My oldest boy [age 9] thinks money is extremely important. He is constantly talking about it. Regardless of what I want for him, he'll probably do something that will lead into making a lot of money." In a sense, the children of divorce had experienced their own private economic depression, and like the generation of the Great Depression, they respond by focussing on upward mobility. Their middle-class mothers met this emphasis with great ambivalence. On the one hand, the sixties mothers believed in the importance of self-reliance and hoped the experience of financial distress would drive home to their kids the importance of being able to fend for oneself. On the other hand, like most parents, they wanted their children to embrace values like their own and were alienated from—not to say dismayed by—the Horatio Alger–like desires of their younger children.

Children who were adolescents at the time of divorce—whose mothers were members of the Depression generation—responded differently to downward mobility. Like teenagers in stable families, they were less tightly bound to their mothers and more heavily invested in the exploits and mores of peer groups.[64] They were oriented toward the world outside the household and were correspondingly less attentive to the transformations occuring within.[65] Their disengagement took on a larger emotional significance in the eyes of their divorced mothers, who looked to their older children as sources of emotional support in times of financial distress, only to find them preoccupied with their own lives:[66]

> My daughter doesn't seem very concerned about the problems I have making ends meet. She is more interested in her friends and in boys. Sometimes I wish she'd think about how hard it is to get by, but I guess that's just the way high school kids are.

The particular set of values which emerged from the teen peer experience was strongly influenced by the "adaptive strategy"— the deliberate plans—that Depression generation mothers pursued in adjusting their families to downward mobility.[67] Two divergent approaches—one stressing continuity with the family's past, the other emphasizing a rapid departure from the "old life"—developed.

Many mothers held on to the old family home, sometimes out of financial necessity: Low mortgages are cheaper to meet than high rents that reflect the recent escalation in housing costs. But most stayed put in an effort to provide their children with as much *social* continuity as possible, believing they needed to protect their kids from any more disruption than they had already faced as a result of divorce.[68] As one mother put it: "Keeping this house was very important. We got to stay in the same community where the boys go to school. Their life-style really wasn't upset since we stayed here. We still live in that middle-class environment."

This strategy often backfired. Instead of forcing an adjustment to downward mobility, protecting teenagers from disruption enabled them to maintain social aspirations and expectations that were inconsistent with the new realities of downward mobility. Staying in the same neighborhood made it possible for teens to hold on to their old friends, but it also drew them into an affluent lifestyle that their divorced mothers could not bankroll.[69] This led to bitter conflict between divorced mothers and their teenagers:

> My children don't seem to realize that we can't afford the kinds of things we had before. They are always asking me for money or clothes, and they sulk if I don't give it to them. . . . What can I do? We can't live the way we used to, and they can't seem to understand that!

Unable to keep up appearances next to their well-heeled peers, adolescents turned their fury toward their fathers, who seemed to be living comfortably while the rest of the family fell from middle class to poor.[70] Resentment built in those teenagers who felt that their old life-style would be within reach if their noncustodial fathers would simply share "the family's wealth" more equitably. Their mothers often agreed. Others saw their fathers as generous because they occasionally provided fancy clothes, while their mothers seemed stingy by comparison as they struggled to provide daily food and shelter.

Because the family is often conceived of as a single unit, a social universe of its own, researchers often assume that families adapt to crises like divorce in a collective fashion.[71] But the notion that parents and children respond to divorce in unison is too simplistic. They live together under one roof, yet each family member moves in different social orbits and cultural directions. For the most part, mothers tried to come to grips with the reality of downward mobility. They understood all too well that they could not sustain the standard of living they had had in their married days. But those who tried to make the adjustment while remaining in the old neighborhood often found that their children failed to bring their expectations into line with the financial realities of the downwardly mobile household. Instead, they continued to behave as if the outside world of their affluent peers defined their own circumstances in life. In maintaining continuity with the past, divorced mothers had unwittingly enabled their adolescents to develop a mentality of entitlement, the feeling that parents "owe" their kids an elevated standard of living.[72]

Boys who stayed in the old neighborhood often became absorbed into upper-middle-class peer groups preoccupied with leisure pursuits. Aspects of this adolescent culture can drive perfectly stable, affluent parents to distraction. But the behavior of these cliques was particularly worrisome for downwardly mobile divorcées of the Depression generation. Their sons were not developing a "hunger" for success, the drive crucial for upward mobility and integral to the personalities of the men the mothers most admired in their own generation. Well aware that they would be unable to transfer financial or professional advantages to their sons, as they might have when they were married, the mothers fretted over their sons' "lackadaisical" attitudes.

Adolescent girls responded to downward mobility in their own fashion. Many developed close attachments to boyfriends that provoked cries of protest from their downwardly mobile mothers.[73] Apart from generational differences in sexual mores, Depression women worried about their daughters' apparent desires to "slip" into traditional male-female relations (capped, in some instances, by early marriages). The mothers saw themselves as "traditional" women and did not want their daughters to suffer the liabilities they had endured. They aspired for their daughters to become "modern": independent, self-reliant, and capable of providing for themselves in ways the divorced mothers had not been. Yet their daughters responded to the insecurity of parental divorce by seeking a source of stability external to the household: a man.[74]

Many families rejected continuity with the past and adjusted to downward mobility by cutting loose from their history. They sold their houses in order to cash in on the equity, escape high mortgage rates, and make a new start in unfamiliar, typically poorer neighborhoods, where their pasts were unknown.[75] Some found that moving left them strangers in a strange land: The physical and social differences between the neighborhoods of the past and the present left them isolated and a bit confused over the loss of their old social rank.[76] Markers of their middle-class upbringing imposed barriers between them and the more working-class peers whom they met in school and on the streets. Jean Seligman grew up in a fashionable part of San Francisco, the child of two educated, cultivated, parents. After her parents separated, she moved to progressively poorer areas of Southern California, where she found herself quite distinctly marked by her origins. Reminiscing years later about the transition, she noted:

> Kids in the neighborhood used to say to me, "You talk funny. You don't talk like us. Why are you using big words, just to show off?" I was raised to speak well. I really didn't know any other way to speak. It was a day-to-day struggle living in a working-class neighborhood and feeling like such an outcast. You know, kids there beat each other up as a major social activity. You can't imagine how different it was from the place I grew up in.

Some adolescents suggested that major adjustments were not worth the effort because their old identities were "real" and these new circumstances were an aberration somehow soon to pass. As Jean put it: "I always had the feeling that it wouldn't always be like that. Sometime we'd get back to a place where everyone acted and spoke just like I did. But it never happened." The discomfort that middle-class kids felt in less affluent surroundings occasionally encouraged closer bonding to their mothers. Peer relations had been interrupted, opening a brief "window of opportunity" for their mothers. But others fitted right in to their new neighborhoods, found new friends, and experienced the relief of no longer having to live poor in the wealthy communities they had come from.

*

The two generations of downwardly mobile divorcées faced fundamentally different opportunities and demands, in part because their families encountered divorce at different points in the domestic cycle. While both "sets" of mothers and children were downwardly mobile in the early 1980s, one generation consisted of single mothers who were themselves fairly young and who had young children, while the other set was older and had adolescent children. These differences naturally molded relations between mothers and children, shaping the character of the emotional bonds tying them together as well as the relative influence of family versus peers.

Age differences, as they are culturally defined, also affected linkages between the divorced women and their own parents. Each generation had to contend with different prospects in the labor market and different opportunities for remarriage. However, *cultural* differences between the cohorts—those shaped by the historical experiences particular to each—define what age differences or domestic cycle positions mean. Generation-bound experience provides a cultural universe within which these groups of women live. Their values and fears, their views of appropriate gender roles, their hopes for their children, and their expectations for their own futures, are products of formative historical events that shaped their lives.

The Depression generation emerged from an early brush with economic disaster to find itself in the middle of one of the greatest boom periods in the country's history and the rush toward domesticity that followed in the wake of World War II. Women were supposed to get out of the workplace, get back to the kitchen, have lots of babies, and settle down to a family life underwritten by their husbands' rising prospects. The sixties generation—products of the postwar baby boom—came of age in a period of affluence and cultural turmoil. Tradition was out, protest was in, and although they did marry and settle down, their background is one that casts a jaundiced eye on the conservatism of the 1950s. Whatever the women's movement may have meant to them when they were young brides, it came to have greater force in their lives as they struggled with the exigencies of single parenthood.

The perceptions of these two generations about what a woman should expect or desire in life—from her man, for her children, and for herself—were shaped by the generational culture in which they had been steeped. It is this changing American culture that defines social roles. The divorced woman of fifty-five (in the 1980s), who grew up in the milieu of the Depression, has one vision of appropriate roles for herself that is different from that of the generation of the sixties. One imagines that when the 60s generation reaches middle age (after the turn of the twenty-first century), their vision of what they want in life for themselves and their loved ones will differ from that of the Depression cohort.[77] Future generations of middle-class divorcees will bring other cultural frameworks to bear. We carry our formative influences with us and they shape our responses to downward mobility just as they define our attitudes toward success.

8

Falling from Grace

Feelings of anger or dismay, a sense of injustice—these are the responses to downward mobility shared by most of its victims. They worked hard for what they had, deferred gratification when necessary, and sacrificed when called upon by their country or their families. But the experience of downward mobility makes it abundantly clear that this is not enough. Attaining a responsible white-collar job, a skilled blue-collar job, or a stable marriage is no key to a lifetime of security. One can play by the rules, pay one's dues, and still be evicted from the American dream. There simply is no guarantee that one's best efforts will be rewarded in the end.

Few people come to this pessimistic conclusion until after calamity strikes. And it is the violation of their older, more optimistic expectations, the uncovering of the naked truth about how precarious comfort is, that makes downward mobility so difficult for them to bear.

Although the middle class is motivated by the rewards of the good life—economic security and a comfortable life-style—to emphasize the material aspects of their quest is to paint too shallow a picture of their values. An integral aspect of middle-class aspirations involves the search for fulfillment, a measure of pride in one's "walk of life." For some that comes from developing the autonomy and status that accompany a professional position. For others that pride derives from meeting a challenge at work, mastering complex tasks, doing what few can do well. Still others feel fulfilled through continuity with the past or the joys of family life. But there is no mistaking the fact that these accomplishments and pleasures are anchored in economic and occupational security. With the loss of financial stability, the achievements of the past and aspirations for the future shatter like so much broken glass.

The downwardly mobile have been betrayed by the forces of the market, by the ambitions of political figures, by husbands who promised a lifetime of partnership or protection, and, in some instances, they feel they have betrayed themselves. Hence downward mobility is not merely a matter of accepting a menial job, enduring the loss of stability, or witnessing with dismay the evaporation of one's hold on material comfort; it is also a broken covenant.[1] It is so profound a reversal of middle-class expectations that it calls into question the assumptions upon which their lives have been predicated. Downward mobility is a bewildering experience not only because it threatens personal identity but because it leaves its victims unsure of what cultural rules to abide by in order to reverse their fall, what lessons to convey to their children so that they may prosper. If the "approved program" of higher education, professional credentialism, craftsmanship, or devotion to home and hearth does not provide security and access to a life of fulfillment, then what does?

Were downward mobility merely a matter of reconciling the ambitions of the managerial man or the air traffic controller with the reality of life's disappointments, it would be hard enough. But economic dislocation casts a wider net than this, encompassing the perceptions and values of the victims and drawing innocent bystanders into the maelstrom. Its prey are whole families and their collective belief systems rather than personal ambitions alone.

The individualistic strain in American culture tends to blind us to the fact that downward mobility thoroughly undermines a family mobility project, not just an individual one. Conventionally, social class is measured by an individual's status in the world of work. But the lives of the downwardly mobile suggest that class identity or social standing is a broader and longer-term phenomenon, one that transcends the individual. When economic displacement strikes, it not only jars the victim's own sense of position, it disrupts a family trajectory, weakening its sense of forward motion or upward mobility. It interrupts what has been, for many American families, a sustained ascent since the Great Depression, the last historical period in which massive, widespread occupational dislocation knocked so many to the ground. It casts fifty years of growing aspirations into doubt and threatens a family's ability to transmit advantages to the next generation.

David Patterson was the first member of his family to receive a college education. His was a night school degree in business, earned while he commuted from home and worked during the day. He was not a son of privilege; he did not have the liberty to pursue comparative literature or history. He had to be pragmatic if he was going to find his way out of the working-class slum in Philadelphia, and he did exactly that. The fact that he was able to achieve so much, starting with so little, confirmed his belief in the validity of the work ethic, but even more important, it enabled his parents to look upon their own lives in terms of sacrifices well spent. They considered their son, the executive, as the bearer of the family standard, proof that the lineage was made of solid stuff.

Patterson's baffling descent into downward mobility calls his parents' confidence and their life's sacrifice into question.[2] What to make of a son who did what they never had the opportunity to do, who built a beautiful home, a reputation to be proud of, and a prosperous family, and then suddenly became unemployed or reduced to taking a menial job? His parents can do nothing to help him, and they have no idea how to explain his predicament to their friends and other relatives. And since they themselves never had much to brag about, they have lost the derivative sense of achievement that their son's status made possible.[3]

David's children are in a similar quandary. For if their credentialed, successful father could stumble and fall, what is to say that they will not repeat the disaster again in their own lives? His fall from grace penetrates their own identities in the form of nagging suspicions that they come from a line that is not destined for success or even for economic stability. Without his occupation (and salary) to provide an anchor for *their* sense of class identity, they are not entirely sure whether they are (or will remain) middle class. If David becomes a permanent refugee from the middle class, it will fall to his children to retrieve the honor of the entire clan, to reestablish the family trajectory that David's life represented. But his experience (and their own resulting financial troubles) leave them wondering how confident they can be of that prospect.

The long reach of downward mobility, the way it envelops the generations above and below the job loser or divorced mother, intensifies the embarrassment and guilt surrounding the entire experience. It also points to the inadequacy of thinking about class or socioeconomic status as a matter of individual occupation. For individuals are defined in terms of those who came before them and those who come after them as much as they are by their own location in the present. And when one person in a long line of upwardly mobile family members suffers dislocation, he "drops the ball" that has been carried by multiple generations. By the same token, he impairs the chances of those who come after him to continue the family pattern of progress and enrichment.

Because a family trajectory is at stake, the individual who suffers downward mobility cannot simply sit in silence or turn inward in his search for the meaning of dislocation. There are others near and dear to whom explanations must be given. However, different forms of American culture refract the experience of downward mobility in distinctive ways, some more damaging to individual self-esteem and family honor than others. Thus, the particular cultural baggage that victims of downward mobility bring to the experience enables them to color it differently for themselves and for the other audiences to whom they must answer.

The meritocratic creed and culture of America's managerial elite provides very little support for the integrity of the rejected manager. Instead it subjects believers who fail to a relentless attack on their personal worth. Either they are unable to reconcile the teachings of meritocracy with their own experience of downward mobility, and are condemned to liminality, or they accept its dictates and judge themselves harshly. Efforts to point the finger elsewhere—at the economy, at a vindictive boss, at the inability of new employers to see what valuable people they truly are—fade in time, to be replaced by self-recrimination or the wagging fingers of others. For meritocracy is so deeply embedded in managerial beliefs and convictions that it leaves no satisfying refuge.

Yet meritocracy has its virtues, even where downward mobility is concerned. At its center lies an inspired individualism that inculcates a tenacious belief in the efficacy of personal striving. It places responsibility on the shoulders of the individual for climbing out of the trenches. This responsibility can be thoroughly debilitating when the dispossessed are unable to find their way out and find no one to blame but themselves. Yet by placing the individual on center stage as the agent of a solution, meritocratic individualism provides displaced managers with a sense that they are, at least potentially, able to alter their fortunes. This stands in sharp contrast to those more collectively oriented pockets of American culture where the individual is subordinated to the actions of larger institutions (such as labor unions) or remote political figures in seeking salvation for the predicament of downward mobility.

Though there are those who see individualism as the leitmotif of American culture, the credo is not evenly distributed throughout the American middle class. There are reasons why executives and managers are its primary believers. There is very little in their ordinary, daily environment that would encourage "collective thinking." Instead of union bargaining, they advance their careers by distinguishing themselves from their colleagues in competition for visibility, responsibility, and promotion. When they suffer unemployment and are occasionally thrust into the company of fellow unemployed managers in places like Forty Plus, they are quite ill at ease. Years of experience have conditioned them to boast their successes and hide their weaknesses, and even when they share a common plight, they find it nearly impossible to let down their guard in front of one another. It is no accident that the conversation at the club is punctuated with jokes. Jokes point to areas of tension in social life, and there is more than enough tension to go around at the Forty Plus Club.

Meritocratic individualism is so powerful that even when a company pushes hundreds of managers into downward mobility, the collective character of their displacement fades from view. In this era of "merger mania," white-collar employees are often trapped in mass shutdowns that are described as necessary downsizing or streamlining and chalked up to the "lean and mean" philosophy of modern management. But the mergers, buyouts, and takeovers that push large numbers of administrators into downward mobility are no more under their control than the shutdown of the Elizabeth factory was for the men and women on the production line. Yet, because managerial workers lack social structures that bind them together into collectivities, they see themselves through the lens of individualism even when they have played no substantial role in their own demise.

While individualism is a crucial element in the national mosaic, it does not dominate the whole of middle-class life. There are pockets of group identity that do not reduce individuals to isolates but define them by common allegiance to organizations, neighborhoods, and communities. It is in this kind of collective context that a brotherhood of the downwardly mobile, forged in the heat of the struggle or in the bittersweet process of retrospection, can develop. Where the brotherhood persists through time, as it has to greater and lesser degrees for the air traffic controllers and the Singer workers, it serves as a bulwark against the crushing self-blame that an ethic of individualism inspires. It directs attention outward, even though the damage of downward mobility goes on behind closed doors.

Yet precisely because a group orientation prevails, individuals often feel helpless to change their own situation in any profound way. The lone Singer worker can do nothing to reopen that factory, much less reverse the decline in northern New Jersey's industrial base. Some air traffic controllers have been able to win their jobs back through individual lawsuits, but they are a very small minority.[4] The vast majority had to await the favor of the politicians in Washington, D.C. Thus mass downward mobility sets up a dynamic of dependency on larger and often more remote institutions and leaves the individual scanning the newspapers for signs of deliverance.

Mass loss that occurs in the context of a residential community also draws a wider population into its orbit. In towns where collective identity is drawn from a now-failing corporation, a community-wide sense of loss and drift often develops. For more than a hundred years, the coal mines of Kentucky and Tennessee have been the center of employment for local residents. The mines defined the region's folklore, its musical traditions, and its bloodiest political battles. When a mine shuts down, much more is lost than simply a community's livelihood. A way of life is lost as well.[5] Company towns whose lifeblood is drawn from this one industry, and whose culture has revolved around its ups and downs for a century, are dealt a harsh economic—and symbolic—blow; their identity as a community is weakened or destroyed.

For the better part of a century, the Singer Company was to Elizabeth, New Jersey, what coal mining is to Appalachia. It was Singer that brought Elizabeth attention as a city of forward-thinking industrialists. It was Singer that provided a measure of prosperity for the townspeople through the ravages of the Depression. With the plant shuttered forever, the soul of the city was diminished. It is the home of other industries now, some of which are prospering. But they cannot replace Singer at the symbolic core; they simply lack the centrality, the intertwined history, that the plant shares with the city.

Both examples of mass dislocation—the Singer workers and the air traffic controllers—show how important community can be in the face of disaster. When one compares them to the isolated manager at home with his answering machine, or the divorced mother trying to cope with downward mobility from the island of her separate household, it becomes clear that fellowship is an irreplaceable source of comfort in the midst of economic dislocation.

Singer workers and air traffic controllers also demonstrate the variety of shapes that communities come in. Traditionally the concept of community has been used to describe people who live in close proximity. Elizabeth, New Jersey, in the person of its Singer workers, is a community of this kind that has persisted in one form or another for nearly one hundred years. The controllers formed a different kind of community. Although most knew their immediate workmates and their union leaders, the remarkable degree of national solidarity they experienced is not a product of residential relations. Theirs was a *community of experience*, tied together by a common fate, bound into an enduring solidarity by virtue of a shared struggle now lost.[6] Shared defeat has left a lasting imprint on their lives. Their effort to survive, and the disappointments they have faced, bind the strikers together even though they may not know each other personally. It is this that encourages a striker who may never again see the inside of a control tower to say of a fellow PATCO loyalist and complete stranger, "I feel we are old friends."

The 1981 controller strike was a national drama that made an indelible impression at the time and continues to be recalled both by the participants and the newscasters who, in 1998, continue to invoke the strike as the beginning of a major decline in the power of organized labor. For the strikers, those events have taken on the character of a crusade for a set of principles—civil rights, loyalty, professional altruism—that gives them a sense of purpose even in defeat. They know why they have suffered downward mobility; they see its cost as a sacrifice on the altar of commitment. This is an honorable state of mind, however tragic and frustrating the consequences have been for the controllers and their families.

The framework of sacrifice developed in the context of mass loss. But there are also individual crusades that drag their protagonists into downward mobility. The whistle-blower who exposes graft and corruption, only to be harassed or fired, often finds that he must adopt a new profession because he is persona non grata in the old one. The price of honesty can be quite steep in this society. Yet the value of personal integrity is high. It can be a tremendous source of satisfaction, even in the face of financial despair. This satisfaction comes from the high moral value that American culture places on honesty and sacrifice for principle. Honor—whether achieved by the lone whistle-blower or the orchestrated actions of group struggle—cannot pay the rent, but it does fortify the soul.

Downwardly mobiles who cannot see their losses as the cost of being committed to a cause, who see themselves as "innocent bystanders," or worse, as victims of the arbitrary actions of others, lack the lifeline of integrity that commitment engenders in American culture. They cannot say that they sacrificed themselves for some higher principle. Indeed, their losses have a capricious quality, as if they could have happened to anyone who was unfortunate enough to be caught in a bad situation. It is difficult to find meaning or sustenance in a toss of the dice or the roll of the roulette wheel. Fatalism is often the only sensible response.

Singer workers have no cause to be committed to, no imagery of sacrifice within which to understand their personal losses. But they do have a collective understanding of why their jobs were taken away. The factory closed because people in power turned their back on the traditions Singer stood for. A covenant was sundered in Elizabeth, for the workers had "promised" to work with pride and commitment, according to the standards of a craft ethic. In exchange they expected employment security and management's recognition of the need to invest in the plant. What they got instead was a speedup and a personal taste of deindustrialization.

It is customary to think of tradition as a conservative force and attachment to it as expressive of a desire to slow the pace of progress or enforce the status quo.[7] But there are other uses for tradition. Singer workers rely upon tradition as an instrument of criticism, a yardstick against which the modern management practices of the company can be measured. From this vantage point, attachment to tradition becomes not a yearning for the past per se, but a desire for a future carved out in accordance with the values of the past.[8] From the vantage point of the Elizabeth factory workers, companies fail because they jettison the craft values of the past.

Traditional communities provide commitments for which people will sometimes risk their lives: "families, friends, customary crafts, and ways of life." In calmer times, the "deep-rootedness of traditional understanding and communal relations" is a conservative force, opposed to modification. But in times of change, "this very conservatism may make traditional communities politically radical, even revolutionary."[9]

The Singer workers are not cut of revolutionary cloth. But there is a middle ground between a conservative appreciation of tradition and the insurrectionary vision that traditionalism may sometimes inspire. The Singer workers took this road in between, which sees tradition not as a catalyst for revolt but as a more passive, yet nonetheless critical image against which to measure the present. They look around the postindustrial world, ask whether it holds a place for them, and discern an ambiguous answer. It remains unclear to what extent they are needed in the modern era. This ambiguity directs their attention to the past, a past that seems to have been a safer time for the working man and woman.

Yet this is a lament rather than a call for action. It cushions the blows of downward mobility, because it locates the moral failures in the Singer management, the world economy, or in political weakness.[10] But it provides little of the moral force that burning commitments and brotherhoods born of a dramatic fight can generate. It is a sorrowful story of betrayed ideals, but one that draws the whole of American industry, and not just the Singer company, into its orbit. But because the abandonment of tradition is seen as so widespread, it is also accepted as a *fait accompli,* an irreversible fact of the economic landscape. And it is not one that holds much promise for recovery from downward mobility.

The Singer workers' attachment to tradition was born of a particular era. They had come of age in a proud, paternalistic company sure of its mission and its superiority in the marketplace, only to see it throw in the towel and retire from the field. This inspired a cynicism toward the company that would have been unthinkable for the generations that came before, those for whom the "company was God . . . the mother, the father. . . ." It is a critical perspective born of a particular generation's experience and observations of the world they live in.

The importance of an era, and of generation-bound experience, also lies at the heart of divorced mothers' interpretations of downward mobility. Each generation of women developed a consistent language that captured the distinct understandings of their fall from grace. The discourse of loss is not invented anew by each woman descending the social ladder in the wake of divorce. It reflects the formative events and the cultural expectations individuals draw from historically grounded experience. Moving through history "together" binds unrelated strangers into cultural groups. Cohorts are another kind of "community of experience," because their members come of age at the same point in time and develop shared visions of American culture that set them apart in some respects from neighboring generations. Women born between the Depression and World War II instantly recognize the values and expectations they hold in common and feel a kinship to their age-mates even though they may never meet. Women marked by the sixties generation are products of an entirely different formative experience. Both groups are composed of women and mothers who must contend with shattered expectations for their own lives and those of their children. But the nature of those expectations, and the ways in which they come to grip with their destruction, is a matter of generational culture.

*

Downwardly mobile refugees from the middle class do, for the most part, grope their way toward stability. For many, it is a stability devoid of promise, short on comfort, and surrounded by the uneasy feeling that there is little in life that one can rely on. They find ways to make ends meet, sometimes just barely. And lacking the benefits they had assumed to be their entitlement—health insurance, retirement pensions, houses appreciating in value—they confront the fact that the rest of their lives will be lived out in patterns more closely resembling those of the working poor than of the solid middle class. They survive, but their culture teaches that mere survival is not enough. Hence they feel perpetually unfulfilled, while their children scramble to reverse this heritage and worry that they too will find themselves dumped on society's junk heap.

Adherents of Adam Smith's laissez-faire doctrine might well conclude that such are the fortunes of a market society. No one is guaranteed a life of comfort and stability. But we would do well to consider the costs that middle-class downward mobility imposes not only on the families involved but on the rest of society as well.

Do we really want to see divorced women who have devoted their lives to hearth and home live in shabbiness or endure years of sleepless nights while they try to figure out how they are going to provide for their children? What is the cost to society of locking capable, experienced people out of the professions they have trained for and served in for twenty years or more? To what better purpose might their talents be put? Adam Smith might answer that the marketplace is driven by the need for efficiency. But there is nothing terribly efficient about the economic displacement these people have undergone. It is hard to see how society benefits from forcing a man who has put in fifteen years as an air traffic controller to spend the rest of his days as a janitor.

The business world does not pay the full cost of throwing experienced personnel down the occupational ladder. The burden of putting these shattered lives back together falls upon the victims, their families, and upon taxpayers. Similarly, the divorced husband all too frequently walks away from his wife and children with the sense that his obligations end on the steps of the courthouse and somehow, magically, "others" will provide.

We should not allow a distorted vision of free-market economics to glorify irresponsibility and lack of commitment. Economists have taught that resources provided below cost are wasted. Employers benefit from society's commitment to provide training and education, in the form of generations of skilled and schooled employees. Some executives seem to want employees to be as disposable as Kleenex—to be used once and thrown away. And indeed, this is a rational move on their part if short-term profitability is the goal. If freshly educated replacements are available when needed and there is no cost attached to jettisoning longtime employees, it becomes all too easy to cast people aside.

We do not accept this kind of logic in other spheres. Companies may no longer dump toxic wastes or other kinds of garbage and expect the community to pay for their disposal. We do not allow them to "externalize" these costs. If employees are reduced to a commodity to be thrown away at will, then there should be a similar responsibility to pay toward the cost of their "disposal." Otherwise we encourage firms that waste human talent and we subsidize the throwaway mentality.

The true costs of downward mobility cannot be fully measured in dollars and cents. Beyond the psychic damage it causes in the lives of victims, downward mobility can ultimately do something even more destructive. It can undermine society's values and threaten its prosperity. Once it becomes known that corporations strand their middle managers in an occupational no-man's-land, or that a company that has taken care of four generations of workers can shut down its factory and never look back, it is but a matter of time before the steadily employed begin to question the wisdom of loyalty and commitment to the employer.

The hidden cost of downward mobility is reflected in diminished attachment to the job and erosion of loyalty to the firm. If employees truly embrace a free-market ideology, they will look out for no one but themselves, and treat the workplace as a resource to be exploited just until a better job is found. "Caveat emptor" will replace "a fair day's work for a fair day's pay," and all notions of pride in product and craftsmanship will disappear.

We have no reliable way of measuring what this means for American business. Will workers who feel like disposable goods contribute new ideas, rise to challenges, give their all for the firm? And if they hold back, will we see the consequences in the form of declining productivity over the long run? Most employers who rely on short-term, high turnover employment practices understand that there is very little they can expect in the way of commitment, and have organized the shop floor with this in mind. High skilled industries that try to function like this will rue the day, for they cannot function at peak levels with perfunctory commitment.

When we train a critical eye on the bottom line, downward mobility adds up to a monumental waste of intelligence, motivation, and aspiration. A nation built on ingenuity, skill, and devotion to the work ethic cannot afford to suspend so many able people in perpetual limbo. They should not be left to suffer in silence or in self-loathing, and we cannot pretend that they have only themselves to blame, or that they can be overlooked. There are too many of them, and they represent far too important a repository of experience and capability. What is more, few of us can say with certainty that we immune to the possibility of falling from grace.

Afterword

"Chainsaw Al Gets the Chop." The gloating in the nation's press began early on the day Al Dunlap was fired by the Sunbeam Corporation for presiding over a $44 million dollar first quarter loss in 1998. By June, the sorry state of Sunbeam's treasury became clear and "Rambo in pinstripes" met his demise. But not before he had cut 12,000 people—half of Sunbeam's workforce—from the payroll. Vindication could not have come too soon for J.E. Smith, Mayor of Bay Springs, Mississippi, a town of 2,000 that weathered the loss of two Sunbeam plants. "I couldn't think of a better person to deserve it. It tickled me to death. We may need to have a rejoicing ceremony."[1] Emery Michael Cole of Mobile, Alabama, a 37-year veteran of the Scott Paper Company "dunlapped" several years before, seconded the motion: "I'm happy the son of a bitch is fired."

Chainsaw Al is a legend in the annals of corporate downsizing. But he is hardly alone: Robert Allen pushed 40,000 AT&T workers out the door in 1996, mainly experienced managers; Louis Gerstner ended the "life time" careers of 35,000 IBM workers between 1993–95; Stanley Gault chopped 12,000 from Goodyear Tire and Rubber over a five-year period.[2] These contractions took place in the midst of a period of sustained economic growth, when unemployment fell to the lowest levels the U.S. has seen for nearly thirty years. The workers who lost their jobs were not the poorly educated, low-skilled labor force that poverty specialists worry about. Most were experienced, well-educated managers who gave the most productive years of their adult lives to these firms, only to be booted out.

Many landed on their feet, particularly those with specialized skills, good contacts, and the accidental virtue of being younger than their middle-aged counterparts. The rest have had to face sliding incomes and painful choices inflicted upon their families. When they come to a skidding halt, the downwardly mobile discover that their experience is more than a lesson in supply and demand. A moral shadow has passed over their lives; they have been sucked down into a vortex that ends in a loss of place, a failed identity, and a prolonged period of psychological wandering for which they are ill prepared. This is no fault of the downwardly mobile. Despite the relentless news of downsizing in the business press, we remain impoverished by our own culture, convinced that worthy individuals rise to the top and the undeserving fall by the wayside. The forces that impinge on workers, that are beyond their control, recede before the American predisposition to define them as masters of their own fate and people who get what they deserve.

In the 1980s, downsizing occurred in the context of an economy that had the flu. American firms were losing market share, profits were down. Unemployment had hit a postwar high of nearly 11 percent when I ventured out of my anthropologist's corner to explore what was happening to the legions of corporate managers, technical specialists, unionized blue collar workers and divorced women who are described in these pages. Most of these people were in shock over the financial distress they were experiencing. They knew well enough that factories were closing all around them, that assembly line workers used to a good wage were watching their jobs disappear overseas. They had not realized that a similar fate was in store for them. They had worked for companies that promised something close to lifetime employment, only to find a new management regime was coming into being: one that embraced outsourcing, temporary workers, and jobs that offered no health, vacation, or pension benefits.

The torrent of downsizing and rising unemployment in the 80s did more than undermine the financial stability of millions of American families. It caused them to wonder whether the country itself was at sea. Broken promises of good fortune were so at odds with expectations built on the strength of post-World-War-II prosperity, that it truly seemed as though the nation was economically rudderless. Still, the wayward economy of the mid-80s convinced even the downwardly mobile that the firms they worked for were in trouble. Through the depression and anger that invaded their lives, they accepted nonetheless the dictum that businesses that are losing money have to take corrective action.

The 1990s told a different story: record profits, a skyrocketing stock market, low inflation, and historic lows in unemployment. On all of these measures, the U.S. economy became the envy of the world. Western Europe was weighted down by double-digit unemployment, Japan entered a steep recession, and the rest of Asia weathered one currency crisis after another, but the United States boomed. The news did not impress former AT&T managers or the refugees from IBM who have found it hard to recover their footing. Why, they want to know, were their lives turned inside out when the companies they worked for enjoyed unheard of profits? And why was it that every announcement of downsizing was greeted with another increase in the value of their firm's stock?[3]

Americans have been admonished that they should expect to change careers five or six times in their working lives. Even if this is true, it still sounds like a bulletin from a brave new world for long-time employees of major American firms. They are not happy with the management mantra that they should "earn their jobs everyday," the need to prove to overpaid CEOs that they deserved to remain employed through their fifties, or the scramble they face in holding on to pensions they thought they could count on. The new regime is not an easy one to accept. It may well have permeated the expectations of generations new to the labor market; to anyone over the age of forty, it remains a hard pill to swallow.

As we learned in the 1990s, that insecurity fueled a hard-hat conservatism, represented by the protectionist voice of Pat Buchanan, who, for a short time, crested to public awareness with the populist message: American jobs for American workers. Free trade be damned. Buchanan's extremism on other fronts caused his popularity to fizzle. But both political parties got the message. Ironically, it was Bill Clinton who benefited in the end from the persistent insecurity of the American workforce. Voters were unsure that Republicans had their best interests at heart, so they let a Democrat back into the White house. Ironically, it was Clinton who pushed through the North American Free Trade Agreement that brought Mexican and Canadian trade tariff barriers down, but opened up the possibility that high wage jobs in the U.S. would resurface as low wage jobs south of the border.

Evidence on the consequences of NAFTA for U.S. workers has proven hard to sort out.[4] Official government reports bespeak tremendous positive outcomes: rising exports to Mexico and Canada,[5] jobs based on export goods growing rapidly,[6] and low cost imports increasing the purchasing power of American households.[7] Yet critics of NAFTA, like the Economic Policy Institute, argue this portrait is completely misleading:

> During the three years NAFTA has been in effect, imports from Mexico rose by $33 billion, eliminating 460,000 U.S. jobs. Exports to Mexico rose $17 billion, creating 210,000 U.S. jobs. *The net loss therefore was 250,000 jobs.*[8]

The giant sucking sound that erstwhile Presidential candidate Ross Perot warned of can be heard along the border. The question, hardly resolved as of the moment, is whether that sound really is so giant or is merely a light wind that will not matter as Mexicans begin to earn enough money to turn around and buy the American label.[9]

Foreign trade is hardly the only culprit or savior at issue here. Forces internal to the United States have led domestic workers to fear for their standard of living. The advent of two-tiered contracts, which leave seasoned employees safe and new workers with jobs that pay much less and have fewer benefits, have become far more common in the 1990s.[10] In the summer of 1997, United Parcel Service employees were asked to swallow the transformation of full-time jobs into part-time jobs which enjoyed neither the wages nor the benefits paid the more senior employees. UPS workers went out onto the picket lines and the nation's shipping system went into a free fall. The strike was settled in favor of the workers, with an outpouring of public support in the background.

Why did the UPS strikers enjoy such public confidence? Media commentators suggested that sympathy sprung from the fact that everyone knows their UPS guy and wanted to support this familiar, helpful figure. This may be part of the answer: the rest lies in the empathy Americans had for a high wage labor force about to be busted down. Enough employees had been through a similar trauma or thought they were in imminent danger to identify with the vulnerabilities of the UPS laborforce. The notion that these strikers were holding their ground as representatives of the threatened American worker resonated with a public grown wary of corporate motives.

This is not to suggest a new militancy, for there is scant evidence that U.S. labor is pushing back at the forces that produce economic insecurity. On the contrary, rosy economic indicators and something close to full employment have left most Americans feeling a peculiar combination of consumer confidence and employment anxiety. We are told repeatedly that we have never had it better, while we recognize that the good times could slip through our fingers because of a merger, the demands of shareholders, the movement of our jobs overseas, or the arrival of a Chainsaw Al in our midst. Since there is truth in both perspectives, we oscillate between optimism and worry.

We can also afford to be a bit less wary because our families have changed to accommodate market pressures. As we saw in Chapter Two, declining median incomes for men have been buffered by the massive increase in the number of working wives. Their contributions go well beyond pin money; they are now major mainstays of the family budget. This trend has important implications where downward mobility is concerned. The loss of a job is a major blow for any worker, but it helps a great deal if a second income is on hand to cushion the fall. This is probably the most important safety net for middle class families in America today and it fundamentally reshapes the problems with which this book deals.

On the other hand, the investment women have made in their careers leaves them that much more vulnerable to the psychological and cultural wounds that open up when their own careers derail. The more they define their identities in the world of work, the more they become subject to its unforgiving assessment. When a woman of Wall Street finds herself out of a job, she is no less devastated than her male counterpart. As we learned in Chapter Two, women who have been displaced from their jobs are less likely to find new jobs at all, much less jobs at the same wage, than the men who work along side them. Once upon a time, this would have made a difference for a family's income but might have spared the woman an identity crisis. She could have retreated behind the honored identity of a mother. We still honor mothers, but working women are now fully invested in their public lives and do not find it any easier than their husbands to contend with the consequences of losing a job or taking a new one that is below their station.

If women have moved into the labor market, changes in the lives of men have been almost as profound. Recent studies[11] tell us that men, particularly middle class men, have moved to take up some of the domestic slack left behind when their wives went out to work. Men are more involved in bringing up baby, devote more time to housework, and do the lion's share of soccer and Little League coaching. The growth of self-employment and telecommuting has meant that many more male professionals are working out of their homes than was true thirty years ago. These trends combine to make men more visible than they once were during the daytime in suburban communities. It has redefined the role of fathers away from the distant breadwinner of the 1950s to the more involved father we know today. Does this lessen the blows of occupational displacement? Only modestly. Men still wrap their identities around their work lives for the most part. Yet they have now acquired other sources of satisfaction, other "jobs" to perform. When they find themselves out of work and the burdens of bread winning fall on their wives, they no longer find themselves the object of pity if it is they who drop the kids off at school or volunteer to help out in the classroom. Among the men interviewed in the preceding chapters, "irregular" gender behavior was a source of great shame and stigma. It is less so now.

*

This book was written before the term "downwardly mobile" was part of the country's cultural landscape. It is now a fixture. We recognize that even in good times, millions of Americans skid down the class ladder. They have to recreate their lives, a task that is more than financial. Downwardly mobile workers and their families have to overhaul their identities as they seek a new footing at a lower standard of living. It is a task easier said than done and for many it is a transformation that is never quite complete. Parents who have lost everything they worked for often find that only in their adult children's lives can they reclaim the kind of class identity that makes sense. If their children are able to become white-collar professionals, and parents can find some way to keep body and soul together, they may cease to think of themselves as former managers or former air traffic controllers, and start defining their lives as the "retired" parents of lawyers or doctors.

Closure is often very elusive, however. For many, the experience of falling from grace remains a watershed that divides their lives into a happy before and a tragic after that stubbornly refuses to resolve into a life they can live with. This is as much a consequence of the way American culture defines moral worth as it is a matter of financial hardship. The great value of meritocratic individualism is that it leaves people feeling they can and ought to exercise control over their fate. Its greatest liability is the way this credo damns those who have not been able to reverse their fortunes, no matter how hard they have tried.

Appendix

Table A1. **Perceived Financial Well-being 1984–1994**

Question: During the last few years, has your financial situation been getting better, worse, or has it stayed the same?

Response	1984	1985	1986	1987	1988	1989	1990	1991	1993	1994
Getting Better	39.1%	39.0%	42.1%	39.5%	41.5%	44.7%	39.9%	36.7%	35.3%	36.6%
Getting Worse	21.6	21.7	20.5	19.3	18.3	17.8	20.0	21.0	25.0	22.3
Stayed Same	39.2	39.3	37.4	41.2	40.2	37.4	40.1	42.3	39.7	41.1
Total # Respondents	1,473	1,534	1,470	1,461	1,470	1,530	1,368	1,508	1,592	2,969

Source: National Opinion Research Center, General Social Survey Trend Table, 1972–1994 FINALTER (Change in Financial Situation by Year, GSS). Storrs, Connecticut: Roper Center for Public Opinion Research. Available on the web at http://www.icpsr.umich.edu/gss/trend/finalter.htm

Table A2.   **Median Income Shifts in the United States 1987–1996 (in constant 1996 dollars)**

Year	Year-Round Full Time Men, Over Age 20	Year-Round Full Time Women, Over Age 20	Families
1987	37,568	24,362	42,775
1988	37,375	24,538	42,695
1989	37,398	24,993	43,290
1990	35,998	24,677	42,440
1991	35,566	24,505	41,401
1992	35,025	24,761	40,900
1993	34,312	24,346	40,131
1994	34,017	24,525	41,059
1995	33,828	24,316	41,810
1996	34,463	24,803	42,300

SOURCE: Historical Income Table P29. Year-Round, Full Time Workers—Persons (all races) 15 Years Old and Over by Median Income and Sex: 1970–1996. Income Statistics Branch/HHES Division, U.S. Bureau of the Census.

Historical Income Table F7. Type of Family—Families (all races) by Median and mean Income: 1947–1996. Income Statistics Branch/HHES Division, U.S. Bureau of the Census.

Table A3. Reemployed Workers by Occupation in February 1994 by Occupation of Job Lost between January 1991 and December 1992 (numbers in thousands)

Occupation of Lost Job	Total Employed[1]	Percent Distribution by Occupation in Feb. 1994					
		Managerial Professional	Technical Sales & Admin.	Service Occup.	Precision Production Craft, Repair	Operators Fabricators Laborers	Farming Forestry Fishing
Total, 20 years and over	2,084	25.6	33.7	8.7	13.2	17.6	1.2
Managerial/ Professional	612	57.9*	28.5	5.0	3.8	4.6	.2
Technical, Sales & Admin Support	613	19.0	66.3*	5.4	3.4	5.8	.3
Service Occupations	103	16.7	11.8	45.8*	9.2	16.4	—
Precision Production, Craft, Repair	340	4.5	15.4	4.7	53.7*	18.3	3.4
Operators, Fabricators Laborers	370	4.9	14.0	12.6	8.4	58.8*	1.3
Farming, Forestry, & Fishing	25	+	+	+	+	+	+

* Percentage of workers reemployed in same occupational category as lost job.

+ Data not shown where base is less than 75,000. Dash equals or rounds to zero.

SOURCE: U.S. Department of Labor, Bureau of Labor Statistics, "Displaced Workers, 1991–92." Bulletin 2464. July 1995. Table D-7, p. 21.

1. Data refer to persons with tenure of three years or more who lost or left a job between Jan 199–Dec 1992 because of plant or company closings or moves, insufficient work, or the abolition of their positions or shifts.

Table A4 **10 Year Merger Completion Record 1987–1996**

Year	# of completed Mergers	% change	Value($bil)	% change
1987	2,517	—	$210.7	—
1988	3,011	19.6%	$291.3	38.3%
1989	3,825	27.0%	$325.1	11.6%
1990	4,312	12.7%	$206.8	−36.4%
1991	3,580	−16.9%	$143.1	−30.8%
1992	3,752	4.8%	$125.3	−12.4%
1993	4,148	10.5%	$177.3	41.5%
1994	4,962	19.6%	$276.5	55.9%
1995	6,209	25.1%	$375.0	35.6%
1996	6,828	9.9%	$550.7	46.8%

SOURCE: *Mergers and Acquisitions* March/April 1997, Vol 31/Number 5, "1996 M&A Profile"

Table A5. **Earnings for Five Cohorts of U.S. Men (in 1996 dollars)**

	Median Income at 30 years	Median Income at 40 years	Median Income at 50 years
Age 30 in 1949	16,683	26,415	34,323
Age 30 in 1960	23,896	35,958	38,079
Age 30 in 1975	30,813	36,976	36,637
Age 30 in 1985	27,713	32,348	—
Age 30 in 1995	24,306	—	—

SOURCE: Historical Income Table P29. Year-Round, Full Time Workers—Persons (all races) 15 Years Old and Over by Median Income and Sex: 1970–1996. Income Statistics Branch/HHES Division, U.S. Bureau of the Census.

Notes

Preface

1. Robert Bellah et al. (1985) spent hundreds of hours interviewing economically secure middle-class Americans about their values and aspirations. Their tour de force, *Habits of the Heart*, suggests that ordinary Americans have lost touch with the philosophical traditions of the past that anchored values to a larger vision of the good society. Bellah argues that the values of the middle class lack richness of meaning and leave many Americans with a feeling of malaise or dissatisfaction. As we shall see, some aspects of meaning in middle-class life become clearer when viewed through the eyes of the downwardly mobile outcasts.

2. The 150 interviews do not constitute a random sample, nor can they be considered "representative" in a statistical sense. Rather, they are an attempt to look for the diversity of experiences that constitute downward mobility in the middle class.

   Where possible, my interviews were supplemented by participant-observation fieldwork in the settings in which the downwardly mobile gather. However, ethnographic fieldwork was not, always possible simply because, for many groups of downwardly mobile Americans, there is no place to gather. In only two cases (discussed at length in chapters 3 and 6) was there anything approaching a bounded community, and it was there that my work most closely matched a traditional anthropological methodology. Elsewhere, I visited people in their homes, in coffee shops, in branch libraries, and on the job to interview them about their lives.

Chapter One

1. Featherman and Hauser (1978): 120. See chapter Two for a more detailed discussion of the evidence for widespread downward mobility.
2. Lamison-White (1997:vii).
3. See Hopper et al. 1985 for a discussion of the adaptations of the truly marginal poor in New York City. The life-style of groups who live below the poverty line is sufficiently distinctive to lead some social scientists (like Oscar Lewis) and some politicians (like Daniel P. Moynihan) to speak of a "culture of poverty." Arguments rage over whether such a culture is transmitted from one generation to the next, conditioning the young for a life of poverty, or whether it is a response each generation develops anew in the face of persistent racial discrimination, segmented labor markets, and the pernicious influence of federal welfare policies (Wilson 1987). The parties to these debates differ over whether poverty creates a self-sustaining culture but agree that the poor are marked by distinctive family structures and survival practices that sustain them in the face of permanent scarcity. The downwardly mobile middle class do not confront economic dislocation with regularized adaptations in hand. It is not part of their "normal" experience. In this respect, and in many others, they can be distinguished from the poor, even when objectively they find themselves in a similar economic position.
4. For an exception to the rule, see Andrew Delbanco (1986).
5. They are suspended in what Victor Turner (1967) called a "liminal state," the period in the middle of a rite of passage during which initiates are usually secluded in order to prepare for their transformation (for example, into adults, into married people, and so on). See chapter Three for a discussion of downward mobility as a form of permanent liminality.
6. Steinbeck's work created a powerful portrait of poverty and despair in an America rich with resources, a literary act that earned him an honored place on J. Edgar Hoover's list of domestic subversives. Steinbeck's experience suggests that in certain periods of American history it can be considered "un-American" to confront the reality of economic disaster.
7. This does not mean that individuals caught in collective downward mobility feel they have no individual responsibility for finding a new job; this is not the case, as the depression era studies and more recent research (for example, Leventman [1982]) show.
8. Some social scientists have argued that changes in family composition are a more significant source of economic dislocation than any other set of factors (Oppenheimer, 1982; Duncan, 1984).
9. This is one of the central conclusions of David Halle's (1984) extensive study of chemical workers in automated factories in northern New Jersey.
10. Cf. Will (1986) and Dionne (1986).

11. To borrow de Tocqueville's phrase.
12. See chapter Two for a discussion of the national survey data on downward mobility.
13. A point made most forcefully by Clifford Geertz in his classic text on symbolic anthropology, *The Interpretation of Culture* (1973).

Chapter Two

1. *Intragenerational mobility,* literally mobility within a generation, refers to financial or social movements up or down within one person's lifetime. It is somewhat analogous to a career. By contrast, *intergenerational mobility* refers to mobility between generations—for example, comparing a father's occupational attainment with that of his adult son. Intergenerational (father-son) studies have predominated in social research. Yet some sociologists contend that this kind of approach is not the best way to understand mobility. Aage Sorenson (1975: 456–457) has argued that "intergenerational data do not represent the actual mobility experiences of any real cohort," they do not measure "fixed attributes of individuals over time," and they are too sensitive to variation introduced by age. Since my concern is precisely to excavate the actual mobility experiences of various groups, my own research takes the intragenerational, within-one-lifetime approach.
2. See table A1 in the Appendix for the NORC data. See table A2 in the Appendix for the data on median income.
3. Duncan et al (1995: 250).
4. Yet this is not necessarily so: A college professor denied tenure who ends up as a successful real estate agent may ultimately triple his salary, even though he has lost a good measure of prestige. However, this is a relatively rare case. For most people, job losses which result in diminished social status also entail a loss of income.
5. Featherman and Hauser (1978: 120).
6. Featherman and Hauser draw on the 1973 "Occupational Change in a Generation Survey II," which enables us to distinguish between those who slide a short distance and those who slide a long distance down the occupational hierarchy. They define long-distance mobility in terms of moving out of one's broad five-category occupational stratum, and short-distance mobility in terms of moving out of a finer seventeen-category occupational stratum. Sixty percent of the downwardly mobile are long movers and 40 percent are short movers.

   The results of the 1973 study were consistent with those of earlier studies of the 1960s by Blau and Duncan (1967), in which one-fifth of men aged 21–53 slid occupationally. 63 percent of them were long movers. See also Kerckhoff et al. (1985).
7. Hauser et al (1996: 9).
8. This had the dual consequence of raising the demands for credentials at the

bottom of the labor force (and therefore cutting the demand for low skilled workers) and stripping away many of the managers who used to sit in the middle of the pyramid.

9. Nearly 11 million people, almost 10% of the civilian labor force, were displaced overall. This figure includes short term workers.

10. The Bureau of Labor Statistics studies from which these figures were taken were particularly concerned with a one subset of displaced workers, namely those with long-term experience in their jobs. They tracked the experience of "stable" or "experienced" workers: those who had held their previous jobs for three or more years before being displaced. This subset constitutes about half of the larger group of persons who lost their jobs on a permanent basis. It is not clear what the implications of the BLS decision to limit analyses to experienced workers might be. One can speculate that these experienced individuals would have a better chance at reemployment than the less experienced displaced workers. If so, the subsequent data on impact may paint a slightly more optimistic picture than is warranted for displaced workers as a whole. In any event, the unemployment figures reported here refer only to the stable or experienced group.

11. Hipple (1997:26).

12. Indeed, Hipple (1997:27) shows that the college educated were more likely to be displaced than those who lack a high school diploma, by a considerable margin in 1993–94.

13. Unless they have the resources to retire. Yet those who retire early often find their income seriously eroded because they have worked fewer years than they need to in order to qualify for full benefits.

14. Farber (1998:118).

15. For the moment, I am lumping together people who might be regarded as voluntarily electing downward mobility by affirmatively choosing part time employment and those who experience the loss as an involuntary consequence of not having the opportunity to secure full time jobs. There is evidence to suggest that the rates of involuntary part-time work have risen in recent year (Tilly 1996).

16. Louis Uchitelle, (1987). These nonworkers are defined as people who are unemployed for reasons other than those we traditionally find acceptable— that is, they are *not* housewives, students, ill or disabled.

17. Based on Table 9 in Hipple (1997:33). Of the 2,213,00 displaced workers with long tenure 1993–94, 146,000 were working part time, 433,240 sustained wage losses of 20% or more, 159,000 were unemployed, and 288,000 were

not in the labor force by 1996. This understates the extent of downward mobility by excluding the displaced who were short-tenure workers.

18. See Table A3 in the Appendix for complete data on the occupations of reemployed displaced workers.

19. When the original Task Force on Economic Adjustment and Worker Dislocation submitted its report on the difficulties facing displaced workers and the deficiencies of American policy in assisting them, it included a dissenting voice: that of Richard McKenzie, professor of economics at Clemson University. Professor McKenzie was of the opinion that the task force had overlooked the ways in which workers are themselves responsible for their difficulties:

> The report of the Task Force . . . is potentially dangerous. It focuses on a social problem, worker displacement, that no one denies exists, at least to some extent. Under the guise of seeking a more "humane society," however, the Task Force effectively treats all displaced workers as victims of markets that have presumably failed to an important degree, unwilling even to acknowledge that at least some workers have contributed to their own job losses and should not, therefore, be entitled to government largesse. The Task Force fails to recognize individuals' and communities' responsibility to solve their own problems . . .

20. Leonard Silk (1978) discussed the issue of whether credit tightening would lead to recession, arguing that Wall Streeters believed recession—stiff enough to reduce inflation and trade deficit but not severe enough to disrupt business expansion plans—would benefit the economy and stock market. The *New York Times* editorial (23 May 1978) noted that an important segment of the financial community foresaw a recession coming in 1978 or 1979 and believed it would be the only remedy for high inflation, that early recession would hurt less than later recession, and that the Federal Reserve should tighten the money supply in order to bring about early recession.

Of course, not all recessions are engineered by the government, and even in those instances when they are, efforts are usually made to control unemployment to some extent. Nevertheless, policy makers are well aware that their actions in clamping down on government spending and tightening the money supply will lead to increases in unemployment.

For more on the political business cycle, see Bluestone and Harrison (1986: 207–208), and Boddy and Crotty (1975).

21. Levitan and Carlson (1984: 59).

22. The Trade Readjustment Act provides for additional unemployment benefits for some workers adversely affected by foreign imports.

23. This index calculates the value of unemployment insurance as a percentage of previous earnings before tax. Implementing the OECD Jobs Strategy: Lessons from Member Countries. Report of the Secretariat to the Ministers

of the OECD. Available on the web at http://www.oecd.org/sge/min/ 97study.htm. Data drawn from p. 10.

24. Implementing the OECD Jobs Strategy: Lessons from Member Countries. Report of the Secretariat to the Ministers of the OECD. Available on the web at http://www.oecd.org/sge/min/97study.htm. Data drawn from Table 2, pg. 11.

25. Labor Task Force (1986).

26. It is often suggested that unemployment is less of a problem for families today than it was during the Great Depression, when unemployment compensation and social security did not exist. Yet a major study of the 1975 recession shows that nearly one-half (48.1 percent of families with an unemployed breadwinner received no income supports in the form of either unemployment or AFDC (Moen [1983]).

27. Ginzberg (1977). There are no critics of the good jobs/bad jobs thesis who argue that Shaiken, Thurow, Kuttner, Bluestone, et al. mischaracterize the changing structure of employment. Medoff (1984) and Medoff and Strassman (1985) suggest that there has been a relative decrease in both middle- and low-paid occupations and an increase in highly paid jobs from 1973 to 1982. This suggests, if anything, a net upgrading of the occupational structure over time rather than a downgrading or polarization (see Attewel [1987] on this point). As we shall see below, this debate continues.

28. Ben Harrison and Joan Fitzgerald (personal communication, July 1998) document this change in their analysis of 485 occupations. They find that 123 of these occupations which had above poverty level wages and above average skill requirements were growing. 22 of the 485 occupations that were below average skill and had sub-poverty wages (less than $7 an hour) grew as well, but at a much slower rate. Their data suggests that the high end jobs are growing faster. But these high end jobs are also seeing falling wages, hence their growth is not generating as much income growth for their incumbents as they once did.

29. This expands the good jobs/bad jobs into very good/good/bad jobs to emphasize the difference (and ever larger one) between managers and professionals and the rest of the labor force. Methodically, most of the allocations are reasonably straightforward except for clericals. This predominantly female field has low pay on average but high educational attainment. Looking at men and women separately however reveals that within genders clerical jobs do fall in the middle. The confusion arises by looking at the average of all workers because women, the bulk of this group, get paid so much less than men. Carnevale and Rose (1998).

30. As recently as 1959 over one-half of the prime age labor force had not fin-

ished high school and now almost 56% have some post-secondary education (ibid). Paradoxically, it may be that the increasing investment in education among workers in the middle range has devalued those very credentials and made it cheaper for employers to hire better educated workers

31. "Share of Employment by Wage Multiples of the Poverty Line, 1973–1996," Economic Policy Institute Data Zone.

32. These people would therefore be at risk for intergenerational downward mobility.

33. The research on trends in income distribution has given rise to a heated debate over the fate of the middle class in America. Blackburn and Bloom (1985) have argued that income data show a substantial decline in the proportion of the population in the middle class. The share of families with middle-class incomes fell from 27 percent in 1969 to 23 percent in 1983 (while upper- and lower-class shares have increased). (Blackburn and Bloom 1985: 21). Levitan and Carlson (1984) argue that this is a "statistical illusion" caused by th entrance of the baby boom into the labor market. We know that people generally experience a rising income as they grow older and that their entry point in the labor market is often much lower than what they will see over time. With such a large generation concentrated at the entry level, Levitan and Carlson argue, overall income statistics are skewed toward the low end of the spectrum. If they are correct, then as the baby boom cohort ages, the income curves should rise. However, there are reasons to dispute this claim, among them that many members of the baby-boom generation are in their forties now, and hardly at the entry level anymore. More telling, perhaps, is their observation that the rise in the number of young, elderly, and single-parent households at the lower end of the income spectrum drags overall household income figures down. Levitan and Carlson suggest that this, rather than fundamental changes in either per capita earnings or the changing nature of the economy, is responsible for the declining number of people "in the middle."

Rosenthal (1985) disputes the declining-middle-class thesis as well, arguing that if we look at individual earners (rather than families), that on nearly all measures only a slight decline can be detected in the fortunes of the "middle third" of income earners, and that, if anything, the net change has been toward an increase in the proportion of full-time workers at the high end of the spectrum. Neither of these critics denies that there has been a decline in middle-class family income. Rather they dispute certain economic explanationas and propose more demographic ones.

At least one economist has argued that income polarization—the disappearance of the middle and the growth of the upper and lower income tiers—may lead to a major depression. Ravi Batra, author of *The Great Depression of 1990* (1985) argues that we are entering an era of extreme income polarization and concentration of wealth whose flip side is high debt and a growth in the poverty population. Debt impairs the banking structure and fuels speculation—both warning signs of depressions. The stock market crash of. October 1987 may well have been a case in point. If Batra is correct, we may all have a date with downward mobility. As he puts it, "Extreme inequality first creates a speculative mania and eventually an economic cataclysm that comes to haunt everybody, rich and poor alike." (Batra 1987)

Frank Levy (1987) argues that the evidence for polarization is weak, but that absolute income decline has taken hold since 1973. Hence, while the proportion of American families in the middle-income group has remained much the same, the income they earn no longer guarantees a middle-class lifestyle. Moreover, it now requires two wage earners to tread water.

McMahan and Tschetter (1986) argue that while the proportion of employment in higher-paying occupations increased for all groups between 1973–1982, the earnings distribution within these occupations shifted to include more lower-paying positions.

34. Ilg (1996:33).

35. Bell (1979).

36. *New York Times,* 14 December 1986.

37. The deindustrialization thesis in not without critics, principal among them Robert Lawrence (1983). Lawrence agrees that job loss has been substantial, but suggests that this does not signal the end of manufacturing industry. He maintains that it could indicate just the opposite: Manufacturers are able to produce more with fewer people—they are more productive rather than less so.

He also suggests that Bluestone and Harrison are measuring the wrong things when they suggest that the country is deindustrializing. Their principal mistake is to examine changes in employment and investment in manufacturing industries (inputs), rather than output. Lawrence argues that if we examine "the output share of goods," the United States remains an industrial (rather than service-dominated) society. What has changed, he notes, is the share of expenditure, employment, capital stock, and R&D devoted to manufacturing, rather than the absolute amount. At the same time manufacturing productivity has risen more rapidly than any other sector. Hence "overall real industrial output has risen . . . but the shares of employment and captial in manufactured goods have declined."

Lawrence suggests that it is "in Europe rather than the United States that employment is undergoing absolute deindustrialization." Between 1973–1980, the United States increased its manufacturing employment more rapidly than did any other major industrial country, including Japan. He also argues that the most recent troubles of U.S. manufacturing are cyclical in nature (having to do with excess capacity and an overvalued dollar) rather than indicative of any long-term changes.

Thus, on nearly every count, Lawrence takes Bluestone and Harrison to task. Bluestone's (1984) rejoinder concedes Lawrence's point that absolute manufacturing employment has not declined to a great degree, but he points to the enormous number of jobs lost and the extent to which they were replaced with jobs that paid comparatively lower wages. He also stresses sectoral differences within manufacturing, with absolute declines in employment in some key industries including tires, household appliances, motor vehicles and parts, textile mill products, apparel, footwear, electrical distribution equipment, and so on (1984: 45). Hence the regions of the United States where these industries are concentrated are not benefiting from areas of growth in manufacturing employment. In fact, they are losing employment rapidly. Thus, while it may be true that the whole country has yet to deindustrialize, there are areas (principally the Frostbelt states of Ohio, New York and Michigan) where the trend is quite strong. What this suggests overall is a high degree of capital mobility from one region to another, leaving communities in the deindustrializating areas to suffer the consequences. Individuals who have been hit by plant closures clearly reap the consequences in terms of wage losses, particularly if they are forced into service sector jobs (Bluestone 1984: 49).

In general, Bluestone argues that Lawrence's optimism is based on the wrong kind of measurement. Aggregate trends do not tell the most important part of the story. The most important evaluation of the deindustrialization thesis comes, Bluestone suggests, from examining "how rapidly and how successfully workers dislocated from so-called sunset industries are reemployed in growing, sunrise industries. The absolute magnitude of output, investment, and employment in manufacturing—the extent to which employment is ahead of or behind that in other developed nations—is by itself not a very useful measure of deindustrialization." (Bluestone [1984]: 51). In the end, Bluestone recommends that we concentrate on "how rapidly employment is shrinking in certain sectors . . . and how rapidly workers are being reabsorbed into equivalent sectors." When looked at in this fashion, we find that downward mobility of job losers is widespread.

One should also note that this debate was, of necessity, limited to data prior to the 1980s. Since 1977 absolute declines have occurred in manufacturing employment. See Roberts (1986).

38. See Table A4 in the Appendix for the data on merger transactions.

39. American Management Association International. October 22, 1997. "Job Cuts, Downsizing Tumble as Major U.S. Firms Opt for Growth." This report presents the findings from the AMA's eleventh annual survey of a sample of its member firms. The sample of 1,168 companies is representative of the organization's 10,000 members which collectively employ about _ of the American workforce. The sample does not reflect the whole of the U.S. economy, but is a reasonably accurate picture of the behavior of its large firms. http://www.amenet.org/survey/pr97survey.htm

40. David Gordon (1996) argues that U.S. corporations did not, in fact, downsize management nearly as much as the popular press would have us believe. He notes that the cuts were indeed deep in the early 1980s, but that overall the ranks of management have increased rather than shrunk.

41. See Table A4 in the appendix for complete data on the occupations of reemployed workers.

42. Valerie Oppenheimer (1982) provides an analysis that both supports and critiques Easterlin's model. As Easterlin would expect, she found that the relative income position of younger men did deteriorate between 1959 and 1969. However, she argues that cohort size is by no means the only factor causing this. She finds, for example, that the decline in the relative position of young male workers is a secular trend that started before the baby boom entered the work force in the early 1960s.

43. The repercussions of the baby boom generation's size continue into the generation it has brought into the world. Although birth rates have dropped, the enormous size of the female population that was of child bearing age in the 1980s and 90s has meant that an "echo boom" or boomlet is filling the nation's elementary schools. They too will face adverse conditions based on the size of their generation.

44. See Table A5 in the Appendix for the actual data on earnings by cohort.

45. Newman (1993) explores the nature of intergenerational downward mobility in detail by looking at the experience of different cohorts moving through the same community, with very different economic prospects and political responses.

46. Duncan's (1984: 18–22) research on the longitudinal Panel Study data showed that composition effects are much more significant in their economic consequences for women than for men. Getting married raised single women householder's incomes by 10 percent in real terms from 1971 to 1978. Those women who remained unmarried faced an income decline of nearly 1 percent. Separation and divorce were (and are) the most widespread financially traumatic events for women. Duncan found that following separation or divorce, women suffered a drop in real income of 9.4 percent in the 1970s.

47. Duncan (1984:148)

48. Howe (1977).

49. Hoffman (1977).

50. Cross-sectional data of this kind do not control for various possible changes in the characteristics of families, for example, in mean age of number of dependents, and thus should be treated with some caution.

51. Oppenheimer (1982).

52. This point is made clear in Phyllis Moen's (1983) study of the impact of the 1975 recession on American families:

Families in the early stages of the family cycle—i.e. with pre-school children—were the most likely to have poverty-level incomes. It is clear that the timing of job loss affects its consequences: Young families are less likely than established ones to have the resources necessary to cope effectively with economic adversity.

53. Table 6. Homeownership Rates by Age of Householder: 1994–1996. (p. 4–5) On the web from Builder Online. http://builder.hw.n4t/monthly/archives/owrat/own0296.htx.

54. U.S. Bureau of the Census, "Average Number of Own Children Under 18 Per Family, by Type of Family: 1955 to Present." Internet release date: May 28, 1998. http://www.census.gov/population/socdemo/hh-fam/htabFM-3 txt.

Chapter Three

1. Nulty (1987:26).

2. *Fortune* surveyed all individuals who had sent unsolicited resumes to E.A. Butler & Associates)an executive search firm with offices around the country) in the first half of 1986. At the end of 1986, the firm "randomly asked a portion of the job seekers for permission to turn over their resumes to Fortune." Two hundred fifty of them agreed and were contacted by phone for interviews on their job search experiences. Most had begun looking for work between mid-1985 and mid-1986. Some were looking for better jobs, while "the great majority . . . had been fired or told by their employers to start hunting." (Nulty, 1987). See also Bureau of Labor Statistics (1985:13).

3. See *Business Week* (1984a:40–41).

4. This is a controversial proposition. Osterman (1986) argues that although the initial impact of computerization may be to depress the employment of white-collar workers, including managers, over time increased productivity creates a higher demand for clerical and managerial employee, albeit in a reorganized bureaucracy. *Business Week* (1984b) argues that the introduction of new technology does "flatten the bureaucratic pyramid—by cutting management layers and redefining work patterns."

5. Main (1984:113).

6. Quoted in Ryan (1985:61).

7. Miner (1963).

8. Forty Plus is one among many self-help organizations for the unemployed, but it is unusual in its restricted emphasis on professional and managerial

workers. The only other organization of its kind discussed in the literature was the Start-Up Program, founded to help Seattle area employees reeling from the impact of the Boeing Aircraft collapse in the late 1960s. Most peer-organized job search clubs focus on blue-collar workers. They typically provide personal and financial counseling, résumé writing advice, phone banks, and perhaps most important, a place for people to go who are accustomed to structuring their lives around the workplace. The Reagan administration's Advisory Council on Private Sector Initiatives pushed for funding of these peer-based clubs from the Commerce and Labor Departments, to be jointly sponsored and managed by local companies and unions (Challenge [1984]).

9. I conducted lengthy on-site interviews with active members of the club during the summer and fall of 1985 and attended the meetings of the membership during most of this period. Working alongside the men and women (who are obligated to spend two and a half days per week minimum working on the various committees of the club), I had ample opportunity to observe interactions between members. Thereafter, I interviewed a sample of former club members who are now reemployed, but in positions that represent a substantial cut in salaries and prestige when compared to their original managerial jobs.

10. Budge and Janoff (1984:29), who have worked as support counselors for the New York Forty Plus Club for a number of years, discuss the importance of this structure, arguing that it takes on "a magical force for the individual, countering the spell of fatalism and immobility, itself a function of feeling lost and worthless" that accompanies prolonged unemployment.

11. These are job counseling and referral organizations that work on a paid contract basis. The most reputable of headhunters work on behalf of corporations who are looking for new employees (who pay these agencies to screen prospective executives for them). A related type of organization, "outplacement" services, works on a contractual basis for corporations that have fired managers but want to see that they receive some help in organizing job searches, writing effective résumés, and learning to tap professional networks (Camden [1982]; Levine [1985]). This is a growth industry, drawing an expanded clientele from among those stranded by the merger wave of the 1980s. More than 75 percent of the Fortune 500 companies use outplacement agencies, paying an average of 15 percent of the total yearly cash compensation per dismissed employee to the agencies (Stybel [1985]).

Beyond the respectable agencies, there are also headhunters who prey on the desperation of unemployed managers, offering them job leads in exchange for hefty fees. They take in résumés but do little with them. Many members of Forty Plus had been through the demoralizing experience of paying a thousand dollars or more for headhunter services, only to find that their offers were bogus, their job files worthless.

12. The literature on unemployment, its causes and its impact on workers, is quite large. It is a research topic that dates back to sociological inquiries of the Depression period (see especially Jahoda et al [1971]; Komarovsky [1940]; Bakke [1940, 1947]). In the last twenty years, the focus of the literature has included the impact of unemployment on individual and community-wide health and social problems, including: mental health (Brenner [1967,

1976]); crime rates (Brenner [1976]); alcoholism and related problems of drunk driving (Kaufman [1982]); heart disease, stroke, and kidney disorders (Kaufman [1982:19]); and suicide rates (ibid: 25, Powell [1958]). Most of this research concerns the experience of blue-collar workers, but a growing number of studies examine the impact on white-collar managerial and professional workers (see especially Kaufman [1982]; Levantman [1982]). Indeed, some scholars would argue that the debilitating effects of unemployment are more serious for higher socioeconomic groups because the latter derive a greater degree of their identity from their work than do lower-status groups (Elder [1974]; Estes [1973]; Komaroff, Masuda, and Holmes [1968]).

I shall make reference to this literature as it applies to the subjects discussed in this chapter, but see Kaufman (1982) and O'Brien (1986) for a comprehensive summary of this research vis-à-vis professional workers.

13. *Permanent* is a difficult word to apply. Few longitudinal studies follow respondents for long enough to know whether they ever find employment again. We know that the longer a period of time out of the labor force, the harder it is to find work, especially equivalent work. If someone has been unemployed for ten years, however, we can reasonably conclude that this is a permanent condition.

14. The club's records are not very reliable for statistical purposes. It is a volunteer organization, with a membership that is constantly shifting and where finding jobs takes precedence over maintaining the kinds of records a social scientist would find reliable. These figures are as accurate a count as I could obtain, but it would be hard to determine how reliable they are.

15. See *Industry Week* (1983). These benefits do not extend down the ranks to middle management, since the purpose of a golden parachute is to make sure that executives "don't have a personal, financial ax to grind when considering bids that would reward shareholders but cost executives their jobs" (*Business Week* [1984c]; Cooper [1982]). As the merger fever spread in the 1980s, so did the use of golden parachutes as a device for protecting shareholder interests. These arrangements often generate the ire of stockholders, because they make companies more expensive to buy out and therefore less attractive as takeover targets.

These arrangements should not be confused with garden-variety severance pay given to lower-level employees on the basis of years of service. Ward Howell International, Inc., a New York executive search firm, did a survey on the extent of golden parachutes and found that 37 percent of the companies protected two to five employees with golden parachutes and 30 percent protected only one. (Savings Institutions [1983]).

16. In discussing corporate references (Stybel [1985:78]) notes that many executives are too embarrassed to tell the dismissed employee that they cannot provide a positive reference. Employees listing these references may be "stabbed in the back" when they use them in job searches.

17. A variety of researchers have described adaptations to unemployment in terms of a series of stages. Eisenberg and Lazarsfeld (1938) writing about the unemployed during the Depression noted that shock is invariably the first response, a point corroborated in more recent studies by Powell and Driscoll (1973), Kaufman (1982), and Budge and Janoff (1984).

18. Briar (1976) (cited in Kaufman [1982]) notes that workers often protect

themselves from feelings of shame by keeping their job losses secret from neighbors and wives.

19. Some students of unemployment go so far as to suggest that professionals who suffer unemployment are initially relieved or suffused with bouyant optimism. They see it as a stroke of good fortune that they were "let go" from a stressful, declining, or pressured work environment (Little [1976]; Fineman [1983]).

20. This does not seem to be uncommon. Wilkes (1975) and Briar (1976) give other examples of fired employees embarking on vacations (see also Kaufman [1982:96]).

21. The most effective networks are those composed of "weak ties" rather than close friends, as Mark Granovetter (1974) has shown in his book, *Getting A Job*. A job seeker's inner circle of friends overlaps too closely the job seeker's knowledge of opportunities and influence in hiring. Hence "strong ties" may be less helpful than one might expect. More distant contacts (who are willing to get involved) are likely to extend the job seeker's knowledge of job opportunities into domains of the business world that he or she was unaware of or unable to exercise direct influence over (Granovetter [1974:52]).

22. See Granovetter (1974:110).

23. Granovetter (1974:85) argues that the length of job tenure influences the shape of work-based networks. He suggests that people who stay a short time in a job may not have had sufficient opportunity to demonstrate their capabilities to potential contacts. On the other hand, he points out that individuals who remain in one job for a long time "may foreclose future mobility by truncating the pool of personal contacts" they might turn to for job leads (ibid:85). I try to develop another side of the contact game. People use their contacts both in an instrumental fashion to help them find new jobs and as sources of emotional support. What may work in the former respect may not for the latter.

24. Kaufman (1982) argues that anxiety over job loss rises during periods of high unemployment, even among those who remain employed.

25. Paula Jaye of Esposito/Jaye Associates, quoted in *Newsweek* (1987b).

26. When the disruption is truly widespread, as it was during the Depression, it is probably still the case that those with a large number of "weak ties" fare better than those who lack them, but further research is needed to know about the resilience of networks in the face of economic downturns.

27. Goffman defines *stigma* as follows: "An individual who might have been received easily in ordinary social intercourse possesses a trait that can obtrude itself upon attention and turn those of us whom he meets away from him. . . . He possesses a stigma, an undesired differentness from what we had anticipated" (Goffman [1963:5]).

28. Robert Murphy (1987) has also discussed the ways in which the physically handicapped are thrust into a stigmatized category and made to feel that they are sociologically damaged goods. People who have damaged bodies can rarely hide their condition. Much as they may want to at times, they cannot conceal their condition except by remaining out of sight entirely. The unemployed are not in this predicament: They can engage in artful

camouflage, hoping that their "secret" is not revealed. But this places them in a different kind of bind: They must actively conceal the truth, either by omitting this aspect of their biographies or by creating a cover story that is often largely a lie. Then they have to cope with guilt about the subterfuge and shame over their dishonesty.

29. Budge and Janoff (1984:27). This is not a new phenomenon. During the Great Depression, the unemployed often felt they could be picked out of a crowd:

> How hard and humiliating it is to bear the name of an unemployed man. When I go out, I cast down my eyes because I feel myself wholly inferior. When I go along the street, it seems to me that I can't be compared with an average citizen, that everybody is pointing at me with his finger. I instinctively avoid meeting anyone. Former acquaintances and friends of better times are no longer so cordial. . . . Their eyes seem to say, "You are not worth it, you don't work" (Zawadski and Lazarsfeld [1935:239]).

30. Yet Komarovsky's (1940) landmark study, *The Unemployed Man and His Family*, found that self-blame was widespread. R. Cavan and K. Ranck (1938:150–151) showed that many people were unaware that there was something called the Depression going on; they knew only that they were suffering unemployment. Lacking a broader picture of the depths of the downturn, families were prone to blame the breadwinner rather than recognize that the whole country, and much of the world, had plunged into serious economic decline.

31. Cohn (1977) has shown that the ways in which the unemployed evaluate themselves change considerably depending on the general level of unemployment. When unemployment is low, the self-evaluations of the unemployed tend to be negative; when the rates are high, the self-evaluations of the unemployed are more positive.

32. Powell and Driscoll (1973:25) discussed the withdrawal of unemployed professionals in terms of life style changes. They note that families often turn social invitations down after a time because they alter their life-styles to suit the father's unemployment. "It was easier for them to stay at home than to be with an acquaintance whose way of life is now very different from theirs." This is an important point. For even when the unemployed can "afford" to socialize, they often find that their status has undergone such a slide that they cannot bear to mix with people with whom they used to share a common social rank.

33. As Goffman (1963:35) put it, "Post-stigma acquaintances may see him simply as a faulted person; pre-stigma acquaintances, being attached to a conception of what he once was, may be unable to treat him either with formal tact or with familiar full acceptance."

34. Professionals frequently turn to job ads as part of a job search strategy, but they are often of little help. As a means of finding a job, researchers have found ads far less effective than either the use of personal contacts or direct applications to employers (Allen [1972]; Azevedo [1974]). For a review of the literature see Kaufman (1982:156–158).

35. Granovetter (1974) gives examples of successfully reemployed professionals

who had used contacts that were of old vintage. This differs from my experiences at Forty Plus where members who remained unemployed for two years either lacked these "weak ties" or found them ultimately unhelpful.

36. Briar (1976) found that feelings of shame and stigma deriving from unemployment lead professionals to isolate themselves socially to protect their self-images. This echoes the findings of researchers working on professional unemployment during the Depression to the effect that social isolation was a common response of higher status employees to the impact of unemployment (Elder [1974]; Jahoda, Lazarsfeld, and Zeizel [1971]; Bakke [1940]). Kaufman (1982:35) argues that withdrawal from social contact is a way of protecting one's self image by diminishing the importance of other peoples' evaluations of one's conduct or situation (see also Cohn [1977]). Estes (1973) and Briar (1976) report that unemployed professionals are less sociable than their counterparts who have not lost jobs. Coyne and Lazarus (1979) and Briar (1976) argue that although the unemployed lose contact with old friends due to the stigma of unemployment, they spend time with new friends who are also out of work. I find no evidence for this last claim among the white collar managers I studied. They did not spend time together once outside the Forty Plus Club, and members who finally found jobs did not keep up contacts with their still-unemployed brethren at Forty Plus.

37. To be sure, some did have obligations to elderly parents, but these did not involve complete financial dependence.

38. One can easily imagine that other kinds of communities could provide similar degrees of support and might offer the same diversity of composition that the gay world offers Lane. Churchgoers sometimes find comfort among fellow members of a congregation. Several Forty Plus people had turned to religion in their despair over not finding a job and did indeed find their religious communities helpful as sources of networks and moral support. But most of the Forty Plus people I interviewed were not active churchgoers.

39. Estes and Wilensky (1978) found that unemployed male professionals who have dependent school-age children manifest stress symptoms far exceeding that of those who are single. Kaufman (1982:67) argues that "even when social support is present, professionals who have primary economic responsibility for others are most likely to be subjected to the highest stress levels as a result of being employed." The gay men at Forty Plus had both strong support systems and low demands placed on them for economic support.

40. There is an extensive literature on physiological effects of unemployment. Most research has been done on blue-collar workers, who show similar patterns of sleep loss, weight disturbance, anxiety, blood pressure problems (Cobb and Kasl [1971, 1977]). Brenner (1976, 1971) has shown that as unemployment rises, death rates due to strokes, heart disease, and kidney failure also rise.

41. The Marienthal study (Jahoda, Lazarsfeld, and Zeizel 1933) was the first to document the ways in which long-term unemployment introduced distortion in the use and perception of time. They argued that joblessness robbed Marienthal residents of a daily structure in their lives and thereby their control over time, leading to a sense of chaos and anomie. In a now-famous phrase they reported that "idleness ruled the day" (ibid: 73). O'Brien

(1986:188–190) has argued that they were wrong. He reanalyzed their data and cites Bakke's (1940) research, to show that the unemployed were active, albeit in costless activities confined to the home.

The symbolic approach I have adopted allows one to see this apparent disagreement as a matter of two perspectives talking past one another. In purely physical terms, the unemployed are not motionless, but in terms of symbolism and meaning (both for themselves and for observers who reflect cultural attitudes) they are idle because their activities lack socially recognized meaning. The unemployed themselves devalue their activities and see them as goalless in comparison to workplace behavior, and hence take little pleasure from them (see also Bakke [1940]). Experientially, they are doing little or nothing; objectively they are involved in many activities.

O'Brien (1986) quite correctly emphasizes that the activities of the unemployed are restricted in part because of lack of money (or poor health) to devote to "active" leisure pursuits. Because he draws heavily on studies of blue-collar workers in the 1930s, he also stresses that the unemployed lacked past experiences of "self-improvement" and "cultural activities" and hence responded to unemployment with "purposeless" activity. He (1986:196) argues that "much of the apparent inactivity and negative mood of the unemployed . . . was a function of *past* [emphasis added] work experiences which left people feeling that they lacked control of their lives."

The managers in my sample were no strangers to education, self-improvement ideologies, high culture, or to jobs in which they were in control. Yet few of them responded to unemployment by studying new subjects or skills, absorbing the cultural richness of New York City, or other forms of self-improvement. This leads me to question lack of prior cultural or self-improvement orientation as an explanation of the lack of routine or purposefulness of the modern professional unemployed.

42. Budge and Janoff (1984:29).

43. These feelings are widespread among unemployed professionals. Little (1973) found that 45 percent of the unemployed technical professionals he studied felt they "just were not a part of things."

44. My notion of categorical fate is conceptually related to an idea often invoked by psychologists: external locus of control. (Rotter 1966). The term is used to describe "people who feel they have little influence over what happens to them and attribute outcomes to outside forces such as fate or luck" (Kaufman [1982:41]; Gurin et al. [1969]). "Externals" are often contrasted to people who are guided by an "internal locus of control." *Internal locus* refers to individuals who "believe that outcomes can be determined by their own behavior." (ibid). The implication of these psychological concepts is that any given individual has a personality characterized by one or the other locus of control, though the strength of his or her orientation may alter depending on environmental circumstances.

The psychological literature on this topic is large and complex (see O'Brien [1986: ch. 7] for a thorough review) and cannot be analyzed fully here. However, a link between locus of control and unemployment has been made by psychologists who have studied the distribution of these personality types among the unemployed, the extent to which these dispositions predispose people to unemployment, and the degree to which the experience of unemployment alters an individual's control ideology.

"External locus of control" resembles my notion of categorical fate to some degree, but important differences between the two perspectives should be pointed out. First, the psychological literature tends to view an individual's orientation as a matter of personality for the most part. There are *some* psychologists who argue that "certain kinds of jobs can affect an employee's relatively enduring beliefs about the determinants of life rewards" (O'Brien [1986:160]). (Hence people in jobs that allow them the chance to use their skills and provide them with high incomes tend to believe that life's satisfactions are a function of personal ability and effort [internal control], while people in dead-end, low-paying jobs that don't provide an opportunity for skill utilization are more likely to believe that external factors "such as other people, social policies or luck" determine their life rewards [external control].) Nevertheless, even psychologists who are sensitive to context tend to see internal or external locus of control as a relatively stable orientation that conditions the way an individual responds to all kinds of situations, including downward mobility.

By contrast, my concept of categorical fate is *not* a personality attribute in the sense of a fixed aspect of an individual's character. It is a culturally conditioned viewpoint which can and does coexist with the opposite orientation (which I have termed manly flaws), or with self-blame. I find that individuals often oscillate between these multiple perspectives. In fact, an individual can hold a categorical fate explanation for why he or she was fired (for example, age discrimination) while holding a different view of why he or she has subsequently been unable to find a new job (for example, manly flaws or, in some cases, self-blame). My view of multiple and shifting perspectives is incompatible with the psychological notion of "relatively enduring" internal or external orientations toward locus of control.

An additional difference is that categorical fate goes beyond a general or abstract notion that one's personal experience is determined by forces "out there" and instead draws attention to one particular force outside one's control, namely stereotyping and the significance of membership in sociological categories that are treated in uniform ways by employers and others. Also at the center of the notion of categorical fate/manly flaws/self-blame is the idea that cultural forces, including the business press, can undermine certain explanations (and defenses) of one's fate while imposing others, that downwardly mobiles may find it difficult to avoid labeling and cultural forces which give a self-blame reading of their fate. This again is quite different from the psychologists' emphasis on stable personality orientations.

Finally, and most importantly, some of the psychological literature implies that well-adjusted individuals are those who take responsibility for their actions and the consequences of them. Hence, for these psychologists, the "choice" between external and internal locus of control is not a neutral one: People who orient toward the former are, in some sense, viewed as running away from personal responsibility for their condition, or making excuses. Anderson (1977) suggests that "externals" do not confront their objective problems and are more dependent on defensive responses (emotional or anxiety reactions) to stress than internals whose coping behaviors are "apparently associated with a more successful solution of . . . problems" (p. 450).

Moreover, in studies of the long-term unemployed, some psychologists have found that "externals" are disproportionately represented compared to employed control groups (Searls et al. [1974]). They also interpret this to mean that the unemployed had this orientation prior to their downward mobility (Andrisani and Abeles [1976], quoted in Kaufman [1982:42] and Andrisani and Nestel [1976]). This implies that somehow "externals" are being disproportionately fired.

In a sense, I advance the opposite perspective. People who consider themselves victims of categorical fate are probably the better "social scientists": They are aware of the ways in which they are perceived by others as exemplars of social groups and are caught up in social processes, like stigmatization of the unemployed, which are larger than themselves, while those who see their lives as entirely a matter of individual control are less acute in their sociological awareness and tend to overlook the extraindividual factors that either rendered them unemployed in the first place or made it difficult for them to find jobs thereafter.

45. This point is supported by a considerable amount of research on age and unemployment. Loomba (1967) and the Batelle Memorial Institute (1971) found that being too old is second only to lack of jobs as the most important barrier to reemployment among jobless professionals.

46. Negative attitudes toward the unemployed are hardly new. During the Depression, it was commonly believed that there was something wrong with a man who couldn't find a job and epithets such as "pampered poverty rats" were spoken loudly, particularly by those opposed to government programs (McElvaine [1984:173]).

47. Little (1973).

48. Little (1973:148).

49. I am not suggesting that no one who is unemployed falls into the sick role, only that such an attitude is not a necessary consequence of invoking categorical fate.

50. Wareham (1987).

51. *Forbes* (1984) notes that 68 percent of white-collar layoffs are based on seniority rather than ability.

52. *Fortune* (1984).

53. *Forbes* (1984:111).

54. Many corporations looking to avoid law suits based on age or race discrimination in firings have begun to make greater use of yearly performance appraisals and numerical rates for management, in order to have measurements of productivity or effectiveness to lean on when they wield the axe. The trend is, in part, a response to the tenfold increase in litigation on the part of fired middle managers over the decade 1972–82 (Miller 1983).

55. Stybel (1982).

56. Fortune (1987:26).

57. See Table A3 in the Appendix for data on the occupations of displaced managers.

58. Liebow (1969).

59. Hartley (1980).

60. Nettle (1971).
61. Hartley (1980).
62. Kanter (1977).
63. There are many reasons why some people lack protective ties, some of which have nothing to do with personality. Managers who work in industries that are volatile or highly mobile—for example, stock brockerage—often find that friends and benefactors they might count on have moved on with such frequency that they are not available when trouble strikes.
64. Revealing the genealogy of the work ethic in Calvinism was, of course, the contribution of Max Weber (1958) in the *Protestant Ethic and the Spirit of Capitalism.* The subsequent evolution of this worldview into a secular philosophy has been charted by Robert Bellah (1975; 1985) in two books, *The Broken Covenant* and *Habits of the Heart.*

   There are important differences between the Protestant ethic in its original and modern secular incarnations. As Bellah et al. (1985) have noted, in its original form, dedication to the work ethic did not have a selfish or materialistic focus. The believer was enjoined not to enjoy the fruits of success but rather to reinvest them. (Weber [1958]). More importantly, the work ethic was part of a larger concern for the well-being of the community in colonial New England. As community members, the elect had obligations of charity and brotherly love toward one another and were engaged in a collective project—the construction of a virtuous society (Bellah 1975:16–18). In this manner, individual salvation was tempered by the demands of civic virtue.

   This Protestant orientation toward serving the greater good has largely passed out of our culture, however, leaving behind a more materialistic and personal rationale for hard work: upward mobility for oneself and family (Bellah et al. [1985]).
65. Psychologists have found that individuals who fail to achieve their aspirations often evaluate themselves as inferior and report feelings of guilt, shame, and depression (Estes [1973]; Kaufman [1982]; Jackson [1962]). They are prone to seeing their situations as evidence of "personal failures" (Jackson [1962:476] quoted in Kaufman [1982:32]).
66. There is evidence to support his views on the demise of middle management. In a survey of large U.S. corporations conducted in 1983 for the Harvard Business School, LdG Associates found that 56 percent of the companies had cut middle management in the previous year. Even highly profitable and fast-growing companies had done so. The findings prompted some analysts to argue that a philosophical sea-change has occurred: "top managers have begun to value middle management less" (Main [1984]).
67. Victor's response was fairly typical, but there were exceptions to meritocratic individualism among my interviewees. George Mahoney, the man who had been let go from the foreign bank responded differently. Mahoney had never given much thought to the privileges he had had in life, nor had he realized how ephemeral success could be. Once he landed a new job, he found himself feeling grateful for both. He also felt sympathy for people he had never given a moment's thought before, people whom he met on the line in the unemployment office. George came to the realization that tragedy can strike almost anyone, that people need protection and rarely find it. The experience reawakened in him a religious sentiment that had

been dormant for many years. George and a few others were brought back to faith as a result of their distress and frustration.

68. McElvaine (1984:172) notes that letters from the unemployed to Eleanor Roosevelt during the Depression frequently complained that they could not keep up appearances and that this was proving a barrier to finding employment. Missing teeth and shabby suits were among the more commonly mentioned problems.

69. Many were actively seeking consulting opportunities and occasionally found a few, but free-lance consulting is hard to come by, and only the fortunate, well-connected few can make a steady living this way.

70. See Goffman (1963:62–66).

71. I excluded from these figures those members of the club who had found jobs and lost them again within the eighteen-month period and were therefore back on "active" status. There were also a number of members who could not be accounted for at all. It is not clear whether they found new jobs or disappeared from the labor force, but it is common knowledge among the active members that people who take low-level jobs are loath to admit it and sometimes "disappear" rather than make public (to their peers) their defeat.

72. This is not surprising in light of the research that has been done on the relationship between age and salary reduction following unemployment. Kaufman (1980) has found that older terminated professionals experience the greatest salary reductions when reemployed. Drucker (1975) found that the older the unemployed professionals, the greater the reduction in the salary they are willing to accept to improve their employability. Within the category of the older reemployed, professional women remain unemployed longer than men (Kaufman [1980]). Moreover, professional women are likely to have learned typing and other skills that enable them to find positions that are well below their previous positions in rank and income (Kaufman [1982:291]).

73. My use of the term *skidding* should not be confused with Harold Wilensky's (1959) usage in his paper "The Skidder." Wilensky used the word to refer to intergenerational downward mobility—a son who failed to match his father's occupational status. I use it here instead to describe the way in which a person hits several intermediary points along the way down the slope of downward mobility.

74. Riesman (1950).

75. It is surprising that an astute observer of corporate life like Rosabeth Kanter (1977) characterizes secretaries in large corporations as praise-addicted, but does not see that the fast-track manager who works sixty hour weeks in the expectation of rapid promotion is no less habituated to recognition from superiors. The form of praise addiction is different in the two cases—managers expect promotion and raises rather than the boss's smile or flirtation. But is the psychological dependency so very different?

76. Kanter (1977) gives a rich portrayal of the various adaptations of managers who find themselves unable to advance.

77. Robert Jackall (1983) has analyzed the survival value of sycophantic behavior in bureaucratic organizations.

78. C. Wright Mills (1951).

79. Turner (1967).
80. Murphy (1987).
81. Douglas (1966).
82. Murphy (1987:131).
83. Cf. Murphy (1987:117).
84. Building on Turner's work, Murphy shows how the disabled enjoy a degree of egalitarianism that would be unthinkable among the able-bodied. The shared identity of disability overshadows distinctions of social rank, occupation, race and—most incredibly—even gender. This introduces a degree of equality that is hard to find elsewhere.

     The downwardly mobile managers differ in this regard. Because there is always the possibility of "climbing out," they hold on to differences of status and continue to think in terms of status hierarchies. Their condition is potentially reversible, unlike that of the permanently disabled, and ironically this prevents them from sharing the comforts of egalitarian social life among themselves. They do not build a community together.

Chapter Four

1. I interviewed people who are now adults (twenty-one to thirty-five) whose families became downwardly mobile during their early to late adolescent years. They were raised in California and in the Northeast. Their accounts are, therefore, retrospective and in some cases involve their reflections on events that took place 5 to 10 years before the interview. I chose this group because I was as interested in the long-term significance of downward mobility for these "adult children" as I was in their immediate experiences at the time, and because access to the children while children was problematic.
2. Voydanoff (1983:95).
3. This should not be overstated. Teenagers are subject to greater peer influence than are younger children. However Ianni (1984) has documented that parents have more influence over teens than the popular stereotype might suggest.
4. Komarovsky (1940) found something similar: Working class families in the Depression would cut back on the least visible expenditures first, hoping to preserve a public face of normalcy as long as possible.
5. See Paula Leventman's (1981) masterful book *Professionals Out of Work* for an account of physicists, engineers, and other technical professionals whose careers were dashed by the cutbacks in federal defense spending in the early 1970s.
6. Mrs. Miller's attitude about food stamps has plenty of historical precedent. McElvaine (1984:176–177) and other historians of the Great Depression have pointed out that the shame of applying for relief was very intense in the 1930s. He notes that relief recipients were roundly condemned as lethargic, docile, listless, and lazy. The same attitude has carried over to the modern-day recipient of food stamps.
7. Indeed, Dierdre's interview for this study was one of the few times she ever discussed her family's economic history with anyone. She was not alone

in this. Survivors of downward mobility in the managerial class often feel so ashamed of their family's problems that they believe no one will understand the situation. They often show surprise that their experiences were similar to others'. They seem to think that their fates are unique.

8. For the generation interviewed in this research, having a downwardly mobile mother was less of a trauma because this was not defined as deviant. Many of the children (who are now between twenty-one and thirty-five) had mothers whose work careers had been interrupted by or sacrificed to full-time family responsibilities. Their children did not view this as a source of shame because it was the norm. This will undoubtedly be less true for future generations. The more middle-class mothers invest themselves in careers, the more their downward mobility will become a problem both for them and their children.

9. Suburbs are notorious for poor public transportation. They are organized on the premise that families will have private cars and little need of a bus system. For the unemployed with a run-down car, this can be a major impediment to the job search process or to keeping a position once found. Cars represent a major investment that can prove onerous for downwardly mobile families struggling to stay afloat.

10. The English workman's love of sugared tea began as status climbing, when sugar was a prestige food consumed mainly by the upper classes (Mintz 1985). Steak functions in much the same way for the American middle class.

11. One of the most persistent worries of Depression era families was the fear of eviction (McElvaine [1984:184]). The downwardly mobile middle class is less likely to encounter eviction but feels much the same sense of deprivation about loss of ownership.

12. Many of the families discussed here were forced into distress sales in the mid-1970s. Housing prices had already begun escalating by then, but many missed out on what later became truly staggering increase in real estate values, which might have guaranteed them much higher profits than what they actually received.

13. It is a truism of downward mobility that the meaning of a loss, be it a house or a job, can only be understood relative to a particular starting point. One man's vision of poverty may be another's undreamed of luxury. Harold Connover (a Forty Plus member) had always lived on the East Side of Manhattan. When Connover's career took a nosedive and he had no income to speak of for over five years, he decided to sell his inherited East Side apartment and move to the West Side of the island. His new home is, by the standards of most ordinary mortals, quite impressive. High atop a new luxury building, he now lives in a three-bedroom condominium that cost nearly a quarter of a million dollars. Still unemployed, he was able to purchase his new home free and clear because the value of the apartment his parents had left him was much greater. Though the area has recently gentrified, displacing the Hispanic families that used to define its character, it is quite a comedown in Harry's mind. It is not the kind of place that "old money" would deign to visit, much less reside in. He is just glad that his parents are no longer alive to see where he lives. They would surely see it as a disgrace.

14. Littwin (1986).
15. *Bergen County Record* (1986).
16. Pooling of resources in the Depression was made all the more necessary by the fact that adult men were often in the industries and occupations hardest hit by the crash. Employers could and did replace them with adolescent males and women workers—who were cheaper to hire. (Eisenberg and Lazarsfeld [1938]). Gender segregation in the job market also meant, ironically, that jobs defined as "women's work" were off-limits for men, despite the widespread prejudice against working women, particularly those who were married (McElvaine [1984:182]; Kessler-Harris [1982]). Hence it was often the formerly dependent members of a household who obtained or were able to hold on to gainful employment, while the father was sidelined by the Depression.
17. The equation of money and power is as clear today as it was in the 1930s. The question of authority, and its foundation (the value of the father's paycheck or the moral authority of his position as household leader), dominated many of the sociological investigations into the impact of the Depression on the American family. Mirra Komarovsky (1940) noted that adolescent boys who went to work while their fathers were unemployed exacted a price for turning over their paychecks: They wanted increased authority and control. They were unwilling to act like subordinates when they were the family's major source of support. They demanded that some power be ceded in recognition of their newfound roles as providers. Komarovsky points to these demands—and the resistance with which they were met by frustrated, unemployed fathers—as a major source of friction in working-class households during the 1930s.
18. Even in this fragile state, Janet could not escape the stigma of downward mobility:

> I had to see a psychiatrist every week. But I had to tell him that we just couldn't pay him. We had to adjust the fees so I'd be paying half-price. It was a big embarrassment on the part of my parents, because they felt he deserved his pay but they couldn't pay it. We were always delinquent. It put a lot of pressure on me to get better quicker.

19. In the last ten years, psychologists have begun to reexamine the assumption that the family constitutes one reality for all its members. Plomin and Daniels (1987) and Daniels et al. (1985) argue that the family is actually an "unshared environment," with each child experiencing the family environment somewhat differently: in terms of their treatment of each other, in their peer interactions, and perhaps in terms of parental treatment. The well-known family composition variables (birth order and gender differences) account for only a small portion of the variance of sibling differences in development.

These studies suggest that prior conceptions of families as single units are flawed. However, they do not consider the prospect that disjunctures in the family experience like sudden downward mobility are sources of variation between siblings, presumably because they assume that these disjunctures hit everyone simultaneously and in the same way. Indeed, Plomin and Daniels (1987) state that "even though the Socioeconomic Status (SES) of families changes, it is unlikely that SES is an important source of differences between siblings." This assumption needs to be reexamined by considering the ways in which changes in SES hit siblings at different points in their development and produce variation between them in personality, behavior, and expectations. And while I have emphasized catastrophic events, less drastic changes would also introduce variation in the family environment to which siblings are exposed in differential ways.

One caveat is in order here: My claim that "multiple realities" emerge when siblings undergo downward mobility is contingent on the age spread in a sibling set and the timing of the disruption of downward mobility. Dierdre's family exhibits multiple realities in part because there are five siblings, representing a long span. In families with only two children who are closely spaced, one would expect less variation in their perceptions of downward mobility simply because their vantage points are comparatively similar. Note that the number of siblings is not, in and of itself, critical: One would expect to find just as much variation between two siblings separated by fifteen years as I found in Dierdre's family (with five).

The timing of the disruption is important as well. Children affected by downward mobility in their early years will share certain characteristics in common, because their vantage points will be similar in many ways, regardless of how many siblings they have. But they will not be identical: The dynamics of protection, envy, and support do differ between smaller and larger siblings sets.

20. Studies of the wives of unemployed professionals document show that substantial numbers do begin to work following their husbands' job loss. Leventman (1981:135) and Little (1976) report that three-quarters of the wives of unemployed male professionals were working.

21. Many accounts of family life during the Depression (for example, McElvaine [1984:180–181]) argue that the loss of the provider role was by far the greatest source of trauma for fathers:

> Since the father's position was based upon his occupation and his role as provider, the loss of his job was likely to mean a decline in his status within the family. The man who was without a position was, well, without a position. It was he who was supposed to provide independence for the family.

The stress laid on unemployment and the erosion of the father's role has been implicitly criticized, however, by other studies (for example, Komarovsky [1940]) that argue strong families were able to withstand these losses without undue damage to the father's role. Families that were, prior to the Depression, riddled with conflict and lack of respect, glued together only by instrumental relations, were the ones in which fathers really suffered once unemployed.

22. See also Kaufman (1982); Wilkes (1975); and Leventman (1982).

23. Beer (1983) argues that household sex roles are no longer guided by deep tradition in the United States and that, in essence, the modern man contributes to housework because he is needed. Others (for example, Berardo et al. 1987) argue that no such shift has occurred. In any case, few of these studies examine the subjective responses of fathers or children to shifts in the household division of labor that are forced by negative circumstances.

24. Elder (1974).

25. Daughters of downward mobility are hardly the only women of their genera-

tion to take a more independent role in the financial management of their families. They have many counterparts in their generation, professional women who also retain finances independent of their husbands. But when asked to explain these practices, the downwardly mobile daughters couch their customs in terms of their observations about the experience of economic loss. The feminist logic is there, but it is comparatively secondary.

26. Demo and Savin-Williams (1983) have argued that as children grow older, socioeconomic position becomes increasingly important as a source of self-esteem. Their research suggests an upswing in awareness of class position between the fifth and eighth grades.

27. This finding echoes Komarovsky's (1940) research as well. She found that fathers who had good relations with their wives and children before the Depression, were more likely to retain the respect of the family than those whose relations had already been tense or based on deference to his purely instrumental role as breadwinner.

28. Ironically, Dierdre's involvement in her father's business created in her a more tolerant and sympathetic perspective of him than her mother had. Her mother was at home with the smaller children in the family and was not as intimately acquainted with the business and her father's efforts as Dierdre.

29. Custom varies widely in this regard. In some households, dinner conversation steers clear of the work domain, since it is considered either too complex, boring, or even too private for adolescent ears. In others, suppertime is an occasion for each family member to report on the day's activities, including Dad.

   Ostrander (1984) reports that in many upper-class households, wives have very little concrete idea exposure to what their husbands do for a living. The work world is a domain entirely apart from the family. The households in question here are not drawn from the very wealthy, and it would be considered aberrant for wives of middle class managers to know nothing about their husbands' jobs. But the extent to which children are incorporated is a matter of family custom.

30. Having an idea of alcoholism's precipitating causes is not the same thing as knowing for sure what caused a parent to fall prey to it. Children (and scholars for that matter) can never be absolutely certain why their parents develop into alcoholics. But it remains striking that some are convinced that alcohol problems preceded the business failures while others are sure that it was the other way around.

31. Bakke (1940:185) and Stouffer and Lazarsfeld (1938:99) make the same point for families in the 1930s.

32. But they can also disintegrate or become severely strained by downward mobility because it is precisely to the family that the economically stressed may turn.

33. See also Marcel Mauss (1954) and Alvin Gouldner (1960).

34. Where the bonds between groups are viewed as tenuous or impermanent, exchanges have to be repeated time and time again to cement the relations between exchange partner. Conversely, where social bonds are inherently permanent (for example, within the family), there is less need for frequent

exchange and an absence of exact reciprocity. Caplow (1982) makes the same point in a different context.

35. Leach (1982:154), Malinowski (1926:48) discussing the Trobriand Islanders, supports Leach's contention that reciprocity is expected, even within the family. Malinowski argued that "the most unselfish relation, that between a man and his sister, [is] founded on mutuality and repayment of services."

36. Some would argue that children have an obligation to return material assistance to their elderly parents, and this might be construed as a "delayed" exchange. But President Reagan discovered that this perspective is no longer widely shared: he suggested that each family should provide for its own elderly (rather than the government) and was met with a hail of objection. At the very least, it can be argued that children are obliged to reciprocate with love and affection in exchange for parental support. For love in the context of exchange theory see Blau (1964).

37. Sahlins (1965:141) sets us a contrast between "exchange" (between families or collectivities) and "pooling" (within a family or collectivity). He argues that "generalized reciprocity, 'pure gifts,' or pooling, alternative names for the kind of sharing found within families, are not based on expectations of repayment. "Failure to reciprocate does not cause the giver to stop giving: the goods move one way in favor of the have-not, for a very long period," (ibid:147). Although based on ethnographic evidence from preindustrial peoples, the model is equally valid for the contemporary American situation.

38. Leach (1982:154).

39. Reciprocity can be an important feature of exchanges, even those that do not involve money. Stoller (1985) has shown that exchange of help among elderly people is also carefully measured between giver and taker. She notes that the inability to reciprocate has a greater negative effect on morale than the need for help in the first place.

40. Glen Elder's study of children in the Great Depression followed the same cohort into adulthood in the 1950s. He found that the economic and status losses of middle-class families provided the children with motivation to achieve in their own adult careers. He notes that "a childhood which shelters the young from the hardships of life consequently fails to develop or test adaptive capacities which are called upon in life crises. To engage and manage real-life (though not excessive) problems in childhood and adolescence is to participate in a sort of apprenticeship for adult life" (Elder 1974:249–250). McElvaine (1984:185) makes much the same argument.

41. A phrase coined by Elder (1974).

42. There are uncanny resemblances between these fiscal conservatives and their own grandparents, who were adults during the Depression and who bear the marks of economic deprivation.

43. I do not claim to have a reliable sample from which to generalize about the frequency of these problems. My purpose here is simply to outline the dimensions of the most common problems that plague the families I have studied, and to describe the more extreme pathologies as well. Moreover, I want to consider some ways in which these pathologies affect the children of downward mobility as they grow up and face the daily ups and downs of adult life.

44. George Vaillant's (1983) longitudinal research on alcoholism has shown that the characterological problems and the marital discord associated with alcoholism typically follow rather than precede the onset of alcoholism. This implies they are usually symptoms rather than causes of alcohol abuse.
45. See Hannerz (1969) and Stack (1974).
46. There is a large literature on the causes of family violence. Among the conclusions reached by some of the leading authorities in the field, is that there is a close connection between unemployment and wife or child abuse (Finkelhor [1983:19, 21]; Straus et al. [1980]).
47. His behavior is consistent with Finkelhor's (1983:19) observations:

> Although [abusive acts] are the acts of the strong against the weak, they seem to be acts carried out by abusers to compensate for their perceived lack of or loss of power. . . . This attempt to compensate is often bound up in a sense of powerlessness, particularly with regard to masculine ideals in our society.

48. It is difficult to know what separates families like Alice's from those who develop only the "normal pathologies" that we might associate with any individual or group under constant stress. Part of the answer lies in the bleakness of the Seattle labor market that followed from the Boeing crash. Eighteen years later, things appear to be returning to normal, but the period of citywide distress was long enough to hurt an entire generation of workers. There were few opportunities for Mr. Pendergast to look forward to and a depressed climate all around him. Moreover, it would appear that the intensity of her father's alcohol abuse was greater than many. Perhaps most important, her family suffered from a degree of social isolation that was more extreme than many. No extended relatives lived near by. Friendships eroded quickly. Indeed, Alice's most painful memories involve the feeling of complete isolation in the midst of misery. No one would help. Even the policemen who responded to her mother's distress calls seemed uninvolved, bored by another domestic dispute.
49. Gelles (1974).
50. I continue to emphasize fathers here, because the adult children of downwardly mobile families I interviewed all came from single-earner households up until the time that their fathers became unemployed. Hence they tie the debacle directly to their father's careers and not to their mothers'. In future years it will undoubtedly be the case that adult children of downwardly mobile families will have gone through this experience as a result of their mother's employment problems as well.
51. Galambos and Silbereisen (1987) make a similar, but not identical, point in analyzing survey data on West German families. They show that fathers and mothers who have undergone income loss tend to adopt "pessimistic life outlooks" that are, in turn, related to "the adolescent daughter's lower expectancy for jobs success." The authors do not dwell on the "genetic" issue, and since their data is quantitative rather than qualitative, the metaphors these daughters might use to describe their lower expectations for job success are not available.
52. This vignette comes from a lecture given by Professor Keller on the occasion of the retirement of Professors Lewis and Rose Coser from the State Univer-

sity of New York at Stony Brook in the Spring of 1986. With Dr. Keller's permission, I have recounted the events from notes of her very moving lecture.

53. Czeslav Milosz, the Nobel Prize winning author from Poland, describes similar experiences in his books *The Captive Mind* (1953) and *Visions from San Francisco Bay* (1982). Indeed, Milosz argues that Americans and Europeans are fundamentally different in outlook and character precisely because the former have not experienced the chaos of invasion on their own soil.

54. The war experience played out somewhat differently for Keller, whose skepticism is directed more toward the world than toward herself. While children of downwardly mobile families feel singled out and fearful of their own capacity for failure, Keller worries that "the world harbors a slow virus for chaos and upheaval" (Suzanne Keller, letter, September 1987).

Chapter Five

1. To unravel the retrospective process, I analyze data drawn from twenty-five intensive interviews of individuals who participated in the air traffic controllers' strike of 1981. This material was collected in the San Francisco Bay area and in the New York/New Jersey area during 1984–1985. These interviews were augmented by analyses of data from two questionnaire surveys (detailed below), archival research in union files, analysis of national newspaper and media coverage of the strike, and interviews with union officials.

2. Jones (1982).

3. Morgan (1984).

4. Only 3–5 percent of the controller work force were women.

5. In this, the military controllers resemble the rebellious, anti-authority orientation described by Paul Willis (1977) in his research on the working class in schools. In many respects, the regimentation of the military was similar to that of the educational institutions from which these men emerged.

6. Britta Fischer (1985:20) argues that air traffic controllers should be regarded as members of the "salaried petty bourgeoisie" rather than as professionals. I chose to adopt the class location controllers themselves adopted when they formed their "professional association" (PATCO) and attempted to distance themselves from blue-collar organized labor. Indeed, it has been suggested that the very act of emphasizing their professionalism cost them the support of the AFL-CIO, among others. Nevertheless, I recognize the difficulty of categorizing a highly skilled occupation that is subject to credentialism and yet lacks the autonomy characteristic of other more typical professions (such as medicine and law).

7. In the last few years before the strike, the controllers were forced to work six-day weeks as well. Many complained that this work load was too stressful, that it exhausted them so badly that their judgment was impaired.

8. Cf. Lipset, Trow, and Coleman (1956).

9. This responsibility is quite personal: Every command a controller issues is tape recorded to permit a postmortem in the event of an accident.

10. A recent GAO (1986) study shows that over 90 percent of the strikers they surveyed would still like to come back to work as controllers. Thus far only 500 have actually been reinstated through administrative hearings and court judgments. These 500 had to be able to prove that they were not "on strike" even though they did not report for work.

11. Indeed, many of the same grievances have surfaced among the current controller work force, the vast majority of whom were either nonstrikers or poststrike hirees (GAO 1986).

12. Morgan (1984); Bowers (1982); Shostak and Skocik (1986).

13. *New York Times* (1981b).

14. These data come from a survey conducted by the General Accounting Office, the research arm of Congress. In 1986 the GAO was asked to survey the current controller work force and a sample of fired controllers in order to provide background information Congress could use in debating one of the many measures that have been introduced in recent years to rehire strikers on a selective basis. [The measures have all been defeated.] The data are the best available information on the occupational fate of the controllers, but the findings must be approached with caution. The GAO pulled a random sample of some 800 fired controllers, but were only able to find addresses for 475. The response rate among these people was a healthy 91 percent. But the inability to locate so many threatens the randomness of the sample. In fact, there is reason to suspect that if anything, the 475 were in better shape than those the GAO could not locate, since the latter are more likely to have been displaced from their homes. Hence the survey probably presents a rosier picture of the controllers' fortunes than a true random sample would.

There is a second survey that has similar problems with the sample. Steven O'Keefe, a fired controller, designed and distributed a survey to the 2,500 members of the United States Air Traffic Controllers organization in 1984. This organization was founded in the wake of the court-ordered decertification of PATCO following the strike. Nine hundred respondents returned the survey (for a 34 percent response rate, which is low but probably unavoidable given the difficulty of tracking a population that suffered this degree of economic dislocation). O'Keefe's findings are very similar to the GAO study, despite the fact that the USATCO membership is undoubtedly a self-selected group of strikers (see Shostak and Skocik [1986] for a detailed analysis of this data).

I have relied on the GAO study because despite its limitations it was drawn from a random sample, rather than from the membership lists of USATCO. The data is therefore, in my judgment, more reliable as a source from which to generalize to the rest of the striking controllers.

15. Forty percent did become managerial workers. But many of these people were in "technical" occupations (such as dispatchers) that fell far short of air traffic control in terms of requisite skill and expertise.

16. U.S. Bureau of the Census (1984:406).

17. Strikers faced federal charges for violating back-to-work orders in fifty-seven federal courts across the country. The government issued criminal complaints against thirty-nine PATCO leaders (Shostak and Skocik [1986:109]).

18. Poli (1982).
19. Interview with Bill Taylor (August, 1985), the director of PATCO Lives.
20. This point should not be overstressed. There were strikers who regretted their decisions and blame themselves for being pressured into the strike. Yet their disagreements were more about the efficacy or advisability of a strike as a tactic, not the question of whether the grievances that provoked it were legitimate. These doubters also focus on Reagan as an enemy, but they add others to the list, including their own union leadership, whom they feel led them astray.
21. USATCO was a nonprofit organization founded after PATCO was decertified and stripped of its treasury by the federal courts. PATCO Lives is a one-man operation in Washington, D.C., which is run by a fired controller, Mr. Bill Taylor. Taylor maintains a hotline and an active newsletter to which 5,300 veterans of the 1981 strike subscribe. His work is funded entirely from voluntary contributions from strikers and their sympathizers.
22. The insistence that money was not at the heart of the strike (a point disputed by some researchers who did surveys for PATCO in 1981 [interview with Shostak]) is interesting in light of the generally held belief that financial well-being is a legitimate, even praiseworthy pursuit in American society. It appears to be inconsistent with notion of purity that is critical to the definition of a crusade.
23. I owe this formulation to a reviewer for *Cultural Anthropology* who provided a helpful critique of Newman (1987). I have taken the liberty of quoting this anonymous colleague.
24. These quotes are excerpted from handwritten comments appended to the anonymous questionnaires distributed by USATCO, discussed in footnote [14] above.
25. Reagan to Poli, quoted in the *New York Times* (1981a).
26. As long as they do not cross certain moral lines.
27. The force of loyalty as a laudable value was given expression is a curious context in 1986, when the famous (or infamous) Washington lawyer, Roy Cohn, died. William Safire, the conservative columnist, berated the "Establishment bar" for sullying Cohn's reputation and praised him posthumously for being a man one could count on:

    > [Cohn] started his career exploiting national disloyalty but wound up an exemplar of personal loyalty. Ask anyone who knew him well, and that's the word you hear, sometimes defensively: loyal. Loyalty may not be the most important trait in a human being, and it can be misplaced; but in a time of coolly calibrated acquaintanceships, it is good to be able to count on someone to fight fiercely for you even if he disagrees with you. Loyalty has moral value and can bring out the best in us" (Safire [1986]).

28. Wilensky (1964).
29. Jane Fonda's film *The China Syndrome* is a fictitious drama built around the same theme, in which a technician who understands the danger of a poorly constructed nuclear power plant is overruled by his bosses, who are more concerned about profit and the political threat to the nuclear industry.
30. Goodwyn (1976).
31. The formulation is reminiscent of the blue-collar worker's cynicism regarding

all politicians: that they are creatures of vested interest, by nature unable to avoid corruption (see Halle [1984]).

32. For a complete list, see *New York Times* (1987c).

33. Will Wright (1975:190) applies this analysis to forty years of Hollywood Westerns, arguing that their heroic themes represent larger American myths about individuality, respect, acceptance, strength, freedom, and goodness that are ways of restating "the conceptual conflicts of modern America." See also Bellah (1985:146).

34. It is important to note that these views were shared both by informants who were supporters of the strike and those who felt it was an ill-advised disaster from the beginning. As one man who had serious and public reservations about the strike at the time put it: "I'm fighting a one-man campaign to let people know what really happened. This is very important. [We need] to counteract all the propaganda and misconceptions people had, to let them know what the real problems were." Thus participation in the present crusade is not contingent on having been a supporter of the strike action in 1981. The attachment of stigma to all of those who lost their jobs binds the strikers together into a moral community in 1988, one devoted at a minimum to retrospective public legitimation.

35. Much of my research was conducted in 1985, a year in which a record number of people were killed in airplane accidents. The controllers I interviewed pointed to these events as proof of the incompetence of those "scabs" who replaced them. Strikers took particular delight in newspaper accounts that the FAA manipulated "near miss" statistics, concealing from the public the deterioration in the air traffic control system (*New York Times* [1987d]; *Wall Street Journal* [1985].

36. The report points out that the problems in the system will intensify in the late 1980s, as the most experience controllers (those who did not go out on strike) reach retirement age (CBS *Nightly News* 1986).

37. *Newsweek* (1987).

38. "Voicing the same complaints that led to a strike six years ago, the nation's air traffic controllers voted overwhelmingly last week to form a new union" (New York Times [1987e]).

39. Various newspaper articles that appeared in 1981 confirmed this perspective, arguing that the move against the controllers was a concerted effort to nip white-collar unionism in the bud (New York Times, 1981b).

40. This quote is excerpted from handwritten comments appended to the anonymous questionnaires distributed by USATCO, discussed in footnote 14 above.

41. From *The Lifeline* (1985).

Chapter Six

1. I discuss the controversies over the deindustrialization thesis at length in chapter Two. See also Cohen and Zysman (1987).

2. Bluestone and Harrison (1982), Cobb and Kasl (1977); Foltman (1968); Gordus et al. (1981).

3. There are studies that assess the impact of plant closures on community mental health, but they are not fundamentally concerned with the subjective

experience from a cultural point of view. See especially Buss and Redburn (1983a, 1983b); Jahoda (1982).

4. The question of whether well-paid blue-collar workers are middle class or working class has been at issue in the sociological literature for decades. By including blue-collar victims of a plant closure in a book on middle-class downward mobility, I put them on something of a sociological par with the managers, the air traffic controllers, and the divorced women (discussed in chapter 7). I take my cue here from David Halle's (1984) book, *America's Working Man*. Halle argues that "affluent" blue-collar workers see themselves as "working men" on the job, where they must endure monotony, a lack of autonomy, and limited opportunity for advancement. But the income derived from well-paid blue-collar jobs makes possible a life-style that overlaps to a substantial degree with occupations associated with middle class. Hence, the chemical workers he studied regard themselves as "working men" who are "middle class." The workers described in this chapter are very similar, even though they worked in a more traditional industry than the chemical plant Halle studied. They were nevertheless homeowners; many of them sent their kids to private parochial schools. Their standard of living often required two incomes (where the controllers or managers might achieve the same with only one), but the resulting life-style was middle class in most respects.

5. See Edward Shils (1981) for an elaborate discussion of the idea of tradition.

6. Cf. Calhoun (1983).

7. The plant moved out of Manhattan in search of larger quarters with ready access to a port and cheaper utilities.

8. Jensen and Davidson (1984) document the prohibitive expense of acquiring a sewing machine and the fears of working-class seamstresses that their livelihood will be destroyed by the coming of the machine.

9. For an analysis of Singer's manufacturing and marketing innovations see Chandler (1977), especially ch. 9.

10. The company moved into everything from educational aids to furniture to space-flight simulators.

11. New York Times (1987f).

12. *Elizabeth Daily Journal* (1939).

13. During World War II, employment rose to over 10,000 in response to government contracts.

14. The club currently has at least 200 active members, who meet once a month in Elizabeth. Once a year the club sponsors a formal dance that is widely attended and is considered an important social occasion.

15. *New York Times* (1982).

16. It should be understood, however, that a middle-class life-style among the Singer workers was generally predicated on two incomes in the household. Hence, where executives and managers were often able to reach this plateau on a single salary, Singer families could only approximate it with the labor of husbands and wives.

17. The Singer company was in the forefront of industrial technology for mass production, and the Elizabeth factory was particularly well known for innovative work:

In 1863 . . . Singer began to mechanize its production processes, building more and more specialized machinery, until by 1880 its American factory—by then at Elizabethport, New Jersey—was manned with automatic and semiautomatic machine tools. . . . Writers throughout the technical literature proclaimed the Singer plant as a progressive establishment (Hounshell 1985:91).

18. The social and occupational costs of plant closures have been documented in a large number of important impact studies based on survey research data. This research provides a much more comprehensive understanding of the fiscal impact of deindustrialization than the life history method employed here, which is primarily valuable for charting subjective responses to a shutdown. For additional data on economic consequences see especially Bluestone and Harrison (1982); Buss and Redburn (1983a, 1983b); Cobb and Kasl (1977); Gordus et al. (1981); Root (1984); Shepard et al. (1960); and Wilcock and Frank (1963).

19. Early retirement cost the Singer workers 4 percent of their benefits for every year they were under sixty-five.

20. Even if financial problems are somewhat mitigated by early retirement, this provides little comfort for the psychological and social problems that attend premature removal from the work force. The feeling that at fifty-five one has suddenly been placed in the category of people who are "over the hill" and no longer needed, combined with the isolation that unplanned retirement brings, can make for considerable difficulty (see Buss and Redburn [1984]).

21. Singer workers qualified for additional federal unemployment benefits under the Job Training Partnership Act of 1982, which added about six months to the standard one year of unemployment benefits. Their only other source of income involved a seniority-based payout from a lawsuit settled in favor of the workers a year or so after the closing.

22. Many of the wives of Singer men worked in clerical occupations that were not well paid; these households were hit hard. The husbands of Singer women were often blue-collar workers who earned more than their wives; these families were comparatively better off, but nevertheless suffered a considerable constriction in their resources.

23. The data for this chapter was collected over a two-year period, 1983–1985. A number of students took part in my research in the spring of 1984 as part of a graduate seminar in urban anthropology. Several generously permitted me to quote from interviews they collected. In particular, I wish to thank Gina Bria, Jan Kubik, Michael McCabe, Ronnie Lichtman, Anastasia Karakasidou, Elissa Tessler, and Lori Traikos.

24. Singer's original world headquarters in downtown Manhattan was one of the first "skyscrapers" in New York City. Completed in 1908, it was forty-seven stories high and was, for a period of eighteen months, the tallest building in the world.

25. The record for duration of employment in the Elizabeth plant was held by Mr. William Buerkle who retired in 1955 after seventy years, ten months, and five days in the factory.

26. In-house publications showed Singer retail outlets high in the Andes mountains of Peru and in distant parts of Asia. Singer was known for its aggressive

overseas marketing operation and its practice of going into partnerships with local (what we would now call Third World) entrepreneurs. This strategy enabled Singer to penetrate remote markets that other companies failed to reach.

27. The UE was known as one of the "left-wing unions" in the CIO because it gave active organizational support to progressive political causes and openly advocated controversial foreign policies at the height of the McCarthyist red-baiting scare. While the UE held the support of the Elizabeth workers during the long and bitter strike, in the end the workers ousted the union and voted instead for a company union that eventually became a local of the International Electrical Workers Union. The UE was ousted from the CIO. During the strike in Elizabeth, intense political pressure was brought to bear on the Singer workers, in effect accusing supporters of the UE of being members of the Communist party. UE leaders were eventually called before the House Un-American Activities Committee and publicly accused of manipulating the union for the benefit of the party.

28. There is a certain inconsistency in their views. After all, the strike itself was a signal that workers and management were at odds.

29. Braverman (1974).

30. David Halle (1984) and Paul Attewell (1987) argue that Braverman's deskilling argument does not hold even for the highly automated industries.

31. Barbara Garson (1975).

32. *New York Times* (1987f).

33. The last labor contract negotiated by the International Union of Electrical Workers on behalf of the Singer local called for management to invest several million dollars in plant modernization. In exchange, the workers agreed to some "give backs." In the end the company failed to put the investment in. The fact that Singer reneged on this agreement was the basis for a lawsuit the union won on the workers' behalf a year after the shutdown; the proceeds were divided among the employees left on the payroll when the plant closed.

34. The Elizabeth factory was hardly alone in its unfulfilled need for investment in production technology. Inefficient or outdated production technology is implicated in nearly half of the nation's recent plant closings, swamping by far the number of shutdowns attributable to lack of sales or high labor costs (Schmenner 1983).

35. The Chrysler advertising campaigns that feature Lee Iacocca guaranteeing his product play upon the sentiment that consumers want to put a face or a company name behind what they buy.

36. The change in management recruiting patterns at Singer is part of a larger trend in the history of American business which has concentrated power in the hands of finance specialists. Analyzing data from the 100 largest firms in the United States between 1919 and 1979, Neil Fligstein (1987:44) argued that:

> Early in the century, large firms were controlled by entrepreneurs or personnel who came up through manufacturing. In the middle decades, sales and marketing personnel controlled large firms. In the past 25 years, finance personnel have become increasingly dominant.

37. These remarks were made in a seminar given by Mr. Barry at the Rutgers University Center for Labor Education in April 1987 and were made available through the courtesy of Professor Michael Merrill.

38. See F.F. Piven and R. Cloward (1972) for an account of the post–World War II mechanization of southern agriculture, and the consequent expulsion of black labor from the rural South. Singer recruited in the south for black labor to run the foundry that was part of the mammoth Elizabeth plant.

39. Though as Walter Barry pointed out, ethnic controls over factory jobs had their darker side. There were few protections for anyone who did not meet with the approval of ethnic leadership in the plant.

40. Evidence from other studies (for example, Halle [1984]; Novak [1971]; Patterson [1977]) points to the persistence of racism among blue-collar whites and the Elizabeth factory appears to be no exception.

41. Elizabeth's geographical neighbor.

42. Ironically, unbeknowst to the white ethnics, nepotistic hiring practices had in fact continued among these new immigrant workers. Many Cuban, Haitian and native blacks who comprised the youngest cohort of workers did what they could to obtain Singer jobs for their relatives. Friends and family members did, in fact, filter into the plant. However, they could not accumulate ties through the generations as the whites had, since in the space of one generation, the plant shut down.

43. Bluestone and Harrison (1982).

44. One man advised me to stay away from the old plant: "Have you taken a ride to the [plant]? Keep your doors locked; if you hear a little bump on your fender, don't get out. If someone steps in front of you, run him over."

45. See Halle (1984) for a much more detailed discussion of contemporary blue-collar culture. His research was done over a seven-year period in a chemical factory in a community immediately adjacent to Elizabeth.

46. See Burawoy (1979).

47. Jahoda (1982); Swimburne (1981); Leventman (1981).

48. Buss and Redburn (1984).

49. The Newark Airport is one of the fastest growing regional airports in the United States. It was the home base of People Express, which was for many years, a growing company (though it has now been through hard times and has been absorbed by Continental Airlines). The airport has revitalized some areas of Newark, providing jobs and investment. But it represents a departure from the manufacturing base that was for such a long time the backbone of the local economy.

Chapter Seven

1. But despite impressive gains in the last decade, most working women are not in managerial and professional jobs. Instead, they continue to populate "pink collar ghettos" where pay and promotion prospects are comparatively low. Reskin and Hartmann (1986:9), Blau (1984). Hence the stories of occupational displacement among well-paid, middle class employees discussed earlier are disproportionately about men.

2. Bane and Weiss (1980); Bradbury et al (1979); Espenshade (1979); Kriesberg (1970); Mott (1977); Ross and Sawhill (1975); Wattenberg and Reinhardt (1979).

3. Peterson's (1996) work represents an important amendment to the original findings of Lenore Weitzman (1985) who found a much larger decline in the income of divorced women relative to divorced men. The two scholars agree on the direction of the findings, but dispute the magnitude of the gender effect.

4. Weitzman found that divorced women from low income families retain a greater percentage of the family income than do women from more affluent marriages, but still have fewer resources to rely on than do their ex-husbands. The figures must be treated with caution, however, owing to methodological problems which her studies have not been able to resolve (see Peterson [1996] for a full account).

5. Census Bureau report P60–187, "Who Receives Child Support" (May 1995).

6. Corcoran et al. (1984) argue that although "women who drop out of the labor force have lower real wages when they return to work than they had when they left work," the net effects are small. Nevertheless, when these losses are tacked on to the fact that women are generally poorly paid anyway, the result is still significant.

7. The U.S. Bureau of the Census (1987a) reports that the wage gap between men and women who work full time is narrowing, mainly because young women (those in their twenties) are entering relatively high-paying occupations (those once dominated by men) in ever-increasing numbers. While this may eventually mean that divorced women reach a par with their husbands in earning power, it is no comfort to the women of the generations examined here. For women forty-five to sixty-four, earnings are still only 60 percent of men's wages. Moreover, it remains to be seen what will happen to the women in the youngest age group as they begin to have children and face the need to interrupt their labor force participation. It will also be interesting to see whether wage rates remain high in the formerly male-dominated occupations as women enter them in increasing number.

   It is entirely possible that the closing of the wage gap within the youngest cohort is an artifact of time spent in the labor market. Brandwein (1987) points out that "at the start of their careers, there is a small gap between the salaries of women and men. . . . However, the longer they are employed, the larger the gap." Hence "unless women's advancement chances substantially improve, we will see, in 10 or 20 years, the earnings gap for this [younger] cohort increasing."

8. Nationwide only 14% of women receive alimony awards and only 7 percent receive it on a regular basis. In New Jersey, where extensive research has

been done on court awards, Bruch and Wickler (1985) discovered that judges generally give wives no more than 30 percent of the husband's salary to maintain themselves and their children, leaving husbands with the remaining 70 percent. New Jersey women rarely receive more than 35 to 40 percent of marital assets. Even so, New Jersey judges are under the impression that alimony is awarded half the time, and have completely unrealistic ideas about the cost of raising children.

9. Weitzman (1985:110) calls these "career assets" and includes among them pension benefits and education. She points out that these are among the most important valuables in the modern economy, but they are not subject to the community property laws (which include only tangible property) and are therefore not taken into account in divorce settlements.

10. Weitzman (1985:15–52).

11. Thirty-four percent of all female-headed families are below the poverty level, and nearly half of them are divorced. If the proportion of the poor who are in female-headed households continues to increase at the same rate that it did in the 1960s and 1970s, "the poverty population would be composed solely of women and their children before the year 2000" (National Advisory Council on Economic Opportunity [1981]).

12. Approximately one in every two American marriages ended in divorce, many of them without children. Yet our cultural conceptions of the family lag behind this reality. The single-parent household has yet to achieve the status of a "normal" family that its numbers might bear out.

13. *New York Times* (1987a).

14. Skolnick (1985).

15. Elsewhere (Newman [1986]) I have coined the phrase *symbolic dialects* to describe the interpretive frameworks that each generation shares. The term *dialect* is apt because generations do not invent American culture anew but rather add new elements, and heighten or downplay existing ones to create distinctive variants of a more continuous national culture. For further discussion of the notion of a generation, and its distinctive experiences see Mannheim (1952), Kertzer (1983), Ryder (1965), and Carlsson and Karlsson (1970).

16. This chapter presents findings from an interview study of thirty white women whose marital standard of living was comfortable but not wealthy. The sample was deliberately restricted to middle-class women because they experience a more dramatic economic loss than their poorer counterparts (Brandwein [1974]; Liker and Elder [1983]). My informants ranged in age from twenty-six to fifty-seven years of age and at the time of the research (1982–83) were living in a northern California coastal community. Most participants were part-time students in a reentry program for "mature women" in a local university, which agreed to facilitate this research.

The focused life-history method was used to compile thirty chronologically organized, open-ended interviews that covered a standard range of subjects from childhood experience through the postdivorce period. The informants were also encouraged to raise topics spontaneously. The data discussed below, then, consist of some ninety hours of life-history material.

17. A cohort is defined as those people within a delineated population who experienced the same significant life event within a given period of time.

The "significant life event" is more often than not birth, in which case the cohort is termed a birth cohort (Glenn [1977:8]).

The concept of birth cohort is closely related to the idea of a "generation"; both refer to a group of people born within the same period. Norvell Glenn (1977:9) explains the relationship between the two concepts as follows:

> The term generation . . . consists of a birth cohort . . . internally homogeneous in some important respect and distinctly different from persons born earlier or later. For instance, persons whose early formative experiences occurred during the Great Depression may be considered a generation in this sense.

Thus a generation is a special kind of birth cohort: a group of similarly aged people who share some important formative experiences. The focus of the term *generation* is on the shared experiences, not on age: "A birth cohort is not the same as an age level, and kinds of cohorts are most precisely identified by the significant life event which defines them" (ibid:8).

18. "Children of the Great Depression" is Glen Elder's (1974) phrase. For additional material on the influence of the 1930s on their subsequent lives, see Elder and Liker (1982).

19. For a thorough review see Garraty (1986).

20. McElvaine (1983), Elder (1974).

21. The oldest cohort, which was represented by thirteen of the thirty individuals in my interview sample, consisted of women born between the years of the Great Depression and World War II (roughly 1930–1940). Ten came from working-class families whose fathers were either unskilled blue-collar workers or skilled craftsmen, while three came from more middle-class families where the fathers were white-collar workers or shopkeepers. The parents of these thirteen women had no formal education beyond high school. Their mothers were predominantly full-time homemakers, though some had had labor force experience either during the depression or World War II.

22. Cherlin (1981:39).

23. Glen Elder (1974), the leading authority on the family during the Great Depression, terms this phenomenon a general "downward extension of adult-like experience" in deprived households.

24. This is, of course, also true for women of the same generation who were not divorced, but whose husbands lost their jobs, placing their wives under the same pressure to support their families (see chapter 4).

25. This follows from the normative expectations of the households they grew up in (Rubin [1976]; Weitzman [1985:192]) as well as the ideals of the "new" middle class of the 1950s, which shaped the dimensions of their married lives.

26. Cf. Cherlin (1981), Easterlin (1980). This generation was represented by seventeen of my thirty interviews. Elder (1974:5) has commented on the sharp differences between this postwar generation and the one raised during the depression: "In a literal sense, these two generations are offspring of contrasting childhoods, one marked by scarcity and the other by affluence."

27. I should emphasize that these women are not the Yuppies of whom so much has been written. They are older than the Yuppie generation, which is a postprotest era phenomenon, composed mainly of people who marry later than their predecessors and are far more career oriented than the

women described here. These women are products of the more turbulent era of social movements so eloquently described by Gitlin (1987).

28. Quoted in Gitlin and Rosen (1987), but see Gitlin (1987) for a more thorough discussion.

29. Weiss (1984:117), Weitzman (1985:333). Specific income data were not elicited in this study. In pilot interviews, informants proved reluctant or uncomfortable revealing dollar amounts, partly because they were unsure of exact figures for their marital years or because they were receiving financial assistance they felt could be compromised. As a result, I decided to ask for present household income as a percentage of marital household income, a strategy that avoided the difficulties discussed above.

30. It also reflects an idiom that was especially salient in California, a state known for cultural innovation. This brings up an important point that I have not explored but is worthy of further investigation. To what extent is a generational culture shaded and colored by regional location? To some extent each generation is exposed to national events that provide continuity across geographical areas in cultural form. But there are variations as well, and the Californian version of the sixties generation is not the only one possible.

31. Fortes (1958) defines the domestic cycle as follows:

> The domestic group goes through a cycle of development analogous to the growth cycle of a living organism. The group as a unit retains the same form, but its members, and the activities which unite them, go through a regular sequence of changes during the cycle which culminates in the dissolution of the original unit and its replacement by one or more units of the same kind.

32. This mirrors national survey findings: Grossman and Hayghe (1982) found that less than half of the mothers awarded child support in 1975 received it regularly. Brandwein et al. (1974) report that 67 percent of fathers cease to provide any financial support after four years.

33. For a discussion of the issue of money and parental contact see Furstenberg et al. (1983).

34. This is precisely the kind of view that newly organized advocacy groups for divorced fathers object to.

35. Weiss (1979:20).

36. Weitzman (1985:192).

37. King and Marvel (1982).

38. One much closer to Weiss's (1979:20) characterization.

39. Comparatively little attention has been paid to the subjective experience of divorce-induced economic loss among women who are heads of households (Brandwein et al. [1974:511]). To the extent that the subjective interpretation of economic loss has been discussed in the sociological literature, it has focused on women's views of "personal fate control." This research makes it clear that the particular mix of household income sources (wages versus welfare, child support, or alimony payments) affects the extent to which women feel they are in control of their lives (Bould [1977]; Brandwein et al. [1974]; Weiss [1979]). The greater the proportion of household income derived from their wages, the more they perceive themselves as masters of their own fate.

40. Cf. Brown et al. (1976); Kohen et al. (1979); Melson (1980); Berman and Turk (1981).
41. Mueller and Pope (1980).
42. Decker (1983).
43. Schneider and Smith (1973:42).
44. Anspach (1976); Cherlin and Furstenberg (1986).
45. In extreme cases (only two in this sample), the assistance of parents to divorced daughters took the form of combining households for a time. Although "doubling up" was a common postdivorce phenomenon in the past, today single mothers from middle-class families are far more likely to form their own households than move in with relatives (Bianchi and Reynolds [1979]; Cherlin [1981]; Colletta [1979, 1983]; Smith [1980]; Sweet [1972]; Beck and Beck [1984]). For the most part, the resources discussed here consisted of cash payments and services in kind from the distance of separate households.

    The changes in divorced women's support networks over time has been the subject of increasing research interest (Arendell [1986]; Leslie and Grady [1985]), but most of these studies do not disaggregate their analyses by age, hence it is difficult to tell where generational differences crop up.
46. Schneider (1980).
47. Yanigasako (1977) has made the point that bilateral kinship networks are often "women-centered."
48. This is hardly surprising. One would be hard pressed to find many women in either of these generations who would have had the economic clout to be in the middle class absent a marriage tie to a man who earns enough money to make such a life possible. Indeed, it is becoming increasingly the case that it requires two incomes to stay afloat in the middle class (Levy [1987]), which will no doubt reinforce the "couple" orientation of the middle class. Hence, although I speak here in terms of a cultural principle, it clearly has a "material" counterpart.
49. Schneider and Smith (1973). The ambiguity of the divorced mother's position is further exacerbated by the discomfort that suffuses friendships after divorce. Friends who populate a married couple's social life often disappear in the wake of divorce. Like other downwardly mobiles, newly divorced women find their social lives contracting; the extended family (siblings, parents, cousins, and the like) often fill in the gap. Blood relations can stand clear of the contaminating effects of divorce, since they do not have to choose one party or the other to side with, as friends often do.
50. It should be clear that I am not arguing that they are not understood to be daughters in the sense of the biological link, but that from a cultural point of view they no longer share the attributes of dependent daughterhood that, in earlier years, would have entitled them to protection, resources, and the like.
51. Lang and Brody (1983).
52. Weitzman (1985:278).
53. See Hannerz (1969) and Stack (1974) for classic studies of networks in poor black communities and Susser (1982) for a discussion of the same topic for poor whites.

54. Anthropologists point to sharing networks to show the folly of "culture of poverty" theories that describe the poor—particularly ethnic minorities—as incapable of deferred gratification, locked inside a "present-day" orientation, and unable to plan or calculate. They also suggest the reasons why poor families find it hard to accumulate enough wealth to remove themselves from the ghetto: To remain part of the insurance scheme represented by sharing systems, one cannot accumulate goods and funds, refusing to share them out.

55. Of course, even older women are beneficiaries of birthday presents and other occasional gifts. But this is not the subject here.

56. Those that do are often downwardly mobile, and they are no better prepared for it in terms of support networks than are divorced women of the middle class. See chapter 3.

57. Liebow (1967); Hannerz (1969); Stack (1974); Wilson (1987).

58. Women in my sample who were wage earners themselves were virtually always secondary contributors to the household's income.

59. This is not to say that "communities of concern," networks of similarly situated single mothers, cannot develop after divorce. The women in the sixties generation were able to connect with other mothers in the same situation through day-care centers, schools, and did, after a period of several years begin to develop stable patterns of reciprocal exchange of services (baby-sitting, transportation, and so on) that were important "Band-Aids" in coping with the limitations of household resources. But even these relations were restricted by middle-class mores that separate the material from the social: Borrowing money, for example, was taboo. These associations were important sources of moral support and were critical in cutting down social isolation, but they could not function as effective replacements for financial resources.

The Depression generation found it more difficult to establish networks of similarly situated women. They were more isolated than their sixties counterparts, partly because they did not have young children, who served as links to other single mothers through day-care centers, schools, and the like. But generational values played a role here as well. The younger group placed a greater degree of importance on commitment to a "community" as a social value. The cultural idiom of the Depression generation revolved around the family to a greater degree. And lacking a family that was complete—according to middle-class, couple-bound definitions—the depression women were often cut off.

60. Weitzman (1985:352).

61. The impact of divorce on child development is a topic of extensive research and debate (Desimone-Luis et al. [1979]; Magrab [1978]; Schlesinger [1982]; Wallerstein and Kelly [1975, 1976, 1980]). Our concern is with a subtopic within this broader problem, namely the effect of postdivorce economic loss on the relations between children and mothers.

62. Schlesinger (1982:9).

63. Cf. Weiss (1979:84).

64. The relative influence of parents and peers on the value systems of adolescents is a topic of some controversy. Recent research by Ianni (1983) reports variation in the extent to which adolescents are dominated by peer groups

according to locale (rural, suburban, and urban) and class. Biddle et al. (1980) argue that both parents and peers exert an influence over adolescents but in different ways and in different domains. Clearly both groups exert pressures for conformity in behavior and normative orientation. Equally clearly, the adolescent is far more subject to peer pressure than are younger children, particularly when divorce disrupts the "normal" degree of parental influence over value formation.

65. Weiss (1979:108).
66. Glasser and Navarre (1965).
67. The term *adaptive strategy* is used here to refer to behavioral and circumstantial changes designed to increase the compatibility of individuals with new environments or changing circumstances in "old" environments.
68. Wallerstein and Kelly (1980:25).
69. Peer groups can act as positive buffers against the negative effects of divorce; they can also assist in the adjustment process (Kurdek and Siesky [1980]; Wallerstein and Kelly [1980]). There is, however, a darker side to peer-group influence.
70. Wallerstein and Kelly (1980:231).
71. See, for example, Buehler and Hogan's (1980:528) discussion of "survival" and "comprehensive" strategies of adaptation to divorce.
72. Divorced women often have little real "choice" in settling their housing problems. Frequently they have few economically rational alternatives.
73. Weiss (1979:117–118) points out that mothers may have other motivations for complaining about their daughters' relations with men. He notes that some mothers regard their daughters as social/or sexual competition or, alternatively, as surrogates whose successes with men can substitute for their own sense of failure.
74. Cf. Hetherington et al. (1979:133).
75. Cf. Carter and Glick (1970:506); Schlesinger (1982:13).
76. I was not able to interview all of the adolescent children whose mothers were informants for this study. Most of the data reported in this section consist of mothers' reports about their children's behavior. However, I was able to interview six adolescents from four different families. The discussion of relations with peers in new neighborhoods is drawn from their comments.
77. Of course, proof of this particular point would depend upon longitudinal data that are not yet available—for example, interviews with the younger cohort in ten to fifteen years time, when it reaches the same point in the domestic cycle that the older group now occupies. Of course, by the time the younger women reach their fifties, the economic and social climate of the world they will inhabit may be entirely different. It is impossible to hold period effects constant while looking at longitudinal differences within cohort groups, as specialists in cohort analysis have often pointed out (see especially Glenn [1977]).

Chapter Eight

1. In his book *The Broken Covenant*, Robert Bellah (1975) uses this phrase somewhat differently, to refer to the breakdown of a traditional moral injunc-

tion to help one's neighbor and take on responsibility toward one's community, which constituted part of the Protestant ethic. I use the phrase in a more secular sense, to suggest the erosion of a cultural or social "contract" to behave in a certain fashion in exchange for the realization of material and social aspirations.

2. Sennett and Cobb (1973) argued that working-class parents, whose children reject the value of upward mobility out of the blue-collar world, end up questioning the validity of the sacrifices they have made in their own lives to further their children's life chances. Patterson's example is a variation on the theme of *The Hidden Injuries of Class*. For here we find people who accepted their parents' demands that they move out of the working class into the white collar world, and who (contra Sennett and Cobb) found fulfillment there, only to see it evaporate through no choice of their own. The parents of these disappointed downwardly mobiles still wonder what their own sacrifices for their children were worth if this is the end their children have met.

3. Arlie Hochschild (1973) has argued that elderly people enter a state of "altruistic surrender" in which they live vicariously through their children and grandchildren. She argues that this provides people who are no longer active in the world a derivative, but no less meaningful sense of accomplishment. By the same token, a child's failures may cast the elderly parent into depression.

4. Approximately 500 out of the 11,500 who went on strike have been reinstated through legal action. Most have had to show that, for one reason or another, they were "out of the office," not "on strike" during the grace period in August 1981 when President Reagan ordered everyone back to work and fired anyone who did not obey.

5. See Caudill (1962) for a moving account of the closing of coal mines.

6. Bellah et al. (1985) invoke the phrase "community of memory" to denote groups of people, and the whole nation in some instances, who have participated in social movements like the civil rights movement.

7. Edward Shils (1981) has spoken of societies that were "in the grip of the past." He has shown how American attitudes toward tradition have oscillated between awe and admiration for the richness of the European past and rejection of traditionalism because it dampens society's freedom to change.

8. In this respect, whatever divergence there may be between Singer workers' views of factory history and the actual working conditions of the past is of little consequence. For tradition is never an exact description of the past. It is a vision of the past which is put to use in the present (Shils [1981]).

9. Calhoun (1983:898).

10. Political weakness is revealed in the unwillingness of the federal government to pass protectionist legislation in the face of massive American job losses stemming from the importation of foreign goods.

11. See Cole (1980) for comparative inter-firm mobility rates.

12. See Labor Task Force on Economic Adjustment and Worker Dislocation, Subcommittee on the Foreign Experience (1986:4).

13. Pascale and Athos (1981:69).

Afterword

1. Deogun (1998).
2. Daniel Kadlec (1998).
3. Useem (1993).
4. See Rodrik (1997) for a helpful review of the debate over the impact of globalization on advanced industrial societies. Rodrik argues that domestic political regimes have a much freer hand than most critics of globalization realize to set social spending priorities which cushion the impact of wage competition. On the other hand, Rodrik suggests that the costs of liberal welfare state policies are growing (especially persistently high unemployment) and may not be supportable in the long run. Employers are unwilling to make job guarantees and pay into the tax coffers to support the unemployed; workers are no less willing to give up the social support they depend upon. Political polarization may be the result in many countries where the gaps between the skill or education rich "haves" and the working class have-nots have grown.
5. Exports of U.S goods to Mexico grew by 37 percent in the three years after NAFTA went into effect, to a record high of $56.8 billion. U.S. sales to Canada increased by $33.8 billion during the same period. Letter from President William J. Clinton, "Report to Congress on the Implementation of the North American Free Trade Agreement," July 1997. Pg. 2.
6. Commerce Department estimates suggest that gains in U.S. exports to Mexico associated with NAFTA support an estimated 90,000–160,000 American jobs. (ibid, pg. 3).
7. "Reduced restrictions on imports also benefit the economy by increasing purchasing power of American consumers, providing them with greater choice in products and services at lower prices . . ." ibid, p. 16.
8. Jeff Faux, "Administration's NAFTA Report Seriously Misleading," Economic Policy Institute report, July 11, 1997, p. 1.
9. The task of evaluating the consequences of NAFTA are complicated by the fact that Mexico experienced a devastating recession in 1995, with real wages plummeting, unemployment skyrocketing, and prices falling, and the peso undergoing a devaluation.
10. Ironically, it was the pilots of Eastern Airlines, who first experienced the back hand of two-tiered contracts—pilots who refused to honor the picket lines of the striking air traffic controllers chronicled in chapter three of this book. Had the pilots' unions respected the line, it is quite likely the strike would have turned out differently. As it is, the controllers' strike is now widely regarded as a major watershed in the history of unionization in the United States: the strike that broke the union movement.
11. Barnett and Rivers (1995), Gerson (1994).

References

Allen, T. L. 1972. "Aerospace Cutbacks: Impact on the Companies and Engineering Employment in Southern California." Ph.D. diss., Massachusetts Institute of Technology.

Anderson, C. R. 1977. "Locus of Control, Coping Behaviors, and Performance in a Stress Setting: A Longitudinal Study." *Journal of Applied Psychology* 62:446–451.

Andrisani, P., and P., Abeles. 1976. "Locus of Control and World Experience: Cohort and Race Differences." Paper presented at the meetings of the American Psychological Association, Washington, D.C.

Andrisani, P., and G. Nestel. 1976. "Internal-External Control as a Contributor to an Outcome of World Experience." *Journal of Applied Psychology* 61:56–165.

Anspach, Donald. 1976. "Kinship and Divorce." *Journal of Marriage and the Family* 38(May):343–350.

Arendell, Terry. 1986. *Mothers and Divorce: Legal, Economic and Social Dilemmas.* Berkeley: University of California Press.

Attewell, Paul. 1987. "The De-Skilling Controversy." *Journal of Work and Occupations* 13(3):323–346.

Azevedo, R. E. 1974. "Scientists, Engineers, and the Job Search Process." *California Management Review* 17(2):40–49.

Bakke, E. Wright. 1947. *Citizens Without Work.* New Haven, Conn.: Yale University Press.

Bakke, E. Wright. 1940. *The Unemployed Worker.* New Haven, Conn.: Yale University Press.

Bane, M. J., and R. Weiss. 1980. "Alone Together: The World of Single-Parent Families." *American Demographics* 2(5):323–330.

Barron, C. 1987. "Down in the Valley." *New York Times Magazine,* 20 September.

Batelle Memorial Institute. 1971. "A Survey of Aerospace Employees Affected by Reductions in NASA Contracts." Columbia, Ohio: Batelle Columbus Laboratories, 20 May.

Batra, Ravi. 1987. "An Ominous Trend to Greater Inequality." *New York Times,* 3 May, B2.

Batra, Ravi. 1985. *The Great Depression of 1990.* New York: Venus Books.

Beck, S., and R. Beck. 1984. "During Middle Age." *Journal of Marriage and the Family* 46(2):277–288.

Beer, William D. 1983. *Househusbands: Men and Housework in American Families.* New York: J.F. Bergin/Praeger.

Bell, Daniel. 1979. "The New Class: A Muddled Concept." In *The New Class?* edited by B. Bruce-Briggs, pp. 169–190. New York: Transaction Books.

Bell, Daniel. 1973. *The Coming of Post-Industrial Society: A Venture in Social Forecasting.* New York: Basic Books.

Bellah, Robert. 1975. *The Broken Covenant: American Civil Religion in Time of Trial.* New York: Seabury Press.

Bellah, Robert N., Richard Madsen, William M. Sullivan, Ann Swidler, and Steven M. Tipton. 1985. *Habits of the Heart: Individualism and Commitment in American Life.* Berkeley: University of California Press.

Berardo, D., C. Sheham, and G. Leslie. 1987. "A Residue of Tradition: Jobs, Careers, and Spouses' Time in Housework." *Journal of Marriage and the Family* 49 (May): 381–390.

Bergen County Record. 1986. "The New Homing Birds." 4: August, 1.

Berman, W., and D. Turk. 1981. "Adaptation to Divorce: Problems and Coping Strategies." *Journal of Marriage and the Family* 43(1):179–190.

Bertaux, D. 1984. "The Life Story Approach: A Continental View." *Annual Review of Sociology* 10:215–237.

Bianchi, S., and F. Reynolds. 1979. "Racial Differences in Family Living Arrangements and Economical Well Being: An Analysis of Recent Trends." *Journal of Marriage and the Family* 41(3):537–551.

Biddle, B., B. Bank, and M. Marlin. 1980. "Parental and Peer Influence on Adolescents." *Social Forces* 58(4):1057–1079.

Blackburn, M., and D. Bloom. 1985. "What is Happening to the Middle Class?" *American Demographics* (January):18–25.

Blau, Francine. 1984. "Occupational Segregation and Labor Market Discrimination." In *Sex Segregation in the Workplace: Trends, Explanations, Remedies*, edited by B. Reskin, pp. 117–143. Washington, D.C.: National Academy of Sciences Press.

Blau, Peter, M. 1964. *Exchange and Power in Social Life*. New York: John Wiley & Sons.

Blau, Peter, and Otis D. Duncan. 1967. *The American Occupational Structure*. New York: John Wiley & Sons.

Bluestone, Barry. 1984. "Is Deindustrialization a Myth? Capital Mobility versus Absorptive Capacity in the U.S. Economy." *Annals of the American Academy of Political and Social Science* 475 (September):39–51.

Bluestone, Barry, and Bennett Harrison. 1986. "The Great American Job Machine: The Proliferation of Low Wage Employment in the U.S. Economy." Study prepared for the Joint Economic Committee, U.S. Congress, December.

Bluestone, Barry, and Bennett Harrison. 1982. *The Deindustrialization of America: Plant Closings, Community Abandonment, and the Dismantling of Basic Industry*. New York: Basic Books.

Boddy, Raford, and James Crotty. 1975. "Class Conflict and Macropolicy: The Political Business Cycle." *Review of Radical Political Economy* 7 (Spring): 1–19.

Bould, S. 1977. "Female-Headed Families: Personal Fate Control and the Provider Role." *Journal of Marriage and the Family* 39(2):339–349.

Bowers, D. 1982. "What Would Make 11,500 People Quit Their Jobs?" *Organizational Dynamics* (Winter):5–19.

Bradbury, K., S. Danziger, E. Smolensky, and P. Smolensky. 1979. "Public Assistance, Female Headship, and Economic Well-Being." *Journal of Marriage and the Family* 41(3):519–535.

Brandwein, R. 1987. "Time Widens Male-Female Earnings Disparity." Letter to the Editor, *New York Times*, 27 September, E22.

Brandwein, R., C. Brown, and E. Fox. 1974. "Women and Children Last: The Social Situation of Divorced Mothers and Their Families." *Journal of Marriage and The Family* 36(3):498–514.

Braverman, Harry. 1974. *Labor and Monopoly Capital: The Degradation of Work in the Twentieth Century*. New York: Monthly Review Press.

Brenner, M. H. 1976. "Estimating the Social Costs of National Economic Policy: Implications for Mental and Physical Health, and Criminal Aggression." Paper prepared for Library of Congress, Congressional Research Service. Washington, D.C.: U.S. Government Printing Office.

Brenner, M. H. 1967. "Economic Changes and Mental Hospitalization." *Social Psychiatry* 2:180–188.

Briar, K. H. 1976. "The Effect of Long-Term Unemployment on Workers and Their Families." Ph.D. diss., University of California, Berkeley.

Brown, C., R. Feldberg, E. M. Fox, and J. Kohen. 1976. "Divorce: Chance of a Lifetime." *Journal of Social Issues* 32(1):119–133.

Bruch, C., and N. Wickler. 1985. "The Economic Consequences of Divorce." *Juvenile and Family Court Journal* 36(3):5–26.

Budge, Scott, and R. Janoff. 1984. "How Managers Face Prolonged Job Loss." *Business* 34(2):22–30.

Buehler, C., and M. Hogan. 1980. "Managerial Behavior and Stress in Families Headed by Divorced Women: A Proposed Framework." *Family Relations* 29(October):525–532.

Burawoy, Michael. 1979. *Manufacturing Consent: Changes in the Labor Process Under Monopoly Capitalism.* Chicago: University of Chicago Press.

Business Week. 1984a. "Office Automation Restructures Business." 8 October, 118–142.

Business Week. 1984b. "White Collar Jobs: A Hot Market Cools." 10 December, 40–41.

Buss, Terry, and F. Stevens Redburn. 1983a. *Mass Unemployment: Plant Closings and Community Mental Health.* Beverly Hills, Calif.: Sage Press.

Buss, Terry, and F. Stevens Redburn. 1983b. *Shutdown at Youngstown: Public Policy for Mass Unemployment.* Albany: State University of New York Press.

Calhoun, Craig. 1983. The Radicalism of Tradition: Community Strength or Venerable Disguise and Borrowed Language. *American Journal of Sociology* 88(5):886–914.

Camden, T. 1982. "Using Outplacement as a Career Development Tool." *Personnel Administrator* 27(1):35–37.

Caplow, T. 1982. "Christmas Gifts and Kin Networks." *American Sociological Review* 47:383–392.

Carter, H., and P. Glick. 1970. *Marriage and Divorce: A Social and Economic Study.* Cambridge, Mass.: Harvard University Press.

Carlsson, G., and K. Karlsson. 1970. "Age, Cohorts, and the Generation of Generations." *American Sociological Review* 35:710–718.

Caudill, Harold. 1962. *Night Comes to the Cumberlands.* Boston: Little, Brown.

Cavan, R., and K. Ranck. 1938. *The Family and the Depression: A Study of One Hundred Chicago Families.* Freeport, N.Y.: Libraries Press.

CBS Nightly News. 1986. "GAO Report on the Air Traffic Control System." 5 March.

Challenge. 1984. "Job Search Clubs for Dislocated Workers." May/June:51–55.

Chandler, A. 1977. *The Visible Hand: The Managerial Revolution in American Business.* Cambridge, Mass.: Harvard University Press.

Cherlin, A. 1981. *Marriage, Divorce, Remarriage.* Cambridge, Mass.: Harvard University Press.

Cherlin, A., and F. Furstenberg 1986. *The New American Grandparent.* New York: Basic Books.

Cherry, Robert. 1981. "What is So Natural About the Natural Rate of Unemployment?" *Journal of Economic Issues* 15(3):729–743.

Cobb, S., and S. V. Kasl. 1977. *Termination: The Consequences of Job Loss*. Cincinnati: National Institute of Occupational Safety and Health (Research report No. 76–1261, June).

Cobb, S., and S. V. Kasl. 1971. Some Medical Aspects of Unemployment. Ann Arbor: Survey Research Center, Institute of Social Research, University of Michigan.

Cohen, S., and J. Zysman. 1987. *Manufacturing Matters: The Myth of the Post-Industrial Economy*. New York: Basic Books.

Cohn, R. M. 1977. The Consequences of Unemployment on Evaluations of Self. Ph.D. diss., University of Michigan.

Cole, Robert. 1980. *Work, Mobility and Participation: A Comparative Study of American and Japanese Industry*. Berkeley: University of California Press.

Colletta, N. 1983. "Stressful Lives: The Situation of Divorced Mothers and Their Children." *Journal of Divorce* 6(3):19–31.

Colletta, N. 1979. "Support Systems After Divorce: Incidence and Impact." *Journal of Marriage and the Family* 41:837–846.

Condon, J. 1986. "Our Unemployment Quandary." *New York Times*. 30 November, F4.

Cooper, Wendy. 1982. "The Spread of Golden Parachutes." *Institutional Investor* 16(8):65–68.

Corcoran, Mary, Greg Duncan, and Michael Ponza. 1984. "Work Experience, Job Segregation and Wages." In *Sex Segregation in the Workplace: Trends, Expectations, Remedies*, edited by B. F. Reskin, pp. 171–191. Washington, D.C.: National Academy of Sciences Press.

Coyne, J. C., and R. Lazarus. 1979. "The Ipsative-Normative Framework for the Longitudinal Study of Stress." Paper presented at the annual meeting of the American Psychological Association, New York, September.

Daniels, D., J. Dunn, F. Furstenberg, and R. Plomin. 1985. "Environmental Differences Within Pairs of Adolescent Siblings." *Child Development* 56:764–774.

Decker, B. 1983. *The Women's Movement: Political, Socioeconomic and Psychological Issues*, 3rd ed. New York: Harper & Row.

Delbanco, Andrew. 1986. "Looking Homeward, Going Home: The Lure of England for the Founders of New England." *New England Quarterly* 59(3):358–386.

Demo, D., and R. C. Savin-Williams. 1983. "Early Adolescent Self-Esteem as a Function of Social Class: Rosenberg and Pearlin Revisited." *American Journal of Sociology* 88(4):763–774.

Desimone-Luis, J., K. O'Mahone, and D. Hunt. 1979. "Children of Separation and Divorce: Factors Influencing Adjustment." *Journal of Divorce* 3(1):37–42.

Dionne, E. 1986. "Experts Discern a Bloc: 'New Collar' Voters." *New York Times*. 20 October, 1.

Displaced Homemakers Network. 1987. *A Status Report on Displaced Homemakers in the United States*. Washington, D.C.: Displaced Homemakers Network.

Douglas, Mary. *Purity and Danger: An Analysis of the Concept of Pollution and Taboo.* London, England: Routledge & Kegan Paul.

Drucker, J. H. 1975. "To Be 60 and Jobless." *New York Times.* 9 July, 36.

Duncan, Greg. 1986. "The Volatility of Family Income Over the Life Course." Unpublished paper, Ann Arbor, Mich.: Survey Research Center.

Duncan, Greg. 1984. *Years of Poverty, Years of Plenty.* Ann Arbor, Mich.: Institute for Social Research, University of Michigan.

Duncan, Greg, Martha Hill, and Willard Rogers. 1986. "The Changing Fortunes of Young and Old." *American Demographics* 8(8):26–33.

Easterlin, R. 1980. *Birth and Fortune: The Impact of Numbers on Personal Welfare.* New York: Basic Books.

Eisenberg, P., and P. F. Lazarsfeld. 1938. "The Psychological Effects of Unemployment." *Psychological Bulletin* 35:358–390.

Elder, Glen, Jr. 1985. *Life Course Dynamics: Trajectories and Transitions, 1969–1980.* Ithaca, N.Y.: Cornell University Press.

Elder, Glen, Jr. 1974. *Children of the Great Depression: Social Change in Life Experience.* Chicago: University of Chicago Press.

Elder, Glen, Jr., and J. Liker. 1982. "Hard Times in Women's Lives: Historical Influence Across Forty Years." *American Journal of Sociology* 88(2):241–269.

Elizabeth Daily Journal. 1939. "Twenty Years of Industry in Elizabeth." 12 October.

Espenshade, T. 1979. "The Economic Consequences of Divorce." *Journal of Marriage and the Family* 41(3):615–625.

Estes, R. J. 1973. "Emotional Consequences of Job Loss." Ph.D. diss., School of Social Work, University of Pennsylvania.

Estes, R. J., and H. Wilensky. 1978. "Life Cycle Squeeze and the Morale Curve." *Social Problems* 25(3):277–292.

Featherman, D. L., and R. M. Hauser. 1978. *Opportunity and Change.* New York: Academic Press.

Fineman, S. 1983. *White Collar Unemployment: Impact and Stress.* New York: John Wiley & Sons.

Finkelhor, David. 1983. "Common Features of Family Abuse." In *The Dark Side of Families: Current Family Violence Research,* edited by D. Finklehor, R. Gelles, G. Hotaling, and M. Strauss, ch. 1. Beverly Hills, Calif.: Sage Publications.

Fischer, Britta. 1985. "Unemployed Engineers and Air-Traffic Controllers: A Systematic Comparison." *New England Sociologist* (Winter):15–22.

Fligstein, Neil. 1987. "The Intraorganizational Power Struggle: Rise of Finance Personnel to Top Leadership in Large Corporations, 1919–1979." *American Sociological Review* 52(1):44–58.

Foltman, Felician. 1968. *White- and Blue-Collars in a Mill Shutdown: A Case Study in Relative Redundancy.* (ILA Paperback No. 6). Ithaca: New York State School of Labor Relations, Cornell University.

Forbes. 1984. "Chopping Dead Wood?" 26 March, p. 111.

Fortes, M. 1958. "Introduction." In *The Development Cycle in Domestic Groups*, edited by Jack Goody, pp. 1–14. Cambridge, England: Cambridge University Press.

Fortune. 1984. "The Recovery Skips Middle Management." Vol. 109 (3):115.

Furstenberg, F., C. Nord, and N. Zill. 1983. "The Life Course of Children of Divorce: Marital Disruption and Parental Contact." *Journal of Marriage and the Family* 48:656–668.

Furstenberg, F., and G. Spanier. 1984. *Recycling the Family: Remarriage after Divorce*. Beverly Hills, Calif.: Sage Press.

Galambos, N., and R. Silbereisen. 1987. "Income Change, Parental Life Outlook, and Adolescent Expectations for Job Success." *Journal of Marriage and the Family* 49 (February):141–149.

Garson, Barbara. 1975. *All the Live Long Day: The Meaning and Demeaning of Routine Work*. Garden City, N.Y.: Doubleday.

Garraty, John. 1986. *The Great Depression*. San Diego, Calif.: Harcourt, Brace Jovanovich.

Geertz, Clifford. 1973. *The Interpretation of Cultures: Selected Essays*. New York: Basic Books.

Gelles, Richard. 1974. *The Violent Home*. Beverly Hills, Calif.: Sage Press.

General Accounting Office. 1986. *FAA Staffing: The Air Traffic Control Work Force Opposes Rehiring Fired Controllers, 9 Oct*. Washington, D.C.: U.S. General Accounting Office.

Gerstel, Naomi. 1987. "Divorce and Stigma." *Social Problems* 34(2):172–185.

Ginzberg, Eli. 1977. "The Job Problem." *Scientific American* 237(5): 43–51.

Gitlin, Todd. 1987. *The 'Sixties: Years of Hope, Days of Rage*. New York: Bantam.

Gitlin, Todd and Ruth Rosen. 1987. "Give the 60's Generation a Break." Opinion–Editorial, *New York Times*, 14 November, p. A27.

Glasser, P., and E. Navarre. 1965. "Structural Problems of the One-Parent Family." *Journal of Social Issues* 21(1):98–109.

Glenn, Norvell. 1977. *Cohort Analysis*. Beverly Hills, Calif.: Sage Press.

Goffman, Irving. 1963. *Stigma: Notes on the Management of Spoiled Identity*. New York: Simon & Schuster.

Goffman, Irving. 1959. *The Presentation of Self in Everyday Life*. New York: Anchor Books.

Gordus, Jeanne, Paul Jorley, and Louis Ferman. 1981. *Plant Closings and Economic Dislocation*. Kalamazoo, Mich.: W.E. Upjohn Institute for Employment Research.

Gouldner, Alvin. 1960. "The Norm of Reciprocity: A Preliminary Statement." *American Sociological Review* 25:161–178.

Granovetter, Mark. 1974. *Getting a Job*. Cambridge, Mass.: Harvard University Press.

Grossman, A., and H. Hayghe. 1982. "Labor Force Activity of Women Receiving Child Support or Alimony." *Monthly Labor Review* 105(11):39–41.

Goodwyn, L. 1976. *Democratic Promise: The Populist Movement in America.* New York: Oxford University Press.

Gurin, P., G. Gurin, R. C. Rao, and M. Beattie. 1969. "Internal-External Control in the Motivational Dynamics of Negro Youth. *Journal of Social Issues* 25:29–53.

Halle, David. 1984. *America's Working Man: Work, Home, and Politics among Blue-Collar Property Owners.* Chicago: University of Chicago Press.

Hannerz, U. 1969. *Soulside: Inquiries into Ghetto Culture and Community.* New York: Columbia University Press.

Harris, Candee. 1984. "The Magnitude of Job Loss from Plant Closings and the Generation of Replacement Jobs: Some Recent Evidence." *Annals of the American Academy of Political and Social Science* 475 (September):15–27.

Harrison, Bennett, B. C. Tilly, and B. Bluestone. 1986. "Wage Inequality Takes a Great U-Turn." *Challenge* (March/April), pp. 26–32.

Hartley, Jean. 1980. "The Personality of Unemployed Managers: Myths and Measurement." *Personnel Review* 9:12–18.

Hetherington, E., M. Cox, and R. Cox. 1979. "The Development of Children in Mother-Headed Families." In *The American Family: Dying or Developing,* edited by D. Reiss and H. Hoffman. New York: Plenum Press, pp. 117–145.

Hochschild, Arlie. 1973. *The Unexpected Community: Portrait of an Old Age Subculture.* Berkeley: University of California Press.

Hoffman, Saul. 1977. "Marital Instability and the Economic Status of Women." *Demography* 14:67–76.

Hopper, Kim, Ezra Susser, and Sara Conover. 1985. "Economics of Makeshift: Deindustrialization and Homelessness in New York City." *Urban Anthropology* 13(2):183–236.

Hounshell, D. 1985. *From the American System to Mass Production, 1800–1932: The Development of Manufacturing Technology in the United States.* Baltimore: Johns Hopkins University Press.

Howe, Louise K. 1977. *Pink Collar Workers: Inside the World of Women's Work.* New York: Avon.

Ianni, F. 1984. *Home, School, and Community in Adolescent Education.* New York: ERIC Clearinghouse in Urban Education, Teachers College.

Jackall, Robert. 1983. "Moral Mazes: Bureaucracy and Managerial Work." *Harvard Business Review* 61(5):118–130.

Jackson, E. F. 1962. "Status Consistency and Symptoms of Stress." *American Sociological Review* 27:469–481.

Jahoda, Marie. 1982. *Employment and Unemployment: A Social-Psychological Analysis.* Cambridge, England: Cambridge University Press.

Jahoda, Marie, P. Lazarsfeld, and H. Zeizel. [1933] 1971. *Marienthal: The Sociography of an Unemployed Community.* Reprint, New York: Aldine-Atherton.

Jencks, Christopher. 1984. "The Hidden Prosperity of the 1970s." *The Public Interest* 77 (Fall):37–61.

Jensen, Joan, and Sue Davidson. 1984. *A Needle, A Bobbin, A Strike*. Philadelphia: Temple University Press.

Johnson, C. 1985. "Grandparenting Options in Divorcing Families: An Anthropological Perspective." In *Grandparenthood*, edited by V. Bengtson and J. Robertson. Beverly Hills, Calif.: Sage Press, pp. 81–96.

Johnson, Greg. 1983. "Shrinking the White Collar Ranks." *Industry Week* 215:55, 58–59.

Johnson, Greg. 1982. "A Flood of Pink Slips for Middle Management." *Business Week*. 20 December: 20–21.

Jones, L. 1982. "Management and Employee Relations Within the Federal Aviation Administration: Report to the U.S. Department of Transportation." Washington, D.C.: U.S. Government Printing Office.

Kanter, Rosabeth Moss. 1977. *Men and Women of the Corporation*. New York: Basic Books.

Kaufman, H. G. 1977. "Factors Affecting the Relationship Between Continuing Education and Performance: A State-of-the-Art Review." *National Science Foundation, Continuing Education Series in Science and Engineering*, pp. 235–245. Washington, D.C.: U.S. Government Printing Office.

Kaufman, H. G. 1982. *Professionals in Search of Work: Coping with the Stress of Job Loss and Underemployment*. New York: John Wiley & Sons.

Kerckhoff, A., R. Campbell, and I. Winfield-Laird. 1985. "Social Mobility in Great Britain and the United States." *American Journal of Sociology* 91 (2): 281–309.

Kertzer, D. 1983. "Generation as a Sociological Problem." *Annual Review of Sociology* 9:125–149.

Kessler-Harris, Alice. 1982. *Out to Work: A History of Wage-Earning Women in the United States*. New York: Oxford University Press.

King, N., and M. Marvel. 1982. "Issues, Policies and Programs for Midlife and Older Women." Washington, D.C.: Center for Women's Policy Studies.

Kohen, A., Parnes, H., and J. Shea. 1975. "Income Instability Among Young and Middle-Aged Men." In *The Personal Distribution of Income and Wealth*, ch. 6. New York: Columbia University Press.

Kohen, J., C. Brown, and R. Feldberg. 1979. "Divorced Mothers: The Costs and Benefits of Female Family Control." In *Divorce and Separation: Context, Causes and Consequences*, edited by G. Levinger and O. Moles. New York: Basic Books.

Komaroff, A. L., M. Masuda, and T. H. Holmes. 1968. "The Social Readjustment Rating Scale: A Comparative Study of Negro, Mexican, and White Americans." *Journal of Psychosomatic Research* 12:121–128.

Komarovsky, Mirra. 1940. *The Unemployed Man and His Family*. New York: Dryden Press.

Kriesberg, L. 1970. *Mothers in Poverty*. Chicago: Aldine Publishing Co.

Kurdek, L., and A. Siesky. 1980. "Sex Role Self-Concepts of Single Divorced Parents and Their Children." *Journal of Divorce* 3:249–261.

Kutscher, Ronald, and Valerie Personick. 1986. "Deindustrialization and the Shift to Services." *Monthly Labor Review* 109(6):3–13.

Labor Task Force. 1986. "Economic Adjustment and Worker Displacement in a Competitive Society." Washington, D.C.: Unpublished report of the Secretary of Labor, December.

Lang, Abigail, and Elaine Brody. 1983. "Characteristics of Middle-Aged Daughters and Help to their Elderly Mothers." *Journal of Marriage and the Family* 45(1):193–202.

Lawrence, Robert. 1984. *Can America Compete?* Washington, D.C.: The Brookings Institution.

Lawrence, Robert. 1983. "The Myth of Deindustrialization." *Challenge* (November/December):12–21.

Leach, Edmund. 1982. *Social Anthropology*. Oxford, England: Oxford University Press.

Leslie, L., and K. Grady. 1985. " Changes in Mothers' Social Support Following Divorce." *Journal of Marriage and the Family* 47(3):663–674.

Leventman, Paula. 1981. *Professionals Out of Work*. New York: Free Press.

Levine, Hermine. 1985. "Outplacement and Severance Pay Practices." *Personnel Administrator* 62(9):13–21.

Levitan, Sar, and Peter Carlson. 1984. "Middle Class Shrinkage?" *Across The Board* 21(10):55–59.

Levy, Frank. 1987. *Dollars and Dreams: The Changing American Income Distribution*. (The Population of the U.S. in the 1980s: A Census Monograph Series). New York: Russell Sage.

Levy, Frank, and Richard Michel. 1986. "An Economic Bust for the Baby Boom." *Challenge* (March/April):33–39.

Liebow, Elliot. 1967. *Tally's Corner*. Boston: Little, Brown.

Liker, J., and G. Elder, Jr. 1983. "Economic Hardship and Marital Relations in the 1930s." *American Sociological Review* 48 (June):343–359.

Lipset, S. M., M. Trow, and J. Coleman. 1956. *Union Democracy*. New York. Free Press.

Little, Craig. 1976. "Technical Professional Unemployment: Middle Class Adaptability to Personal Crisis." *Sociological Quarterly* 17 (Spring):262–274.

Littwin, Susan. 1986. *The Postponed Generation: Why American Youth Are Growing Up Later*. New York: William Morrow.

Loomba, R. 1967. "A Study of the Unemployment Experience of Scientists and Engineers Laid Off from 62 Aerospace and Electronic Firms in the San Francisco Bay Area During 1963–1965." San Jose, Calif.: Manpower Research Group, Center for Interdisciplinary Studies, San Jose State College.

Magrab, P. 1978. "For the Sake of the Children: A Review of the Psychological Effects of Divorce." *Journal of Divorce* 1:233–245.

Main, J. 1984. "The Recovery Skips Middle Management." *Fortune* 109(3):115.

Malinowski, Bronislaw. 1926. *Crime and Custom in Savage Society.* London, England: Routledge & Paul.

Malinowski, Bronislaw. 1922. *Argonauts of the Western Pacific.* New York: E. P. Dutton.

Mannheim, K. 1952. "The Sociological Problem of Generations." In *Essays on the Sociology of Knowledge,* edited by P. Keckskemeti, 276–322. New York: Oxford University Press.

Mauss, Marcel. 1954. *The Gift.* Glencoe, Ill.: Free Press.

McElvaine, S. 1983. *Down and Out in the Great Depression.* Chapel Hill: University of North Carolina Press.

McMahon, P., and J. Tschetter. 1986. "The Declining Middle Class: A Further Analysis." *Monthly Labor Review* 109(9):21–27.

Medoff, J. 1984. "The Structure of Hourly Earnings Among U.S. Private Sector Employees: 1973–1984." *Computer and Business Equipment Manufacturers Association Industry News,* December.

Medoff, J., and P. Strassman. 1985. "About the Two-Tier Workforce and Growth of Low-Pay Jobs." *Computer and Business Equipment Manufacturers Association Industry News.* March.

Melson, G. 1980. *Family and Environment: An Ecosystem Perspective.* Minneapolis, Minn.: Burgess.

Mergers and Acquisitions. 1987. "Almanac and Index" 21(6).

Miller, Arthur. 1949. *Death of a Salesman.* New York: Viking Press.

Miller, William. 1983. "How To Fire an Executive." *Industry Week* 211(2):28–32.

Mills, C. Wright. 1951. *White Collar: The American Middle Classes.* London, England: Oxford University Press.

Milosz, Czeslav. 1982. *Visions From San Francisco Bay.* Translated by R. Lourie. New York: Farrar, Strauss & Giroux.

Milosz, Czeslav. 1953. *The Captive Mind.* Translated by J. Zielonko. New York: Vintage Books.

Miner, C. 1963. *How to Get an Executive Job After 40.* New York: Collier.

Mintz, Sidney W. 1985. *Sweetness and Power: The Place of Sugar in Modern History.* New York: Viking Press.

Moen, P. 1983. "Unemployment, Public Policy and Families: Forecasts for the 1980's." *Journal of Marriage and the Family* (November):751–760.

Morgan, D. 1984. "Terminal Flight: The Air Traffic Controllers' Strike of 1981." *Journal of American Studies* 18(2):165–183.

Mott, F. 1977. "The Socioeconomic Status of Households Headed by Women. Results from the National Longitudinal Surveys" (R & D. Monograph 72). Washington, D.C.: U.S. Department of Labor.

Moy, J. 1985. "Recent Trends in Unemployment and the Labor Force, 10 Countries." *Monthly Labor Review* 108(8):9–22.

Mueller, W., and H. Pope. 1980. "Divorce and Female Remarriage Mobility: Data on Marriage Matches After Divorce for White Women." *Social Forces* 58(3):726–738.

Murphy, Robert. 1987. *The Body Silent.* New York: Henry Holt.

National Advisory Council on Economic Opportunity. 1981. *The American Promise: Equal Justice and Economic Opportunity* (Final Report). Washington, D.C.: U.S. Government Printing Office.

National Opinion Research Center. 1986. *General Social Survey 1972–1986: Cumulative Codebook.* Storrs, Connecticut: Roper Center for Public Opinion Research.

Nettle, J. P. 1971. "Consensus or Elite Domination: The Case of Business." In *Politics and Western European Democracies: Patterns and Problems,* edited by G. Byrne and K. Pederson. New York: John Wiley & Sons.

Newman, Katherine. 1987. "PATCO Lives! Stigma, Heroism, and Symbolic Transformations." *Cultural Anthropology* 2(3):319–346.

Newman, Katherine. 1986. "Symbolic Dialects and Generations of Women: Variation in the Meaning of Post-Divorce Downward Mobility." *American Ethnologist* 13(2):230–252.

Newsweek. 1987a. "Year of the Near Miss," 27 July.

Newsweek. 1987b. "A Jolt for Wall Street's Whiz Kids." 26 October, 55–58.

New York Times. 1978. "The Forces that Favor Recession." 23 May, A18.

New York Times. 1981a. [Flight Attendants' Paid Advertisement], 16 August, 12.

New York Times. 1981b. "Execution of a Vision." 19 August, 14.

New York Times. 1982. "Singer Plant Closing: A Way of Life Ends." 19 February.

New York Times. 1986a. "America's Service Economy Begins to Blossom—Overseas." 14 December.

New York Times. 1986b. "Singer May Bid Sewing Adieu." 19 February.

New York Times. 1987a. "Average Child Support Payment Drops by 12%." 23 August, 26.

New York Times. 1987b. "Women Reduce Lag in Earnings But Disparities With Men Remain." 4 September, 1.

New York Times. 1987c. "Espousing "High Morality," Living With Scandal." 15 May, B10.

New York Times. 1987d. "Near Collisions of Aircraft Among Signs of Safety Crisis, Many Experts Say." 17 May, A28.

New York Times. 1987e. "A New Union for Controllers." 14 June, E4.

New York Times. 1987f. "Joseph B. Flavin is Dead at 58: Led Overhaul as Singer Chairman." 8 October, B5.

Norwood, Janet. 1987. "The Job Machine Has Not Broken Down." *New York Times,* 22 February, D5.

Nossiter, Daniel. 1982. "Oh, Those Golden Parachutes." *Barron's* 62(48): 15, 26.

Novak, Michael. 1971. *The Rise of the Unmeltable Ethics.* New York: Macmillan.

Nulty, Peter. 1987. "Pushed Out at 45—Now What?" *Fortune* 115(5):26–30.

O'Brien, Gordon. 1986. *Psychology of Work and Unemployment.* New York: John Wiley & Sons.

O'Neill, D. 1987. "Low Wage Jobs." Letter to Editor, New York Times. February 22. p. A18.

Oppenheimer, V. K. 1982. *Work and the Family: A Study in Social Demography.* New York: Academic Press.

Osterman, Paul. 1986. "The Impact of Computers on the Employment of Clerks and Managers." *Industrial Labor Relations Review* 39(2):175–186.

Ostrander, Susan A. 1984. *Women of the Upper Class.* Philadelphia: Temple University Press.

Parnes, H., and R. King. 1977. "Middle-Aged Job Losers." *Industrial Gerontology* 4(2):77–95.

Pascale, R., and A. Athos. 1981. *The Art of Japanese Management: Applications for American Executives.* New York: Basic Books.

Patterson, Horace. 1977. *Ethnic Chauvinism.* New York: Stein & Day.

Piven, Francis Fox, and Richard A. Cloward. 1971. *Regulating the Poor: The Functions of Public Welfare.* New York: Vintage Books.

Plomin, R., and D. Daniels. 1987. "Why Are Children in the Same Family So Different from One Another?" *Behavioral and Brain Sciences* 10(1): 1–60.

Podgursky, Michael. 1984. "Sources of Secular Increases in the Unemployment Rate, 1969–1982." *Monthly Labor Review* 107(7):19–25.

Poli, Robert. 1982. "Why the Controllers Strike Failed." *New York Times.* 17 January 28.

Powell, E. H. 1958. "Occupation, Status and Suicide: Toward a Redefinition of Anomie." *American Sociological Review* 23: 131–139.

Powell, D. H., and P. F. Driscoll. 1973. "Middle Class Professionals Face Unemployment." *Society* 10(2):18–26.

Redburn, F. Stevens, and Terry F. Buss, eds. 1981. *Public Policy for Distressed Communities.* Lexington, Mass.: D.C. Heath & Company.

Reskin, Barbara, and Heidi Hartman, eds. 1986. *Women's Work, Men's Work: Sex Segregation on the Job.* Washington, D.C.: National Academy of Sciences Press.

Riesman, David. 1950. *The Lonely Crowd.* New Haven, Conn.: Yale University Press.

Rones, Philip. 1984. Recent Recessions Swell Ranks of Long-Term Unemployed. *Monthly Labor Review* 107(2):25–30.

Root, Kenneth. 1984. "The Human Response to Plant Closures." *Annals of the American Academy of Political and Social Science* 475 (Sept.): 52–65.

Root, Kenneth. 1979. *Perspectives for Community Organizations on Job Closings and Job Dislocation.* Ames, Iowa University Press.

National Opinion Research Center. 1986. General Social Survey, 1972–1986. Cumulative Codebook. Storrs, Connecticut: Roper Public Opinion Research Center.

Rosenthal, Neal. 1985. "The Shrinking Middle Class: Myth or Reality?" *Monthly Labor Review* 108(3):3–10.

Ross, H., and I. Sawhill. 1975. *Time of Transition: The Growth of Families Headed by Women.* Washington, D.C.: The Urban Institute.

Roszak, T. 1969. *The Making of a Counterculture: Reflections on the Technocratic Society and Its Youthful Opposition.* New York: Doubleday.

Rotter, J. B. 1966. "Generalized Expectations for Internal versus External Locus of Control." *Psychological Monographs* 80(1; 609).

Rubin, L. 1976. *Worlds of Pain: Life in the Working Class Family.* New York: Basic Books.

Ryan, P. 1985. "Age 47 is a Crisis Point for White Collar Terminations." *Business* 35(3):60–61.

Ryder, N. 1965. "The Cohort as a Concept in the Study of Social Change. *American Sociological Review* 30: 841–861."

Safire, W. 1986. "About Roy Cohn." New York Times. 4 August, A17.

Sahlins, Marshall. 1965. "On the Sociology of Primitive Exchange." In *The Relevance of Models for Social Anthropology.* ASA Monographs 1, pp. 139–227. London: Tavistock.

Savings Institutions. 1983. "Regulated Executives Apt to Fly Without 'Golden Parachutes,'" August:, 109.

Schlesinger, B. 1982. "Children's Viewpoints of Living in a One-Parent Family." *Journal of Divorce* 5(4):1–23.

Schmenner, R. 1983. "Every Factory Has a Life Cycle." *Harvard Business Review* 5(2):30–35.

Schneider, D. 1980. *American Kinship: A Cultural Account.* 2nd edition. Chicago: University of Chicago Press.

Schneider, D., and R. Smith. 1973. *Class Differences and Sex Roles in American Kinship and Family Structure.* Englewood Cliffs, N.J.: Prentice-Hall.

Searls, D., G. Braucht, and R. Miskimis. 1974. "Work Values of the Chronically Unemployed." *Journal of Applied Psychology* 59:93–95.

Sennett, Richard, and Jonathan Cobb. 1973. *The Hidden Injuries of Class.* New York: Vintage Books.

Shack-Marquez, Janice. 1986. Earnings Differences Between Men and Women. *Monthly Labor Review* 107(6):15–16.

Shaiken, Harley. 1984. *Work Transformed: Automation and Labor in the Computer Age.* New York: Holt, Rinehart & Winston.

Shepard, Harold, Louis Ferman, and Seymour Faber. 1960. *Too Old To Work— Too Young To Retire: A Case Study of a Permanent Plant Shutdown* (Report to the Special Committee on Unemployment Problems, United States Senate). Washington, D.C.: U.S. Government Printing Office.

Shils, Edward. 1981. *Tradition*. Chicago: University of Chicago Press.

Shostak, A., and D. Skocik. 1986. *Winning and Losing: Lessons from the Air Traffic Controllers Strike*. New York: Human Sciences Press.

Silk, Leonard. 1978. "Will Credit-Tightening Lead to Recession?" *New York Times*. 27 April, D3.

Skolnick, Arlene. 1985. "The Paradox of Perfection." In *Marriage and Family in a Changing Society*, 2d Ed., edited by J. Henslin, pp. 59–66. New York: Free Press.

Smith, M. 1980. "The Social Consequences of Single Parenthood: A Longitudinal Perspective." *Family Relations* 29: 75–81.

Sorenson, Aage. 1975. "The Structure of Intragenerational Mobility." *American Sociological Review* 40 (4): 456–471.

Spanier, G., and F. Furstenberg. 1982. "Remarriage After Divorce: A Longitudinal Analysis of Well-Being. *Journal of Marriage and the Family* 44(3):709–720.

Spanier, G., and P. C. Glick. 1980. "Paths to Remarriage." *Journal of Divorce* 3(Spring):283–298.

Sprinkel, B. 1987. "Let's Not Torpedo the Growth of Jobs." *New York Times* 4 June, A35.

Stack, Carol B. 1975. *All Our Kin: Strategies for Survival in a Black Community*. New York: Harper & Row.

Steinbeck, John. 1939. *The Grapes of Wrath*. New York: Viking Press.

Stoller, E. A. 1985. "Exchange Patterns in the Informal Support Networks of the Elderly: The Impact of Reciprocity on Morale." *Journal of Marriage and the Family* (May):335–342.

Stouffer, S., and P. Lazarsfeld. 1937. "Research Memorandum on the Family in the Great Depression" (Bulletin 29). New York: Social Science Research Council.

Straus, M., R. Gelles, and S. Steinmetz. 1980. *Behind Closed Doors: Violence in the American Family*. Garden City, N.Y.: Doubleday.

Stybel, L. 1985. "Does Outplacement Really Work?" *Business* 33(4):55–57.

Stybel, L., et al. 1982. "Planning Executive Dismissals: How to Fire a Friend." *California Management Review* 24(3):73–80.

Susser, Ida. 1982. *Norman Street: Poverty and Politics in an Urban Neighborhood*. New York: Oxford University Press.

Sweet, J. 1972. "The Living Arrangements of Separated, Widowed and Divorced Mothers." *Demography* 9:143–157.

Swimburne, P. 1981. "The Psychological Impact of Unemployment on Managers and Professional Staff." *Journal of Occupational Psychology* 54:47–64.

Taylor, Bill. 1985. "The Lifeline." Washington, D.C.: PATCO Lives, October.

Turner, Victor. 1969. *The Ritual Process: Structure and Anti-Structure*. Ithaca, N.Y.: Cornell University Press.

Uchitelle, L. 1987. "America's Army of Non-Workers." *New York Times*, Business Section, 27 September, 1.

U.S. Bureau of the Census. 1986. "Characteristics of the Population Below the Poverty Level: 1984." *Current Population Reports* (Series P-60, No. 152). Washington, D.C.: U.S. Government Printing Office.

U.S. Bureau of Labor Statistics. 1986a. "Reemployment Increases Among Displaced Workers." Press release, 14 October.

U.S. Bureau of Labor Statistics. 1986b. "Displaced Workers: One Year Later." *Monthly Labor Review* 109(7):40–43.

U.S. Bureau of Labor Statistics. 1985. *Displaced Workers 1979–83* (Bulletin 2240). Washington D.C.: U.S. Government Printing Office.

Vaillant, George E. 1983. *The Natural History of Alcoholism*. Cambridge, Mass.: Harvard University Press.

Voydanoff, P. 1983. "Unemployment: Family Strategies for Adaptation." In *Stress and the Family, Vol. II: Coping With Catastrophe*, edited by C. Figley and H. McCubbin, 90–102. New York: Brunner/Mazel.

Wall Street Journal. 1985. "Near Collisions Aloft Are Said to be Rising as Air Traffic Picks Up." 20 April, 1.

Wall Street Journal. 1986. "Stepping Down in Size But Up in Rewards." September 15. New York: Dow Jones Reprint.

Wallerstein, J., and J. Kelly. 1980. *Surviving the Breakup: How Children and Parents Cope With Divorce*. New York: Basic Books.

Wallerstein, J., and J. Kelly. 1976. "The Effect of Parental Divorce: Experiences of the Child in Later Latency." *American Journal of Orthopsychiatry* 46:256–269.

Wallerstein, J., and J. Kelly. 1975. "The Effect of Parental Divorce: Experiences of the Preschool Child." *Journal of the American Academy of Child Psychiatry* 14:600–616.

Wareham, John. 1987. "How to Hire Incompetents." *New York Times*, 7 June, C3.

Wattenburg, E., and H. Reinhardt. 1979. "Female-Headed Families: Trends and Implications." *Social Work* 24:460–467.

Weber, Max. 1958. *The Protestant Ethic and the Spirit of Capitalism*. New York: Charles Scribner's Sons.

Weiss, R. 1984. "The Impact of Marital Dissolution on Income and Consumption in Single-Parent Households." *Journal of Marriage and the Family* 46(1):115–128.

Weiss, R. 1979. *Going It Alone: The Family Life and Social Situation of the Single Parent*. New York: Basic Books.

Weitzman, Lenore. 1985. *The Divorce Revolution: The Unexpected Social and Economic Consequences for Women and Children in America*. New York: Free Press.

Wilcock, Richard, and Walter Frank. 1963. *Unwanted Workers: Permanent Layoffs and Long-Term Unemployment.* Glencoe, Ill.: Free Press.

Wilensky, Harold. 1964. "The Professionalization of Everyone?" *American Journal of Sociology* (September):137–158.

Wilensky, Harold. 1959. The Skidder: Ideological Adjustments of Downward Mobile Workers. *American Sociological Review* 24:215–231.

Will, George. 1986. "New Collars, New Values." *Newsweek.* 24 November, 100.

Willis, Paul. 1977. *Learning To Labor: How Working Class Kids Get Working Class Jobs.* New York: Columbia University Press.

Wilkes, P. 1975. "Jobless, In the Suburbs." *New York Times Magazine* 8 June, 79–86.

Wilson, William J. 1987. *The Truly Disadvantaged: The Inner City, The Underclass, and Public Policy.* Chicago: University of Chicago Press.

Wright, Will. 1975. *Six Guns and Society.* Berkeley: University of California Press.

Yanigasako, Sylvia. 1977. "Women-Centered Kinship Networks in Urban Bilateral Kinship." *American Ethnologist* 4:207–226.

Zawadski, S., and P. Lazarsfeld. 1935. "The Psychological Consequences of Unemployment." *Journal of Social Psychology* 6:224–251.

Zussman, Robert. 1985. *Mechanics of the Middle Class: Work and Politics Among American Engineers.* New York: Columbia University Press.

Additional References

Barnett, Rosalind and Caryl Rivers. 1995. *She Works/He Works.* San Francisco: Harper.

Carnavale, Anthony and Stephen Rose. 1998. "Education for What? The New Office Economy," unpublished paper. Princeton: Educational Testing Service.

Clinton, President William J. 1997. "President's Report to Congress on the Implementation of the North American Free Trade Agreement." July.

Deogun, Nikhil. 1998. "No Tears for a Chainsaw." *Wall Street Journal,* 16 June, B1.

Duncan, Greg, Timothy Smeeding, and Willard Rodgers. 1993. "W(h)ither the Middle Class?" In *Poverty and Prosperity in the USA in the Late Twentieth Century,* edited by Dimitri Papadimitriou and Edward Wolff. Annandale on Hudson: The Levy Institute, pp 240–267.

Farber, Henry. 1998. "The Changing Face of Job Loss in the United States, 1981–1995." *Brookings Papers:Microeconomics 1997:* 55–142. Washington, D.C.: Brookings Institution.

Faux, Jeff. 1997. "Administration's NAFTA Report Seriously Misleading." Economic Policy Institute press release. July 11. Washington, D.C.

Gerson, Kathleen. 1994. *No Man's Land: Men's Changing Commitments to Work and Family.* New York: Basic Books.

Gordon, David. 1996. *Fat and Mean: The Corporate Squeeze of Working Americans and the Myth of Managerial "Downsizing."* New York: Free Press.

Hauser, Robert, John Warren, Min-Hsiung Huang, and Wendy Carter. 1996. "Occupational Status, Education and Social Mobility in the Meritocracy." Unpublished paper, Department of Sociology, University of Wisconsin-Madison. Available on the web at HYPERLINK http://www.ssc.wisc.edu/cde/cdewp/96-18.pdf www.ssc.wisc.edu/cde/cdewp/96-18.pdf

Hipple, Steven. 1997. "Worker Displacement in an Expanding Economy." *Monthly Labor Review* (December): 26–39.

Howell, David, Margaret Duncan and Bennett Harrison. 1998. "Low Wages in the U.S. and High Unemployment in Europe: A Critical Assessment of the Conventional Wisdom." Unpublished paper, Center for Economic Policy Analysis. New School for Social Research, New York.

Ilg, Randy. 1996. "The Nature of Employment Growth, 1989–95." *Monthly Labor Review* (June): 29–36.

Kadlec, Daniel. 1998. "Chainsaw Al Gets the Chop." *Time Magazine*, 29 June, 46–47.

Lamison-White, Leatha. 1997. "Poverty in the United States, 1996." Current Population Reports on Consumer Income. Series P-60-198. U.S. Bureau of the Census.

Levy, Frank. (in press) *The New Dollars and Dreams.* New York: Russell Sage Foundation.

Meisenheimer, Joseph. 1998. "The Services Industry in the 'Good' Versus 'Bad' Jobs Debate." *Monthly Labor Review* (February) 22–47.

Newman, Katherine. 1993. *Declining Fortunes: The Withering of the American Dream.* New York: Basic Books.

Peterson, Richard. 1996. "A Re-evaluation of the Economic Consequences of Divorce." *American Sociological Review* 61 (June): 528–536.

Rodrik, Dani. 1997. "Sense and Nonsense in the Globalization Debate." *Foreign Policy* (Summer): 19–36.

Tilly, Chris. 1996. *Half a Job: Bad and Good Part-Time Jobs in a Changing Labor Market.* Philadelphia: Temple University Press.

Useem, Michael. 1993. *Executive Defense: Shareholder Power and Corporate Reorganization.* Cambridge: Harvard University Press.

Index

322 Index

Downward mobility, *cont.*
mobility, 8, 15–16, 23–24; as a social
problem, 11, 21–23, 230, 236. *See
also* Income Data, and Income Loss
Drucker, J. H., 269n72
Dual-career families
median family incomes, 38; Singer
employees and, 282n22
Duncan, Greg, 21, 23, 250n8; 251n4;
251n5; 251n6; 258n54; 258n56
Duncan, Otis, 252n10

Earnings, for three cohorts of U.S.
men, 247
Easterlin, Richard, 35, 258n53; 287n26
Eisenberg, P., 262n17, 272n16
Elder, Glen, Jr., 261n12; 264n36;
273n24; 275n40; 275n41; 286n16;
287n18; 287n20; 287n23; 287n26
Elizabeth, New Jersey, 176–181
immigration history of, 192–194;
neighborhood decline in, 196
Employment policy
affirmative action, 194–195; laissez-
faire, 29; OECD nations, 28–29;
West German and Japanese companies, 240
Entrepreneur
archetype of, 73–75; downwardly
mobile children as, 133
Espenshade, T., 285n2
Estes, R. J., 261n12; 264n36; 264n39;
268n65
Ethnicity, among Singer workers, 192–
197
Exchange
Kula ring, 125; reciprocity among
kin, 125–128; 274n34, 275n35,
275n37, 275n39
Executive wives, 113–115
Executive unemployment
breaking the news to the family, 51–
52; Forty Plus Club, 44–48, 83–86;
meaning of time during, 63; social
isolation and, 58–60; treatment by
potential employers, 55–56. *See also*
Managerial culture

Failure
American culture and, 10–11; children's assessments of parental failure, 122–124; expectations of "ge-

netic" transmission, 141–142,
276n51
Families
generalized sharing within, 126; impact of downward mobility on, 95–
103, 230–232; relations with extended kin, 125–128
Families, pathological, 134–140
alcoholism, 134–137, 274n30,
276n44; violence, 276n46; 276n47
Family home
loss of, 271n11; meaning of, for De-
pression-era divorcees, 211–213;
real estate values and, 271n12; as a
symbol of social status, 102
Family trajectories, 231–232
Featherman, D. L., 250n1; 252n8;
252n9; 252n10
Federal Aviation Administration
(FAA), 144
response to firings, 145; standard-
ized training program, 146
Feminism, downward mobility and,
119–120
Fineman, S., 262n19
Finkelhor, David, 276n46; 276n47
Fischer, Britta, 277n6
Flavin, Joseph, 188–189
Fligstein, Neil, 283n36
Foltman, Felician, 280n2
Fonda, Jane, 279n29
Foreclosures
farms, 11; homes, 46
Fortes, Meyer, 288n31
Forty Plus, 259n8, 261n14; 269n71. *See
also* Executive unemployment
Furstenberg, Frank, 288n32

Galambos, N., 276n51
Garraty, John, 287n19
Garson, Barbara, 283n31
Geertz, Clifford, 251n13
Gelles, Richard, 276n49
General Accounting Office (GAO),
278n10, 278n11, 278n14
Generational culture, 275n42, 286n15,
287n17, 287n26, 288n30
baby-boom generation, 35–37,
255n40, 258n53; boomerang generation, 105; definition of social roles
and, 228; Depression-era divorcees,
210–213; divorced women and, 18;
labor market problems and, 258n50;